A VIEW OF EPPING FOREST

For Imogen and Louis,

best wishes

Nicholas Hagger

A VIEW OF EPPING FOREST

Nicholas Hagger

BOOKS

Winchester, UK
Washington, USA

First published by O-Books, 2012
O-Books is an imprint of John Hunt Publishing Ltd., Laurel House, Station Approach,
Alresford, Hants, SO24 9JH, UK
office1@o-books.net
www.o-books.com

For distributor details and how to order please visit the 'Ordering' section on our website.

ISBN: 978 1 84694 587 8

A CIP catalogue record for this book is available from the British Library.

Design: Stuart Davies

Printed and bound by CPI Group (UK) Ltd, Croydon, CR0 4YY

CONTENTS

BOOKS PUBLISHED BY NICHOLAS HAGGER

The Fire and the Stones
Selected Poems
The Universe and the Light
A White Radiance
A Mystic Way
Awakening to the Light
A Spade Fresh with Mud
The Warlords
Overlord
A Smell of Leaves and Summer
The Tragedy of Prince Tudor
The One and the Many
Wheeling Bats and a Harvest Moon
The Warm Glow of the Monastery Courtyard
The Syndicate
The Secret History of the West
The Light of Civilization
Classical Odes
Overlord, one-volume edition
Collected Poems 1958 – 2005
Collected Verse Plays
Collected Stories
The Secret Founding of America
The Last Tourist in Iran
The Rise and Fall of Civilizations
The New Philosophy of Universalism
The Libyan Revolution
Armageddon
The World Government
The Secret American Dream
A New Philosophy of Literature

Acknowledgments

I acknowledge the memory of the poets Tennyson and Clare, who both lived within Epping Forest, and of the British intelligence agent T.E. Lawrence who wanted to print *Seven Pillars of Wisdom* in his hut at Pole Hill, Chingford. (The hut now stands in the Warren.) I acknowledge the memory of Sir William Addison, author of books on Epping Forest who often, with a friendly smile, guided me to texts on its *flora* and *fauna* when I visited his bookshop as a boy.

I am grateful to Tony O'Connor, Curator of the Epping Forest District Museum, Waltham Abbey, who discussed hill-forts with me and kindly asked to see a very early draft of Part One of this book; and to P.J. Huggins, who led the 1984-91 excavations at Waltham Abbey, for answering my questions. I am grateful to Terence Mallinson for sending me a booklet about the White House, Woodford; to Eric Dixon, who kindly lent me one of the twelve copies of Waller's *Loughton in Essex*; to Harry Bitten, Leader of the Centenary Walk for 28 years and Tricia Moxey, who helped run the Epping Forest Conservation Centre (now the Field Centre), for their observations about the Forest and, in Tricia's case, for lending papers and providing a c.1945 map of High Beach and painting of Edward Thomas's cottage; to Loredana Morrison and Marian Delfgou, archivist of Chigwell School, who supplied illustrations from the Chigwell School archives; to Austin Darby of Fairmead Farm (previously Fairmead Cottage) for information on Dr Allen's asylum; and to many other local people who have at various times provided snippets of information, including Chris Pond and Richard Morris of the Loughton & District Historial Society.

I am grateful to John Hunt for understanding that a local area becomes national if (like Wordsworth's Lake District) it features in the work of poets and international if the poets have a following overseas – and if the world descends on its borders to watch the Olympic Games. I am also grateful to my P.A. Ingrid who helped me research and write the book in just over six months (from 4 May to 8 November 2011) while we worked on other projects.

"Fair seed-time had my soul."

Wordsworth, *The Prelude*, bk 1, line 301

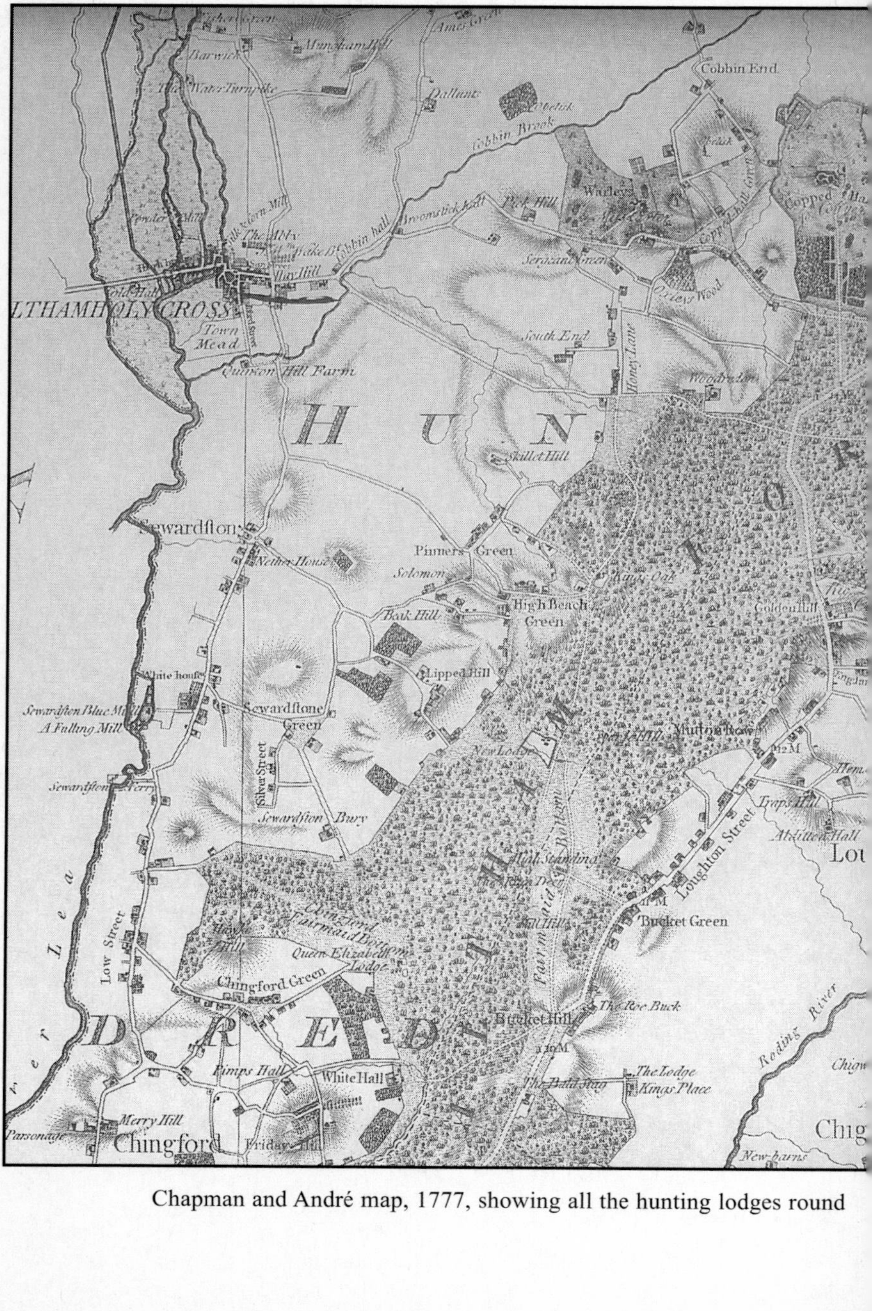

Chapman and André map, 1777, showing all the hunting lodges round

Fairmead (see pp.66-70), and Loughton's seven hills (see p.101).

Prologue: History Shaping Places

I have known Epping Forest since 1943. It was the cradle of my growth, and it has hardly changed since my childhood. This book tells the story of Epping Forest's history, places and institutions. It is not a guidebook, detailing every region of the Forest, but more a reflection of the Forest's variegated history which still confronts us wherever we look.

Objective narrative

As I draw on decades of personal experience this book has the flavour of a personal memoir. However, I see it as an objective narrative as it tells the story of Epping Forest's history and the evolution of its places and permanent buildings. Even the most objective narrative must inevitably be coloured by the personal observations of the narrator, and in my objective narrative the personal and the objective are intertwined. The personal element is in the "view" of the book's title, the objective in its focus on the Forest.

View

This book presents a view of Epping Forest, of 6,000 acres of ancient woodland. It is *a* view, just one of a number of possible views, *my* view, for the Epping Forest I describe is the one I have known.

According to the *Shorter Oxford Dictionary* a 'view' has two main components in its meaning. The first, referring to the view that can be seen from a window, is "a sight or prospect of some landscape or extended scene; and extent or area covered by the eye from one point". The second, referring to a reflective opinion, is "mental contemplation, a single act of contemplation or attention to a subject; a particular manner or way of considering or regarding the matter or question; a conception, opinion or theory formed by reflection or study".

My 'view' presents both a description of the landscape of Epping Forest from the single point of my eye and a reflection (or contemplation) on the Forest that leads to a "conception, opinion or theory".

The description and reflection are inextricably entwined in my view of the Forest.

Perspectives: four periods of history

The theme of this book is that the places of the Forest cannot be fully appreciated without a firm grasp of four periods of history which have shaped them. These four periods are conveyed in Part One as pairs of contraries or opposites: Celts and Romans; Anglo-Saxons and Normans; Medievals and Tudors; and enclosers and loppers. In Part Two I attempt to show how history has shaped the main Forest places in my Loughton, Chigwell, Woodford, Buckhurst Hill, Waltham Abbey, High Beach, Upshire, Epping, the Theydons and Chingford Plain. The Appendix reproduces some of my poems about these places.

I am partly known as a local educator, and I have taken the opportunity to include my three Oak-Tree schools, which form a triangle largely within Epping Forest, and to put little-known facts on public record as although thousands of local people have been through these schools over the years published information on the schools is relatively scanty and often factually incorrect.

The book thus presents different perspectives of the Forest: the four very different periods of history; the continuity of the flow of historical tradition; the effect of the cumulative tradition on individual places; and my reflective contemplation on the places in my Epping Forest in poetry. I blend history, recollection and poetic reflection in a quest for a rounded view of the Forest.

Whole sweep

As a Universalist, in my works I present the whole sweep of history and its context. I use what Coleridge called the "esemplastic power of the imagination". (The Greek *eis en plattein* means "to shape into one".) Such a historical mind shapes conflicting events into one and understands the progression that leads to the present. I have used this approach in writing of the rise and fall of civilizations;[1] of a period of history;[2] of an episode in history and its consequences;[3] and of the evolution of local history.[4]

The historian who knows that all history is ultimately a unity wants to find out what really happened by close reference to historical texts and sources, and presents local history in terms of a whole. I am not a local historian in the mould of W.C. Waller and the producers of booklets for the Loughton & District Historical Society who publish records, documents and diary entries – in themselves useful sources – without much attempt to relate them to a narrative that reflects a whole view. Writers on Epping Forest must be able "to see the wood for the trees". A view of Epping Forest has to be "wholist" rather than partialist while necessarily being eclectic.

My approach is closer to Sir William Addison's. He wrote of Epping Forest's literary and historical associations, focusing on well-known individuals or "Essex worthies". His topic-based *Portrait of Epping Forest* is supplemented by its companion volume, *Figures in a Landscape*, which dwells on the Forest's landscape, people and history and retells anecdotes. He recorded the social whims of his figures but was alert to the movement in the age behind the sweep of local events and fortunes of local notables. As a Universalist I look for the underlying movement of each age and relate it to the actions of its significant individuals.

Sources

Unfortunately, Addison did not provide his sources. In this day and age sources are crucial, and writing must be evidential. I endeavour to be accurate and meticulous in locating sources.

I have found that many of the books on Epping Forest get facts wrong and repeat and perpetuate mistakes made in other books on blind trust, without scrutinising or supplying sources. For this reason I have made a fresh start. I have resolved not to trust anything for which there is no source. Wherever possible I have gone back to original sources and looked at them with an open mind. I have ignored the consensus of books that do not give sources. When books say, for example, that there is no connection between Ambresbury Banks, Loughton Camp and

Celtic or Roman occupation I have re-examined the sources and have sometimes come to surprising conclusions. I hope that there will be a broad welcome for a fresh approach that explores the history of Epping Forest as if coming to it anew.

I present evidence, probe behind the surface and revise any judgement that is not soundly based. I challenge orthodoxy when necessary and iron out inconsistencies to arrive at the truth. This is the method I have used in my historical works.

What the Forest means

Epping Forest has meant different things in different ages. To the Neolithics it was a dark, forbidding place, and primitive humans were happy to settle along the Roding. To the Romans it was wild and dangerous, and hid hostile Celts. To the Normans the Forest of Waltham was at first a place from which Saxons could launch attacks and then became the hunting-ground of kings. The 14th-century forest of *Sir Gawayne and the Grene Knight* was wild and inhospitable, removed from the fire on the lord's hearth. The Norman and Tudor forests, including Waltham (later Epping), Forest, were dangerous places: hunting zones, entry to which was illegal and might result in fines or death. In the Elizabethan Age, like Shakespeare's forests Waltham (or Epping) Forest was a place of natural beauty in whose solitude transformation could take place and individuals could discover inner truths. To the German and English Romantics forests were holy and uncorrupted by the taints of civilization. In reality, during both these times Epping Forest was haunted by footpads and highwaymen, and locals had to venture in to lop branches for firewood to keep warm. Nevertheless, to Tennyson and Clare Epping Forest was a place of natural beauty and purity.

Epping Forest has meant something different, again, to me. It is a place of inspiration. It teems with life and reveals Nature's system and the universal order. It offers still ponds that reflect the universe. It flows with the seasons, from winter bareness to smiling spring's tender green, to summer profusion and autumnal tints in myriad reddening and yellowing leaves.

Like an oak

The places of Epping Forest have been shaped by the history and tradition of the Forest just as the branches of a tree are shaped by its trunk. Epping Forest is like one of its ancient oaks: its roots are in prehistory, its trunk is the tradition of the last 2,500 years and its branches are the Forest settlements and communities that have grown out of its evolving history.

I, too, am like one of its oaks. And I am happy that one of my acorns has grown into these leaves that are prints of its parent and of the long tradition and history of Epping Forest.

PART ONE

The Roding Valley and the Stirrings of History

1

Celts and Romans

Epping Forest, the sweep of banked trees, lush green in spring, reddening and orange in autumn, stretches for twelve miles (nineteen kilometres) from Forest Gate to Epping along the north side of the River Roding.

The Roding valley

The Roding rises four miles north-west of Great Dunmow at Mole Hill Green, and flows towards the Thames. My Roding extends north-west through low flood meadows from the bridge in Roding Lane, Buckhurst Hill back towards its source. On the Chigwell side there are willows. On the Loughton side, in autumn, there are thistles with bearded seed, purple loosestrife and nettles. Beyond the humpback bridge I used to push my bike over when cycling to school can be seen viper's bugloss, teasle, burdock and purple mallow, and there are red haws on the hawthorn bushes. There I have seen a flock of whitethroats and a pippet.

Roman Roding

The Romans settled along the Roding, and further along on the Chigwell side, parallel to Abridge Road, was a Romano-British settlement and cemetery under what is now Woolston Hall estate. In Roman times a large stone was placed by the river so that Roman families could wash their wool and clothes, hence the name "Woolston".

Nearby, on land north-east of the Epping Forest Country Club, a Roman bathhouse complex[1], corn-drying ovens and cremation urns[2] have been found, along with Roman pottery, figurines and coins. The site, referred to in a 1777 map as "Little London", seems to have extended to Abridge and is thought to have been part of the Roman town of Durolitum,[3] which is known to have lain on one of the Roman roads between London and Chelmsford.

Roman remains have been found at High Beach and Warren Wood (across the road from Ambresbury Banks).[4] Traces have been found of Roman villas on the other side of the Roding in Loughton[5], Theydon[6] and Abridge, at Hill Farm.[7] From Abridge the river meanders through marshy meadows filled with reeds back towards Passingford Bridge and Ongar.

Invasions and Epping Forest

This tiny part of Essex has an amazing history. The Roding valley and Epping Forest have been swept by several of the historical tempests of the last 2,500 years – Celtic invasions and inter-tribal wars, two Roman invasions and a tribal revolt, Saxon and Norman conquests – and have been ruled by East Saxons, Danelaw and Normans and visited by many kings and queens: Edward the Confessor, Harold II, William I, (probably) William II, Henry I, Henry II, Richard II, Henry VIII, Mary, Elizabeth I, James I, Charles I and II and Queen Victoria.

Important events have taken place around the Forest. Direct evidence that some of the events can be conclusively linked to the Forest places may be lacking but a close reading of the circumstantial evidence suggests that it is highly likely that some of these events directly impacted on, or even took place in, these places, as we shall see.

The Roding valley contrasts with, and complements, the Forest. It dictated its geology and now smiles serenely in the sun.

Prehistory

Epping Forest has been shaped by ice.

Ice sheet forms Epping Forest

The glacial ice sheet which covered Northern Europe c.18,000BC slid down the east of England but split in the region of Epping Forest where the Roding villages are now located. One half gouged out the Lea (or Lee) valley, the other half scraped out the Roding valley, leaving a ridge of clay topped with loam between the two valleys. The split ice may have squeezed up the earth between the two valleys into this ridge.

This ridge formed the base of Epping Forest. It extended from Epping (the highest point being near Ambresbury Banks, 384 feet or 111 metres) to Pole Hill near Chingford (299 feet or 91 metres). High Beach, 300 feet above sea level, is a beach-like expanse of Ice-Age sand and gravel: gravel on the surface with underlying deposits of Bagshot Sand from an unknown river that may have flowed north from the Weald of Kent, as the (correct) spelling 'Beach' (an early English description) rather than 'Beech' reflects.[8]

The lower slopes of the ridge, at Loughton, Buckhurst Hill and Woodford, are of clay with low hills formed of glacial (as opposed to pebble) gravel. Loughton alone had seven of these hills. (See p.101.) The Old Stone-Age people lived along the river valleys.

The glacial ice sheet was a treeless tundra of Arctic moss and lichen-covered ridges, among whose birches and willows roamed mammoths, reindeer and Arctic foxes. There were settlements at Great Clacton and Jaywick during the interglacial period c.500,000BC. In Epping Forest Palaeolithic man left traces that predate the melting of the ice that severed Britain from the Continent at the Straits of Dover, creating an island c.6,000-5,000BC. Evidence has been found of flint tools that once belonged to hunters in the Roding and Lea valleys about 150,000 years ago. Four Palaeolithic handaxes, a handaxe tip and nine flint flakes were found at Woodford during work on the M11.[9]

Mesolithic hunters

As the ice receded c.11,000BC, plants grew and soon there were woods. By the Mesolithic (or Middle Stone-Age) time from c.10,000BC, there were birch and pine trees, hazels, aspens and alders on the Epping-Forest ridge. Oaks, elms and small-leafed limes grew later. There were heaths and moorland.

Mesolithic hunters cultivated land with stone hoes and sticks. Along the Roding there are signs that soil was turned over to receive seed during this time, and early farming began. The hunters fed off fish, game and wild plants. Traces of a Mesolithic shelter have been found at Hill Wood near High Beach, where wild boar and red and roe deer were hunted. There was a Mesolithic site in the Lea valley, near Waltham Abbey.

Epping Forest may have been continuously covered by trees since the retreat of the glaciers at the end of the Ice Age c.11,000BC, and certainly since Neolithic times.

Neolithic farmers

The Neolithic (New Stone-Age) people from c.4500BC practised animal husbandry, and traded. Late Stone-Age farmers invaded across the Channel by boat. There was a peat bog near the gates of Copped Hall in Lodge Road, Upshire. Analysis of the pollen shows that the bog was formed very early, c.3350-2600BC or from c.2340BC,[10] by the creation of a wooden causeway to act as a path.

The Early Bronze-Age Beaker peoples came to Essex from Holland and the Rhineland c.2300-1700BC. They made pots of metal (first copper, then tin-bronze) and buried their dead under round mounds or barrows.

Celts

The Iron Age began in Britain c.700BC, when bronze and iron were introduced to Britain. Ninety per cent of the trees in Epping Forest were then small-leafed limes. Pollen studies show that there was continuity of woodland cover in what is now Epping Forest from the Neolithic period to the present time, and that there was no significant decline in tree species during the Iron Age, suggesting that Belgic settlers made little impact on Forest vegetation.[11]

Ambresbury Banks and Loughton Camp

The main evidence of prehistoric occupation in Epping Forest is the Iron-Age earthworks at Ambresbury Banks, Epping and Loughton Camp, both of which date to perhaps c.700BC[12] and certainly to c.500BC, with evidence of Belgic or late Iron Age reoccupation.[13] Both have areas of about four hectares (nearly ten acres). Both were on high ground, and Ambresbury Banks was on the highest part of the Epping-Forest ridge with a commanding view across the plain in front of it (see p.35).

Earthwork walls in Loughton Camp (left) and Ambresbury Banks (right).

The earthworks only had one wall and may not be sufficiently protected to have been forts. On the other hand, they were too elaborate to have been animal pens. Ambresbury Banks, which is 384 feet above sea level at its highest point, had a ten-foot-high rampart wall with a timber palisade and walkway on top, and a moat or ditch 26-30 feet wide and 6-10 feet deep. The entrance had a stone revetted passageway, or passage faced with masonry (found by the 1958 excavation), and a causeway (found by the 1956 excavation).[14] There was evidence of a collapse of the revetting wall on the north-east side of the passageway, which spilled stones on to the butt (or thicker) end of the ditch and beyond. There were three courses of stonework below the entrance with post holes for wooden gates.[15] A trackway for carts was developed after the collapse of the revetting wall, and there are traces of wheelruts. The lowest ruts contained 13th-century potsherds, iron nails and a buckle, suggesting that the cart track was medieval.[16]

The earthworks do not seem to have been continuously occupied and may have been used as communal refuges (rather than settlements) in disturbed times for the people who lived in pile dwellings in the Lea valley and in farmsteads in the Roding valley.

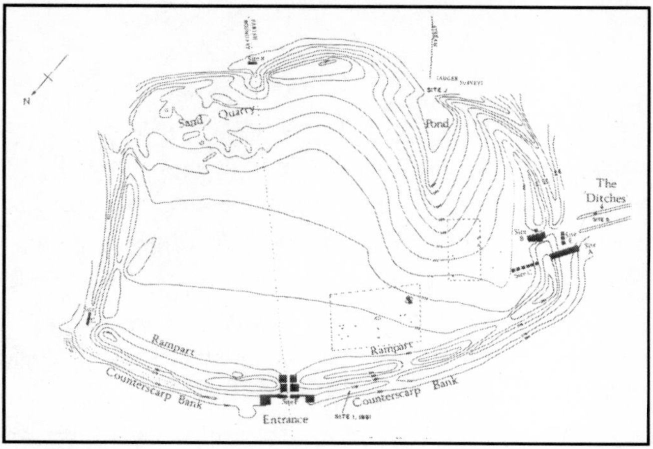

Ambresbury Banks, contoured plan showing rampart, entrance and excavation sites.

It has been suggested that the earthworks were constructed by rival groups – by a tribal group settled by the River Lea and another tribal group settled by the Roding – and may have faced each other across a boundary line. In fact, there are likely to have been symbols of power, warning potential invaders against attack, and at the same time secure trading centres where traders could bring their merchandise without fearing that they might be robbed.[17] They may also have had a religious significance: they may have included shrines that acted as early temples.[18]

There is some evidence that there was a defensive line, a kind of Hadrian's Wall, that extended south of the Thames from Caesar's Camp on Keston Common to Woolwich; and north of the Thames to Uphall Camp beside the River Roding where it flowed into the Thames at Ilford; on to these two earthworks in Loughton and Epping; and on to the site of the Iron-Age hill-fort and Roman temple located on a low hill in the bend of the River Stort near Harlow; and to Wallbury Camp, an Iron-Age hill-fort near Bishop's Stortford.[19]

It has been claimed that Ambresbury Banks was refortified after the Romans and took its name from Ambrosius Aurelianus, a British warlord who fought the Saxons in 450.[20]

Excavations

In archaeological excavations since General Pitt-Rivers' excavation of 1881, including those of 1926-7, 1933, 1956, 1958 and 1968,[21] flints and Iron-Age potsherds have been found in both earthworks along with flint arrowheads and lumps of burnt clay. Pitt-Rivers reported that he found potsherds of "Romano-British" type near the entrance to Ambresbury Banks, in site I (the site of the 1881 excavation).[22] It is not known what happened to his finds. In Loughton Camp, which is in Monk Wood just off the Green Ride, an Iron-Age stone quern (for grinding grain) has been discovered. Many spearheads and arrowheads have been found in Fairmead Bottom (not far from the tea hut between the Robin Hood roundabout and High Beach), where there seems to have been a 'flint factory'. Flint tools, weapons and post holes suggest some sort of a windbreak.

No systematic archaeological investigation of the whole of the two earthworks has ever taken place. The earthworks have never been properly excavated, and digging has been confined to trenches here or there. A British encampment of the same period was discovered during the building of the Lea-valley reservoirs near Walthamstow.

The peaceful Trinovantes and Epping Forest

The earliest Celts of the Iron-Age Hallstatt culture from Austria (the Iron Age A culture),[23] spread to Britain from the 8th century BC. They settled in many parts of Essex, including the Lea valley, and these two Epping-Forest earthworks are attributed to them.

They were the tribe of Trinovantes, who were peaceful farmers based in Colchester. Their name is thought to come from the Celtic 'tri' and 'novio' meaning 'very new', or 'newcomers'. However, Geoffrey of Monmouth claims in his *Historia Regum Britanniae* that they derived their name from 'Troinoventum' or 'New Troy', a reference to the legend that Britain was founded by Brutus, a Trojan who had arrived in Britain (near Totnes in Devon) as a refugee after the Trojan War. The native British absorbed this influx.

The next wave of Celts, the fierce La Tène culture from Switzerland (the Iron Age B culture) reached Britain during the 3rd century BC but did not spread as far eastwards as Essex.

The warlike Belgic Catuvellauni conquer the Trinovantes
Beginning around 150BC a third wave of Celtic settlers came from Belgic Gaul (the Iron Age C culture),[24] the Belgae, who initially settled in Kent, Essex and Hertfordshire. The most powerful group were the Catuvellauni, who occupied much of Essex and Hertfordshire and had their capital at St Albans. The River Lea was a frontier between the Catuvellauni and the Trinovantes, who used the Epping-Forest earthworks. By 75BC they were harrying the peaceful Trinovantes, who undoubtedly sought refuge in times of peril in the two hill-fort earthworks on the Epping-Forest ridge.

The aggressive Catuvellauni pushed towards the Trinovantes' capital at Colchester, and developed Camulodunum ('the fort of the Celtic war-god Camulos') in part of their capital. The Belgae used the heavy plough with share, had wheeled vehicles and made pottery on a wheel. They were more advanced than the Trinovantes, their eastern neighbours.

Did the invading Catuvellauni occupy the two Epping-Forest hill-fort earthworks of the Trinovantes c.75BC? An open-minded inquirer looks at the larger picture, of their sweep from Hertfordshire to Colchester, and sets out the circumstantial evidence. Would the Trinovantes not have resisted them in these two hill-forts?

Romans

Roman Impact on Celts
At the time the Romans arrived in Julius Caesar's expeditions of 55 and 54BC, the inhabitants of Essex, the Trinovantes, were considered the most powerful Celtic tribe in Britain.

The Catuvellauni are at war with the Trinovantes

Caesar, in his *De Bello Gallico* (*Concerning the Gallic War*) says that the king of the Trinovantes was Imanuentius. The Catuvellauni were at war with them to the west. The Catuvellauni were ruled by Cassivellaunus, who was based in Braughing (in contemporary Hertfordshire).

Julius Caesar's first invasion of Britain in 55BC

During the first Roman invasion of Britain (55BC) Caesar was based in Kent at a camp his men built that extended more than a hundred acres somewhere near Deal. They had not found a natural harbour, and their fleet was wrecked in a storm on the nearby beach and at anchor. The camp was attacked by the Britons. The Romans fended the Britons off but did not venture far inland.

Julius Caesar's second invasion of Britain in 54BC and Epping Forest

Mandubracius, son of the king of the Trinovantes, appeals to Caesar

By the time of Caesar's second expedition in 54BC Cassivellaunus, king of the Catuvellauni, had overthrown Imanuentius, king of the Trinovantes, whose son Mandubracius fled to Gaul and sought Caesar's protection. He promised to support the Romans if Caesar would restore them to power.

Did the Catuvellauni occupy Epping-Forest hill-forts?

During this year of peril, of Cassivellaunus's advance, the Trinovantes undoubtedly used the hill-fort earthworks in Epping Forest: Ambresbury Banks, from which there was a view across the River Lea into the Catuvellauni's Hertfordshire and almost to the Chilterns, and southwards towards the Thames; and Loughton Camp, from which there was a view across the Roding valley towards the Thames Estuary and the hills of Kent, monitoring the arrival of Romans invading from the south. It is likely that the two hill-forts were captured from the Trinovantes and occupied by Cassivellaunus's invaders shortly before the arrival of Caesar's second expedition.

Was this the case? Again, an open-minded inquirer looks at the larger picture of Cassivellaunus's advance from Hertfordshire to Colchester, and sees that these two hill-forts were in his path. There is circumstantial evidence that it is likely that Cassivellaunus occupied these two hill-forts.

Caesar's march

In the second Roman invasion of Britain (54BC), Caesar arrived with 800 ships and landed several miles north of the previous landing-place, somewhere between Deal and Sandwich. His men built an enormous camp and engaged the Britons twelve miles away. Another storm snapped the chains of the ships and smashed them into each other, throwing them up on the beach, destroying 40. Caesar had planned to sail up the Thames, but now he had to march inland. His troops marched in an awesome column four abreast stretching several miles.

Caesar's spin

Caesar left an account of his expeditions to Britain. We have to be cautious in reading it as it was probably an assembly of dispatches sent from the front to the Senate back in Rome, with a view to retaining the support of Roman senators. Caesar presented his campaign in a good light, with a considerable element of "spin". It seems he wrote for the senators and was not concerned to give precise locations or details of his engagements.

Caesar crosses the Thames

Caesar states that the infantry and cavalry crossed the Thames in pursuit of Cassivellaunus (V,18). Writing of himself in the third person, Caesar tells us: "On learning the enemy's plan of campaign, Caesar led his army to the Thames in order to enter Cassivellaunus' territory. The river is fordable at one point only, and even there with difficulty. At this place he found large enemy forces drawn up at the opposite bank. The bank was also fenced by sharp stakes fixed along the edge, and he was told by prisoners and deserters that similar ones were concealed in the river-bed. He sent the cavalry across first, and then at once ordered the infantry to follow. But the infantry went with such speed and impetuosity, although they had only their heads above water, that they attacked at the same moment as the cavalry. The enemy was overpowered and fled from the river-bed."[25]

Seeing the Romans ford the Thames, the Britons who lined the northern bank fled. Caesar marched north of the Thames: "Cassivellaunus had now given up all hope of fighting a pitched battle. Disbanding the greater part of his troops, he retained only some four thousand charioteers, with whom he watched our line of march. He would retire a short way from the route and hide in dense thickets, driving the inhabitants and cattle from the open country into the woods wherever he knew we intended to pass. If ever our cavalry incautiously ventured too far away in plundering and devastating the country, he would send all his charioteers out of the woods by well-known lanes and pathways and deliver very formidable attacks, hoping by this means to make them afraid to go far afield."[26]

Cassivellaunus was mounting guerilla attacks. "During this march" the Trinovantes sent envoys asking Caesar to protect Mandubracius. Five tribes (the Cenimagni, Segontiaci, Ancalites, Bibroci and Cassi) sent embassies and surrendered. From them Caesar learned that he was near Cassivellaunus's stronghold.

Caesar defeats the Catuvellauni at their stronghold

Caesar continues (V,21): "He [Caesar] marched to the place with his legions and found that it was of great natural strength and excellently fortified. Nevertheless, he proceeded to assault it on two sides. After a short time the enemy proved unable to resist the violent attack of the legions, and rushed out of the fortress on another side. A quantity of cattle was found there, and many of the fugitives were captured or killed."[27] Caesar had defeated Cassivellaunus.

Caesar describes hill-forts used by the Britons:

"The Britons apply the name 'strongholds' (*oppida*) to densely wooded spots fortified with a rampart and ditch, to which they retire in order to escape the attacks of invaders." [28]

"They hid in the woods where they occupied a hilltop, having improved its natural strength, in preparation, no doubt, for some war among themselves, since all the entrances had been blocked by felled trees laid closely together." [29]

Was the final battle at Ambresbury Banks?

Caesar tells us that the Britons "hid in woods", and it is likely that their "strongholds" (*oppida*) were partially hidden in dense forest, secret places of refuge from which they rushed out to conduct guerilla attacks. These hill-fort strongholds would have provided grazing for animals and, in the case of Ambresbury Banks, a water supply from a spring.[30] In times of danger it is likely that a warning beacon was lit nearby that could be seen for miles around, a signal for those in surrounding villages to leave their homes and gather in the hill-forts, which now became communal places of safety. The hill-forts could be seen from afar but were on the verge of dense forest where the Britons could hide.

Scholars have had their eye on hill-forts in Surrey as the site of Cassivellaunus' defeat, such as the one at Oldbury Hill near Ightham (which was captured by the Romans from the Belgae in AD43); Anstiebury near Dorking; Holmbury; and Hascombe.[31] However, Caesar tells us that he crossed the Thames, and though some conclude that he forded the Thames west of London and fought Cassivellaunus near Wheathampstead in Hertfordshire, according to other scholars Caesar forded the Thames at Westminster and doubled back towards the mouths of the Lea and Roding, and fought the decisive battle in a 20-30-mile swathe north of the Thames at one of only four fortified sites: Ambresbury Banks; Loughton Camp; Uphall Camp (which can be rejected as being too close to the Thames); and Weald Park Camp or Wallbury Camp, Great Hallingbury, to reach which would have required a much longer march from where Caesar crossed the Thames.[32]

It is therefore not impossible that Caesar's final battle against Cassivellaunus took place in Ambresbury Banks or Loughton Camp, Trinovantes camps going back to at least 500BC which Cassivellaunus and the invading Catuvellauni can be presumed to have occupied. The "territory of Cassivellaunus", to which Caesar says he led his army (V,18), would therefore have been in West Essex.

Was Cassivellaunus at one or the other, or both, of the Epping-Forest hill-forts in 54BC? We have seen that there is circumstantial evidence that this was likely. Did Caesar fight his decisive battle against Cassivellaunus in Epping Forest? There is a long-standing oral tradition that Cassivellaunus held Ambresbury Banks against the Romans.[33] An open-minded inquirer looks at the larger picture and sets out the circumstantial evidence which makes it a possibility and, in view of the textual evidence that Caesar crossed the Thames and was in the Epping-Forest area, perhaps a likelihood. There will be no direct evidence until there is a thorough systematic archaeological investigation of the two hill-forts.

Caesar restores Mandubracius

Having defeated Cassivellaunus during his second expedition, Caesar restored Mandubracius as king of the Trinovantes.

Caesar imposed a peace. He established client relationships with some British tribes, particularly the Atrebates south of the Thames, and in Augustus's time client relationships were extended to other tribes, particularly those who sought to resist the expansion of the Catuvellauni, notably the Trinovantes and the Iceni.

The Catuvellauni twice conquer the Trinovantes

The next king of the Trinovantes was Addedomarus, who came to power c.20-15BC and moved the capital back to Camulodunum (Colchester). However he too seems to have been conquered by the Catuvellauni as their king c.20BC, Tasciovanus, issued coins from Camulodunum, suggesting that the Catuvellauni had once again displaced the Trinovantes.

Addedomarus was restored, and c.10-5BC was succeeded by his son Tubnovellaunus, but a few years later the Trinovantes were again conquered by Tasciovanus or his son Cunobelinus (or Cynobelin, Shakespeare's Cymbeline).

Gold coins have been found near Ambresbury Banks relating to Tasciovanus and his son Cunobelinus. Four gold staters of Tasciovanus and seven gold staters of Cunobelinus, dated between c.20BC and 10AD, all found near Ambresbury Banks, were on display at the Epping Forest District Museum, Sun Street, Waltham Abbey, on loan from the British Museum, in September 2011.

Around the end of the 1st century BC, possibly by c.AD5, when Cunobelinus succeeded his father, and certainly by c.AD10,[34] the Catuvellauni imposed their rule on – conquered – the Trinovantes and established themselves at Camulodunum. (Camulodunum has been put forward as a possible site of Arthur's Camelot as a result of all the activity there at this time, but it is likely that if Arthur was a real person and not just a fictional character, he was a Roman Briton who resisted the Saxons at least five centuries later.)

Cunobelinus conquered the Cantii in Kent and ruled south-east England as King of the Britons until he died in AD40 or 41. He was succeeded by his sons Caratacus (less correctly, Caractacus) and Togodumnus, whose north-eastern neighbour was the Iceni in Norfolk.

Claudius's Invasion of Britain in AD43 and Epping Forest

Aulus Plautius defeats the Catuvellauni

The Romans had conquered Gaul and were concerned that under the Catuvellaunian supremacy raiders from Britain sometimes arrived in Gaul and that refugees left Gaul for Britain. The Catuvellauni were a threat to the stability of Roman Gaul. The Romans were also very interested in Britain's mineral resources.

Claudius, found cowering in terror by the praetorian guard who made him Emperor, needed a triumph to establish himself as Emperor. Britain was the ideal place to achieve this as the Trinovantes had appealed to Claudius, asking him to restore them against the

Catuvellauni.

In AD43 the Roman conquest of Britain took place at the direction of the Roman Emperor Claudius. Four legions invaded under Aulus Plautius. Some 50,000 men landed unopposed near Richborough in Kent. Some perhaps landed in Fishbourne near Chichester, where there are traces of Roman barracks beneath the palace of the later Roman client king Tiberius Claudius Togidubnus (Cogidubnus in Tacitus's *Agricola*).[35] Plautius defeated the Catuvellauni at the battle of the Medway. Caratacus fled to Wales. His brother Togodumnus was killed. The two sons and successors of Cunobelinus had been removed.

Claudius and Plautius take Camulodunum

Plautius halted at the Thames. Cassius Dio, in his *Roman History* (written in Greek) states: "The Britons retreated to the River Thames in the area where it empties into the Ocean and at flood-tide forms a lake."[36] This seems to refer to the estuary, but the lake could be the Tidal Pool of London east of the present-day Tower Bridge, below which the Romans may have thought that the Thames emptied into "the Ocean" (the North Sea).

Although Plautius waited, it is likely that he secured the north bank of the Thames – he describes how German auxiliaries swam across – and that elephants were shipped across to the north bank before Claudius arrived in Britain. The tribes were already submitting. The Roman Emperor Claudius arrived to take personal command of the end of the campaign.

He crossed the Thames, probably at Westminster and, led in by armoured elephants which evoked Hannibal, personally took possession of Camulodunum (Colchester) and received the formal surrender of the British kings: Cogidubnus of the Regni and Prasutagus of the Iceni. According to Cassius Dio, Claudius's campaign only lasted sixteen days. A Roman city was built in Camulodunum with a temple to Claudius.

Ambresbury Banks and Loughton Camp abandoned

Claudius wanted to annex the arable south-east of Britain, not the whole island. The Romans overran the south-east in AD44. The two Trinovantes' hill-fort earthworks at Ambresbury Banks and Loughton Camp were abandoned about this time, and were perhaps demolished by the Roman conquerors.

The scanty archaeological evidence supports this view. Potsherds near the entrance to Ambresbury Banks show that the hill-fort earthwork was used, or re-used, by the Belgae – the Catuvellauni – during the 1st century AD.[37]

Pacification

Caratacus continued the resistance in Wales. Aulus Plautius was succeeded as commanding officer by Ostorius Scapula, who crushed Caratacus's forces. Caratacus fled to the Brigantes, whose territory covered much of northern England, and was handed over to the Romans by their queen, Cartimandua, in AD50.

The previous year the 20th legion founded a veteran settlement – a colony (known as *Colonia Claudia Victricensis*) for retired Roman soldiers – at Camulodunum. The rest of Britain took another 80 years to conquer, and the sway of the conquest would last until the fall of Rome in AD410.

Roman Roads and Towns

Trunk roads and sub-roads

The Romans built roads to transport goods from Londinium (London) to the Roman towns and bases. There were six trunk roads from Londinium:

- The Devil's Highway went west to modern Exeter via Portway and Ackling Dyke.
- Watling Street went to modern Chester, north Wales and Anglesey via St Albans (Verulamium).
- Watling Street continued to Canterbury, and Richborough and the Kent coast.
- Ermine Street headed north to Scotland (via Lincoln and York).

- The Great Road led to Colchester, via Gidea Park and Chelmsford, and continued into Norfolk.
- Stane Street went to Chichester and Fishbourne.

Three sub-roads were important to the Epping-Forest region:

- Stane Street branched off Ermine Street and properly began at Braughing. It passed through Dunmow and Braintree and reached Colchester, following the route of today's A120 from near Standon, which is not far from Braughing, the Catuvellauni's capital in Hertfordshire.

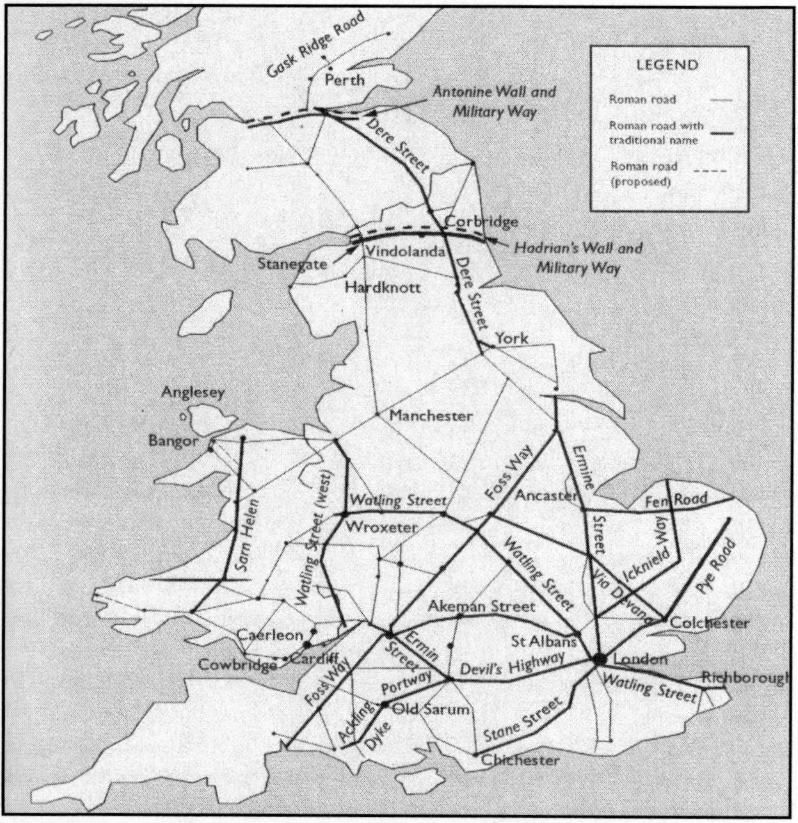

The six Roman trunk roads from Londinium.

- Another sub-road passed through the Roding valley. It began near the Roman marker-stone beneath the High Stone near the Green Man roundabout, Leytonstone ('Lea-town stone') and passed through Roding Lane North, South Woodford (the site of the Roman road at Woodford Bridge)[38] and part of Chigwell High Road (near the Roman building in Chigwell)[39] to Abridge, Abbess Roding and Dunmow, where it intersected with Stane Street. This sub-road passed between Epping Forest and Hainault Forest.
- Another sub-road from London to Norfolk passed through Abridge, Hobbs Cross farm, Theydon Garnon, Coopersale, Wintry Wood (along what became the medieval Old Stump Road, so-called because its course through boggy terrain is marked by tree stumps), and Thornwood before reaching Harlow.

Roman remains in Epping Forest

Roman remains have been discovered in all the places I have just mentioned. A Roman road has been found at Abridge along with a site of Roman cremation and a poppy-head beaker.[40] Evidence of a Roman settlement has been found at Abridge.[41] In Abridge, a hypocaust (the hollow space under a Roman floor into which hot air was sent to heat a room or a bath) suggests a villa or bathhouse.[42] A Roman lead coffin has been found in Abridge,[43] along with a Roman ditch, a timber-lined well, a site of Roman cremation and a Roman coin.[44] At Hobbs Cross Roman ditches have been found along with a Roman tile, brick and stone, a Roman kiln site[45] and a lead coffin.[46] In Theydon Bois and Theydon Garnon two Roman villas have been found[47] along with Roman pottery,[48] Samian pottery[49] and the site of a Roman tile kiln.[50] At Coopersale Street Roman pottery has been found.[51] At Thornwood Common the Roman road has been found, along with a Roman settlement site,[52] and the remains of a Roman pottery kiln.[53] A coin of Domitian has been found in a garden in Allnutts Road, Epping.[54]

Oak trees were probably felled in the south-western tip of Epping Forest during the construction of these last two sub-roads. Essex had no stone which could be used in road construction, and timber had to be used instead. The trees were squared off to build Roman wharves near London Bridge.

Triangle of trunk roads

The three most important Roman towns in the south-east, London (Londinium), St Albans (Verulamium) and Colchester (Camulodunum), formed a triangle, and trunk roads led between them: from London to Colchester, from London to St Albans, and from St Albans to Colchester along a sub-road that came out to Stane Street. Within this triangle were the Lea and Roding valleys and the sub-road that serviced them.

The Catuvellauni and Trinovantes both had a presence within this triangle. Harlow was a Roman town of some significance. It was within the territory of the Catuvellauni but on the frontier of the territory of the Trinovantes. The Trinovantes had co-operated with the Romans and formed a *civitas* in Roman Britain. Their chief town was now Caesaromagus ('Caesar's plain', Chelmsford).

Boudicca's Revolt against the Romans in AD61, and Epping Forest

Rome annexes the Iceni's land

The Iceni of Norfolk had agreed to act as a Roman client kingdom. But they had been forced to pay an indemnity after a minor rising, and had been harried by Roman tax-collectors.

Their king Prasutagus had died in AD60. The Romans expected a client king to leave his kingdom to Rome in his will. The Roman historian Tacitus tells us in *The Annals* (book XIV, ch.31) that he divided his kingdom equally between his two daughters, who shared one half, and the Roman Emperor, who had the other half, hoping that this arrangement would lead to tranquillity. This was not acceptable to Rome.

Roman centurions forcibly annexed the territory of the Iceni and confiscated Prasutagus's estate under the pretence of carrying out the terms of his will, as the Roman Emperor was part heir. Roman soldiers ravaged his kingdom and plundered his house. They flogged his widow Boudicca (also wrongly spelt Boadicea) and raped her daughters. The king's relatives were treated like slaves and the Icenian chiefs were deprived of their hereditary estates.

There is evidence that the Romans broke the Iceni's weapons, a great insult in Icenian culture. The retired soldiers at Camulodunum treated the Trinovantes abominably, driving them from their homes and their land and insultingly calling them prisoners and slaves. The priests at the temple of Claudius were looting the country's wealth.

Queen Boudicca's rebels burn Camulodunum

Boudicca, queen of the Iceni, rallied her people and other tribes, including the Trinovantes who resented the loss of their lands to retired Roman soldiers.

The Romans had been able to leave the retired soldiers in Camulodunum and concentrate on the pacification of Wales. Suetonius Paulinus, Roman governor from 59 to 61, invaded Anglesey (then known as Mona) and levelled the groves of Druids. Then news came that the Iceni had rebelled and that the whole province was up in arms.

The retired soldiers sent to Catus Decianus, the procurator (imperial agent) of the province, for reinforcements. Only 200 incompletely armed men could be spared and these were added to the small garrison. The temple was protected but no other preparations were made, and the elderly and women remained in the garrison.

It was easily overrun by the Iceni, and Camulodunum was burnt. The garrison barricaded itself into the temple, which fell two days later. The commander of the 9th legion, Quintus Petillius Cerialis, marched to relieve Camulodunum but the Iceni routed him and massacred his infantry. The procurator, Catus Decianus, fled to Gaul (France).

The Iceni sack Londinium and Verulamium

Dismayed by the news, Suetonius marched from Anglesey to Londinium (London). There he decided he had too few soldiers to do any better than Cerialis, and he withdrew. The Iceni sacked Londinium, which was largely unprotected as the main army was returning from Wales, and slaughtered the population. They then went on to

Verulamium (St Albans), where there was no Roman garrison, and massacred the population. In all, Tacitus says in *The Annals* (XIV, ch.33) 70,000 citizens or allies of Rome were massacred.

Suetonius engages the rebels

Suetonius put together an army. His 14th legion, the veterans of the 20th legion from Camulodunum and nearby auxiliaries (soldiers from the provinces) amounted to nearly 10,000 men, Tacitus informs us. He moved to engage the rebels. Tacitus says (XIV, ch.34):

> "He decided to attack without delay. He chose a position in a defile with a wood behind him. There could be no enemy, he knew, except at his front, where there was open country without cover for ambushes."[55]

Other translations say: "He chose a spot encircled with woods, narrow at the entrance, and sheltered in the rear by a thick forest." Or: "He chose a place approached by a narrow ravine, and in the rear enclosed by a wood."

Suetonius, Tacitus continues, "drew up his regular troops in close order, with the light-armed auxiliaries at their flanks, and the cavalry massed on the wings". The British numbered 80,000. Their "cavalry and infantry bands seethed over a wide area". In other words they formed no regular line of battle. They were so self-confident that they had "confidently brought their wives to see the victory, installing them in carts stationed at the edge of the battlefield".

Boudicca drove round all the tribes in a chariot with her two daughters in front of her. She cried out that she was fighting for her lost freedom and to revenge the flogging she had received and the rape of her daughters. She reminded them that a Roman division had already been defeated and that the Romans were afraid. She pointed to the numbers of the British, who outnumbered the Romans 8 to 1. Suetonius also spoke, drawing attention to "the clamours and empty threats of the natives".

Suetonius gave the signal for battle. Tacitus says (XIV, ch.37):

> "At first the regular troops stood their ground. Keeping to the defile as a natural defence, they launched their javelins accurately at the approaching enemy. Then, in wedge formation, they burst forward. So did the auxiliary infantry. The cavalry, too with lances extended, demolished all serious resistance. The remaining Britons fled with difficulty since their ring of wagons blocked the outlets. The Romans did not spare even the women. Baggage animals too, transfixed with weapons, added to the heaps of dead....According to one report almost eighty thousand Britons fell. Our own casualties were about 400 dead and a slightly larger number of wounded. Boudicca poisoned herself."

Other translations say, "The narrow defile gave them the shelter of a rampart," and "The legion kept their ground immovably, sheltering themselves within the defiles as with [within] a bulwark; till the enemy, having come near them, had received all their darts [i.e. javelins], discharged at a sure [i.e. safe] distance, when they sallied out upon them in a kind of wedge." It is clear that the Romans used the "defile" as a "natural defence" or "rampart".

Suetonius's defile and Ambresbury Banks

There are differing claims as to where Boudicca's last stand of AD61 took place. There is a strong local tradition that it happened at Ambresbury Banks, Epping, and Epping Upland.[56] (Epping Upland is now a village north-west of Epping, and it may be mentioned because there is a green and forest in the background. But in some sources 'Epping Upland' is the civil parish created in 1896 that includes the high ground on which Ambresbury Banks stands, and it may refer to the terrain around Ambresbury Banks.)[57] Others have said that it took place at King's Cross[58] in London, somewhere near Watling Street, or at Mancetter in Warwickshire, or in Northampton, or near Milton Keynes. But the British had moved from London, which they had sacked, to St Albans. They surely did not go back to London, where the Romans were returning, and there was no need to head north to Warwickshire or Northampton or Bedfordshire as Tacitus tells us that

Suetonius had already arrived in London.

The capital of the territory of the Trinovantes was Caesaromagus (Chelmsford), and it is likely that the retired Roman soldiers of Camulodunum (Colchester) had dispossessed them of some of their lands at Chelmsford. It would have made sense for the British to return from St Albans with a view to making their way back to Chelmsford to massacre any Romans there, and to Colchester (Camulodunum), which the Trinovantes would want to secure from any Roman counter-offensive. The Iceni would then return to Norfolk to consolidate their newly independent tribal region, having thrown off the Roman yoke.

The strongest local Epping-Forest tradition (supported by the 18th-century Essex historian Philip Morant, author of the two-volume *The History and Antiquities of the County of Essex*, 1763 and 1768)[59] is that the battle took place in the hill-fort earthwork at Ambresbury Banks, which archaeological evidence suggests was occupied from 700BC to AD43.[60] Thomas Wright in *The People's History of Essex* (1861) says: "Morant and others, whose authority is decisive say – 'The famous battle between Suetonius and Boadicea was fought somewhere between Epping and Waltham, near which a fine camp remains.'"[61] There is a local tradition that Boudicca poisoned herself by eating berries, and an even stronger local tradition that she picked hemlock growing alongside Cobbin's Brook, Upshire. In the park at Warlies Hall, Upshire, near which Cobbin's Brook trickles a mile north-west of Ambresbury Banks, there are two 18th-century obelisks erected during landscaping that mark the spots where Boudicca is alleged to have taken poison and died. This story was supported by the Waltham-Abbey local historian William Winters.[62] Some sceptics assert that the owner of Warlies Hall invented this story in the 18th century.

Roman remains round Ambresbury Banks

Roman remains have been found all round Ambresbury Banks. A bronze figure of Hercules[63] has been found in Epping along with a Roman pottery kiln,[64] Roman pottery[65] and a Roman tile kiln.[66] Samian pottery (fine red pottery from the Roman Empire, especially Gaul, from which Caesar launched his expedition in 54BC) has been found in Epping.[67] and in Epping Upland.[68] There was a Romano-British settlement in Epping.[69] Roman pottery has been found at Copthall Green, Upshire,[70] along with Samian pottery.[71] Roman remains have been found in the Warren Wood across the B1393 from Ambresbury Banks[72] and at High Beach.[73]

High Beach pillow mounds as funeral pyres?

The Waltham-Abbey area and High Beach are also associated with Boudicca's defeat. William Addison writes in a 'Topographical Note' at the end of *Epping Forest, Its Literary and Historical Associations* that the pillow mounds at High Beach were linked to both Ambresbury Banks and Loughton Camp, according to Hazzledine Warren, the Loughton archaeologist who conducted excavations at High Beach in 1925 and studied the prehistory of the Forest for many years. Warren believed that the pillow mounds were ritual structures, remains of the funeral pyres of men killed in battle.[74]

This is a controversial interpretation as the collective wisdom now is that they formed artificial rabbit warrens, the Iron-Age potsherds having been brought up from underground by rabbits, see p.37. However, there are pillow mounds (so described on the Ordnance Survey map) on Dartmoor surrounded by Bronze-Age settlements and roundhouses, and these pillow mounds were not artificial rabbit warrens but are regarded as prehistoric features.

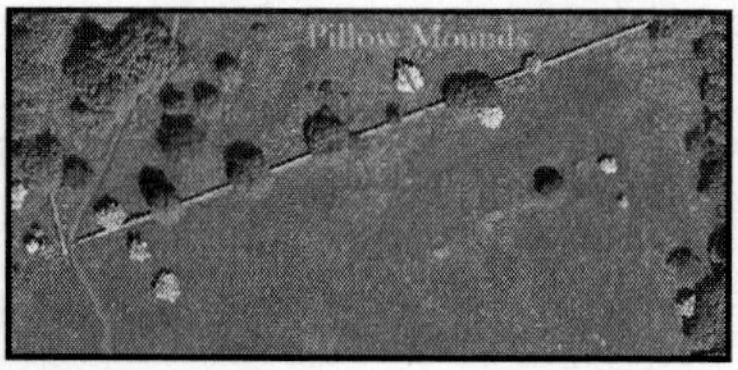

High Beach pillow mounds.

It has to be said that there is no direct evidence for any of the aspects of this local tradition, as many books point out. However, there is a good deal of circumstantial evidence, and a moment's thought can give a plausible explanation for these disconnected references, connect them up and present a coherent account of what *might* have happened.

What might have happened

Boudicca may have left St Albans (Verulamium) with her vast army, and headed towards London down Watling Street. She may have branched off on the sub-road that connected with Ermine Street to meet up with Britons she had left to mop up in London, who had advanced to rejoin her, and may have been set to proceed to Chelmsford and then Colchester. This route would have taken her towards Waltham Abbey, where a Roman road and traces of a Romano-British settlement have been found, along with much Roman pottery,[75] Roman brick,[76] Samian pottery,[77] Romano-British pottery and a coin.[78]

In the vicinity of Waltham Abbey, five kilometres from Ermine Street by the River Lea, they may have turned inland and headed up to the high ground of High Beach, which is 300 feet above sea level and overlooks the River Lea. Here there was a third hill-fort with a single defensive bank.[79] Beyond this was one of the Trinovantes' Iron-Age hill-fort earthworks, Loughton Camp, which had been abandoned eighteen years earlier in c.AD43. High Beach has been thought to have been used as a look-out for Loughton Camp before it was abandoned.

Iron-Age remains have been found all round this area: a hoard of Iron-Age coins and gold coins at Theydon Bois,[80] a gold coin at Coopersale Common,[81] a coin at Chigwell,[82] gold coins at Chingford[83] and Iron-Age pottery at Abridge.[84]

The rural Iceni and Trinovantes would have been happy to camp out in the open on this plateau. Their homes were not in towns, which were a Mediterranean invention. They were used to country living. Some 80,000 of them would have been spread along the high ground which commanded a view over the River Lea, from High Beach to Bell Common, Epping, with a view to resting, sleeping on the open plain near their wagons and reorganising themselves before continuing to Caesaromagus (Chelmsford), the one large town in the area they still had to rid of retired Roman soldiers. As the crow flies, High Beach is almost directly midway between St Albans and Chelmsford.

Boudicca herself may have rested not in Ambresbury Banks, as local tradition asserts, but in nearby Loughton Camp. She would have known of both Iron-Age earthworks and may have used them after they were abandoned, seemingly in AD43.

In Londinium (London) Suetonius Paulinus would have been told by his spies where Boudicca was heading. He would have had to position his force between Boudicca and Chelmsford, the next place to be defended. His force of nearly 10,000 either advanced up Ermine Street to the Waltham area (marching in the opposite direction to the one Boudicca's army had come from), or travelled by ship up the River Lea from where it flows into the Thames near Bow. At Waltham there was a causeway across the river that linked to Ermine Street. Suetonius and his army would also have turned inland and, either arriving before Boudicca's army or outflanking it, placed themselves to the Chelmsford side of where the Britons would sleep.

Outnumbered by eight to one, he needed a defensive place with a rampart and ditch which he could defend.

We have seen that Tacitus writes of a "defile with a wood behind it" which served as "a natural defence", which can also be translated as "a narrow ravine, and in the rear enclosed by a wood", "a spot encircled with woods, narrow at the entrance and sheltered in the rear by a thick forest", a "narrow defile" that "gave them the shelter of a rampart". Tacitus makes no mention of hills. A defile is defined in the *Concise Oxford Dictionary* as "a narrow way through which troops can only march in file". A defile suggests a narrow opening, so narrow that an army may have to march in single file to pass through it.

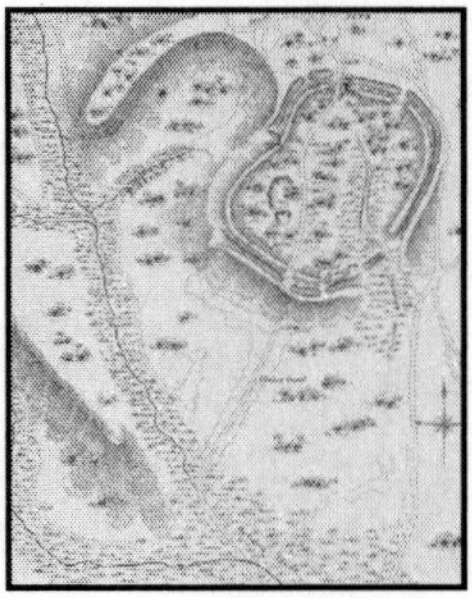

Loughton Camp showing possible defile (gap between walls).

There are not many places in the High Beach-Loughton-Epping area that fit this description, where 10,000 could be protected by a narrow defile and yet be able to draw themselves up in a long line behind it, which has led some to hazard a guess that the defile was not in the Epping-Forest area. We are looking for a place where 10,000 can gather behind a narrow defile, draw themselves up behind it in a long line, infantry in the middle and cavalry at either end, and then rush out of it in one, two or three files. There has to be enough space to run out and form a "wedge". Such a place could not have been the sloping hillside between Earl's Path and Loughton Camp. That terrain is too steep to have been the plain on which 80,000 Britons could camp.

Tacitus and Agricola

It must be remembered that Tacitus's father-in-law was the Roman general Gnaeus Julius Agricola, who had served as military tribune on the staff of Suetonius Paulinus, governor of Britain from 59 to 61 before himself becoming governor of Britain from 77 to 84. Tacitus was not present at the battle, and was writing more than 50 years after the event and based his account on descriptions that had reached Rome. He was not an eyewitness of the "defile", although his father-in-law Agricola had probably been an eyewitness. Tacitus may have discussed the battle with Agricola before Agricola's death in 93. Tacitus also had access to the State sources: the *acta senatus* (senate minutes), the *acta diurna populi Romani* (news of government decrees), Emperors' speeches and other literary and historical sources.

It must be said that Tacitus's narration of specific events that have attracted scholarly interest and close scrutiny has been regarded as accurate, for example his reference to Christ and Pontius Pilate while describing the fire that burnt much of Rome in 64, which he wrote about c.116 in his *Annals* (book 15, ch.44). Just as his account of the fire has been accepted as accurate and authentic even though it was written fifty-two years after the event, so too his account of the defile, which may have been based on Agricola's information, may be equally accurate and authentic although it was written equally long after the event. It must not be forgotten that the physical geography of Epping Forest has changed during the last two thousand years, and what was then a plain can be proved to have been subsequently covered by trees. However, the geography of the "defile" will not have changed: the contours that create a narrow area will still be present.

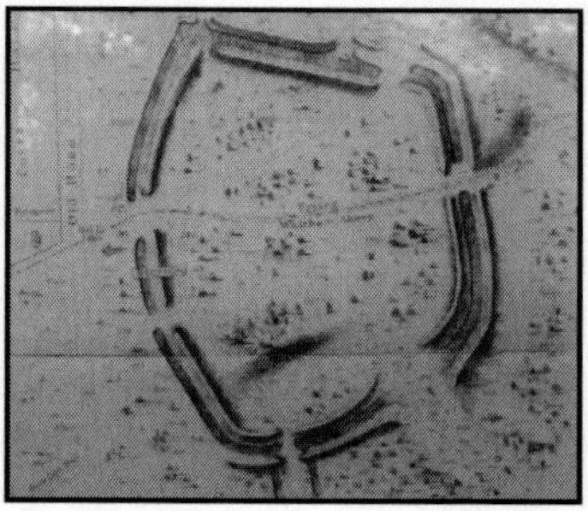

Ambresbury Banks showing the defile (entrance gap between walls).

Tacitus's rampart as Ambresbury Banks?

Tacitus's description fits the abandoned Iron-Age hill-fort earthwork of Ambresbury Banks, which is horseshoe-shaped with a narrow opening where (it was established by the 1958 excavation) double wooden gates once stood over central post holes before the hill-fort was abandoned.[85] The fort was surrounded by a wood on three sides and there is a sloping valley behind it beyond Jack's Hill. The wall is now six feet high with a surrounding ditch.

In 43AD, before it was abandoned or sacked, the wall would have been 10-12 feet high with a 12-30-foot-wide, 6-10-foot-deep U-shaped moat or ditch (see p.12), and the front would have commanded a view of the plain or plateau, across what is now the Epping Road (B1393). Such a prospect from Ambresbury Banks has been confirmed by evidence of wild service trees[86] before the front of the earthwork, which indicate a regrown forest. Morant says that the battle was fought near where a "fine camp remains", and this plain between Epping and Waltham would accord with his view of the battlefield.

A "rampart" is defined in the *Concise Oxford Dictionary* as "a defensive wall with a broad top and usually a stone parapet" and as having "a walkway on top of such a wall". A "parapet" is defined as "a defence of earth or stone to conceal and protect troops".

A "rampart" is a defensive wall with a walkway on top, here the earth wall of the abandoned hill-fort earthwork. The Roman troops could have lined up within the horseshoe near the front entrance of the camp behind the "rampart" with a "defile", infantry in the middle and cavalry at each wing, confident that with trees on three sides they could not be taken from the rear.

The Britons would be visible on the plain in front of them, which would have extended beyond the Epping Road for a wide area from High Beach to Bell Common. Outnumbering the Romans by eight to one the Britons would have been confident of annihilating the Romans, having defeated Cerialis's ninth legion and anticipating a push against the Roman occupiers of Caesaromagus (Chelmsford).

Suetonius had chosen a site for the battle that allowed for battle discipline, and the rebels played into his hands by accepting his choice of site, which required them to be spread out. Suetonius gave the signal for battle.

Roman regular troops hurled their javelins, "keeping the defile as a natural defence". In other words, they were still within the horseshoe. And the Britons had come within javelin range, lured onto Suetonius's chosen site. Then in wedge formation the regular infantry burst out from the horseshoe, followed by the auxiliary infantry and the cavalry. They pushed the Britons in two directions: towards High Beach and towards Upshire, both of which were a mile and a half away in different directions. The ring of wagons would have penned the Britons in along the edge of the high ground at High Beach and along towards Bell Common. The Romans slaughtered 80,000 Britons for the loss of only 400 Romans.

Boudicca would have been driven back towards Upshire, and picked hemlock (or poisoned berries) on the bank of Cobbin's Brook, a tributary of the Lea, near Upshire, and then ridden back to the site of the main obelisk near Copped Hall, which was a vantage point from which she could view Ambresbury Banks a mile and a half away. She saw that her army had been massacred and took the poison. Some Britons may have fled to what is now the village of Epping Upland. Suetonius had prevented Chelmsford from being sacked like Colchester, London and St Albans.

The dead had to be removed. The Romans probably ignored the

Britons and made funeral pyres for the 400 Romans. The 20 long "pillow mounds" that can be seen in front of the King's Oak, High Beach today may have begun as earthwork funeral pyres for the Roman dead.

I have said that the 1925 excavator, Hazzledine Warren, pronounced the mounds to be historic ritual structures as they were found to contain many flints and Iron-Age potsherds. (See p.31.) I have said that they are now thought to be artificial rabbit warrens built by the Normans or people who lived between c.1550 and 1850, rabbits being blamed for the presence of Iron-Age potsherds within them found by Hazzledine Warren in 1925. But they may have begun as Roman funeral pyres and been converted into rabbit warrens by the Normans or post-c.1550 locals.

If that is so, the presence of Iron-Age potsherds within the pillow mounds is due to the scooping and mounding of funeral pyres from earth strewn with fragments of pots broken during the slaughter of the Britons. I follow William Addison's suggestion that the pillow mounds were originally raised-earth funeral pyres for some of those fallen in battle.

Suetonius recalled to Rome

After his victory Suetonius Paulinus acted harshly. Having massacred 80,000, he conducted a series of merciless reprisals, and the new procurator of the province, Julius Classicianus arranged for him to be recalled to Rome. Classicianus sought a more peaceful and harmonious partnership between the Britons and the Roman Empire, and Suetonius's repressive methods had become a liability.

Tacitus, writing about his father-in-law, the Roman general Gnaeus Julius Agricola, in *De vita et moribus Iulii Agricolae*, ch.30, has the British chieftain Calgacus address his warriors about Rome's appetite for conquest and plunder: "*Ubi solitudinem faciunt, pacem appellant.*" ("Where they make a desert, they call it peace.")

Was Suetonius at Ambresbury Banks?

Was Suetonius briefly in the abandoned Ambresbury Banks in AD61?

An open-minded inquirer, looking at the larger picture, sets out the circumstantial evidence of where the Norfolk-based Boudicca may have headed from St Albans and of the Roman need to protect Chelmsford. Does the terrain accord with Tacitus's description? Would there have been trees behind Ambresbury Banks in AD61? Had knowledge and maps of the abandoned hill-forts been passed down to Suetonius from the records of Caesar's expedition in 54BC and Claudius's in AD43? It would make sense that he would head for a *known* "defile" if Boudicca's forces were camped out in the open on the plateau rather than have to find a suitable place from scratch with the enemy nearby.

Direct evidence will not be available until a fully systematic archaeological investigation of Ambresbury Banks has taken place.

Roman Occupation and Loughton

The conquest of Britain

The Roman conquest proceeded. Wales was conquered by 78. In c.90 three legions remained permanently based in York, Chester and Caerleon. Scotland was a problem, and Hadrian built his stone wall (c.122-130), the most impressive frontier work in the Roman Empire and the permanent frontier of Roman Britain. There was an attempt to occupy Scotland.

Then Septimius Severus, the Roman Emperor from Leptis Magna in Libya, built permanent bases on Scotland's east coast. He died during a campaign in Britain in 211.

Caracalla

His son by a Syrian (Julia Domna), Caracalla, Emperor from 211 to 217, extended Roman citizenship to almost all the inhabitants of the empire in his *Constitutio Antoniniana de Civitate* of 212 (a device to collect more taxes).

Caracalla was not himself present in Britain once he had become Emperor, but his coins were. I know, for when I was a pupil at Oaklands School, Albion Hill, Loughton in the autumn of 1946 (I would think) I remember leaving school one afternoon, crossing the High Road, standing by the red pillar-box and looking down at the sloping waste land that adjoins the top of The Crescent, near its junction with the High Road. A mechanical digger, a forerunner of a JCB, was gouging hard clay and depositing it. I saw something gleam and fall during a deposit, and when it was safe, tiptoed down across wild grass and retrieved it from the edge of the clay.

It was a copper or bronze coin. When I washed the mud off I saw its reverse said SC (an abbreviation for "*senatus consultum*", "a formal resolution of the senate") within a wreath. On the front was a small worn head facing right with stamped lettering that began on the left and disappeared overhead as the stamp was not central.

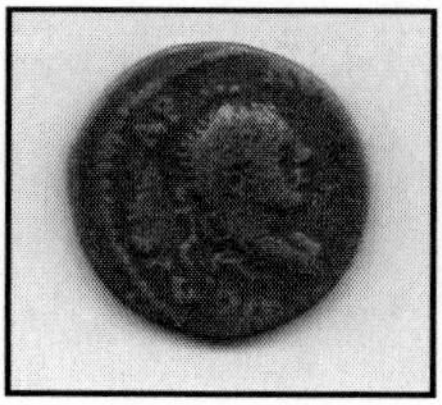

Coin of Caracalla.

Later I had the head identified by Seaby's as Caracalla's, possibly colonial coinage. A coin of Caracalla in Roman Britain, proof that a Roman (or Briton) had dropped it on the hillside, perhaps proof that there was a Roman settlement on the hillside across the High Road from Albion Hill in the early 3rd century. It would have lain near the Roman villa in Loughton[87] and the Roman building at Loughton's Long Shaw;[88] near the Roman remains in High Beach; not far from a Roman villa's *tesserae*, hypocaust and flue-tile on the north-west bank of Perch Pond, Wanstead Park;[89] not far from Roman ditches and pottery found in Chingford[90] and another villa there near Roman ditches[91] and Roman buildings;[92] not far from the Roman remains in Warren Wood (just across the road from Ambresbury Banks) and Copthall Green, Upshire; and not far from the Roman tile kiln near St Margaret's Hospital, Epping. I still have the coin.

2

Anglo-Saxons and Normans

Soon after the withdrawal of the Romans following the fall of Rome in 410, Essex, and Epping Forest, fell under the rule of new invaders. Their invasions began before the Romans left.

Anglo-Saxons

Angles

The region of the Trinovantes was invaded by old Germanic tribes. Angles (Latin '*Anglii*') from Schleswig-Holstein occupied East Anglia and parts of modern Essex by the end of the 5th century.

Saxons supplant Angles

Saxons from Northern Germany (Old Saxon 'Sahson', Old English 'Seaxe') raided by boat between the 5th century and 850, and superseded the Angles in Essex. Their boats came up the tributaries of the Thames and they established communities in the Lea and Roding valleys.

The local people were now under Saxon authority. The Saxons built wooden houses round an open space which acted as their village green. They cultivated a couple of fields for their own use. Each family was allowed a few strips in fields belonging to the community, and their cattle, sheep and goats grazed the surrounding area which was in common, a concept that was to persist in Epping Forest. Pigs ate acorns and beech nuts in the Forest. The number of oaks rapidly increased and their leaves were shunned by animals and their seedlings resisted being ripped apart by animals' feet.

Essex is ceded to Saxons

Essex was ceded by the Britons to the Saxons in c.460, according to the account in book 6 of the 12th-century *Historia Regum Britanniae* by Geoffrey of Monmouth, who based his information on the 9th-century *Historia Brittonum* by the Welsh historian Nennius.

After the Romans left Britain, the High King of the Britons, Vortigern, allowed Anglo-Saxons, probably Jutes from Jutland, under Hengist and Horsa to settle in the Isle of Thanet. They agreed to serve as mercenaries against the raiding Picts and Scots. Hengist and Horsa took advantage of Vortigern, forcing him into allowing many more settlers to arrive and granting them the territory of Kent.

A peace treaty was to be cemented by the marriage of Hengist's daughter Rowena to Vortigern. In return for this intermarriage, Essex and Sussex were ceded by the Britons to the settlers, along with Kent. A banquet was arranged in modern Wiltshire, in the vicinity of Salisbury Plain. Saxons, Angles and Jutes arrived with their long knives (*seaxes*, the swords on the Essex county shield) hidden under their clothing. At a given command during the feast, the Saxons drew their long knives and killed all the Britons except for Vortigern and one other. The Saxons' treachery came to be known in Welsh as "*Brad y Cyllyll Hirion*" ("The Treachery of the Long Knives").

Seven kingdoms of Anglo-Saxons

According to sources, including Bede, the Angles founded kingdoms in north England (Northumbria), east England (East Anglia) and middle England (Mercia). The Jutes from Jutland founded a kingdom in Kent in the 6th century and also settled the Isle of Wight. Four separate Saxon realms emerged:

- The East Saxons created the Kingdom of Essex in 527.
- The Middle Saxons created the Province of Middlesex.
- The South Saxons created the Kingdom of Sussex.
- The West Saxons created the Kingdom of Wessex.

The Kingdom of Essex soon expanded into Middlesex and from c.500 to 850 there were effectively seven kingdoms in Britain, which were known as the Anglo-Saxon Heptarchy:

- the three kingdoms of the Angles: Northumbria, East Anglia and Mercia;
- the kingdom of the Jutes: Kent;
- the three dominant kingdoms of the Saxons: Essex, Sussex and Wessex.

Eventually the Normans called the English tribes collectively "Anglo-Saxons", and their name has stuck.

The East Saxons' Kingdom of Essex, 527-825

Essex was the largely wooded kingdom of the East Saxons, taking its name from the '*seaxe*', the sword that still appears on the county shield. The first king of Essex was Aescwine, who according to tradition first led the East Saxons across the North Sea. The kingdom he founded in 527 included most of the lands in the modern counties of Essex, Hertfordshire and Middlesex. It included the remains of the Roman capitals of Camulodunum (Colchester) and Londinium (London), and also Verulamium (St Albans). It was the successor state to the Trinovantes.[1]

The Saxons brought their gods, Thor and Woden. The Kingdom of Essex claimed descent from Woden. It had been briefly converted to Roman Christianity following the landing in Kent of the missionary Augustine in 597, but had returned to heathenism in 616. Oswald, King of Northumbria, had brought missionaries from Iona to spread the Celtic Christian faith from Northumbria. In Essex King Sigeberht II, the Good, received St Cedd, a monk in Lindisfarne in Northumbria who had been sent to Essex as a missionary, and the Kingdom of Essex was converted to Celtic Christianity in 653.

The Kingdom of Essex grew by absorbing other Saxon tribal groups who had formed sub-kingdoms. Such sub-kingdoms are thought to have included the Rodings ('the people of Hrotha')[2] and Epping (Uppingas, 'the people of Epp', according to one derivation, although there is another derivation – see below.[3]

At the beginning of the 8th century the Kingdom of Essex included Kent, and the Essex kings issued their own coins (*sceattas*). After the loss of Kent, Essex's northern and southern borders were those of the modern county of Essex. By the mid-8th century the Kingdom of Essex ceded territory west of the River Lea, including London, to Mercia. The reduced Essex was now subordinate to Mercia.

Essex annexed by the West Saxons' Wessex

For most of its life the Kingdom of Essex was subservient to an overlord. Besides being ruled by Kent and East Anglia at different times, it was ruled by first Northumbria, then Mercia, and finally Wessex. Wessex (the West Saxon Kingdom) conquered the country. In 825 Egbert, King of Wessex, defeated Mercia in battle and was accepted as king of Kent, Surrey, Sussex and Essex. The last king of Essex, Sigered, ceded the kingdom to Egbert, who annexed it in 825.

In the 9th century Essex was part of a sub-kingdom of Wessex that included Sussex, Surrey and Kent. In 886 Alfred, king of Wessex, became lord of all the non-Danish-ruled lands in England. Alfred conquered the country and prepared the way for the founding of the Kingdom of England.

By the middle of the ninth century trees had been cleared back from the banks of the Lea and the Roding more or less to where they are today. The East Saxons left few archaeological traces, but they shaped the terrain we see.

Saxon names in Epping Forest

There are philological traces of Saxon names in many villages surrounding Epping Forest. Saxon settlements had names ending in -ing ('people of'), -ton ('town') and -ham ('home'). Thus:

- Epping meant '*ybbe ingas*', 'upland dwellers' – it was an early (probably 7th-century) East-Saxon settlement;
- Loughton comes from the Saxon Lukintone ('Luca's *ton*, town')

or Lukintune, ('Luca's *tun*, settlement'); and
- Waltham or Waldham (one of the oldest Saxon settlements in the Epping-Forest region),[4] *weald ham*, meant 'wood settlement', 'forest dwelling', 'forest homestead'.

Saxon villages also end in -field ('open country'), -stead ('place'), -ford ('river crossing'), -hurst (Anglo-Saxon *hyrst*, Old High German hurst, 'wood, thicket, wooded hill'), -don ('hill') and -ley ('clearing' in the sense of a clearing within trees or a wood'). Thus:

- Finchingfield meant 'open country of Finc's people'.
- Greensted, *grene stede*, meant 'green place'; Wanstead, *waen* or *wenn stede*, meant 'wagon or mound place'; and Stansted, '*stansteda*', meant 'stony place'.
- Chingford, meant either *cegingaford*, 'the dwellers by the stumpy ford', or *Chingelford*, 'chingelford' or 'shingly ford' [through the Lea] or 'ford through the river Ching', 'crossing of the Ching' (perhaps 'King's Ford', 'Ching' being Norman for 'King'); and Woodford meant 'ford [through the Roding] by the wood'.
- Buckhurst (originally 'Bocherste', *boc hyrst*) meant 'beech-wood'. (A reference in 1135 to La Bocherste reflects the Norman influence on Epping Forest. Later it was known as 'Bucket Hill', 'a hill covered with beech trees'.)
- Parndon, *peren dun*, meant 'pear-tree hill'.

Other examples in Essex but not in Epping Forest include:

- Great Bentley, *beonte leah*, which meant 'bent-grass clearing'.
- Roydon, *rygenan dun*, which means 'rye hill'; and Maldon, *mael dun*, which meant 'hill with a cross'.

Theydon, *thaec dene*, meant 'thatch-reed valley', referring to Theydon's southern boundaries on the Roding which abounded in reeds good for thatching. Roding, originally Roothing, meant 'the territory of Hrotha's people', as we saw on p.42.

Saxon Common Land

During the Saxon period hunting became very popular. Huntsmen used nets, traps, bows and dogs to catch deer, wild boar and hares. The Anglo-Saxon kings claimed pieces of common land as their own, justifying this by asserting that it would be for the common good if waste land could be supervised under royal charter.

Such land was called '*boc*-land'[5] or 'common land', and a king could hunt on it. (I have just said that in 'Buckhurst Hill', *boc hyrst* meant 'beech-wood', but it might also mean 'common wood [owned by the king]'. We shall see that in Tudor times the monarch treated Buckhurst Hill as his own hunting-ground. See pp.66-70.) What a royal huntsman caught on such land therefore went to the king, in return for which the huntsman was fed and clothed and might receive a small gift.

When ruled by the Celtic Trinovantes, the Roman conquerors and the East Saxons, the Epping-Forest region was prominent in the emergence of the Kingdom of England. This prominence continued under the Danes.

Danish Vikings

The Danish Viking raids had begun on a small scale in the 790s. In the early 9th century they turned into larger plundering incursions. The Vikings took their booty back to Denmark and Norway, and spared Essex at first as it was not considered a rich area. But in 851 the raiders wintered in England and made their first attacks on Essex, which they now dominated.

In 865 a large Danish army came to East Anglia, intent on conquest. In 871, having already seized York, it attacked Wessex. Alfred, who came to the throne of Wessex that year, made peace but during the 870s the Danes took over Mercia. They were forced out of Wessex in 877 but attacked Wessex again in 878. Alfred defeated them, and their king Guthrum was converted to Christianity and took his forces to East Anglia.

Essex under Danelaw, 878-920

In 878 by Alfred's Treaty of Wedmore with the Danish leader Guthrum, all lands east of Watling Street, including Essex, became part of the Danelaw (*Danelagh*). Essex became part of the kingdom of Greater East Anglia which Guthrum's Danish army founded.

In 886 Alfred pushed the Vikings back north of the Thames, captured London and was recognised as leader by all the English living outside the Danish areas. The Thames and Lea now formed the boundary between Saxon England and the Danelaw. The Vikings had taken control of Essex, and of Epping Forest, and both were under Danelaw. Essex was used by the Danes as a base from which to raid Saxon England.

After King Guthrum's death in 890, the Danes made more attacks on Alfred's kingdom. In 895 Hasten's Danes towed ships up the Lea and created a Danish military base near Hertford, twenty miles north of London. Alfred built forts in London on either side of the River Lea, and in 896 diverted the river so the Danish boats upstream were stranded in shallow water and were captured by the Saxons.

Alfred's successor, his son King Edward the Elder, began the reconquest of the Danish areas. In 912 he marched into Essex. In 917 he expelled the Danish garrison from Colchester. In 920 he reconquered Essex, which became part of a united England.

By now the hundred system had emerged in Saxon England. It was a traditional Germanic system described by Tacitus in his *Germania* in AD98. Introduced by the Saxons between 613 and 1017, a hundred had enough land (a hundred fields) to sustain a hundred households who managed all local issues under a hundred-man or hundred *eolder*. Essex was divided into 20 hundreds for the purpose of local government, courts and taxation. The hundreds developed into parishes, which were to survive a thousand years as a tier of local authority.

Essex again under Danelaw, 1016-1042

King Edward's successors (Athelestan, Edmund I, his brother Edred, Edmund's son Edwy, Edwy's brother Edgar the Peaceable, his son

Edward the Martyr and Ethelred II, the Redeless or Unready) all defended United England. Then in 991 sea-raider Danes attacked Ipswich and turned towards Essex. They defeated the English at the Battle of Maldon, at which the Saxon Byrhtnoth (or Brihtnoth), *ealdorman* (alderman) of the East Saxons of Essex, and his thanes, fought to the death.

The Danes rampaged into Essex. Ethelred tried to buy them off by paying Danegeld. He ordered a massacre of all Danes in England in 1002, and triggered the invasion by Sweyn of Denmark in 1003.

During the next ten years the Danes ravaged England, and Ethelred fled in 1013. Sweyn was now King of England. Both Ethelred and Sweyn died soon after, and their sons Cnut (Canute) and Edmund Ironside fought at Assundune (thought to be Ashingdon, Essex on the River Crouch rather than Ashdon near Saffron Walden).

Cnut defeated the English, killing Edmund, and became King of England in 1016. England was under Danish rule, an Anglo-Danish state, until 1042, and during Cnut's reign Essex was linked with East Anglia under Earl Thurkill.

To create a good impression among his English subjects, Cnut made gifts to monasteries. His Danish standard-bearer, Tovi (Tofig) the Proud, a powerful man with many estates, is often said to have founded the church of Waltham Holy Cross in the Epping-Forest region in 1030. Tovi possessed estates at Waltham and founded a hunting lodge there c.1020. A building called Viking Hall was excavated north of Waltham Abbey in 1969-71, which may be this hunting lodge.[6] A marble black stone cross found on his estate in Montacute, Somerset, was loaded onto an ox-drawn cart. The oxen drew the cart and headed in the direction of Waltham. As if by divine intervention it stopped there. Although he is said to have built the small church at Waltham to house the cross and to have granted some of his lands to the church, see p.174 for evidence that Tovi did not found or build the church at Waltham but merely housed the Holy Cross within it c.1030.[7]

Essex was under the Danish rule of Cnut; then of his natural son Harold I; and then of his son Hardacnut, who, a year before he died of overeating at a marriage feast in 1042, invited his half-brother Edward the Confessor to court.

Normans

Harold II and Waltham: The Norman Conquest and the End of the Saxon Line

Edward the Confessor succeeded Hardacnut as king in 1042, restoring the old Saxon line. England had reverted to the Saxon dynasty, and Viking attacks were renewed.

When Tovi died (in or after 1043) his estate, including the church of Waltham Holy Cross, passed to his son, Athelstan. It has been said that Athelstan fell into debt and that he was too weak to run the church. Athelstan forfeited his Waltham lands to Edward the Confessor, who granted them to Harold.[8]

Harold, son of Earl Godwin, was the most powerful man in England after the king. His powerful family had risen to prominence under Cnut. Godwin was the Earl of Essex, Wessex and Kent and his wife's supposed brother was the son-in-law of Sweyn I and father of Sweyn II. Harold's sister became Queen Consort of Edward the Confessor, who had no children of his own.

Because of this connection Harold became Earl of East Anglia in 1045. He accompanied his father Godwin into exile in 1051 and succeeded him as Earl of Essex, Wessex and Kent in 1053. He became Earl of Hereford in 1058, by which time he was the most powerful man in Essex, East Anglia, Wessex, Kent and now Hereford – in a large part of England.

Earl Harold rebuilds Waltham Holy Cross

Harold had been cured of paralysis by the Holy Cross at Waltham, and wanted to express his gratitude by upgrading the church, which was now in Edward the Confessor's hands. This may explain how he came to be granted the Waltham lands. Edward the Confessor asked Harold to rebuild the church of Waltham Holy Cross.

In 1060 Harold refounded and rebuilt the church at Waltham Holy Cross, employing Norman builders brought to England by Edward the Confessor. He endowed it with the lands of 17 lordships, gave it ornaments, plate and books and installed a Dean and a secular college of 12 lay canons (priests who lived in their own houses in the town of Waltham). He did this while Edward the Confessor was building Westminster Abbey.

Until it was supplanted by Westminster Abbey Harold's church of Waltham Holy Cross was the finest church in England. Edward attended the consecration of the church of Waltham Holy Cross in 1060.

Earl Harold holds Loughton and gives it to Waltham Holy Cross

We need to look more closely at Harold's endowment of 17 manors, which took place in 1060. Tovi's estates at Waltham, which passed to Harold via Athelstan and Edward the Confessor, amounted to 40 hides (2,400-4,800 acres) and the estate in Northland, Waltham amounted to 3 hides (180-360 acres). Harold held other lands and manors besides these.

Harold held four manors in and around Loughton. In honour of the consecration, in the same year, 1060, Harold gave all the lands in Lukintone or Lukintune – the 1062 Anglo-Saxon Loughton which had two manors and was described as the single-manor Lochintuna in the 1086 *Domesday Book* – and the manors of Alderton (Aelwartone) and Debden (Tippedene) to the 12 secular canons of Waltham Holy Cross, which already held the soil of Waltham Forest. Edward the Confessor confirmed the gift in 1062.[9] In addition to Loughton Harold gave Waltham Holy Cross the manor of Woodford and fifteen other manors.[10]

Loughton can thus look back to Earl Harold as the lord of four of its manors before 1060 and to the 12 lay canons of Waltham Holy Cross (after 1184 Waltham Abbey) as the lord of most of the land in the parish of Loughton from 1060 until 1540. For Loughtonians the Abbey building brings together its two main 'lords of the manor' at this time,

Earl Harold and the lay canons of Waltham Holy Cross (later the Augustinian canons of Waltham Abbey).

Waltham Abbey from west (left) and south (right).

Edward the Confessor promises William the English throne

Edward the Confessor had spent over twenty-five years in exile in Normandy during the Danish occupation of England, and he had got to know William, Duke of Normandy. In 1051 Earl Godwin (Harold's father) raised an army against King Edward the Confessor. The Witan (or Witenagemot, the Anglo-Saxon assembly of wise men which served England from before the 7th century to the 11th century) averted civil war by agreeing that Harold Godwin and his sons should be banished from England. They returned in 1052, and the end of the dispute was sealed when King Edward the Confessor was persuaded to marry Edith, Earl Godwin's daughter and Harold's sister. In the same year, probably before the dispute had been resolved, William, Duke of Normandy, visited Edward in London, and Edward, still disenchanted with the Godwins, seems to have promised him the throne.

Earl Harold's oath to William

Harold had been shipwrecked at Ponthieu, Normandy in 1064 and was allegedly taken to William, Duke of Normandy. He swore an oath of loyalty to William over the concealed bones of a saint. Harold did not realise that he was standing over bones, but from William's perspective he would perjure himself if he broke his oath.

There are other versions of what happened. According to one, Harold had been sent to Normandy by the childless Edward to appoint William, his maternal kinsman, as his heir. According to another, he was seeking to release members of his family held hostage since his father Godwin's exile in 1051. According to a third version, he had been driven across the Channel by a storm while fishing off the English coast.

Edward the Confessor puts England under Earl Harold's protection

Edward the Confessor now confused the issue of the succession. On his deathbed at the end of 1065, before he slipped into a coma, he ambiguously commended his widow and his kingdom to her brother Harold's "protection", and left his Waltham estate to Harold on condition that a monastery was built there. Edward died on 5 January 1066, and the Witenagemot (the Witan assembly) selected Harold to succeed. Harold was crowned probably in Westminster Abbey, the next day and ruled as Harold II.

Vikings from Norway invade England

The death of Edward the Confessor triggered the last Viking invasion by sea. Harold's brother Tostig, Earl of Northumbria, had doubled taxation on Northumbria in 1065. The Northumbrians revolted against their earl and, bowing to the demands of the rebels, Harold gave Tostig's earldom to Morcar of the House of Mercia. Tostig was now Harold's most bitter enemy, and he allied with Norway. Harold had driven his brother Tostig into the arms of Harald III Hardraade (or Hadrada), King of Norway, who wanted to conquer England as part of a colonial expansion that had seized Orkney, Shetland and the Hebrides islands.

Harald and Tostig invaded England and defeated Harold's wife's brothers Edwin, Earl of Mercia and Morcar of Northumbria (Tostig's replacement) at the battle of Fulford. Harold marched from London to Yorkshire in four days.

There is a story in Snorri Sturluson that before the battle a man (Harold), presumably with his face concealed, rode up to Tostig and offered him his earldom back if he would turn on Harald Hardraade. Tostig asked what he would give Harald. Harold replied, "Six feet of ground or as much more as he needs, as he is taller than most men." This story may be apocryphal as Harold's victory depended on surprise.

Harold defeats the Norwegians

On 25 September 1066 Harold attacked the Norwegian army at Stamford Bridge on the Derwent, killing Harald Hardraade and his own brother Tostig and sinking many ships. The Norwegians withdrew in their remaining twenty-five ships.

William invades England

On 1 October Harold heard that William, Duke of Normandy, who had been building 700 warships and had won the backing of the Church for his claim to the English throne, had landed at Pevensey and was marching on London. Still tired from fighting the Norwegians, Harold marched 241 miles to Hastings.

Harold prays at Waltham

On the way, he stopped at Waltham. There he prayed for victory in the church he refounded, Waltham Holy Cross. He marched on and reached Hastings on 11 October.

Harold killed at Hastings

On 14 October, twenty-four days after the defeat of Mercia and Northumbria by the Norwegians, Harold's exhausted army attacked the Norman army of William. The English battle-cry was "Holy Cross", a reference to Harold's stopping at the church of Waltham Holy Cross on his way to Hastings. After a battle lasting nine hours, Harold was killed when he was within half an hour of victory.

According to tradition and interpretations of the Bayeux Tapestry, he received an arrow in an eye and was then trampled by horses and mutilated beneath a horse's hooves. Some sources claim that he was found on the battlefield by Edith Swan-neck (*Swannesha*), or the swan-necked, the 'wife' he had married in a ceremony recognised by Danish law. The ceremony was not recognised by the English clergy, who regarded her as his mistress. He had had six children by her.

Perhaps because as king he needed a wife who would be recognised by the Church, in January 1066 Harold had married Ealdgyth and had two sons (perhaps twins) who were born in November 1066, after his death at Hastings.

There are conflicting traditions as to what became of Harold's body. According to one tradition it was buried in the church at Bosham, his birthplace near Chichester. A stronger tradition is that he was buried in the church at Waltham Holy Cross, and a marker stone points to the approximate location of his tomb outside the present Waltham Abbey – within the sanctuary of an older church, whose demolished walls left it out in the churchyard.

There is a story that Henry I (who came to the throne in 1100) met a monk called Harold at Waltham Holy Cross who was Harold II as an old man, a claim that he was not killed in the Battle of Hastings. However, the monk may have been one of Harold's posthumous twin sons, Harold Haroldsson. It has been suggested without evidence that this Harold occupied the Waltham tomb. See pp.183-93 for a further examination of the burial of Harold.

As a result of the Norman victory at Hastings, Harold's Saxon dynasty came to an end.

Norman Epping Forest

William was crowned at Westminster Abbey as William I, and was known as the Conqueror. Saxon Essex, which had become Danish Essex from 886 until 920 and again after twenty-five years of semi-occupation by the Danes, from 1016 to 1042, had now become Norman, as had what is now Epping Forest. During the Danish time Epping Forest, which was powerfully linked to Harold II through Waltham Holy Cross, had been fought over on and off by both the Saxon and

Danish sides.

King William I confiscates land

William swiftly established himself on the English throne as King of England. He lived at Barking Abbey not far from Epping Forest while the motte-and-bailey White Tower of the Tower of London was built as his headquarters.

William I dictatorially claimed legal ownership of the entire realm. Land was confiscated from English landowners and given to Normans. To bolster his position he handed out English lands to knights of the Norman aristocracy who had supported him. One such knight was Robert Gernon, who received lands in Chingford, Loughton and Leyton.

Domesday Book *and Epping Forest villages*

In 1085 William's power was threatened by the prospect of an invasion from King Canute of Denmark and King Olaf of Norway. He needed to reassess Danegeld to maximise his revenue. To learn about his new kingdom with a view to increasing taxation William ordered a survey of all lands. This became the *Domesday Book* of 1086, which found that there were some 70,000-80,000 people in Essex, settled in 440[11] places, out of an English population of 1.25 million. Essex is included with Norfolk and Suffolk in the *Little Domesday Book*, which compares conditions in 1086 with those at the time of the 1066 Conquest.

The entries for the Epping-Forest region show that the Saxons and Danes had cleared lands near the Lea and the Roding and created the Forest villages of Leyton, Walthamstow, Chingford, Wanstead, Woodford, Loughton, Chigwell, Theydon, Epping and Waltham Holy Cross. William I owned all lands in England, and the entries show who held the villages in demesne from him as tenants-in-chief, who were under-tenants and how many fisheries or mills there were. Each village had three arable fields, which could be tenanted by separate tenants-in-chief and let on to separate under-tenants. The survey shows that:

- Cing(h)efort (Chingford) had six manors, one of which was held by the canons of St Paul's before and after 1066, another of which was held by Robert Gernon (Ordgar being under-tenant), and there were 6 fisheries and a mill.
- Wenesteda (Wanstead) had two manors, the main one of which was held by the Bishop of London (Ralph FitzBrian, or son of Brian, being under-tenant) and there was a mill.
- Wodefort (Woodford) had two manors, the main one of which was held by the canons of Waltham Holy Cross before and after 1066, and there was a mill.
- Lochetuna/Lochintuna (Loughton in the 1086 *Domesday Book*, known as Lukinton in Edward the Confessor's charter of 1062 which granted estates to Waltham Holy Cross, as Lukintune elsewhere by the Saxons, as Luketune or Luketon in the 13th century, as Loketon or Lughton in the 14th century, as Loghton in a 1384 will and as Loughton in the 16th century)[12] had six manors (excluding Alderton and Debden), two of which were held by the canons of Waltham Holy Cross before and after 1066, one by William I's reeve, one by Robert Gernon (W. Corbun being under-tenant) and two by Peter de Valognes (Ralph and, in 1086, Leofcild being under-tenants, Ralph's land being near North's Farm, Buckhurst Hill),[13] and there was a mill.
- Cingheuuella (Chigwell) had eight manors, the main one of which was held by Earl Harold until 1066, and then by Ralph de Limesi, and there was a mill. It had seven adjoining manors.
- Taindena/Teidana (Theydon Bois, Theydon Garnon and Theydon Mount) had four manors, which were held by William FitzConstantine, son of Constantine, Swein of Essex (Robert being under-tenant), Eudo the Steward (who had replaced the pre-1066 Ulmar and held lands in Theydon Garnon),[14] and Peter de Valognes, and there were 18 beehives, 2 mills, 3 cobs, 3 foals, 92 pigs, 157 sheep and 15 goats.
- Ep(p)inga/Ep(p)inges (Epping) had three manors held by the

canons of Waltham Holy Cross before and after 1066 (land in the centre and south of Epping), Count Alan (Osbern being under-tenant) and Ranulf, brother of Ilger (two free men being his under-tenants). Some of the estates listed as being under Waltham Holy Cross extended into Epping.

- Wal(t)ham had eight manors, the main one of which (40 hides, a hide being 60-120 acres) was held by the Bishop of Durham, who seemed to have some control over Waltham Holy Cross,[15] and there were 3 mills, 5 fisheries, 12 London houses and a gate.[16]
- Waltham Holy Cross (later Waltham Abbey) was not mentioned in the *Domesday Book* as Church property was not taxable. In c.1086 Harold's college held only half a hide in Waltham (i.e. 30-60 acres).[17] Harold's endowment of Northland in Waltham amounted to three hides (180-360 acres).[18]

We now need to be very careful to distinguish the canons of Waltham Holy Cross from the manors of Loughton, Woodford and Northland[19] which Harold endowed to the canons; the manor of Northland which Harold endowed, most of which William seems to have confiscated; the remainder of Harold's lands in the parish of Waltham, which William confiscated; and, of course, Waltham Abbey, which did not come into existence until 1184, as we shall see. By making these distinctions we can pick our way through Waltham's tangled medieval history and grasp what actually happened.

Landholdings in Waltham

William I owns the canons of Waltham's lands in the parish of Waltham, 1066-1075

Waltham Holy Cross had been deprived of some of its landed property, notably its lands in the parish of Waltham, soon after the Norman Conquest because of its connection with King Harold. From 1066 to 1075 these lands belonged to William I. Harold's endowment of Loughton and Woodford does not seem have been confiscated. These manors continued to be held by the canons of Waltham Holy Cross.

William I gives lands in the parish of Waltham to Odo

William I temporarily put the confiscated lands in the parish of Waltham in the possession of his half-brother, Odo, Bishop of Bayeux and Earl of Kent, the builder of Bayeux Cathedral where the Bayeux Tapestry was found. It is thought that the Bayeux Tapestry was commissioned by Odo and stitched between 1070 and 1077. The confiscated lands in the parish of Waltham were therefore owned by the reputed commissioner of the Bayeux Tapestry while it was being created.[20]

William I gives lands in the parish of Waltham to the Bishop of Durham in 1075

In 1075 William I granted the remainder of Harold's lands in the parish of Waltham (some 40 hides) that were not a part of the manor of Northland in Waltham – or of the other lands endowed by Harold to the canons of Waltham Holy Cross (including Loughton and Woodford) – to Walcher, Bishop of Durham, to give him a home in London. Walcher also acquired 2½ of the 3 hides held by the college in Northland, and established some control over Waltham Holy Cross itself.[21] In 1086 these Waltham lands were held by his successor William of St Calais.

Canons of Waltham Holy Cross biggest landholder

The *Domesday Book* had found the Epping-Forest region to be occupied by small farming communities. Now the canons of Waltham Holy Cross were the biggest local landholder. They held 600 acres in Woodford alone, as well as four manors in the Loughton area. Much of Epping Forest, then known as Waltham Forest was owned by Waltham Holy Cross just as much of Hainault Forest (which meant 'wood belonging to a monastic community', a name dating from the 13th century) was owned by Barking Abbey.

William loved hunting and selected the countryside with the most deer for his own pursuit of hunting. It is thought that he hunted in Hainault Forest and Epping Forest while staying at Barking Abbey.

William I returned to Normandy and died in 1087, a year after the

Domesday Book, at the age of sixty. He was succeeded by William Rufus, who ruled as William II. He lacked his father's stature and authority, and eventually died in mysterious circumstances in the New Forest in 1100.

William II owns lands in the parish of Waltham, 1088-1091

In 1088 William II was in dispute with Bishop William of Durham as the Bishop had failed to oppose an unsuccessful rebellion against the king by Odo of Bayeux and others, and he took back the Waltham lands until 1091, and probably stripped the church of Waltham Holy Cross of its precious furnishings and sent them to St Stephen, Caen.[22]

The Bishop of Durham owns lands in the parish of Waltham, 1091-1177

In 1091 the lands in the parish of Waltham were returned to the Bishop of Durham, who, despite a further dispute when the Bishop of Durham's lands were again in William II's hands and were granted in dower to several successive queens, retained them until 1177.

Henry II owns lands in the parish of Waltham, 1177-1189

In 1177 the secular canons established by Harold II at Waltham Holy Cross were dissolved. The lands in the parish of Waltham were taken away from the see of Durham and were owned by Henry II, who re-established Harold's college of Waltham Holy Cross as a priory for Augustinian canons. He gave it abbey status in 1184 as part of his penance for the murder of Thomas à Becket.

Manor of Waltham held by its abbot and canons, 1189-1540

In 1189 Richard I succeeded Henry II, and for 300 marks granted the whole manor of Waltham, including the great wood and Harold's park, to the abbot and canons of Waltham Abbey. The canons had now gained possession of the lands held in 1086 by the Bishop of Durham and the lands in Epping and Nazeing mentioned in the *Domesday Book* as being held by Ranulf. From 1189 Waltham Abbey was controlled by its own administrators. There is no evidence that the Bishop of Durham had held any part of Epping, and the Epping manor held by the canons of Waltham Holy Cross remained in the possession of Waltham Abbey along with the manor of Waltham until the Dissolution in 1540.[23]

Norman Feudal System

The Normans had brought the feudal system to England.

Lords and vassals

The king owned all lands. A lord who held his lands direct from the king as opposed to another nobleman or prominent member of the clergy, was a tenant-in-chief, and he paid scutage (a tax) to the king and passed the cost on to his under-tenants. On his death his honour (i.e. lands) reverted to the Crown until his heir paid a sum of money to renew it.

This manorial system gave lords of the manor powers over the lower orders. It had begun in the Frankish Kingdom of the 8th century and had spread with the Frankish conquests. The social system of rights and duties was based on land tenure and personal relationships. Land was held in fief by vassals from lords, to whom they gave services and were bound by personal loyalty.

Peasants

In Essex, life for peasants became harder as they paid for the hire of their land by performing tasks, such as ploughing, weeding, reaping, hedge cutting, for their lord and by giving him a share of their produce. Thus, a share of all corn ground in the lord's mill and baked in his bakery had to go to his store. Those in the higher order, on the other hand, paid rent for their land and were relatively free; not in bondage.

Peasants were tied to their manor and could not leave it without their lord's consent. The farming system they worked in was based on rotation of crops in three fields, one of which was left fallow. The other two fields were prepared by ploughs pulled by teams of eight oxen. Barley or oats was sown in one field in spring, wheat or rye was sown in another field in autumn. Peasants had to give their lord an animal each year, and in return their animals were allowed to graze on the common lands. This applied to the common lands around Epping Forest. The peasants had the right to lop wood in Epping Forest to fuel the fires on which they cooked and which kept them warm.

Waltham-Forest Laws

William the Conqueror's Normans introduced the concept of 'forest', which differed from the tree-covered landscapes we understand by a 'forest'.

Norman meaning of 'forest'

The Norman '*foris*' meant 'outside' or 'without', and the legal phrase '*forestem sylvam*' meant 'outside the wood'.[24] A wood surrounded a palace, castle, monastery or manor house, and was enclosed. Land 'outside a wood' was common land or 'forest'.

Our 'forest' may derive from this Norman concept of '*foris*', but may also derive from the Norman '*feresta*' that was based on the Latin '*ferarum statio*', which was the tree-covered habitation of beasts. According to this view the 'forest' was land that included woods, cultivated land, common land and villages that had by-laws to protect the King's deer. Its boundaries were marked by officials during what was called their 'perambulations'.

Norman aristocracy

The Normans were soon integrated into English life, like the Anglo-Saxons before them. The Normans formed the new aristocracy. Thus, Geoffrey de Mandeville, a baron under Stephen, was created the first Norman Earl of Essex in 1140. (Harold I had been the last Saxon Earl of Essex.)

Laws protect king's rights in Royal Forest

What is now Epping Forest was a Royal Forest by 1104, and was covered by Forest law after c.1130. The laws were strictly enforced in the Forest areas to protect the king's hunting.

The laws of the Norman Carta de Foresta, or Lawes Forrest, 1217, protected the king's "right to vert and venison" (trees and deer).[25] Forest courts had challenged the right of commonage, and until Henry III's reign killing a deer was punishable by the loss of a limb, or by death. After 1217 protests were no longer allowed against the severity of the Forest laws, and fines were substituted for extreme penalties. The Carta de Foresta stated: "No man shall henceforth lose either life or member [i.e. limb] for killing our Deer. But if any man be taken and convicted for taking our Venison, he shall make a grievous fine, if he has anything whereof; and if he have nothing to lose, he shall be imprisoned a Year and a Day."[26] Hawking was introduced.

In what is now Epping Forest the Crown owned the Forest rights, but at this time not the soil (which, as we saw on p.49, was owned by the canons of Waltham Holy Cross). The Crown owned part of Hainault Forest, including the soil.

The Forest of Waltham had first been mentioned in 1205: "*foresta nostra prope Waltham*".[27] The abbot of Waltham Abbey had to allow the king to hunt on his lands if he chose, but he was allowed to send 960 sheep into the Forest and to turn 770 acres in the north of the Forest into farmland, following a precedent established in 1189-90 (after Richard I had sold the manor of Waltham to the abbot and canons). This land ran from Wintry Wood to Epping Long Green, Galleyhill Wood and back to Copped Hall.

Beeches now dominated the Forest. Oaks and birches were plentiful, and hazels, alders and hornbeams were more common.

In King John's time, in the early 13th century, the Forest of Waltham comprised 60,000 acres[28] against Epping Forest's 6,000 acres[29] today. In 1215 Magna Carta removed the King's prerogative to hunt in all forest lands.

Soon afterwards, Waltham Forest was surrounded by a border, known as a purlieu, of 7-foot-high banks adjoined by deep ditches. This marked the boundaries of the Forest where the King had exclusive hunting rights. It was a barrier to trespassing poachers and prevented deer from escaping. Remains of the purlieu can be seen in Gernon

Bushes, Coopersale; to the east of Theydon Bois golf club; in Lower Forest; and in the northern part of the Forest at Gibbons Bush Green.[30]

Waltham Abbey's importance

Because of the Holy Cross and its powers of healing, Waltham Abbey was visited by pilgrims and became prosperous. It grew in importance. Queen Eleanor, wife of Edward I, died in Nottinghamshire in 1290 and was brought to rest in Waltham Abbey. This was symptomatic of the Abbey's importance in the 13th century.

The Norman feudal system was still dominant and had strengthened the social position of the Church. However, its repressive form of bondage had brought much hardship to the people of Epping Forest.

3

Medievals and Tudors

Medievals

Medieval Waltham Forest

Life in medieval Forest of Waltham was hard. The Church and monasticism drew strength from the manorial system, and there was more focus on Waltham Abbey.

The Black Death and Peasants' Revolt

It is often asserted that the Black Death, or bubonic plague, of 1348-9 killed a third of the country's population of about 4 million. This may be an exaggeration: five to ten per cent may be a more realistic figure. Even so it had a catastrophic effect in decimating the population in many regions.

The plague spread to London from the southern counties in September 1348, and swept through Essex to East Anglia. Attempts have been made to retrieve the local picture from county archives, but local instances remain sketchy.[1] The effects of the Black Death on Essex are still buried in county archives, diocesan registers and manorial records, awaiting a comprehensive study.

A consequence of the Black Death was a shortage of labourers to work in the fields. A tenth had died and many had fled from their villages to safer areas. This meant that surviving labourers were in demand and could theoretically increase the pay for their labour. But they were trapped in the feudal system of duties to their lord, and discontent intensified.

Poll tax

In 1380 King Richard II was only fourteen. His advisers, including John of Gaunt, the acting regent, and the Archbishop of Canterbury, urged him to enforce a new poll tax, the third in four years, allegedly to fund military campaigns overseas. The first poll tax in 1377 was a flat rate of one groat (four pence). The second poll tax of 1379 was graduated, a basic groat (or four pence) with more for the richer. This third poll tax of 1380 was three groats (twelve pence or one shilling) and while some poor were allowed to pay a reduced rate other poor had to pay the full tax, which seemed unjust.

Attack on Waltham Abbey

Essex was a focal point for the Peasants' Revolt of 1381. The revolt began in Brentwood, Essex on 30 May. It spread through Essex and Kent. Many of the peasants from manors owned by Waltham Abbey – including Chingford, Loughton, Epping and Waltham itself – attacked Waltham Abbey and burned every document in the Abbey,[2] hoping to destroy evidence of their feudal bondage so that they could become free men.

Ball's rhyme

By mid-June, 100,000 peasants under Wat Tyler and John Ball had captured Canterbury (seat of the Archbishop of Canterbury Simon Sudbury, adviser to the young king) and marched to London to put their grievances before King Richard II. John Ball gave a sermon at Blackheath in which he declared: "When Adam dalf [delved] and Eve span,/Who was then a gentilman?"[3] The rebels captured the Savoy palace of the King's uncle, John of Gaunt (another hated adviser of the young king), London Bridge and the Tower of London.

Richard bravely refused their demands. There was a night of rioting and the next day he met the peasants again at Mile End and promised to make concessions.

Many of the peasants returned home but some remained and there was more rioting. Richard met them again at Smithfield.

Wat Tyler

Wat Tyler, the peasants' leader, now demanded the confiscation of

Church lands. There was fighting and Tyler was wounded. His supporters carried him to St Bartholomew's Hospital, but he was dragged away on orders from the Lord Mayor of London and beheaded. Richard issued a command that order should be restored throughout the country.

Richard II meets rebels at Waltham Abbey

On 22 June Richard rode to Essex at the head of an army and met a deputation of rebels at Waltham Abbey to restore order. He told the rebels that he had no sympathy with them and that his promises had been made under duress and were null and void. He said, "Villeins you were and villeins you are; in bondage you shall abide, and that not your old bondage, but one incomparably worse."[4]

There was a second rising in Billericay in which 500 rebels were killed, and another uprising in Colchester. Then the leaders were beheaded, and John Ball was executed at St Albans.

Slow decline of manorial system

The Peasants' Revolt did not break up the Norman manorial system, but it marked the beginning of its end. The struggle against manorial servitude continued into the 15th century, especially in the Forest parishes around Epping.[5] The Waltham-Forest villages remained full of impatient discontent during the slow decline of the manorial system.

The baronial clashes of the Wars of Roses had little impact on Waltham Forest, but there had been minor ecological changes. By the beginning of the Tudor Age wolves were extinct in Waltham Forest. Rabbits introduced by the Normans – and possibly encouraged to inhabit the pillow mounds of High Beach, as we saw on pp.31 and 37 – were now rife. A quarter of the trees in the Forest were now beeches, another quarter were birches, a fifth were oaks. A tenth were hornbeams and another tenth were elms. Willows, and alder and hazel trees, were increasing.

Tudors

Tudor Waltham Forest: Henry VIII's hunting lodges and deer park

Henry VIII hunted in Waltham Forest

In the Tudor time, Henry VIII used to hunt in Waltham Forest. He knew the Forest area, was a regular visitor and stayed at Waltham Abbey with Anne Boleyn during hunting trips in nearby Waltham Forest.[6] It is recorded that Henry left Greenwich for Waltham Abbey with Queen Catherine of Aragon and Anne Boleyn in May 1528,[7] that he took Anne Boleyn on progress in July 1529, during which he visited the Abbey, and that he and Anne Boleyn stayed at Waltham Abbey for five days during the summer progress of 1532.[8] There had been a royal stable there since 1294, and there was still a royal stable there in 1541.[9]

Knowing the Forest area, Henry decided to create a new royal deer park in Chingford, where he owned some manorial lands. He commanded that a new royal park should be laid out at Fairmead.

Waltham Abbey closed in 1540

Waltham Abbey had been dissolved on Henry VIII's instructions, the last Abbey in the country to be dissolved. Its deed of surrender was signed by the last abbot of Waltham, Robert Fuller, and it was closed down in 1540. All Waltham Abbey's possessions, including the parish of Lochentuna (Loughton) and the soil of Waltham Forest, reverted to the Crown. The Abbey was no longer available and as a result hospitality would have to be provided within the deer park.

Deer park at Fairmead

Some 300 acres were cleared of trees between 1540 and 1543, and the resulting heath was enclosed as the King's deer park of "Fayremeade". Sir Richard Rich (later Lord Rich) was keeper of the new park and of its lodges. In its heyday as a deer park, the heath stretched from Chingford's Fairmead to Chingford Plain, High Beach and Buckhurst Hill as far as the Roe Buck Inn (later, the Roebuck); to Loughton's Fairmead including the

Warren; and to Debden and down to the River Roding.[10]

Loughton's Fairmead Bottom extended from Hill Wood south across Warren Hill almost to the Roe Buck Inn. Contemporary maps show Fairmead Bottom as extending northwards (towards Epping) from Rangers Road, but the Chapman and André 1777 map of Essex, surveyed in 1772-4 and compiled before Rangers Road was constructed, shows Fairmead Bottom (weirdly labelled "Fairmaid Bottom"), continuing southwards (towards Woodford) into the private gardens now south of Rangers Road. These gardens lie in a direct line between the now demolished Roe Buck Inn on the other side of the hill and Henry VIII's Great Standing, now known as Queen Elizabeth's hunting lodge.

There was already a small network of hunting lodges nearby which can be found on the Chapman and André 1777 map (see pp.x-xi):

- *Little Standing*
  Henry used a two-storey hunting lodge called Little Standing ("High Standing" on the Chapman and André 1777 map) in the centre of Fairmead. It eventually became a keeper's lodge and was rebuilt as the Reindeer Inn, which was pulled down and replaced by the Warren.[11] The remains of Little Standing are now embedded in the fabric of Warren House.

- *Pimp Hall*
  Henry also used Pimp Hall (originally Pymp's Hall) below Friday Hill in Chingford. The timber-framed and plastered building was pulled down just before the Second World War. The 16th-century dovecote can still be seen.

- *Poteles or Langfords*
  There was also Poteles or Langfords, a palace with a hunting lodge annexed to it that was later known as King's Place Farm and stood at the foot of what is now Palmerston Road, Buckhurst Hill.

Poteles was bought to be a palace by the Crown (Edward III through his son John of Gaunt) c.1360, and was mentioned in 1372 and 1378, when custody of it was granted, free of rent in return for repairs, to Alan de Buxhull.[12] Edward IV bought a house and lands adjoining it from Robert Langford in 1476. The combined estate of 92 acres came into the possession of the Duke of Clarence, and when he died it returned to the ownership of the Crown. Soon afterwards Edward IV granted custody of it for life to Sir John Risley, and in 1485 Henry VII confirmed the grant. Risley died without a male heir and in 1513 it was granted tail male to William Compton.[13] Henry VIII is thought to have subsequently visited it frequently while staying at Waltham with Anne Boleyn.[14]

The estate was sold to the National Freehold Land Society in 1853 and was broken up for building development. Langfords Hall was demolished in the late 1950s – William Addison reports that traces of the original hunting lodge could be seen in the cellars[15] – and its name is commemorated in 'Langfords', a close where there are at least twelve houses, and in the nearby King's Avenue.

- *New Lodge*

Fairmead Lodge, the rebuilding of New Lodge.

There was also New Lodge, which may have been the oldest of the Forest lodges. It was mentioned in records in 1341 and later in 1367, when it was called the King's New Lodge,[16] its name suggesting that it was a replacement for an 'old' lodge. In 1378 its custody was granted to Alan de Buxhull on condition that he kept it repaired. It was surveyed in 1589, with a view to repair.[17] It was at the northern (High Beach) end of Fairmead Park. It was rebuilt in 1725 and called Fairmead Lodge, and was demolished in 1898.[18]

- *Great Standing (Queen Elizabeth's Hunting Lodge)*
  Henry now ordered the building of the three-storey Great Standing (Greate Standinge, 'grandstand'), known today as Queen Elizabeth's hunting lodge, from which to view hunting. This grandstand was built from 1542 to 1543 in modern Chingford. Sir Richard Rich, keeper of the new park, paid £30 to George Maxey of Chingford Walk for work on Great Standing and for laying out the new park. (For illustration, see p.257.)

Now that the trees had been cleared to create his deer park there was open heath between Great and Little Standings and it was possible to ride or walk from Little Standing to Great Standing, skirting the swamp that would in due course become Connaught Water and fording the Ching at its narrowest point, at the foot of what is now the steep green slope that descends past today's Warren Wood pub. (Trees grew again when the deer park was abandoned in 1553, and this green ride was cleared back to its pre-1543 state within living memory.)

It is not known whether Henry ever used his Great Standing as his health was not good during the last four years of his life. But he is thought to have visited the other hunting lodges nearby, which were in existence before Great Standing. There is a local tradition that Henry and his party left Poteles or Langfords and processed up the hill along the route of what is now Palmerston Road, turned right in the direction of Loughton at what is now the High Road, processed to the vicinity of the later Roe Buck Inn (more recently the now demolished Roebuck Hotel), turned left into the deer park across the present cricket field at the top of the hill and either processed down to ford the Ching and ascend to Great Standing, or turned right and headed to Little Standing in the middle of Fairmead Bottom.

As the hunting party processed, beaters would flush out deer for the lords and ladies to shoot at with crossbows while on horseback. They would dismount at one of the lodges to view the day's hunting and again shoot at deer flushed near them. Great

Standing was the most spectacular grandstand with an open third floor, from which they would watch, shoot and enjoy the food and hospitality.

Copped Hall (Copthall), the Waltham Abbot's country house in the Forest, passed to the Crown in 1536/7 shortly before Waltham Abbey was dissolved in 1540. Henry added Copped Hall and estates he had bought in Chingford to his deer park at Fairmead to create the massive heath that now extended from Chingford to the outskirts of Epping, and spent many days at his park.[19]

Edward VI inherited the estates, but, not being interested in them, sold them to Sir Thomas Darcy of Chiche (St Osyth). In 1553 they were acquired by Princess Mary, later Queen, who abandoned the idea of a Fairmead deer park and lived in Copped Hall. The Chingford estates were given to a lady of her bedchamber (Susan Tonge).

Great Standing eventually passed to Elizabeth I, who used it as a grandstand for watching hunting. There is a local tradition that she rode up the stairs to the top floor on a white palfrey to celebrate the English victory over the Spanish Armada in 1588.[20] In 1589 she had Great Standing renovated as a hunting lodge.

Those on the lodge's open top floor shot at deer driven towards them: hunting from a standstill for ladies who did not want to ride. The Queen could hit a deer as it bounded past the grandstand "with great surety".[21] But she still rode out to hunt. It was reported in 1602 that the she hunted on horseback at the age of 69. Edward North Buxton observed in 1923, "All true foresters believe further that she was in the habit of riding up the staircase and dismounting at the top. Nor would this be a very difficult feat, as each step is a solid oak beam, and they are laid in short flights and at a moderate angle."[22]

Edward de Vere, Lord Warden of the Forest of Waltham

Since Henry II Waltham Forest had been administered by the Lord

Warden of the Forest of Waltham, an office held by the Earls of Oxford until it was taken away from them by Henry VIII. In July 1603 James I restored the Wardenship to the 17th Earl of Oxford, Edward de Vere, who was Lord Warden for nearly a year, until his death in June 1604. Oxfordians believe that Edward de Vere wrote Shakespeare's works, and that none other than Shakespeare himself was in charge of what is now Epping Forest in 1603-4.

Tudor and Stuart Great Houses

The Elizabethan Age was one in which great houses flourished around Epping Forest, some of which are no more.

Copped Hall

Copped Hall was originally in the manor of Eppinga. (For illustration, see p.73.)

Early history of Copped Hall

Before the Norman Conquest Harold II gave the manor of Eppinga to the canons of Waltham Holy Cross. Although William the Conqueror took lands in the parish of Waltham away from Waltham Holy Cross because of its association with Harold II and gave them to his own half-brother, Odo of Bayeux (who commissioned the Bayeux Tapestry, see p.57), the manor of Eppinga remained with the canons of Waltham Holy Cross. Odo brought Waltham Forest under his severe Norman laws, and the locals were forced to cut wood and hunt game.

In c.1150 the new manor of Copped Hall was held in fee (i.e. as a feudal benefice, land held under the feudal system) by the canons of Waltham Holy Cross's foresters, the Fitzaucher family. In 1184, as we have seen, Waltham Holy Cross was given abbey status by Henry II. In 1337 the reversion of Copped Hall was conveyed to Sir John Shardlowe, who exchanged it with Waltham Abbey for lands elsewhere.[23] From 1350 Waltham Abbey owned the Copped Hall estate.

Henry VIII at Copped Hall

Henry VIII frequently visited Waltham Abbey and probably stayed at the monks' Forest retreat at Copped Hall.[24] In the grounds there was an avenue of yew trees which eventually had a statue of Henry at one end and of his son Edward VI at the other end.

There is a local tradition that Henry paced up and down this walk during the morning of 19 May 1536, waiting for the cannon to signal that his second wife Anne Boleyn had been beheaded.[25] When he heard the cannon he was said to have mounted his horse and ridden to the moated Theobalds Palace (now outside Cheshunt), where Jane Seymour was waiting for him. In 1999 there was an experiment to see whether a cannon fired at the Tower of London could be heard in the Copped-Hall yew walk, and despite the M25 traffic the gun could be heard. (There are also traditions that Henry heard the cannon from Queen Elizabeth's hunting lodge; from High Beach, where there would have been a view over the River Lea towards the Tower of London; from under the Fairmead Oak on the lower slope of Hill Wood, where Henry is said to have breakfasted; and from Windsor.)

In 1536-7 Copped Hall became the property of the Crown (see p.216). When Waltham Abbey was dissolved in 1540, Henry VIII took possession of Copped Hall and visited the house. He probably hunted from it in his deer park.

Mary and Elizabeth at Copped Hall

Copped Hall passed to Edward VI. Mary lived there during his reign, almost a prisoner. She was forbidden to celebrate the Catholic Mass. When she became Queen in 1553, England became Catholic.

In 1558 Copped Hall passed from Mary to Elizabeth I in poor repair. In 1562 (the year she caught smallpox, requiring her face to be covered in white-lead lotion) Elizabeth set up a Commission to plant trees in "our park", and in 1564 granted Copped Hall to Sir Thomas Heneage, a courtier who became no.2 to Walsingham in the English secret service and, in 1590, Chancellor of the Duchy of Lancaster, intending that he would pay for the repairs. He pulled much of the old house down and rebuilt a new house on its site (which is not in existence). Elizabeth visited, and stayed in, Copped Hall in 1568, and in May 1578 she returned when the minor royal progress brought her back to Copped Hall.

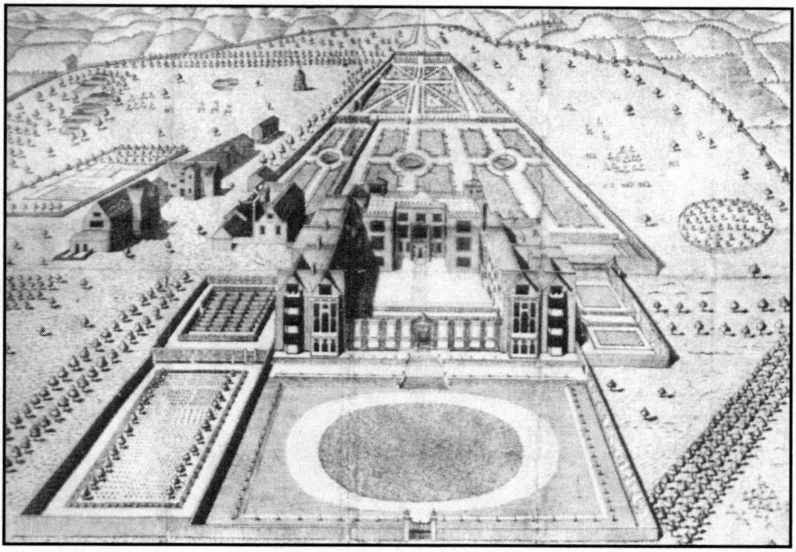

Sir Thomas Heneage's Copped Hall, which he rebuilt 1564-68.

Heneage marries Southampton's mother at Copped Hall

In 1594, having lost his first wife, Heneage remarried Mary, Countess of Southampton, the mother of Shakespeare's patron, the 3rd Earl of Southampton, who lived at Titchfield. When the theatres closed due to plague in 1592, Shakespeare had written verses (*Venus and Adonis*, *The Rape of Lucrece*) and, as one did in Elizabethan times, had sent them to an aristocrat, hoping for patronage that would replace the loss of his theatre income. Southampton's name appears as dedicatee on these two works, and in 1594 Shakespeare may have been living at Titchfield. According to A.L. Rowse and some other scholars, Shakespeare wrote *A Midsummer Night's Dream* for the marriage between Heneage (Duke Theseus) and the Countess of Southampton (Hippolyta), which took place on 2 May 1594.

The marriage may have been conducted at Southampton House in the Strand, and the reception is reported to have taken place in Copped Hall (which the couple spelt 'Coppt Hall'), where *A Midsummer Night's Dream* was performed in the 56-yard-long gallery. It is possible that the play was performed over several days, beginning and ending in the long gallery at Copped Hall, with moonlit forest scenes, specific banks of wild thyme, oxlips and violets, and specific smells of musk-rose and eglantine being located in the grounds and Forest near Copped Hall.[26] If the writing of *A Midsummer Night's Dream was* linked to Shakespeare's connection with the Earl of Southampton, and if the play *was* first performed at Copped Hall, then Shakespeare was undoubtedly present at the wedding reception to oversee the performance of his work.

The couple were in frequent contact with Sir Robert Cecil of Hertfordshire, son of William Cecil, Lord Burghley, Elizabeth's chief minister (whose role he took over in 1598, effectively becoming prime minister for the first nine years of James I's reign).

Hill Hall

Hill Hall, Theydon Mount, which has survived, was rebuilt during the 1550s and completed in 1557. (See illustration on p.249.)

Sir Thomas Smith, who lived there, had been Vice-Chancellor of Cambridge and served Protector Somerset, who led an architectural group that implemented a Renaissance style that was inspired by France rather than Italy. In 1562 Smith became Ambassador to France, and in 1572 Secretary of State to Elizabeth I. His *De Republica Anglorum* (*Concerning the State of the English*) set out the constitution of Elizabethan England.

About the same time as Smith three minor Elizabethan poets flourished in the area: George Gascoigne and his stepson Nicholas Breton in Walthamstow and Thomas Lodge, who wrote *Rosalynde*, on which Shakespeare based *As You Like It*, in Leyton.

Wanstead House

The grandest of the great houses was Wanstead House (no longer in existence).

Wanstead House.

Mary and Elizabeth at Wanstead House

Mary, about to be crowned queen, stopped there on 1 August 1553 and received her sister, Princess Elizabeth, and a thousand nobles who had ridden with her. Queen Elizabeth I had visited Wanstead House in 1561, when it was in the possession of Lord Rich.

In 1577 it became the home of Robert Dudley, the Earl of Leicester, Elizabeth's suitor and favourite, who held it until his death in 1588. Elizabeth revisited Wanstead House during her progress in May 1578, and in 1588 Leicester accompanied her to Tilbury, where she made her famous speech rallying her Navy against the Spanish Armada.

Loughton Hall in the Wroths' time (left) and Lady Mary Wroth (right).

Loughton Hall

In 1522 the manor of Loughton had been leased by Waltham Abbey to John Stoner (or Stonard) on an 80-year lease. After the Dissolution in 1540, the ownership of the manor passed to Mary Tudor from 1553 to 1558, with the Stoners still as lessees. In 1558 the Duchy of Lancaster annexed the ownership of Loughton, and Elizabeth I visited the lessee John Stoner at Loughton Hall in 1561. She visited him again at his other house, Luxborough Hall in Chigwell, in 1576, and again at Loughton Hall in 1578. He died in 1579 and the lease passed to his daughter Susan and her husband Robert Wroth. His heir, Sir Robert Wroth succeeded him in 1606 and bought the manor of Loughton from the Duchy of Lancaster for £1,224 in 1613. The manor of Loughton then descended within the Wroth family.[27]

Lady Mary Wroth, Sir Philip Sidney's niece, at Loughton Hall

To the Loughton Hall of that time (no longer in existence) came Mary Wroth, who married Sir Robert Wroth on 27 September 1604. She was the daughter of Robert Sidney, who in 1618 became Earl of Leicester, a title that had come to an end with the death of his uncle, Elizabeth's suitor Robert Dudley, the Earl of Leicester, of nearby Wanstead House.

Her father, unsurprisingly as he was the younger brother of the poet Sir Philip Sidney and son of the poet Mary Sidney (who also happened to be the sister of Robert Dudley), was himself a poet although his verses were not discovered until the 1960s.

Ben Jonson at Loughton Hall

Mary had acted in Ben Jonson's *Masque of Blackness* and three years later in his *Masque of Beauty*. She was a personal friend of Jonson's and after her marriage to the second Sir Robert Wroth in 1604, when she became Lady Mary Wroth, she lived in Loughton Hall. She received James I when he visited Loughton Hall in 1605,[28] and on several occasions Ben Jonson, who dedicated *The Alchemist* (1610)[29] and 'A Sonnet, To the Noble Lady, the Lady Mary Wroth' to her; and section III of his poem 'The Forest' to Sir Robert.[30]

George Chapman, who some regard as Shakespeare's rival poet, wrote her a sonnet which prefaced his 1611 translation of the *Iliad*.[31] He is thought to have visited Loughton Hall. She was the subject of a poem by George Wither. Not surprisingly as she was a niece of Sir Philip Sidney and granddaughter of Mary Sidney, she was also a writer. In the reign of James I she wrote *Urania* (1621) on the theme of fidelity, a hundred poems and twenty songs. Widowed at 27 in 1614, she remained in Loughton Hall until soon after 1642.[32]

There has been speculation that Lady Mary Wroth was Ben Jonson's mistress, and the "Celia" addressed in sections V, VI and IX of Jonson's poem 'The Forest'.[33] However there is no evidence.

Lady Wroth's two children by William Herbert

There *is* evidence that she had been the mistress of her first cousin William Herbert, the 3rd Earl of Pembroke – the possible dedicatee of Shakespeare's *Sonnets* (Mr. W.H.), one of the two dedicatees of the 1623 *First Folio*, and Ben Jonson's patron – as she had two illegitimate children by him. It is known that she was staying at Baynard's Castle with William Herbert in September 1608 and that she was reluctant to return to her sick husband in Loughton. She made a brief visit and then returned to Baynard's a week or two later.

Statue of the 3rd Earl of Pembroke, William Herbert, in the courtyard of the Bodleian Library, Oxford.

William Herbert was a patron of poets, and must have had dealings with Shakespeare, whose *Sonnets* were being prepared for their first publication in 1609. Even if William Herbert was not the Mr W.H. of the *Sonnets* (who is usually thought to have been the 3rd Earl of Southampton), he was in Shakespeare's circle and it is not unlikely that, like Ben Jonson, Shakespeare knew Lady Mary Wroth and found his way to Loughton Hall. He may have got to know the area from his time at Copped Hall, and as he himself had certainly acted in Jonson's *Every Man in His Humour* and probably in his *Sejanus*, he would have been very interested in the literary life of Loughton Hall and the presence of Jonson there.

The decline of the Royal Forest

James I at Loughton Hall

Ben Jonson says that James I hunted from Loughton Hall during his visit in 1605.[34] James I continued the royal hunting in Waltham Forest – to excess. He tightened the Forest laws and imposed tolls. He spent more and more time hunting, basing himself at Theobalds Palace, his favourite palace. In 1612 he introduced dark fallow deer to Epping Forest, and is thought to have continued the use of Queen Elizabeth's hunting lodge until 1625.[35] Charles I used it less often.

Under the Commonwealth the Forest lost its splendour. Most of the deer disappeared.

Samuel Pepys

The Restoration did not restore the Forest to its former glory. The diarist Samuel Pepys, when Clerk to the Navy Board, recorded that he rode to Waltham Forest on 18 August 1662 to see how trees were cut and measured. Most of the timber for the Navy was in fact taken from Hainault Forest.

Charles II at Chingford

Charles II visited Waltham Forest less frequently than the Tudors. Nevertheless, he hunted in Chingford woods and, sheltering in the former manor house or at nearby Pimp Hall during a snowstorm at Christmas, is said to have been fed a loin of beef which pleased him so much that he knighted it "Sir Loin". (The same story is told of James I, and an oak table in Friday Hill House, built in 1835-6, was inscribed: "All lovers of roast beef will like to be informed that on this table a loin was knighted by King James I on his return from hunting in Epping Forest.")[36]

The glow in the sky from the Great Fire of London of 1666 could be seen from Pole Hill, Chingford. By now the Forest had become a bystander, a spectator of events that happened elsewhere.

4

Enclosers and Loppers

Waltham Forest first came to be known as 'Epping Forest' during the 17th century.

Attitudes towards the Forest that came to be known as Epping Forest had changed due to new social conditions. The Forest was no longer a welcoming place where kings hunted deer and enjoyed hospitality in the sun at a network of lodges. It was now a menacing place. It now sheltered outlaws and the roads through it became increasingly impassable.

Enclosers

The Enclosure of Epping Forest

Concerns to improve public safety developed into plans to provide safe roads and build on Forest plots, and led to the idea of enclosing parts of the Forest.

Outlaws

After the Civil War the Forest was occupied by outlaws, retired soldiers who blackened their faces, poached the king's deer and robbed travellers. A gang known as the Waltham Blacks lived in the Forest. Trees were cleared by the side of some roads to protect travellers, as happened alongside Golding's Hill in Loughton.

Dick Turpin

In the 18th century, the highwayman Dick Turpin lived in the Forest. He had married at 22 and had set up a butcher's shop near the Roebuck Hotel, Buckhurst Hill (no longer in existence). He joined the Gregory Gang of deer stealers who sold stolen meat, some of which he sold in his shop.

After a year in prison they took to robbing people in Woodford, Chingford and Loughton. Turpin is said to have roasted an old woman over a fire at Traps Hill Farm, Loughton, to find out where her money was hidden, and many houses in Loughton put "Turpin traps" at the top of their stairs, wooden flaps that were let down and kept in place by a pole wedged between the floor and ceiling above so that it was impossible for an intruder to go beyond the stairs.[1]

In 1737 Dick Turpin became a highwayman. In April 1737 he and two other men robbed a traveller of his horse and money near the Green Man, "Layton Stone" (i.e. Leytonstone).

Turpin took to the Forest and hid in a cave, possibly a hollow in undergrowth by a bank or hollow tree in Loughton Camp, possibly a cave behind the Turpin's Cave pub, High Beach.[2] He was caught in York for selling stolen horses under the name John Palmer and, his face pocked from smallpox, was hanged as a horse thief in April 1739.

Large houses

During the 18th century a number of large houses were built or rebuilt round Epping Forest. One of the largest was at Copped Hall, where in 1751 the old Tudor house was demolished and the Conyers family built a new house to the south-east. Other houses were rebuilt about this time, including Coopersale Hall in c.1776. With the rebuilding of substantial houses came plans to improve the system of safe roads.

Roads

The roads had been ruined by troops during the Civil War, and Turnpike Trusts raised money and built improved roads along which coaches could travel. In the 1790s there were 46 coaches to Epping a week, and it was possible to travel from Epping to London via Buckhurst Hill, Woodford Green, Snaresbrook and Whipps Cross.

From 1829 to 1834 the Woodford New Road and the Epping New Road were cut through Epping Forest along the route of an old Roman Road, bypassing Loughton, and soon 25 coaches a day were arriving at Epping. Clay excavated during this work was deposited by the side of the road, creating the Wake Valley pond.

Wanstead House and enclosures

The 18th century was marked by the enclosure of parts of Epping Forest. The German Hanoverian kings had not been interested in the Forest or its deer, and enforcement of the Forest laws had lapsed.

Lord Warden and Tylney family

The locals still exercised their right to cut firewood and graze their cattle in the Forest. More and more local people made applications to enclose Forest lands, and their pleas were heard by the Lord Warden of Epping Forest, who had administered the Forest laws since late Norman times. This office was now held hereditarily by the Tylney family of Wanstead House.

The Duke of Wellington's nephew bankrupts Wanstead House

In 1812 the young Tylney heiress of Wanstead House, Catherine Tylney Long, married the nephew of the Duke of Wellington, William Wellesley Pole, who now called himself William Pole Tylney Long-Wellesley. By his marriage he became Lord Warden of Epping Forest. He was dissolute and squandered her fortune. He fell so deeply in debt that Wanstead House and its contents were put up for sale, and when there were no buyers Wanstead House was demolished so that money could be recovered from the sale of the masonry.

As Lord Warden Long-Wellesley agrees to massive enclosures

As Lord Warden, William was an equal disaster. The Forest laws were not enforced and of the 9,000 Forest acres in 1793, 3,000 were enclosed and the verderers were unable to defend them. There was then less firewood available to be lopped.

The lords of the Forest manors now saw their lands as their own property, and did not see why some of them could not be enclosed so long as locals could continue to use some of their land. The government encouraged farming and housing and saw enclosure as creating more land to farm and build houses on.

The Crown was lord of the manor of Hainault Forest and sold its soil and hunting rights for agricultural land. Lords of the manors of Epping Forest were allowed to enclose their lands without objection from those administering the Forest laws. The open spaces of Hampstead Heath and Wimbledon Common were also threatened.

Resistance to enclosures

The Commons Preservation Society was founded in 1865 to safeguard common land for public use. As a result of pressure from the public, plans were made to preserve the Forest and save it from being enclosed. The poor took to visiting the Forest on Sundays, congregating on Chingford Plain. Some came on foot, many came by railway, which reached Loughton in 1856, Epping in 1865 and Chingford in 1873.

Loppers

William Whitaker Maitland and Willingale

Nevertheless, enclosers prospered. The Crown was keen not to be involved in heavy expenditure on the Forest.

William Whitaker Maitland encloses 1,377 acres

In 1825 there was a new lord of the manor of Loughton. Miss Anne Whitaker of Loughton Hall bequeathed her Loughton estate to her cousin John Maitland of Woodford Hall, a descendant from a branch of the Norman Maitland family that produced the border clan of Maitland and the Duke of Lauderdale (a member of the CABAL Administration or Cabinet council under Charles II).

John Maitland died six years later and his son William Whitaker Maitland inherited the manor of Loughton and Loughton Hall. In 1836 Loughton Hall was gutted by fire and remained a shell until it was demolished and rebuilt in 1879.

In 1851 there were 5,928 acres of waste land in Epping Forest.[3] In 1857 through the Commissioners of Woods, Forests and Land

Revenues, the Crown agreed to sell 1,377 acres of the Forest to William Whitaker Maitland, along with the hunting rights and use of its rabbits. In October 1858 Maitland paid £5,468 and received a conveyance to him and his heirs or assignees.

Loughtonians' right to lop

Loughton householders believed they were granted a right to lop Forest trees by Queen Elizabeth I. Monk Wood's 98 acres and Loughton Piece's 7 acres were both owned by the lord of the manor of Loughton and could not be lopped by commoners, though they could be lopped by the lord's tenant farmers. Breaches of this law resulted in fines. As far back as 1630, a Thomas Britten had been fined for felling trees. In 1828 Thomas Willingale had been brought before a Forest Court for having felled an entire tree and regarding it as his possession.

Under a tradition going back to before 1753 lopping began on 1 November (All Saints' Day) and ended on 23 April (St George's Day). But the calendar changed in 1752, when 3 September was relabelled 12 September, and the Court Leet of 1753 changed the lopping dates. Lopping could begin on 12 November.

Loughton householders believed they would forfeit lopping rights for ever if they did not begin lopping at midnight on 11 November. They assembled for drinks in the King's Head public house, then took ladders and cut boughs with long-handled lopping axes. The boughs had to be at least 7 feet above the ground. Once cut, they were loaded onto a sledge and drawn by two horses – more than two were not allowed. The wood could only be used as domestic fuel. It could not be used commercially.

Thomas Willingale carries on lopping

In about 1840, like many of the poor, Thomas Willingale, an illiterate labourer, had built himself a cottage on the edge of the Forest, one of the small houses near Wroth's Path on the south side of Baldwin's Hill, on land owned by the lord of the manor of Loughton, and he had enclosed a small garden with a 'fence' of brambles. For 16 years he had defied the lord of the manor by lopping wood, which he sold to the parishioners from his woodyard in Whitakers Way, Baldwin's Hill. He was not allowed to sell lopped wood commercially.

On 11 November 1859 an agent for the lord of the manor of Loughton, named Richardson (nicknamed the Bulldog) held a dinner at the King's Head, Loughton and invited all the loppers. Through his agent, Maitland had tried to get Willingale and his cronies drunk so that no lopping could happen at midnight on 11 November, in which case their lopping rights would be forfeited for ever.[4] Willingale, now over 60, remained sober enough to go to Staples Hill and cut a branch which he took back and presented to Richardson.

Richardson offered Willingale sums of money to stop lopping, but Willingale stood his ground.

Rev. John Whitaker Maitland and Willingale

In 1861 William Whitaker Maitland died, owning 1,120 acres of unenclosed land in Loughton.[5]

Rev. John Whitaker Maitland's war on lopping

His third son, the Rev. John Whitaker Maitland, who had become Rector of St John's Church, Loughton in 1856, became lord of the manor of Loughton. He believed that his father's purchase meant that his tenants had lost their rights to use the waste or common lands of his Forest estate. Lords of the manor were selling common lands for development and in 1863/4 he tried to exclude his tenants from grazing on, or lopping wood in, common lands.

Rev. John Whitaker Maitland

Rev. John Whitaker Maitland encloses 1,100 acres of waste land

The Rev. John Whitaker Maitland offered to compensate his tenants if they would give up their rights as commoners. He gave money to some, the freeholds of their cottages and gardens to others and land on which to build extensions for new homes to yet others. Maitland sold off bits of common land to his parishioners. The new owners increased their boundaries by growing bramble hedges, and cutting back on the inside each year after the bramble had grown outwards. Having granted 300 acres on this basis, he enclosed 1,100 acres.[6]

The Crown was concerned that the Forest was shrinking but did not want to incur expense. In 1864 a letter was sent to the Metropolitan Board of Works offering to allow it to enclose the Forest as a place for recreation. The Board of Works declined.

Rev. John Whitaker Maitland sells common land

In 1864 the Rev. John Whitaker Maitland arranged a sale of bits of common land at the Plume of Feathers, a public house on the outskirts of Loughton on the road to Epping.

Now the Treasury Secretary wrote to the Office of Woods to say it should control the Crown's rights over Epping Forest, to preserve it as an open space for hunting deer and wild animals.

Loughton's population had expanded from 540 in 1763 to 1,333 by 1841, and it would reach 2,851 by 1881. The lord of the manor, the Rev. John Whitaker Maitland, fenced in 1,316 acres of Forest in 1865 alone.[7]

The Rev. John Whitaker Maitland resolved to prosecute anyone who cut wood within the newly enclosed parts of the Forest.

The conflict between the lords of the manor of the Forest and the local villagers came to a head in December 1865, when Maitland took Willingale to court in Epping for injuring Forest trees. The charge was dismissed.

Three Willingale relatives imprisoned

Four months later Willingale's son Samuel and his nephews (Samuel's cousins) Alfred Willingale and William Higgins, were summoned to Waltham Abbey court on a charge of trespass. They were prosecuted for injuring trees and stealing wood from land Maitland had enclosed, which the previous year had been lopwood from the Forest common land to which they were entitled. They were fined 2s.6d. each with 11s.

costs and damages, or seven days' imprisonment if they defaulted. They refused to pay and chose to spend seven days in Ilford jail. They were widely regarded as martyrs.

Samuel Willingale (left), Alfred Willingale (centre) and William Higgins (right).

The Rev. John Whitaker Maitland's policy in 1866 was to offer the poor homes with gardens where they could grow their own food rather than poach and steal from his Forest land.

John Whitaker Maitland offers to build Willingale a new cottage

He offered to build Thomas Willingale a new cottage. Willingale accepted but insisted that Maitland should buy back his brambled garden, two perches of which he had gained by cutting brambles and encroaching outwards. As we have just seen, Maitland had enclosed 1,100 acres of Forest waste land – to sell as building plots on Baldwin's Hill. In the manor of Loughton there were only 50 acres of unenclosed land left for villagers to cut firewood and graze animals.

Willingale v. Maitland

The 6,000 acres of the Forest in 1850 had dwindled to 3,500 acres by 1870. In 1866 the Forest had dwindled to nearly this acreage.

Opposition to enclosures by Willingale's supporters

Concerned at the reduction of the Forest, the Board of Woods' solicitor, Philip Lawrence, travelled to Loughton and sought out Willingale. He and Edward North Buxton (a leading member of the Commons Preservation Society and soon-to-be author of a best-selling book *Epping Forest*, 1885) encouraged a stand by the loppers (or commoners) against the enclosers.

They were supported by the solicitor to the City of London, Thomas Nelson, who would prepare material for the Corporation of London's lawsuit against the lords of the manor. Sir Thomas Fowell Buxton of Warlies, Upshire, the brother of the author Edward North Buxton, was also opposed to Maitland's enclosure of Forest land in his manor. He offered financial assistance to Thomas Willingale to take legal action against Maitland to prevent him from enclosing any more of the Forest.

Maitland buys Willingale's rented cottage and evicts him

Willingale lived in a cottage owned by a man called Grout, which he rented. In May 1866 the Reverend Maitland (retaliating for the defiance of the illiterate Willingale and his family) purchased the cottage from Grout for £105. On 12 October 1866 Maitland and his agent issued a summons against Willingale, evicted him and won possession of his cottage.

Willingale goes to court to preserve lopping rights

In October 1866 Willingale's solicitor, Philip Lawrence, filed a bill in Chancery, Willingale v. Maitland (and others), to preserve the lopping rights of the "labouring poor". A complaint to the court of Chancery was in order if it could be shown that the common law did not provide a remedy for a problem. Anyone wanting to start a suit in Chancery had to employ a solicitor to draw up a bill of complaint, or petition, which he submitted to the Lord Chancellor.

Willingale's case

The illiterate Willingale claimed that Loughton was within the royal Waltham Forest, and that Elizabeth I had granted by royal charter that the people of Loughton could lop wood on the bits of waste land in the Forest, to use for themselves or to sell to others in Loughton for fuel. In his complaint he argued that the enclosures were unlawful, and that Maitland's cutting down of trees and selling waste land as building ground encroached on the right of the people of Loughton. He said he had been warned that if he pulled down any houses built unlawfully on these plots of ground he would be committing a criminal offence. Maitland answered the bill and the lawsuit continued.

It was pointed out in a letter in the *Woodford Times* (15 December 1866) that Willingale had himself encroached on two perches of Forest for the 27 years of his residence in Baldwin's Hill. He had claimed ownership of these perches by squatter's right and had insisted on being paid for them when he was re-housed.

Maitland's case

Maitland argued that there was no evidence of any royal charter granting lopping rights to Loughton inhabitants. He said he had inherited the land from his father, who had bought Forest rights from the Crown. He said it was customary for the lord of the manor to sell waste ground. The Staples Road school building had been built on such waste land. He had compensated all tenants who gave up their lopping rights, including the owner of the cottage Willingale lived in (i.e. Grout). Willingale therefore had no right to lop.

Willingale replied that there was evidence of the charter in Forest court records, which had been lost. He said he had lopped for 25 years, and had helped his father to lop before that. He said he had lived in his cottage for 27 years (i.e. since 1840) and did not know it had been built on waste ground.

Maitland said he did know, and that Willingale was not telling the truth.

Willingale then complained that he had been evicted by Maitland from the cottage he had rented from Grout.

Willingale claims lopping rights for all Loughtonians

In 1868 Willingale amended the bill to claim lopping rights for all Loughton householders. In August 1868 Maitland answered the bill.

Maitland demolishes Willingale-occupied cottages to end lopping rights
In 1869 Maitland demolished the cottage he had bought from Grout in May 1866. He also bought three cottages from Thomas Willingale's son, William Willingale in 1869 for £275 and demolished them. Maitland considered that all lopping rights of Willingale and his family had ceased with the demolition of these four cottages. Four new cottages were built and rented out for 3 shillings a week, with no lopping rights. One of these was the new cottage Maitland had offered to build Willingale. Willingale was not offered any of the newly-built cottages. He moved to Lower Road, Golding's Hill, into a cottage vacated by Elizabeth Tyser, who had accepted land at Earl's (or Earle's) Path in compensation for the extinction of her lopping rights. Willingale then exercised lopping rights from his new abode, even though they were supposed to be extinguished.

During the late 1860s Maitland offered to settle out of court, but Willingale would not be bought off. In 1870 Willingale died before the case came to court, and the case lapsed.

The Corporation of London saves Epping Forest
The Corporation of London had become involved in the Forest. In 1854 it had bought 200 acres at Aldersbrook Farm, and this purchase entitled it to graze cattle.

1871 test case in Court of Chancery
In 1871, following the lapse of Willingale v. Maitland, it took action against enclosures of Forest land. It brought a test case before the Court of Chancery against 16 of the 19 lords of the Forest manors.[8]

The lords of the manor argued that each manor was separate and its commoners only had rights within their own manor. The Corporation of London argued that cattle could wander everywhere in the Forest, across manor boundaries.

The Corporation of London stops enclosures
In 1874 the Court of Chancery ruled in favour of the Corporation of

London. It ruled that all lands enclosed after 1851 should be returned to the Forest unless they had been built on or were attached to a house. The land of High Beach church was excluded from this ruling.

Epping Forest Acts

In 1871 the first Epping Forest Act was passed. It stopped all lawsuits regarding enclosures and established commissioners to report to Parliament. In 1872 the second Epping Forest Act was passed.

The Corporation of London buy 19 manors

Starting in 1875, the Corporation of London systematically bought the 19 manors of Epping Forest and now undertook to maintain the land as an open space.

The Corporation of London become Conservators in place of Crown, 1878

The Epping Forest Act of 1878 gave the Corporation of London the right to administer the Forest as Conservators and abolished the hunting rights of the Crown and the jurisdiction of the Forest courts. The Conservators had a duty to keep the Forest unenclosed as an open space for public recreation and enjoyment.

The Corporation of London buy back enclosed land

The Corporation of London purchased all common lands that had been enclosed, and all commoners' rights to lop wood. Those who had been granted common land by the lord of the manor of Loughton now found it was owned by the Corporation of London, and that the enfranchisement compensation they received was not as much as they hoped.

There should now be no cutting of wood, and no clay, sand or gravel could be removed. Two features of post-Norman woodland management stopped: coppicing (felling a tree so that several tree-trunks grew from the stump) and pollarding (coppicing above head height to leave it clear of animals).

The Corporation of London acquire Queen Elizabeth's hunting lodge
There was no provision for the financial management of the Forest, and the Corporation of London took this upon itself. An Epping Forest Fund was established from the proceeds of levies on corn and other produce, and this enabled the Corporation to fund these changes. The Corporation acquired Queen Elizabeth's hunting lodge.

Maitland compensated
Maitland was compensated for his legal defence against the Corporation of London, and in 1879 he rebuilt Loughton Hall, which had been destroyed by fire in 1836.

Removal of Maitlands' fences
The fences were to be removed at Maitland's expense. However, William Willingale, Thomas's son, took it upon himself to remove the fences. For four days he and an opponent of the enclosures, George Burney, who contributed four horse buses, drove round the Forest, cutting down the lord of the manor's enclosing fences. The loppers may have lost their lopping rights, but, led by William Willingale, Thomas's son, they demolished the enclosers' fences.

Conservators based at the Warren
The Conservators of the Corporation of London, like the old Forest court, were allowed to rationalise lands by selling small strips and buying others. Based at the Warren, their duty was to keep the Forest unenclosed and manage ancient remains, install land drains and improve footpaths and roads.

Lopping ends
Defiant lopping continued for a while: in 1880 seventeen were fined 5s. but had their sentences suspended on condition that no further lopping took place. In 1881 eleven were fined £2, and some were imprisoned in default of payment. Lopping soon petered out.

Compensation for Loughtonians

The Act did not compensate the people of Loughton for the loss of their lopping rights. They eventually received £7,000 from the Corporation of London for this loss. Records show that 522 houses were involved, but that 72 had been built on waste land since August 1851 and 25 had already been compensated by Maitland. A Committee of Householders decided that 280 householders should receive £3.11s. and that the rest of the £7,000 put up by the Conservators of the Corporation of London should be spent on building and maintaining a public hall which would benefit all Loughton inhabitants.

Queen Victoria's visit to Chingford and High Beach

Queen Victoria made a highly publicised visit to Epping Forest on 6 May 1882. Travelling with her youngest daughter, Princess Beatrice, the Queen arrived by train at Chingford station at 4pm, and was greeted by a 21-gun salute. A hundred carriages had gathered round the station. She drove past the Royal Forest Hotel and Queen Elizabeth's hunting lodge, along the newly-built Rangers Road, past the swamp that would become Connaught Water the following year to the Epping New Road, and along the Green Ride across Fairmead past the Strawberry Hill and Earl's Path ponds to High Beach, where there was a grandstand and beyond it a view of the Lea valley. Half a million people cheered her along the route. Arthur, Duke of Connaught; his wife, Princess Louise (Louischen); his sister, Princess Louise; and the Lord Mayor accompanied her.

Queen Victoria spoke from her carriage: "It gives me the greatest satisfaction to dedicate this beautiful Forest to the use and enjoyment of my people for all time."

The Forest was already no longer hers to give. Under the Epping Forest Act of 1878 it had been invested in the Corporation of London. The day ended with fireworks behind the Royal Forest Hotel.

Management of Forest

The management of the Forest improved. Ranger's Road was

constructed in 1881[9] at the Corporation of London's expense and named after the Duke of Connaught's position as Ranger. The swamp near Chingford Plain was drained to create Connaught Water (named after the Duke of Connaught). The extraction of sand and gravel ceased from 1885 to 1895, and the gravel pits left behind turned into Loughton's ponds: the two ponds on Strawberry Hill (where extraction of sand and gravel ceased in the 1880s) and the Blackweir (or Lost) Pond near Baldwin's Hill (where extraction of sand and gravel ceased in 1895).[10]

The Conservators fund Lopping Hall

The foundation stone for the public hall to be funded by the Conservators was laid in September 1883. The Rev. John Whitaker Maitland opened the ceremony, which was attended by the Lord Mayor of London, with a prayer.

In the speeches the Arbitrator said that all who had appeared before him had gone away poorer, but that Loughton was full of nice people as they did not seem to mind. Maitland said that Loughton now had a huge hall and hoped it would be used for educational purposes and temperance meetings. And Edward North Buxton said that the lord of the manor and the poor woodcutter had both lost, but that Nature conservation had won and the Forest would now be preserved.[11]

Lopping Hall, c.1933.

Lopping Hall, a redbrick building with a clock tower, was opened in 1884.

Records of Loughton: Waller

The Rev. John Whitaker Maitland seems to have undergone some sort of rehabilitation during the last years of his life before he died in 1909, still rector of St John's church, Loughton. In 1900 the Loughton historian and Inner Temple barrister W.C. Waller brought out 12 copies of *Loughton in Essex*. One of these is in the possession of St John's

Loughton, access to which was made available to me. It consists of Waller's notes on the history of the manor and parish, and lengthy appendices on legal and parish data: court and assize rolls, Forest records, abstracts of title, rectors, vestry minutes, charters, rentals and wills that he used to research into earlier centuries.

Waller's work on early Loughton estates

In his Preface he says he began to contribute short notes on parish history to the Loughton Parish Magazine in 1889, amplifying on the findings of Morant and other local historians. He derives Loughton from the 1062 Lukinton (see p.55) and, quoting from the replies to questions on which the *Domesday Book* was based, he identifies eight Loughton estates including Alderton and Debden that were held by the canons of Waltham Holy Cross (see p.55). Much of the work he did on the early manors has been reused by later historians. He says he was loaned a 1739 survey of the manor of Loughton – by the Rev. J.W. Maitland, the encloser of the Forest.

Waller's letters to John Whitaker Maitland

Two original letters from Waller to Maitland are in the front of the St John's book. The first (17 September 1899) begins: "Dear Mr Maitland, I don't remember having any intention of republishing my Loughton notes, and they are too dis-jointed to make it worthwhile to do so, even if the cost were not prohibitive – there are, in all, over 200 pages of small type. But I have 12 copies printed on large paper, and one of these it was my intention to offer you, that it might pass on as an heirloom with the Hall. A book of which only 12 copies have ever existed is something of a rarity." There is a note at the end, "P.S. The venison was *excellent*." The second letter (20 December 1901) includes the following paragraph: "With this note I send you the promised copy of my notes on the history of the parish. You will see by the little deed of gift inside it that you are, so to say, the lift-tenant, as I wish it to go with the Hall. Whatever its demerits, the book will be a Great Auk's egg [i.e. very rare] for collectors in time to come: as most of the copies will go to Public Libraries." He signed both letters "Believe me", which was how Sir John Biggs-Davison, MP, always signed off the many letters he wrote me. (In the Victorian Age one could use "Believe me" as a natural rather than an excessive expression of sincerity.)

Waller says in his first letter that his "notes" are barely in publishable form, and certainly that is the impression his book gives. They cover events from 1086 to the 16th century, discuss sources and dwell on individuals. Waller makes it clear that his "notes" should be lodged at Loughton Hall by the Rev. J.W. Maitland as a historical record of documents relating to Loughton. In doing so Waller rehabilitates the reputation of the Rev. J.W. Maitland.

Waller's notebooks

Waller also wrote in notebooks filled with jottings made between 1850 and 1917. There are seven notebooks in all in the Essex Record Office, and selections of his notes have been made into two small pamphlets, *Notes on Loughton 1890-1895* and *Notes on Loughton II: 1896-1914*. Waller lived in Loughton from 1874 until his death in 1917 and constantly researched the history of Loughton during this time. His notes are anecdotal diary entries about buildings in Loughton and local life. In 1903 Waller read a paper on the history of Loughton at the Loughton Club Literary Society, and 100 copies were printed of a pamphlet *Loughton, Essex: A Brief Account of the History of the Manor and Parish, from Domesday to 1900.*

Waller's record of Loughton's buildings

Waller also wrote *An Itinerary of Loughton*, a record of Loughton's building compiled for future historians. It was unfinished at his death in 1917, and its incompleteness is evident as there are obvious omissions: the east side of the High Road, Albion Hill, Staples Road, Upper Park, Lower Park, Algers Road and Station Road. It was lost for 83 years as it descended within his family. It was rediscovered in 2000 by Richard Morris and has been republished verbatim as *Loughton, A Hundred Years Ago*.

Waller's records of Loughton offer local history as documents from past times and observations on current buildings and the minutiae of local life rather than the whole sweep that, following Addison, I have favoured in this work. The whole view includes the parts, but the partial view does not include the whole.

Unenclosed Epping Forest

After the Epping Forest Act of 1878 previously enclosed areas of the Forest were now unenclosed. They included the Stubbles and Chingford Plain, where furrows from Forest land turned into enclosed cornfields can still be seen. Baldwin's Hill Road, Staples Road and Nursery Road were all created from encroachments on the Forest. Ironically, the Debden estate built after the Second World War to re-house bombed-out victims from the East End on the Maitlands estate between Loughton High Road and the Roding encroached on the Forest on a much larger scale than any of the Maitlands' enclosures.

Grazing could continue throughout the Forest. Verderers would still be elected but they were to represent the local people. The Crown was allowed to appoint a Ranger. Queen Victoria chose her third son Arthur, Duke of Connaught, who was interested in trees. He was a 28-year-old soldier in 1878, and married Princess Louise of Prussia the next year.

Some 450 different species of flowering plant were recorded in the 1880s. Sadly a third of these have since disappeared as a result of the public's recreational use of the Forest.

Did the conservation movement begin in Loughton?

Nevertheless it can be argued that the international conservation and ecological movement began with the people of Loughton's victory over the enclosers and the safeguarding of the Forest that began in 1878. Willingale's lopping was not ecologically-motivated and the right to lop was justifiably abolished in 1878. However Willingale's defiance awakened the spirit that led Queen Victoria to declare that the Forest should be enjoyed by the people of England "for all time".

*

History and timelessness

The Forest looks so still and calm. Its perennial presence is so reassuring, and wears a constant beauty. Its trees put out leaves, yellow water-lilies flower in its ponds which reflect the sky. It feels so timeless. Yet time after time it had witnessed the stirrings and to-ing and fro-ing of troubling human events: the conquest of its Trinovantes, the coming of the Romans, successive phases of Saxon rule, oppressive Danelaw, the Norman extinction of the Saxon line, cruel feudal bondage, the doomed Peasants' Revolt, kings' and queens' thrill of the chase, enclosing lords and defiant loppers.

It has remained serene above all these trials, a constant inspiring backdrop to the personal yearnings and troubled aspirations of all who saunter and muse, a massive presence that soothes with its comforting endurance. "I have suffered untold tribulations," it whispers to the sick of heart. "If I can endure and flourish, you can overcome your afflictions."

The stirrings of history have been mere ripples across the still surface of its timeless pools. Its banked horizons enfold the places where people have made their homes within its view, and have shaped their earliest memories and unspoken lives. We woodlanders who live beside it can never escape it. We go away but return to its permanence, and nowhere else would be as good.

PART TWO

Forest Places

5

Loughton

"How blest art thou, canst love the country, Wroth,
Whether by choice, or fate, or both.
And though so near the city, and the Court,
Art ta'en with neither's vice nor sport."

Ben Jonson, 'The Forest', III,
To Sir Robert Wroth, lines 1-4.

My Epping Forest enfolds most of the places of its troubled past. I first knew it at Loughton, where my family set up home in 1943, during the Second World War.

History of Loughton

Loughton nestles beneath the Forest-clad rim of a crater whose east side has collapsed into the flat meadows of the Roding. It lies between the Forest and the Roding. In those days Loughton was a village with houses and shops on either side of a tree-lined through-road. At one end, at the foot of Buckhurst Hill, were the fields that would become Oaklands School's, and at the other end, at the foot of Church Hill, was the cricket field.

In the 19th and 20th centuries, roads had been built off the through-road, the High Road. The arrival of the railway in Loughton in 1856 – the Eastern Counties Railway, later the Great Eastern Railway – had doubled the population (which was 681 in 1801)[1] and had accelerated Loughton's development, and new buildings filled in gaps in the old village. The west side of the High Road was developed between 1881 and 1914, and the east side was developed between 1901 and the Second World War.

Seven hills

The seven hills of Loughton are the slopes up the three-sided crater to the rim. They are (see 1777 map on pp.x-xi):

- The Crescent/Spring Grove to the east (the end of the descent to the flat meadows) – in 1777 known as Bucket Green;
- Buckhurst Hill – known in 1777 as Bucket Hill;
- Manor Road/Warren Hill/Albion Hill/Ollards Grove;
- Robin Hood Lane or Earl's Path/Strawberry Hill/Staples Hill;
- York Hill, Woodbury Hill/Baldwin's Hill/Church Hill;
- Sedley Rise/Golding's Hill;
- Trap's Hill/Alderton Hill.

The Forest curved like a bow from the Roebuck on top of Buckhurst Hill, round the Epping New Road to Baldwin's Hill at the top of Golding's Hill and round to the top of Trap's Hill. The Forest enfolded the village on three sides and could be seen above the rooftops, in some places looming large on the skyline, and well before the Second World War roads up the seven hills of Loughton connected the High Road to the Forest's curved ridge. The railway transported Londoners out to the Forest, including the poor East-End children brought in parties by the Ragged School Union, and a small tourist industry of tea-rooms for trippers appeared before the Second World War.

Wartime Loughton

My father came to work in Loughton at the Council Offices in Old Station Road. He had been appointed to the Treasurer's Department of the Chigwell Urban District Council, and in March 1943 he rented 52 Brooklyn Avenue, a semi-detached house in a road built in the 1920s and 1930s with a stream at the bottom of the garden, Loughton Brook, that was hidden by tall trees. My grandmother owned a large house in East Grinstead, Sussex, her late husband having created a family business in Sussex and Kent, but there was no question of my parents' buying a house in Loughton during the war. There was risk of air attack and at any time a bomb could wipe out a house and the investment that went into it. Two people had been killed by German bombing in The Drive in July 1940 and on the first day of the Blitz, 7 September 1940, a Hurricane had crashed on an air-raid shelter in Roding Road. Farms in Loughton and Debden had been damaged in a raid in 1941; and a gun battery at Loughton Hall had been bombed, killing a soldier.

The Maitlands owned much of Loughton, and my father rented from the Maitland family. In January 1944 I was sent to school at Essex House with the Miss Huntleys. They occupied 258 High Road, which was pulled down and replaced by a utilitarian block in 1958, now occupied by The Olive Tree restaurant.

Council offices, Loughton, 1937.

Living in Brooklyn Avenue, during the war years I was often taken to the High Road. We cut through a passage by the Post Office (now the Last Post public house) to walk to the Food Office on the corner of High Beech Road (from which I could see the low white fence in front of the Crown). We walked to the greengrocer, Gladys, who wore a white overall and mittens and, at her open-air stall opposite St Mary's church, weighed potatoes on scales which held a battered, oval pan, and to the butchers (Dewhurst's, near The Drive).

Such trips were anxious occasions because of the threat from enemy planes. We were in Prime Minister Winston Churchill's constituency, and it was widely believed that the Nazis targeted the Epping-Forest area to undermine Churchill. The Battle of Britain was over, but occasionally there were dogfights high in the sky during the day and we could see tiny parachutes drifting down. When the police-station siren wailed for at least a minute and died back down we hurried home.

One late afternoon in March 1944 my father said I could go with him to post a letter. It was nearly dark as he shut the front door and I ran ahead to the gate. The police-station siren wailed and immediately a white flash lit up the sky – I can still see it now, everything was suddenly as bright as day – and behind me there was a tinkling as glass fell out of our windows. My father had reached the gate. He turned and without a word, with a fiercely determined look on his face that I can still see, hurried back to the front door and I chanted excitedly, "A bomb, a bomb." A string of German bombs had fallen in the Forest, and six fell on the cricket field some 200 yards away, gouging out the crater in the corner where Trap's Hill joins the High Road.

Nicholas Hagger (left) aged 4, after windows were blown out by a German bomb in March 1944.

The old Oaklands

The bombs had landed just across the road from the old Oaklands School, a double-fronted Regency-looking house (with protruding bay windows and a fanlight over the front door) that had opened as a school in 1937, and had caused some damage. (A house can be seen within its footprint on the 'shops side' of Trap's Hill on the 1777 Chapman and André map. This may have been an earlier house, or perhaps the old Oaklands was older than it looked and had a facelift in the Regency time.)

Because of this damage classes had to be moved to the Methodist church hall the other side of the High Road for a short while. I had been moved to the old Oaklands for the start of the summer term in April

1944, and found myself in the church hall for the first few days. (About this time I was taken on Sunday mornings to Loughton Methodist church, a 1903 building with pews, bare walls and a clock on the wall whose small hand crawled too slowly between XI and XII.)

The old Oaklands.

The old Oaklands was repaired, and in the summer of 1944, about the time of D-Day, at a first-floor assembly we all sang, "We plough the fields and scatter/The good seed on the land," which placed us all within the rhythms of Nature. I spent morning breaks playing in the walled garden. The co-owners both supervised: Miss Elizabeth Lord, the Headmistress (who owned three-fifths), and Miss Mabel Reid, who taught one of the classes (and owned two-fifths). There was a quince tree, and we 60-odd pupils often had quince jam with our elevenses. There were a couple of white tents pegged on the lawn.

There was an iron Morrison air-raid shelter (named after the Labour Minister of Home Security Herbert Morrison) in the garden. It had a sturdy iron top with see-through iron mesh on either side. When the police siren signalled a possible air raid we were led out to sit on a rug in the shelter near the high Georgian blackish-brick garden wall. I can recall lying on my front on a rug near a teacher and a boy called Robin Fowler, who swapped his Japanese hundred-*yen* bank note with a picture of brown cattle on the back for a sweet I had brought from home. I still have the note.

V-1s

Daylight raids were a trial, but the night raids were worse. In June 1944 the first V-1 rockets (doodlebugs) landed in the Epping-Forest area. I often lay in bed in Brooklyn Avenue, listening, and when I heard the whine of an approaching pilotless doodlebug I would wait for its engine to cut out and would start counting. By the time I had counted to ten there would be an explosion. I would be relieved that the flying bomb had not fallen nearby. I knew that any night one of the V-1 rockets could fall on our roof and wipe us all out. Perhaps those evenings cowering under my bedclothes stimulated my sense of the ephemeral, which coloured my writing in later years.

Trees

The Forest had an impact on me in the days following D-Day. Its trees were everywhere and filled me with wonder. We walked up to the Strawberry-Hill pond. My father took us to the Stubbles, open heath lands still ridged from being enclosed and sown for wheat in furrows, and we played football near the central clump of trees we knew as the Witches' Copse. Brooklyn Avenue had trees at intervals in its pavements, some of which had blossomed in the spring.

The new Oaklands

In September 1944 Oaklands School moved to its present premises in Albion Hill, and I moved with it. The old Oaklands has since been pulled down and replaced by a parade of shops, and there are now utilitarian garages behind them where that garden stood.

The new Oaklands was then a large rambling, ivy-clad house. I was later told that it had been built in 1837, but it has been assessed as dating to c.1885.[2] It was one of the large old houses on the south side of Albion Hill, and was at first known as Fir Bank (or Firbank). It had a garden, and years later had acquired the use of two fields carved out of Forest land between Albion Hill and Warren Hill that had been enclosed in 1862. During the war it was occupied by the Belgian Refugees. After the war the two fields were full of buttercups in which we lay in the warm autumn sun under a huge oak that was reputed to be 800 years old: the oak on the school badge.

The fields were part of the Forest of Waltham when Peter de Valognes owned land nearby in 1086 and later formed part of Epping Forest. They were enclosed in January 1862 when the Rev. J.W. Maitland granted them to Edward Vickers of The Pollards, and the iron railings that surround them may have dated from their enclosure that year. The fields are shown on a map of enclosures in Loughton manor that accompanied the Preliminary Report of the Epping Forest Commissioners in 1875, They formed plot 359, "garden and pleasure ground attached to the Pollards", which were "released from Crown rights into the ownership of Edward Vickers". On 3 February 1882 they were re-awarded to Edward Vickers (in return for £550) by Sir Arthur Hobhouse, the Arbitrator who had compensated Loughton after the Epping Forest Act of 1878 and had presided over the building of Lopping Hall. One field passed down to Bernard Howard, owner of Fir Bank before it became Oaklands, and the other field to Sir Geoffrey de Freitas, who became a Labour MP in 1945 (see p.120). De Freitas lived in Greengates in the grounds of The Pollards, a palatial house demolished in 1960 whose wide stone garden balustrade and Roman-style fountain (reputedly built by 14 Italian men c.1862) have survived along with a mosaic floor that peeped through grass at the end of the war.

The new Oaklands fields with oak tree (left) and railings (right).

Oaklands was not the first house in Albion Hill to have been turned into a school. Across the road from Fir Bank was the 16th-century Albion Hall (now 9-11 Albion Hill), part of which was a school in the 1820s and 1830s. It is therefore possible that Oaklands was built earlier than c.1885. (Loughton's historian W.C. Waller does not record the buildings in Albion Hill.) Francis Worrall Stevens took over the running of this school from his father in 1827 when he was 20 and ran it until 1834. In 1833 he wrote to Lord Althorp, Chancellor of the Exchequer, proposing an adhesive penny stamp bearing royal arms. About this time his assistant was Rowland Hill, who worked with him for five months while recovering from an illness. After Stevens emigrated to New Zealand, Hill proposed the idea of a penny post with the sovereign's head on stamps, an innovation for which he took the credit (having apparently stolen the idea from Stevens).[3]

I was in a class with the children of some of the better-known Loughton figures, such as Mark Liell, JP, the local solicitor, and Dr Walker, our GP. It must have been in the winter of 1944 that I was invited to have tea with the son of the architect Kenneth Lindy, who exhibited designs for the rebuilding of the City of London in 1944, and the son of the architect Charles Frederick Clark, who lived at Ripley Grange in Debden Lane.

V-2s

In early 1945 we were attacked by the soundless V-2 rockets, which struck without warning. Several fell in the Forest. One enlarged the pond by Butler's Retreat next to Queen Elizabeth's hunting lodge, and another the pond by the Rising Sun public house. The fall of Berlin and the death of Hitler were greeted with euphoric relief.

Churchill in Loughton

In April 1945 Prime Minister Churchill toured his constituency for the coming General Election. He began in Woodford and drove by car along a crowded Loughton High Road to King's Green in front of the King's Head. He spoke from the war memorial, standing on the first step and facing the cricket field with Mrs. Churchill at his side. It was drizzling. I was there, standing very near Churchill. A photograph appeared in the *Gazette* (as the local paper, now known as the *Guardian*, was then called), showing half my head. My mother has written "Nicholas" on the cutting which is framed on my study wall, and has an arrow pointing to my head. I am near the Methodist Minister, Mr Allwood, and his wife, who are also labelled. Churchill congratulated his constituents on surviving rockets and flying bombs and said that if he was called away during the election – a reference to the coming Potsdam conference – Mrs. Churchill would stand in for him. It was at Potsdam that Churchill learned he had lost the election and been rejected by the British people after delivering victory over the Nazis.

Churchill speaking in Loughton in 1945, with Nicholas Hagger out of view (bottom left).

That speech of Churchill's at Loughton has become a benchmark. I go to a dentist in King's Green, Norman Roback, whose window is within view of the war memorial. We sometimes discuss how a true "old Loughtonian" can be identified. Anyone privileged to have heard Churchill that day is among the oldest of Loughton's "old Loughtonians".

Post-War Loughton

In July 1945, after the end of the war, my family moved to Journey's End in Station Road, one of the original 1870s houses in that road (which had been marked out around 1871).

Journey's End

Journey's End had been occupied by the ARP (Air Raid Protection, which had been founded in 1935) and the WVS (Women's Voluntary Service, which had been founded in 1938). It was empty when we moved in, with cut telephone wires sticking out of the skirtings and green lino on the upstairs floors. Initially we rented it from Commander J.W. Maitland, the last Loughton descendant of the 19th-century Maitlands who had enclosed the Forest, and in early 1949 we bought it from him.

After the war Commander Maitland sold the 644-acre Debden estate, which his family had owned since 1825, to the London County Council. The Council filled it with rows of prefabs to rehouse bombed-out East-Enders. The prefabs were in due course replaced by small houses. The Maitland family left Loughton and relocated to Harrington Hall, Spilsby in Lincolnshire, which had connections with Tennyson, where their son Sir John Maitland later lived. (My daughter lived as a tenant there for a while – weirdly, like her grandfather a tenant of the Maitland family – and went shooting with Sir John.)

Under the tenure of my parents Journey's End became a green house. It had green timber frames on three white gables, and green porch doors. There were green lime trees on either side of a green gate. At the back on a green lawn stood a green pear tree with another pear and apple tree nearby, behind green gooseberries and raspberries.

At the end of Station Road stood the pyramidal four-faced clock of Lopping Hall, a peace offering to the people of Loughton from the Corporation of London's compensation fund to make up for the loss of their lopping rights and of the Maitlands' right to enclose. Beyond it, on the skyline, was the dark green Forest around Loughton Camp.

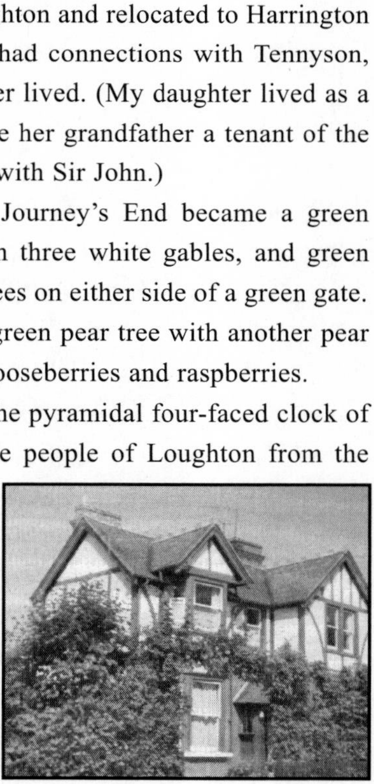

Journey's End, Loughton.

In the mid-1940s it was a rather splendid house, double-fronted and full of character. Sadly today all the green has gone, and I cringe when I walk past as its timber-framing has been rendered with plaster and its front garden has been turned into a plasterer's yard.

It was on the back lawn, before we had moved in July, that my mother held a sixth birthday party for me in May 1945. We had been given permission to use the kitchen, and tables with starched-white tablecloths were set out on the lawn in a U shape on a hot sunny day. All my Oaklands classmates sat up to a sumptuous tea even though there was still rationing. I sat with my back to redcurrant bushes, not quite in the shade thrown by the pear tree. There was a feast on the white tablecloths and one of the helpers spilt damson jam on it about a foot from my plate. I can see my mother, slim in a summer dress, stooping on the other side of the table, scraping the damson jam with a knife and then rubbing salt onto the stain. I can see the scene so clearly that I can almost put my arm into it and help rub salt on the stain.

Addison's Bookshop

It must have been that birthday when I was first given a five-shilling book token. I took it to Addison's Bookshop (which is now marked by a blue plaque next to the Café Rouge), a small book-lined room, and encountered the tall, stooping figure of William Addison. He had just completed his first book, *Epping Forest, Its Literary and Historical Associations*, in Easter 1945, and published it later that year. I can see him leave his high dark desk and walk three paces to me, clerical and avuncular in a suit, bend and put his hand on my shoulder, guide me to the shelf where the *Observer's* books were kept and suggest that I bought the *Observer's Book of Trees*, putting me on course to connect with the Forest (and write this book). He believed that children should spend book tokens on books that enhanced their observation of Nature. After later birthdays and Christmases he encouraged me to buy other Observer's books: the *Observer's Book of Butterflies*, the *Observer's Book of Flowers* and the *Observer's Book of Birds*.

The Forest

The Forest, bare, humped and sullen in winter and lush-green and smiling in summer, had us under its spell. It enfolded Loughton and drew us towards it. We often walked up Station Road, crossed over to Forest Road and ran towards the stream at the end where the Forest began. There we caught sticklebacks and minnows in nets made of canes, wire and sewn-together flour bags. My aunt used to speak of "the lure of the Forest" for us children. My brother and I would walk to the Stubbles off Nursery Road, in those days a heath with wild flowers and brambles where I could catch butterflies with a net: azure blues, small tortoiseshells and red admirals. There were dozens of purple and green grasshoppers, and the whole heath was full of their chirping and each footstep we took was accompanied by their jumping.

The Stubbles.

Nature

The next two years I either walked to school or caught a number 20 double-decker red bus from the Crown to Albion Hill. At Oaklands School we were taken on Nature walks, sometimes round the grounds past the prehistoric plants that grew at the bottom of the main field, beyond the ancient iron railings, and sometimes to the mosaic in grass that survived from the old Pollards house along with the balustrade and fountain of Buckingham-Palace proportions which still stands in a hollow between gardens, now a folly left over from a grander age. Sometimes we crossed Warren Hill and listened to the birdsong and learned to identify willow-warblers and wrens.

Sometimes we were taken up to the two ponds on Strawberry Hill. The Earl's-Path pond was half-covered in lily-leaves with white or golden water-lilies. The inner pond on Strawberry Hill was ringed by Forest trees and had a fallen beech that lay just above the water. We could walk out on the trunk, holding on to a branch, and look down on either side for frogspawn. Opposite the fallen beech, by reeds, there was clear water near a bank, and there we fished for dragonfly larvae, caddis, tadpoles and newts. We brought back Canadian pondweed and put it in the aquarium on the Nature table. We drew it with great precision along with sycamore seeds and spotted red toadstools, which we had found. I found a stag beetle and put it in a matchbox pierced with air holes and drew its horned claws.

Oaklands, school photograph with Nicholas Hagger inset, 1946.

There was a bird table on our garden lawn, on which I put bacon rind. I kept a bird diary, drawing all the birds that visited it: finches, tits, sparrows and starlings. Knowing my love of Nature, at auction my parents bought a specimen cabinet with a dozen drawers that held pinned butterflies and moths, and two glass cases containing birds' eggs, each in a tiny labelled compartments.

The Journey's End garden teemed with life. The two pear trees and apple tree dropped windfalls, which attracted wasps. A fence of trailing honeysuckle was full of humming bees. There were roses and Michaelmas daisies. There were gooseberries and red currants, and we grew peas, which I would pick and shell, and runner beans. There was a fence of ivy, and I pruned the lime trees at the front with a long-arm. At Oaklands School the fields were full of buttercups, and the hawthorn bore may blossom which brightened the summer term. There were foxes and squirrels, and a badger's set. I was alert to the changing colours of leaves in autumn.

In those days after the war there were no televisions or computer games to amuse children. We developed our own interests to make good use of our time, and getting to know Nature was a very important interest. The Forest was the cradle of my soul, and all those hours of observing trees, leaves, fruit, birds, butterflies and insects turned me into a woodlander and gave me a lifelong love of Nature and a familiarity with all the various species which would later find their way into my poems, stories and other writings.

Loughton Camp and the Lost Pond

I continued to live in Loughton during the rest of my school days. I can recall two or three walks through Loughton Camp, scuffling through last year's leaves between the Iron-Age banks and peering into the hollow tree thought by some to be Dick Turpin's "cave". We had no fear of being kidnapped; in the 1950s the Forest was not a dangerous place. I was invited to a couple of parties in Baldwin's Hill, near where Willingale had lived, and recall playing a form of hide-and-seek on the green there in summer evenings. I can recall running down the slope to the Lost Pond where the sculptor Jacob Epstein, who also lived in Baldwin's Hill, sometimes painted. (He exhibited a hundred paintings of the Forest in 1933, and continued to paint the Forest during the war.)

Baldwin's Hill Pond

On a couple of occasions we went to Baldwin's Hill Pond, near Blackweir Hill, which was formed by the damming of Loughton Brook and once served as Loughton's reservoir. It was full of rushes and water violets, gypsywort and water horsetail. It overflowed at one end into a drain, a grating perhaps ten feet below which there was a curved tunnel open at the far end. A sluice allowed Loughton Brook to continue and carried it under Clay Road into Loughton, and in due course past the bottom of our garden in Brooklyn Avenue. We always climbed into the tunnel and, stepping on either side of the steady trickle of overflow water, reached the end and stood under the grating, the water pouring down at the pond end in a small waterfall. I would imagine I was in a subterranean prison or dungeon, an image I was later to use in my poem 'Orpheus-Prometheus in the Blackweir Region of Hell'. (See p.309.)

Howard Carter's brother

My first dentist was Dr Carter, a silver-haired man in horn-rimmed spectacles who wore a white dentist's tunic. He practised in one of the large houses on the High Road between Meadow Road and Lower Park Road, Glendale (the second house in from Lower Park Road). The dentist's chair was in the room to the left of the front door, looking from the gate. As he was about to drill my teeth he would tell me a story about his brother, Howard Carter, the archaeologist. I can recall him describing how Howard Carter opened Tutankhamun's tomb – "hold on a minute, just a little drilling" – and then how he entered the tomb and saw "wonderful things". There was more drilling before he told me what the wonderful things were. His stories about his brother, told to take my mind off the pain of the drill, gave me a lifelong interest in Egyptian history.

Railway

When I was eight I started at Chigwell School. I travelled by steam train from Loughton station. After the electrification of the railway line from Loughton to London, when tubes replaced steam trains in 1948, I made occasional visits to London during the school holidays. I was very interested in Roman history and used to visit a seller of Roman coins who had a rejects box in which slightly damaged coins were priced at 6d (2.5p), and in the course of many visits acquired coins of most of the Roman emperors.

Churchill again

On 25 October 1951 Winston Churchill came to the Loughton High School for Girls (now Roding Valley High School) to speak in the General Election campaign. I stood at the top of the steps, on the left as you face the school, and stepped out as he approached at the head of his entourage, bent over his stick, in coat and hat, and held out my autograph album and a pen. I asked him for his autograph and he signed "W. Churchill" in a spidery, uncertain hand and beamed at me before entering the school. His warm smile stayed with me and coloured my re-creation of the last year of the Second World War in *The Warlords* and *Overlord*.

Studies

But it was the Roman and Greek war leaders who then caught my imagination. At Journey's End, where the pear tree was patterned on my bedroom wall by the street light at night, I steeped myself in the classical world to pass my 'A' levels, and got into Oxford to read Law. My father planned that I would become a solicitor, and arranged for me to spend a week sitting in Mark Liell's solicitors' office in Loughton so I could decide whether I wanted to spend my life in the Law. I was more interested in reading Chester Wilmot's *Struggle for Europe* about the Second World War. I spent a gap year commuting to a solicitors' office near Chancery Lane. I read voraciously on the tube and was now more interested in European literature than in the Law, and, knowing I would become a writer, I changed to English Literature as soon as I could.

Staple's Hill and John Ezard

The Forest was important to me when I returned to Loughton for the university vacations. Besides the English Literature syllabus, which ran from Anglo-Saxon to the 19th century, I was reading the best-known works of French, German, Russian, Italian and modern English literature and I discussed these with John Ezard, an Old Chigwellian who was reading English at Cambridge and who went on to become Arts correspondent for the *Guardian*. We would meet up in The Hollybush opposite Lopping Hall. Some afternoons I would call on him in The Drive, Loughton and we would walk up to the cut-through to Staple's Hill, where the local people had exercised the right to lop during the Maitlands' time as lords of the manor. We would discuss books such as Huysmans' *A Rebours* (*Against Nature*), and I said I preferred Wordworth's view of Nature. Yeats, Kierkegaard, Dante, Goethe, Camus and Sartre were just some of the writers I can recall discussing during those afternoon walks when we sometimes walked on from Staple's Hill to the Earl's Path pond.

Strawberry Hill and Earl's Path ponds

During the 1960s I taught English Literature at universities abroad, in Iraq, Japan and finally Libya. I wanted to experience the world's cultures and civilisations and witness the Cold War at first hand.

I took a look at the fallen beech by the Strawberry Hill pond before I left for Iraq. There I implemented Churchill's unification of Sunnis, Shiites and Kurds, who co-existed in my classes, and visited the ruins of ancient civilisations.

I walked round the Strawberry Hill pond before I left for Japan. My father had just died and, still raw, I had a profound experience when the trees mirrored in the water blended with the sky and I sensed the unity of Nature beyond reason and words. In Japan I represented the West. I absorbed the wisdom of the East and during a visit to Communist China in March 1966 got first wind of the Cultural Revolution.

Past holders of Loughton

In 1966 I came back on leave from Japan for ten weeks and rented my brother's house, 55 High Beech Road. In Japan I had found myself as a poet, and I wrote poems during this visit. It was a short walk to the Stubbles and Strawberry Hill, and I delved into Epping Forest. I marvelled at the number of historical figures who had once held or owned Loughton. As we saw in Part One, Earl Harold (before he becamed Harold II) gave Loughton (Lukintune) to Waltham Holy Cross, and from the 13th century its land was known as the manor of Loughton, and was valued in 1254 at £11.12s.[4] It passed into the possession of Henry VIII in 1540, was owned by Edward VI until 1551, and was given to Mary Tudor in 1553 and then to the Duchy of Lancaster in 1558. In 1613 it was bought from the Duchy by Sir Robert Wroth for £1,224. Loughton had therefore been held by Earl Harold and Waltham Holy Cross (later Waltham Abbey), owned by Henry VIII, Edward VI and Mary, and held by the Duchy of Lancaster; and the first local lord of the manor had received Ben Jonson. I felt a direct link with Harold II and Henry VIII by being in a place they once held or owned, and felt equivalent links with Tennyson and Clare, two poets who had lived in Epping Forest.

British School and Matthew Arnold

I noted that Matthew Arnold had visited Loughton in 1867, the year of 'Dover Beach', when he was working on *Culture and Anarchy*. As Inspector of Schools, he had visited the British School that was established in 1844 in 40-44 Smarts Lane, Loughton,[5] and reported that 87 children were presented for examination and that the average attendance for the year was 69.[6] The school closed in 1888. I also noted that Kipling had lived opposite Golding's Hill Pond.

The British School visited by Matthew Arnold.

Walks

I took a last look at the fallen beech at the Strawberry Hill pond before again leaving for Japan. On my return I lived in Crescent View, off The Crescent, on the other side of the road from where I had found the Roman coin. I often walked up Albion Hill with my young daughter, who now attended Oaklands School, and along Nursery Road to the Stubbles. Sometimes we went on to Strawberry Hill.

I left again to work in Libya, and after more leave in England, found myself grappling with Gaddafi's tyranny and, a representative of the West, narrowly escaping execution, a story I recounted in *The Libyan Revolution*.

I had always returned to the Forest between postings and renewed my bond with Strawberry Hill. I often looked into the mirror of Earl's Path pond, in which both reflected sky and muddy ground could be seen at the same time. I put this experience into 'Clouded-Ground Pond', which is in fact the Strawberry-Hill pond (see pp.309-11).

Strawberry Hill pond (left) and Earl's Path pond (right).

Absence in London

In the 1970s I lived and taught in London. I was Head of English and Senior Teacher at a large London school. I had a Department of 25 and helped run the school. I was in charge of the public examinations and arranged coverage for absentee staff. It was a heavy load – there were over 2,000 pupils and 140 staff – and I dreamed of returning to Epping Forest. I always had to have a tree outside my London window, and a key to the gardens of the nearest London square.

High Beach church

My two sons were christened at High Beach church and my mother held family gatherings at Journey's End. At the last of these the Headmistress of Oaklands, Miss Lord, was present.

Miss Lord offers Oaklands

My mother had suggested that she should be invited, and it was over a cup of tea in the garden, standing near the pear tree about where I had sat for my sixth birthday party when the damson jam was spilt, that she asked if I would buy Oaklands from her, appoint my wife (a trained teacher) as Headmistress and run it. The negotiations proceeded very slowly and Miss Lord carried on running the school until she was nearly 82. By then it had taken five years for the transfer to take place.

Miss Lord eventually visited my mother at her new house – long widowed, my mother had sold Journey's End and moved to a more manageable house, 54 High Road – and asked what she thought of Oaklands' passing to a past pupil, her son.

Sadly my mother died in 1981, ten months before my wife and I took over at Oaklands. Her funeral took place at St Mary's, Loughton, where my father's funeral had taken place in 1963. She died before knowing the details of our tenure at Oaklands, but she knew our tenure would happen.

Oaklands School

We were to take over at Oaklands in the autumn term of 1982. The building needed modernising, and at the start of the summer holidays we spent ten days painting and renovating, working from 8am to 10pm each day. We decorated ten rooms: two coats on all ceilings, walls and doors. We installed central heating and made many improvements.

Miss Lord (left) and Ann Hagger, 1982.

Fields

Initially we rented the two fields. The main field had been conveyed to Miss Lord by Bernard Howard in January 1954 and the second field had been conveyed to her by Sir Geoffrey de Freitas (a 1945-intake Labour MP and later diplomat who lived on the Pollards estate) in November 1953. Miss Lord had clearly rented the main field that I played in as a child from the Howard family from 1944. I had to keep the grass cut. I bought a ride-on mower and cut the grass myself, starting on the outside and reaching the centre in ever-decreasing circles.

The front of Oaklands School with Wren doors, and Oak House on left under blue acacia cedar.

Running the School

I had to continue my teaching in London for the first two or three years. We put our London house on the market and moved to lodgings in a house across the road from the school, and I commuted to work from Loughton each day. I got up at 5.45am every morning and left at 6am, having swallowed breakfast prepared overnight, stopping to gaze in wonder at the sunrise and sun shafts through mist beyond the massive blue acacia cedar which stood near the School's front door. I returned about 7pm when, after a quick supper, I would start again and cope with the Oaklands finances: settle invoices, calculate the staff's salaries and keep the accounts. All staff had a contract signed by me, and I oversaw the legal and insurance side of the school's activities.

We achieved a lot in those first few weeks. We met the parents and got to know the staff. We modernised the curriculum. The school had always taken boys to seven and girls to eleven. My wife Ann had taught English and Maths to eleven-year-olds at her previous schools in London, and had an excellent grasp of what girls needed to do to pass exams to enter independent schools at eleven. We set about raising standards and lifting the roll, which had dropped to 156 when we took over. I was concerned to raise it to around 240. Meanwhile the children ran happily in every morning, as had happened when I was at school, and worked within the context of Nature: the trees and birds in the grounds. They played out under the trees and ran in the main field each break and lunchtime, and took part in after-school activities, which we expanded. We set high standards of work and made as much use of the Forest and grounds as possible.

Lunches

Each school day at Oaklands we put on nearly 200 lunches. My wife and I shopped for the next week at Makro (in Charlton) and at a frozen food store every Friday evening. After a hard week in London I carried the tins down to the cellar storeroom. I often went to Creeds, next to the Post House Hotel on the way to Epping, to buy two heavy sacks of potatoes for the next week, and humped them into my car boot and the other end down the basement steps. We had in-house staff on our payroll who prepared the lunches.

One-way traffic flow

The road outside the school, Albion Hill, was narrow and there were frequent traffic jams at peak times. At the end of October I held an evening meeting in the school hall for local residents, parents, councillors and our community policeman (PC Giddings), and we all agreed to make Albion Hill unofficially one way down the hill to ease the flow of traffic. I asked Epping Forest District Council to make the one-way arrangement official, but the Council administration declined to do so. In fact, my unofficial arrangement has operated smoothly since 1982. Word has spread, and two or three generations of parents have known to come in down the hill at peak time.

More improvements

I had been granted planning permission to build a house in the school grounds between Miss Lord's house and the school building, where we would live. We moved the Art Room from what was now a building site and tacked it on to the Garden Room, doubling the space for the Kindergarten. I had begun negotiations to buy the two fields, which I had been renting and cutting, and in July 1983 Miss Lord agreed to sell. We spent the summer half-term redecorating around the school hall and a week in the 1983 summer holiday painting classrooms. By now the new house was waist-high.

Steps

The school steps incongruously led down to the new house, and we had to move them to take staff, children and parents down to the grounds at the back, which are at a lower level than the school building. In the middle of the steps was a gigantic half-ton slab of York stone, and the builder husband of a member of staff, his son-in-law and I discussed how we should move it. With Stonehenge as our model, we improvised. The husband prised with a garden fork, his son-in-law jacked with a pickaxe and together we slid the slab onto boards and pipes, makeshift rollers borrowed from the building site, and inched it several yards to its present location. Within a few days we had a new flight of steps, which is still in use.

Oaklands steps and Wren doors.

Wren doors

The school's front door was really a side door, and we replaced a window near the Head's study with the present pair of white-painted wooden doors. I acquired these at London Architectural Salvage, which was based in a disused church in Shoreditch. There were umpteen parts of buildings stacked along the sides of the church, and all could be bought. I found the original front doors of St James, Piccadilly, a Wren church and drove them home protruding from the open rear door of my wife's estate car. We made them fit. They are still in use and have the old Wren locks and ironmongery on them.

Upgrading

Every holidays we carried out building improvements. The Garden Room (Kindergarten) complex was added to, and the kitchens were upgraded with industrial flooring and equipment. The basement area was made more hospitable and salubrious, and now included a new staff room. Two other rooms in the basement were improved, including the store-room. The assembly hall was redecorated – by me and a volunteer parent (Martin Wickham, then owner of the Trumps record shop chain). We picked out ceiling features in gold. A curved brick retaining wall was built at the back to shore up the plateau of land on which the school stood and the path running round it. All the paths were tarmaced. Perimeter fencing was renewed.

Purchase of fields

The two fields were completed, and became ours, on 8 December 1983. I continued mowing them and derived great pleasure from regarding them as an 1862 Forest enclosure. The ancient iron railings around the main field would have been erected in that year. An adviser from the Conservation Centre (now the Field Centre) visited us and said that there was very ancient woodland at the bottom of the main field: dog's mercury, wild garlic, wood arums and Star of Bethlehem.

House

We moved into our new house in February 1984. It became the School's Head's house. My wife now lived next door to the School. In May 1984 I secured planning permission to build a three-classroom extension for our reception class. The building was completed a couple of years later in 1986, and is still in use. It stands to the right of the front gate.

Tom McAlister

I gave up teaching in London at the end of the spring term, 1985. I could now play football with the seven-year-old boys. Tom McAlister, the West Ham goalie, one of our parents, had agreed to take football. I had got to know him. The previous September he had dropped in complimentary tickets for me to take my two boys to watch him play at Upton Park. Once a week I put on a tracksuit and played up one end while he played at the other. He was good value, feigning to miss so that our small boys who had seen him on Match of the Day could score against him.

Local police constable

On one occasion the local police constable, PC Giddings (whose wife served me every week as the cashier at the bank), called in on a social visit and asked if he could play. He hung his helmet on a goalpost and, still in uniform, kept goal for my side, hacking the muddy ball with his uniformed right foot. He let three goals in and the trousers of his uniform were very muddy when he apologised to our side for not doing better, replaced his helmet on his head and plodded off.

John Dutchman

John Dutchman, the former Pegasus footballer and Chigwell School master, now took football. One of our seven-year-olds was more interested in picking daisies than in playing football, and I recall Dutchman making one forty-yard-long inch-perfect pass that arrived as he took a step forward. The ball cannoned off his right leg into the goal. He had never scored a goal before and beamed when he realised what he had done (or had had done to him).

Lord Murray

Around this time Lord Murray of Epping Forest, formerly Len Murray, the TUC's general secretary who had retired in 1984 and become a life peer, walked past our house most days on his way to the Forest. We often had a chat on the political state of affairs. On one occasion he helped my elder son Matthew into the car giving him a lift to school, making sure that his violin case was safely inside the door. Sometimes when I was waiting for a tube on Loughton station I would feel my elbow squeezed and would turn to find myself face to face with Murray. We would sit together and talk in the tube carriage. He came to my aunt's landmark birthday parties, which I held for her. He would have been the first to say that his title gave him no monopoly on Epping Forest.

Purchase of allotment area

In early 1987 I arranged to buy the allotment area beyond the second field on the corner of Warren Hill from the former co-owners, Miss Lord and Miss Reid. Completion was on 26 May 1987. I hired a JCB and supervised the gouging-out-of a pond, leaving an island for ducks. A new pond has to be puddled, trodden many times, to seal its bottom. Our new pond was puddled by ten parents from the Parents' Association, who turned up one weekend in wellingtons to tread and (in some cases with bare feet) seal the earth. Mabel Reid gave us reeds and pondweed, and soon there were frogs, fish and water-beetles – and enormous leeches.

After her retirement Miss Lord sometimes wandered into the Head's study for a chat. One day I heard the sound of an electric saw in the second field. I followed the sound and found a woodsman up a ladder sawing a branch off the very large oak that grew near the Old People's Home adjoining the second field. I asked him who had given him permission. He said, "The owner of the Old People's Home as the branch is overhanging his land." He said, "I went to the School and asked for the Headmistress. I was shown into a room where an old lady was sitting. I asked her if I could lop the branch and she said, 'Yes.'" In her mind, Miss Lord was still Headmistress.

Caravan

I acquired a red gypsy caravan as a birthday present to my wife. I arranged for the vendor to tow it by tractor to the School. The tractor entered through the Warren Hill gates. I was standing in the doorway of the caravan, and we crossed the main field where a game of rounders was in progress, astonishing the children and staff, halting the game, and stopped by the wooden gate at the top of the field. The tractor uncoupled and left, and the red caravan has stood there ever since. It has been a base for school events. It housed the PA system during fireworks night in November and has been a changing-room for school fêtes in June. On one occasion Vicki Michelle used it to change into her *'Allo 'Allo!* outfit before opening one of our fêtes.

Geoff Hurst

In June 1986 the Parents' Association put on a barbeque on a hot Sunday. The West Ham goalie, Tom McAlister, wore a French apron and served sausages cooked on a grille over half an oil drum on a stand under the oak tree of the school badge. Another parent-footballer, Geoff Hurst, was there – an ex-West Ham player – and I recall speaking to Giles Watling, son of the actor Jack Watling who had lived in Alderton Hall.

Geoff Hurst opening a fête at Oaklands, with Nicholas Hagger, 1987.

In June 1987 the Parents' Association's annual fête was opened by Geoff (later Sir Geoff) Hurst, who was best known for scoring a hat-trick when England won the World Cup in 1966. He had a daughter in my wife Ann's class. I chatted with him during the country dancing and then introduced him to the crowd on the microphone. He said a few words and judged a contest. I walked with him to the second field and we discussed his hat-trick, and he said perceptively: "It's a twentieth-century record that looks safe. I can't see England getting to the Final again before the end of the century, let alone anyone scoring in a World Cup Final."

School keepers

From the start there was a wonderful can-do spirit at Oaklands. In those pre-Health-and-Safety days staff coped with everything. If an outside drain was blocked with leaves, staff saw the problem, rolled their sleeves up and fished the leaves out. There was no waiting for a school keeper.

We had inherited an odd-job man from Miss Lord, who was in his early eighties and very handy with a screwdriver but incapable of heavy work. We eventually hired a Cockney called Les. In July 1987, during the summer holidays, we painted the outside of Oaklands, including the high second-storey gable overlooking the tennis-court. He had been used to running up the rigging in the Navy during the war and he scampered up the ladder while I kept my foot on the bottom rung. He encountered a problem and wanted me to go up and have a look.

When I had reluctantly climbed about fifteen feet the ladder pulled away from the wall. Les had been keeping his foot on the bottom rung. Clinging to a vertical ladder I looked down and saw Les struggling to keep the ladder upright so I did not fall over backwards onto the sloping rockery and rose-bushes beneath. He eventually managed to push the ladder back. Had I gone over backwards I would probably have broken my back and my neck.

Les was remarkable for his toughness. One day he came in two hours late, saying, "I've just had all me teeth out. I told the dentist, 'I don't want to bother with them no more, take the lot out.'" "Did you have gas or injections?" I asked. "Oh neither, nothing. I just had the lot out. Went home and lay down for a bit and I'm fine now."

Eventually Les emigrated to Australia in search of better weather and was replaced by Ernie Peake, an ex-soldier who was among the first to enter Belsen concentration camp with his Crocodile flamethrower in 1945.

We discussed his qualifications for being a school keeper. He had been a sentry in the war, and had shot and killed a Nazi Colonel who failed to halt. He was court-martialled, and his defence was: "He looked like Hitler with a peaked cap, and he wouldn't stop, he was coming straight for me." He was acquitted. Back on sentry duty he challenged a car late at night which did not stop. He opened fire and the car came to a halt. A German girl got out and called, "You have shot the English Colonel." The English Colonel had been smuggling a German girl back into base and Ernie had killed him. He was court-martialled a second time, and again acquitted. I said, "I reckon your skills will enhance the School's security." Ernie loved the Forest, and we had many chats about the wild life. I kept an eye on the two bullfinches that lived in the hedge by the greenhouse, and on the nuthatch that came to the bird feeder.

Hurst again

The Oaklands 1987 summer fête was again opened by Geoff Hurst. It was an overcast, windy day. I again introduced him after the country dancing, and while he opened the fête I noticed our MP, Sir John Biggs-Davison standing in the middle of the tennis-court steps wearing a large blue rosette and holding an umbrella, trying to be noticed as there was a General Election in five days' time, doing his best to upstage Hurst, without much success.

50th anniversary

Soon afterwards the 50th anniversary of Oaklands was celebrated. The Parents' Association put on a barbeque in the main field on a baking hot June day. Five hundred attended. Parents sat in groups all over the main field basking in the sun, revelling in the atmosphere of togetherness. No one left until well after 6 and many stayed until 8.

Several of my Oaklands school friends came back, including Peter Liell, son of Mark Liell, now a lawyer himself. Christopher and Andrew Imms, who had lived next-door-but-one to Journey's End, also attended.

Jack Straw

I received a letter from Jack Straw, MP, wishing the School well. He had been a past pupil in the Kindergarten – his mother had been a teacher at the school in those days – and he was principally remembered for falling through the ice of the shallow pond beyond the iron railings at the bottom of the main field. "Jack Straw was a *naughty* boy," Mabel Reid (Miss Lord's co-owner) used to say of the future Foreign Secretary. "He was told not to skate on the ice, and he disobeyed and fell through and was marched, blubbing his eyes out, to sit outside Miss Lord's study and be told off."

Disasters

The tennis-court had been re-tarmaced. It had to be repaired almost immediately for when parents sat in the tennis-court to watch a dancing display on the grass under the apple trees in scorching sun, the tarmac melted and some of their benches and chairs became embedded.

Then the great storm of October 1987 unleashed a hurricane which passed across the school grounds around midnight and felled a large chestnut tree across the tennis-court netting, which collapsed beneath it. The eye of the storm ripped out many tiles from the Oaklands roof. Woodsmen were around the School for days sawing branches for logs while roofers swarmed up ladders and crawled on the roof.

The Howards

I received a letter from Tom Howard, whose father Bernard Howard, a verderer, owned Fir Bank before it became Oaklands from the First World War to 1929. He then moved to Little Pollards. The letter paved the way for the visit by two of Tom's sisters, Mary and Jean, who came to look round their former home with Mabel Reid. Bernard Howard had married Elizabeth Jane Fox and had five daughters (two of whom were my visitors) and two sons.[7]

The Howard family had made its money from Howard's Aspirins. Their factory was at Ilford, within the site of the Uphall Camp (see p.13). I was greatly impressed that a family that had owned Oaklands should have built its workplace in the centre of an Iron-Age hill-fort. Tom's brother was killed when a German bomb dropped on the factory during the Blitz, and his mother was killed a month later.

The family came from a line of Quakers and gave its name to the Howard League for Penal Reform. They were friendly with the Fry family who lived over the road and were descended from Elizabeth Fry, the Quaker philanthropist who inspected prisons and died in 1845.

Before the First World War it was not uncommon for families to marry into neighbours' families. Before the Howards, Fir Bank was owned by the Sturges, and about 1900 Florence Sturge married the son of the Harris family who lived in Albion Park House across the road.

The Howard sisters told how during the First World War they played records in the cellar, dined in the present library (from which there was a door to the garden), used the Headmistress's study as a den and slept in the attic to the right of the top of the stairs, lighting their way with candles as there was no electricity, and gas stopped at the first floor. Three maids lived in the attic to the left of the top of the stairs. The sisters' parents' bedroom was at the top of the first flight of stairs on the right, and there was a nurse's room next door. The nursery was the large classroom that had been Mabel Reid's and was later Ann Holland's. They described a fire-drill out of their top-floor bedroom window during the First World War, when, though little girls, they had to abseil down on ropes.

Bernard Howard.

Bonfire night

Throughout the 1980s, the Parents' Association put on a bonfire night on the main field. In those pre-Health-and-Safety days parents came in the previous week, dug out a large square of turf and built a 20-foot-high wigwam of old bits of wood. It was lit after dark and sparks flew high into the air. Then parents put on a firework display with announcements over the public address system (often by me). Nowadays a company comes in and lets off the fireworks, and there is no fire.

Sports Day

I was often on the microphone for Sports Day, which was held on the main field. Sitting under the oak tree of the school badge, we prided ourselves on the slickness of the races. As one lot of runners set off, the next race stepped up to take their place. The parents stood along the far side of the track silhouetted against the trees at the bottom of the main field, and watched wave after wave of runners. The first, second and third of each race came to receive badges while I announced the results of the previous race and introduced the next one.

On one occasion in the 1990s a member of the British women's relay team stepped forward to run in the mothers' race. I announced that she was to be given a handicap: she had to start at the top of the steps (the ones we had moved), leap the iron railings and catch the others up. I should have enforced the handicap as she won by half the length of the course.

Rod Stewart

On another occasion one of our parents, the singer-songwriter Rod Stewart, attended with his then wife Rachel Hunter. We had their daughter for most of the summer term, when they were not in Los Angeles. Rod had taken to collecting his daughter at 12 o'clock, sitting on the low window-ledge nearest the front gate wearing shorts and sandals while he waited for the door to open. From the house window I sometimes saw a dozen mothers, carefully dressed and heavily made-up, standing near him and ignoring him as much as he ignored them.

In the mothers' race, Rachel Hunter ran barefoot like the wind and came second. One of the parents said to me, "Don't you realise her legs are insured for five million? If she'd tripped and broken her ankle the insurance company would have made a claim against the School." It was the first indication I had had that we were moving into a compensation culture.

I did not think that Rod Stewart's legs were insured for that amount and I called the fathers' race and said that Mr Stewart was making his way to the starting line. In fact, Mr Stewart was lying face down on the grass, exhausted after entertaining a huge audience in Paris the previous evening, and he did not stir.

Those days were full of sunshine and on the main field, surrounded by trees and grass, we felt that the races were taking place in the Forest itself rather than in an enclosed part of the Forest.

Carol service

Every year there was an afternoon carol service at St Mary's, Loughton, which had been built in 1871. In December 1992 my wife, as Headmistress, was greeting parents at the door. I arrived and asked her where I was sitting. She said, "You're not. The vicar hasn't turned up, you're taking the service."

The church was packed. I had to go down to the front and welcome everyone, and introduce the hymns. I sat with the staff during the nativity play. But at the end there was still no sign of the vicar.

"You'll have to do the blessing," one of the staff said (Ann Holland, a fellow pupil of mine at Oaklands in 1947).

So I stood up and, with some of the staff trying not to giggle, said, "May the Lord bless you and keep you and make his face to shine upon you and give you peace. Amen." There was a chorus of "Amens". I walked to the door and shook hands with my departing flock.

At that point the vicar turned up. "Oh," he said. "Oh. Who took the service?"

"I did," I said.

"Oh."

Later I worked out that my blessing should have been worded, "May the Lord bless *us* and keep *us*." I had not been struck down.

Death of Miss Lord

At the beginning of January 1993 Miss Lord admitted herself to a private nursing home, Marcris in Theydon Bois, while her niece Marion, who looked after her, was in hospital having chemotherapy. Elizabeth Lord knew deep down that Marion would not be able to continue to look after her – she in fact died the following September – and she lost the will to eat. I received a phone call from another relative saying that Elizabeth was only expected to live for a few minutes, would I visit her.

Ann and I left straightaway, but we were too late. I sat with her by myself for some while, and thought of all the young souls (including mine) who had passed through her hands.

She was eventually cremated and there was a memorial service at St Mary's immediately afterwards, at which I read *Matthew* 5, 14-16; 18, 1-5; and *Proverbs* 3, 13-18, pausing at every word that suggested her life. Mark Liell, one of the Loughton worthies of my boyhood, came up to me at the end, white-haired and old, no bowler hat now.

Mabel Reid was present. Soon afterwards she sold her house and moved into another private nursing home, Forest Place in Buckhurst Hill, and she died aged over 90 in 1996. Her memorial service on 1 July was also at St Mary's.

Prize-giving: Tony Little

Prize-giving was held at that time at the Hawkey Hall off Woodford High Road. It was named after Sir James Hawkey, Churchill's constituency chairman, and opened on 26 March 1955. Churchill arrived for the opening ceremony in a coat and hat, holding a stick, in the last month of his premiership, and a picture that first appeared in the *Evening News* survives of my younger brother in short trousers applauding him. I had been taken to hear Churchill speak from the platform there on another occasion.

During prize-giving I would sit on the platform with the guest speaker, and we would then descend to the hall and watch the children put on a concert to demonstrate their artistic skills. In July 1999 the guest speaker was Tony Little, then Headmaster of Chigwell School. As I sat next to him waiting for the concert to begin I said, "There's a vacancy at Eton. You went there, you should apply." He looked at me, smirked and said nothing.

A few years later he returned to Chigwell as Head Master of Eton, having started there in 2002, and told me, "I'd just had the interview and had been told I'd got it and that I should keep quiet and not tell anyone until an announcement was made, and you came out with what I was trying to keep secret. I wondered if you are a mind-reader."

Oak-Tree Group of Schools

The Oaklands waiting-list grew so long that I founded Coopersale Hall School (see pp.223-43) and I later acquired Normanhurst School, Chingford (see pp.261-70) to create the Oak-Tree Group of Schools (which form a triangle largely within Epping Forest). Establishing a group enabled resources to be pooled and regular contact to be maintained between teachers on one staff and their opposite numbers on the other two staffs, which would raise standards. During the 1990s I left Loughton each morning for Epping to help Coopersale Hall through its growing phase, and spent less time at Oaklands.

Mottoes

Normanhurst had a Latin motto, and I was called on to come up with Latin mottoes for the other two schools. For Oaklands I found "*E pluribus unum*", "out of many, one". I had just finished writing *The One and the Many* when I chose this motto. The phrase suggested that a school has one identity out of many different pupils and races, and that pupils should find their way to their own unique identity among the many impressions and bits of knowledge they would assimilate.

The phrase came from a Latin translation of a variation of Heracleitus's 10th fragment ("everything is one") that reads "out of all things, one, and one out of all things" ("*ek panton hen kai ex henos panta*"), suggesting the One that unifies the universe, the unity behind plurality and opposites. In a poem attributed to Virgil, '*Moretum*', colour is "*e pluribus unus*" (i.e. blends many shades into one), and "*ex pluribus unum*" is used by St Augustine in his *Confessions*, book 4. In the 1770s the phrase was used by *The Gentleman's Magazine* to suggest many articles in one magazine, and it was recommended to the committee designing the American Seal by Pierre Eugène du Simitière. It appears on the American Great Seal, and on some American coins, to suggest, 'out of many states one nation'. It has been used by Benfica football club since 1908 to suggest one team out of many players, and on 14 September 2011 Portuguese fans unfurled a huge banner proclaiming this phrase at Benfica's UEFA Champion's League home tie against Manchester United. It is a Universalist phrase with connotations of world government ('out of many nations, one world').

All these associations added layers of meaning, but in its educational sense the Oaklands motto means: "Develop one unique identity out of many bits of knowledge, within one school that contains many different pupils, and within one Reality behind a universe consisting of many natural phenomena."

Matthew Hagger

My wife was called on to advise in the new schools, and stood down as Headmistress in July 1996 so that she could be free to put energy into all three schools. Our son Matthew, who had gone through Chigwell and after university had trained as a teacher, joined the Oak-Tree Group of Schools as Managing Principal in July 2001. Matthew bought the house next to ours, which had once been Miss Lord's house. It was adjacent to the school land and Matthew shadowed my day-to-day work. I gradually handed over the day-to-day running to him and when he was ready became a semi-retired figurehead, spending more and more time each day writing books.

Matthew Hagger.

More building

We did more building, which Matthew supervised. We built a long Art Room block below the curved retaining wall and built extra classrooms on the first floor of the school. At the same time access to all first-floor classrooms was changed so that they could be entered from a long through corridor. (In the Victorian house some rooms could only be entered from other rooms.) My wife and I moved out of our house in the grounds, which now became an administration area with rooms for small children and support staff and a large IT area. It was renamed Oak House. Matthew made many more changes, continuing my policy of perpetual upgrading and improvement.

Bank

I still did the banking in Loughton High Road, and as I went to and fro each week I would occasionally be stopped by past Oaklands parents who told me what their children had gone on to do.

My connection with the bank spanned six decades. In the summer of 1946 when at Oaklands I was friendly with Gwen Thomas, and was invited to tea where she lived: at Barclays, for her father was the local bank manager. My father banked with him. Aware of this, after tea Mr Thomas took me into the foreign currency room where there was a mound of foreign coins, about knee-high to me as I was then. I believe they had been brought back by returning servicemen at the end of the war. Mr Thomas said I could keep as many as I could hold in two hands. I plunged in my hands and carried my handfuls towards a wall. Out fell African coins with holes in them, Indian coins shaped like diamonds, Arab coins with serrated edges, coins with magnificent crowned heads and legends with mysterious currency units: rupees, piastres and mills. This would have been a few months before I found the coin of Caracalla. I still have my two handfuls.

I banked at the same branch while I was at university, from 1958, and had been with the branch ever since. In July 2008, when the branch had had a decorative make-over and the latest manager wanted a formal opening, I was invited to cut the tape. I was given a tour of the bank beyond the cashiers' windows and worked out that I picked up my two handfuls in what is now an open-plan area that can be seen from the innermost cashiers' windows.

Inspections

I still took part in the dinners we put on for the staff after school inspections. Each Independent Schools or Ofsted inspection we had was harder to get through than the last one as the inspectors raised the bar each time, and each time we had more "excellents" and "outstandings". In 2010 I took part in a dinner we held for the Oaklands staff in the large room above Café Rouge. The school's pastoral care had been found excellent, and there was talk of Jade Goody, the Oaklands parent who had died in March 2009. Oaklands had provided some stability for her two children who were our pupils before she died.

75th anniversary

Oaklands' 75th anniversary, and the 30th anniversary of the Haggers' involvement in running the school, were due to be celebrated in 2012. In 2011 one of my contemporaries, both at the old Oaklands opposite the cricket field and at the present school in Albion Hill, visited from America. Gordon Roberts had not seen the school since he left to go to Chigwell in 1946. I met him by the front gate. He was with his American wife, and I took them down to the main field. We sat on a seat and looked at old school photos I had brought in a carrier bag. He named faces from the early to mid-1940s. The years rolled back as we pored over my magnifying glass and tried to identify each face.

Continuity

He remarked on how little the setting had changed. In truth, he was right. The oak tree of the school badge, the two fields and the trees around us had hardly changed at all. If we ignored the adventure playground and distant equipment, there was a continuity that had lasted our entire lifetimes: of setting standards, of values and of a way of living.

Loughton has retained a similar continuity, which has survived the intrusion of new buildings and new machines. I can sense that continuity in the bank, by the waste ground where I found the Roman coin, by the war memorial steps on which Churchill stood, on the cricket field with the filled-in hollow where a bomb fell, in the echoes in the old Fir Bank house – and on the Oaklands fields.

6

Chigwell, Woodford and Buckhurst Hill

"Chigwell, my dear fellow, is the greatest place in the world. Name your day for going. Such a delicious old inn opposite the churchyard – such a lovely ride – such beautiful forest scenery – such an out of the way, rural place – such a sexton! I say again, name your day."

Charles Dickens, letter to John Forster,
25 March 1841

Chigwell

We saw on p.55 that Chigwell had eight manors, that the main manor had been held in 1066 by Earl Harold and that after the Conquest it was given to Ralph de Limesi. The descent through many generations is in *The Victoria History of the County of Essex*.[1] In 1550 Edward VI sold the manor to Sir Thomas Wroth, and the manor of Chigwell descended within the Wroth family of Loughton Hall until 1669.[2]

Chigwell was the place I came to know best after Loughton in the Epping Forest area. Loughton and Chigwell were formally linked with the establishment of the Chigwell Urban District Council, which included Loughton and Buckhurst Hill from 1933 to 1974. I got to know Woodford after I knew Chigwell.

Post-war Chigwell

My first memories of Chigwell were of Chigwell School.

First visit

In early 1946 when I was still six I was taken by my parents to be interviewed by the Headmaster Dr Robert James (who left soon afterwards to become High Master of St Paul's and later Head Master of Harrow). I can see him sitting at his desk opposite me in a suit and waistcoat.

There are three letters signed by him in March 1946 regarding my entry in September 1947. One says that the School had offered "a number of places annually" to Essex County Council, under the Direct Grant scheme which had just begun. (At this time about a quarter of the cost of tuition at Chigwell School came from Essex and the central government, and this included arrangements for local day-boys.)[3]

Entrance exam

The entrance exam took place in Chigwell's New Hall on a warm Saturday afternoon in the spring term of 1947. I can see rows of desks facing open doors and the lush green grass of Top Field. I sat about fourth from the front and slightly to the left of centre. There must have been a maths paper, but I can only recollect the composition. Arnold Fellows, a giant with white hair, announced that we could turn over our papers. There was a choice of two compositions: 'The London Clapham Omnibus'; and 'Newts'. I did not know what an omnibus was – I knew what a bus was – or that in Latin it meant 'for all', and I did not know about Clapham or, at the age of seven, that there is a memorial tablet to the inventor of the bus, George Shillibeer, in St Mary's church, Chigwell, to which I had never been. I wrote on newts, having watched them in the aquarium on the Oaklands Nature Table under the window

Memorial to George Shillibeer including "omnibus".

that was replaced by the Wren doors. I knew all about the great crested newt with its speckled underbelly and dragon-like back; the palmate newt; and the common or smooth newt. I knew about their lizard-like webbed hands and feet, their feeding habits and living patterns. I got into Chigwell on my knowledge of newts.

First day

My first morning at school in September 1947 was traumatic. I was a day-boy, the youngest boy in the school, aged eight years three months. My mother accompanied me on a steam train on a misty morning. She put her bicycle in the guard's van at Loughton, retrieved it and then did the same again when we changed trains at Woodford. She pushed her bicycle from Chigwell station up to the school with my bulky kitbag on the handlebars. (The kitbag was a cylindrical bag that contained our sports clothes and football boots. Our troops were sometimes filmed carrying kitbags on their shoulders as they boarded a ship to go overseas, and Chigwell kitbags were an echo of wartime, and post-war, military life.) I walked beside her in my new uniform, cap and blazer sporting a white mitre. There was no sign of any master inside front quad (the School's main entrance), where just a few boys were standing around.

My mother spoke to one of these and was directed to a changing-room (near the carpentry workshop) where my kitbag had to be hung, padlocked to a peg. She spoke to an older boy nearby, into whose care I passed. He told me firmly that I was a "new bug" and took me to New Hall, where morning prayers were about to begin as the chapel was still closed due to war damage. It soon dawned on me that everyone taking part was several years older than me – I had lost my way into morning prayers for the senior school – and it was only after much kneeling down and standing up again and being startled by communal responses I did not know that I mustered the courage at the end of prayers to ask where I should be. Then an older boy took me to Hainault House, a Victorian building, and installed me, correctly, in Miss Crabtree's class. There I sat at the one desk that was unoccupied. Nowadays great care is taken over the reception of new pupils to make sure they do not become lost.

Well

'Chigwell' comes from the Saxon 'Cicca's well', and the *Domesday Book*'s *Cinghuuella*.[4] Its name has been said to derive from a lost 'king's well'. The well may have referred to medicinal springs in Chigwell Row.[5] According to an 18th-century local historian, Nathaniel Salmon,[6] the 'well' derived from *weald*, Anglo-Saxon for 'wood' or 'forest', rather than *wielle*, Anglo-Saxon for 'well', but that derivation is now discredited.

Ancient buildings

Chigwell to me then was a few ancient buildings strung along the High Road: on one side the 1874 Hainault House, the 1820s Haylands (the Head's house from 1948), the village shop, the 1853 almshouses, the 1620s red-brick school front either side of the porch, including the first Latin Master's house to the right and the later Latin Master's house at right angles to it (which was occupied from 1772 and now includes the white front door), the buildings behind it (the chapel, library, New Hall, its classrooms and the armoury), Church House and the originally Norman parish church, St Mary's; and on the other side the 1485 Harsnett's House, and the 1547 King's Head and 17th- or early 18th-century Grange Court. From there it was a long walk down to the station, past the rebuilt red-brick Chigwell Hall on the right and the William the Fourth pub on the left. Of course, there were other parts of Chigwell: the shops near the station and the large houses in Vicarage Lane, Pudding Lane and Manor Road. Chigwell had always been a scattered parish; it had 72 houses in 1391, 168 houses in 1671 and 396 houses by 1851.[7]

Chigwell School in the 1940s

Among these ancient buildings I slowly found my feet and learned to be streetwise amid games that echoed past wars.

Marbles

At break the muddy ground near Hainault House became a marble pitch. Many boys had bags of marbles, of oners and glarney fourers, sixers, eighters and twelvers, and there were gullies (gouged-out bowls of earth) into which, once there had been four cannons, marbles were flicked. The winner was the last to flick a marble into the gully. A oner had to beat a fourer four times to win, a fourer had to beat a twelver three times, and so on. Games began with a statement of the rules: "You lay [i.e. you throw your marble down first], four cannons [i.e. we have alternate flicks until there have been four hits], nothing in the game [i.e. no clearing away twigs or obstacles on the ground], keeps [i.e. the winner keeps the loser's marble]." The cannons referred to hits but probably, dashingly and with bravado, also to the firing of ships' cannon-balls in the French Napoleonic wars.

Conkers

Each autumn round the marble pitch boys played conkers. Two boys each dangled a skewered conker threaded on to a string or a bootlace. Conkers were preferably oven-baked to be durable when hit. One boy held out his conker and turned his face away to protect his eyes while the other boy swung his conker, hoping to smash it into pieces so it shattered off the string. Then the other boy held his conker out while the first boy walloped his conker. Before the contest, each boy established the value of his opponent's conker for in the event of a win the total would be added to his own tally. If a boy had a sixtier and he beat a forty-fiver, he would have a hundred-and-fiver to flaunt before his next game. Games began with one saying, "Bags froggy wallop," a reference to the French Napoleonic wars and to Napoleon's practice of being the first to attack.

Auctions

The Latin tradition of the school had extended to classroom auctions. We had our own desks in our classroom. They were filled with exercise books, textbooks and clutter. Sometimes between classes a boy, tidying the inside of his desk, called with the lid up, "*Quis*?" ("Who?", meaning "Who wants this?") and there would be a chorus of "*Ego*" ("I"). An unwanted object would then be given to the boy collectively deemed to have answered first.

Bumps

I soon learned that being streetwise meant keeping quiet about one's birthday, for at break a birthday boy would be fallen upon by a dozen classmates and given the bumps, one for each year of his life. Many hands held on to different limbs and, acting in unison, threw the boy, arms and legs splayed, four feet up into the air, dragged him back down, then threw him up again, chanting "One-two-three-four" and so on while the victim's stomach lurched.

Cold

The winter was bitter and some days were as cold as the previous winter of 1946-7, when there were snowdrifts ten feet deep. The new Headmaster, Donald Thompson, had started in January 1947, and over sixty years later his wife Dickie, who was then in her mid-nineties, described to me how shortly after they had arrived the School's lights went out after dark and she and her husband hunted for the fuseboard. No one seemed to know where it was, and unless they found it the School would be freezing the next morning. Despite the cold weather rules remained rules, and on games days we were forbidden to wear vests under our football shirts. Our fingers numb from the sub-zero temperatures, we shivered our way through football, playing with occasional half-hearted kicks and thinking only of keeping warm.

Grange Court

The following September my class moved down to Grange Court, which had been bought as a memorial to the fifty Old Chigwellians who had given their lives in the Second World War. It stood on the site of the 15th-century Ringleys, and was a 17th- or early 18th-century three-storey Georgian yellow-brick house that had been remodelled in 1774,[8]

Grange Court.

with lower side wings. In charge of Grange Court was the Housemaster and Second Master, Arnold Fellows ('A.F.'). He held assemblies in the wide corridor below the staircase, off which was my Form-2 classroom. A.F.'s study was near the staircase, and there he marched off any boy with an unsatisfactory grade and caned him. We heard the crack while standing in assembly, and, paralysed by fear, no one made a sound. No one is caned today.

A.F. taught us Latin and English at the same time. His dedication to learning was immense. He sometimes placed a pile of sixpences on the master's desk, and if a boy answered a question correctly he flicked a sixpence to him through the air. If the boy caught it he could keep it. If he dropped it he had to return it to the pile on the master's desk.

Arnold Fellows, 1924 (left) and 1950 (right).

King-he

In the large walled garden at the back there was a flight of steps and a large lawn on which we played 'King-he'. A boy, designated 'he', was given a tennis-ball. When he threw it and hit a boy, that boy became a 'he'. In the end 'hes' would lob the ball to each other and 'non-hes' would jump and attempt to fist the ball away from the 'hes', often with a handkerchief tied round their knuckles. The game ended when the last 'non-he' was made a 'he'. At the end of break A.F. would appear on the steps, cup his hands round his mouth and call, "Hoi, all in." Such was his authority that the game would immediately stop and everyone would run in.

Extract from Chigwell School photograph showing Nicholas Hagger (front row, centre), 1949.

A.F.

A.F. was a character. He drove a Morris 12, registration number AVW 124. On one occasion the village policeman stopped him in the High Road and said of his running-boards, which rose and fell as the car moved, "They're very dangerous, sir." He meant, "Get them fixed." "Ah, yes, I see," A.F. said, and he lifted the running-boards off and put them in the back seat of the car like skis.

The Founding of Chigwell School

Eventually my class moved to the main school, and got to know the original one-storey building opposite the main entrance: Big School.

Big School

Big School's porch doorway has a stone shield bearing a mitre and the date AD1629. In fact, as Godfrey Stott pointed out in *A History of Chigwell School*, the School was actually founded between 1619 and 1623, a dating reflected in the listing of the main building by British Listed Buildings: c.1620.[9] The land was purchased, and the first schoolhouse erected, in 1619, and the first Latin Master – Peter Mease, M.A., a Bachelor of Divinity from Jesus College, Cambridge – was appointed in 1623.[10]

Big School, 1910.

Samuel Harsnett

The purchaser of the land and appointer of Mease was Samuel Harsnett, a Colchester baker's boy who became Bishop of Chichester, then Bishop of Norwich and finally Archbishop of York and Vice-Chancellor of Cambridge University. He had been vicar of Chigwell parish church, St Mary's, from 1597 to 1605. Both his wife and daughter had died in 1601. He had carried on living at Chigwell, buying a house and estate there. His 15th-century house, Stickmers (or Stickmarsh), was near the first house after Grange Farm on the way to

Abridge. (It was destroyed by fire in 1938.)[11] In 1619 he had bought more land in the parish, three roods on which he founded first a Latin School, and then an English School.

The creation of a school

It is now possible to form a clear view of the founding and establishing of Chigwell School. The land for the Latin School was bought on 13 October 1619. The Latin School seems to have started between 1620 and 1623, the year when Mease became Latin Master. It comprised Big School One (the right-hand side of Big School when viewed from the road), which it occupied from 1629 to 1868. The Latin Master's house was next to it on the right when viewed from the road, within the same frontage (the present praefects' room, lobby and the bedrooms above, which served as the Latin Master's house from 1629 to 1772).

The English School began in July 1627, when Archbishop Harsnett bought Harsnett's House across the road from the Latin School as an English Master's house and presented it to the School. Its orchard, which was behind it, could not be occupied as it was sublet. (In recent years, it was a boarding-house and then the house of the Head of the Junior School, and I was invited to dinner there by Robin Parfitt in 1987 when he was Head of the Junior School.) Big School Two (the left-hand side of Big School when viewed from the road) was added as the English School soon after July 1627 and housed the English School from 1629 to 1868. The first English Master, Richard Willis, finally arrived in 1628[12] or 1629 and served as usher to the Latin Master.

It seems that the English School was not part of Harsnett's original intention as it would have been more natural to house the English Master at the left end of Big School Two when viewed from the road, to counter-balance the Latin Master's house on the right end of Big School One. The English School seems to have been an afterthought.

The two schools were put together in 1629, when a new school that combined the two existing schools, the Latin and English Schools, Chigwell School, was founded. The date over the porch doorway, AD1629, refers to the founding of this new school which combined the two previous schools.[13] Harsnett died in January 1631. Mease left in 1633 and was replaced by Willis, who now became Latin Master.

As the founding of Chigwell illustrates, founding and establishing an institution is a process that can take months, years or even a decade. As we shall see, I put Coopersale Hall School together by making three separate purchases (the Coopersale Hall building, Orchard Cottage and the private drive), and a later purchase of a field, and I sometimes reflect that to some extent I was treading in Harsnett's footsteps when I founded Coopersale Hall School piecemeal in 1989 and the following few years.

Harsnett's ordinances

Harsnett's ordinances laid on the requirements of a good Head: "I constitute and ordain that the Latin schoolmaster be a graduate of one of the universities, not under seven-and-twenty years of age, a man skilful in the Greek and Latin tongues, a good poet of a sound religion, neither papist nor puritan, of a grave behaviour, of a sober and honest conversation, no tippler, nor haunter of alehouses, no puffer of tobacco, and above all that he be apt to teach and severe in his government."[14] The scholars should be taught the classics, "the ancient Greek and Latin poets, no novelties nor conceited modern writers". The English Master should "teach *gratis* to read, cipher and to cast account".[15]

William Penn

In 1629 there were 16 "poor, clever" scholars. They were taught in Big School. William Penn, the Quaker who went to the New World and founded Pennsylvania, was a pupil there during the Puritan rule, from 1650 to 1654, and, according to John Aubrey, at the age of 11 he had a mystical experience in his room at the top of the school, "being retired in a chamber alone".[16]

Two restructurings

In 1772 the School was restructured. The Latin Master's house was moved to the building now at right angles with it, that contains the main entrance and white front door. His previous house was allocated for school use.

In 1868 the School split into two. In 1869 the wall between Big School One and Big School Two was removed, and teaching took place in one large room (Big School One and Big School Two).[17] The English School was rehoused in a new single-storey building behind the English Master's house (Harsnett's House). Local children studied reading, writing and arithmetic there, but in 1881 the English School was returned to the main School across the road. In 1898 the new building was used as a laboratory. I was taught chemistry in it in the 1950s. The building was later used as a workshop and in 1981 was sold to become a private house (now called Dickens Lodge).[18] The Latin School remained in Big School, where the Latin scholars were taught.

Motto

On Michaelmas Day 1868 the reorganised Chigwell School opened. At a gathering to mark the occasion the Archdeacon of Westminster, Christopher Wordsworth, nephew of the poet William Wordsworth and previously Head Master at Harrow, asked the Chigwell Headmaster, Henry Mowld Robinson, if he had a motto for the School. Robinson replied, probably uncomfortably, that he had not found or made one. Without hesitation Wordsworth proposed "*Aut viam inveniam aut faciam*", a Latin phrase, meaning "Either I shall find a way or make a way" or, more simply, "Find a way or make a way".[19]

I have shared Robinson's discomfort at being asked about a motto. One of my three schools already had a Latin motto. I chose Latin mottoes for the other two. One I found and the other I made. It took me a long time, and a lot of thought, until I came up with, or made, "*Superans conando*" for Coopersale Hall: "Overcoming (or prevailing) by striving (or trying)". In finding and making Latin mottoes for two schools I have remained true to the spirit of the Latin School.

Chigwell School's motto is attributed to Hannibal, who is supposed to have replied in these words when his generals told him that it was impossible for elephants to cross the Alps. Hannibal would have spoken in Punic, but his words may have been translated into Latin. More than 200 years later Seneca showed that he knew the phrase in his *Hercules Furens* (2.1.276): "*Inveniet viam, aut faciet*", "Let him find a way or make a way".

Did Wordsworth's nephew know his Hannibal? Or did he know the phrase from elsewhere? The motto is under the arms of an old Scottish family, and has been adopted by an Indian regiment (the 34th Sikh Pioneers) and by the University of Pennsylvania (presumably to connect William Penn with Harsnett's Chigwell). It is a chapter heading in a novel by Scott and is said to adorn the oratory W.E. Henley built.[20]

School song

The motto features in the school song written by a Chigwell vicar, the Rev. T. Marsden, between 1885 and 1892. This is still sung by Old Chigwellians at ceremonial events such as reunions on Shrove Tuesdays. It has five verses, with a chorus sung after each, and it begins:

> Which is the way to be happy?
> Not only the long-living day,
> To keep sound in your mind and your body,
> And hard at your work and your play.
>
> *Chorus*
> Find a way, or make a way!
> Brave old Harsnett's son!
> The upward way, the onward way,
> The way the founder's gone.

Big School partition

In about 1950 Latin was still taught in Big School, which could be divided by a partition that we boys operated. One day, after much tugging, the folded-back partition between the old Latin and English Schools suddenly straightened with my right index finger still in it and my nail was ripped up from its surrounding skin, perhaps portending (or punishing in advance) my future defection from Latin to English in 1959. That finger has not been straight ever since though it has participated in the millions of English words I have written.

Inside Big School, 1907.

Harsnett's bust

In Big School One there is a bust of Archbishop Harsnett wearing his mitre. It was copied from the brass which had covered his grave, and is now on a wall in the church, by a Chigwell lady, Miss Ada Palmer.[21] It was unveiled on 28 July 1887, and, sitting at desks in rows rather than at the sideways-on tables with high sloping sides of c.1850, I was often able to study the face. Harsnett is believed to have sat for the brass image, and it is believed to be a true likeness of him.

Samuel Harsnett, brass (left) and bust (right).

Harsnett and Shakespeare

In his life Harsnett was known for his Church-of-England opposition to Puritanism and popery, and for his scepticism regarding witchcraft. His *A Declaration of Egregious Popish Impostures* (1603), published while he was vicar at St Mary's, Chigwell, condemned exorcisms by Catholic priests in the 1580s and was read by Shakespeare, who put phrases from it into Edgar's mouth in *King Lear*. In due course it was used by Milton when he wrote 'L'Allegro'.

Free will

The founder had a very positive message for his pupils that is embodied in the motto: nothing is impossible, free will can solve all problems. He would have agreed that (like Goethe's Faust) one can overcome by striving.

Chigwell School and Village in the 1950s

Lessons

Latin up to 'O' level was almost always taught in Big School One or Two, the 1620-29 building with partition doors. There I was taught Latin by (among others) Godfrey Stott, the author of *A History of Chigwell School*, who sat under the Harsnett bust. (I believe that I was tugging the partition doors to enable him to begin a Latin lesson.) Working in this high-ceilinged 17th-century schoolroom during my 'O' level Latin lessons and later, under David Horton, during my 'A' level Latin, Greek and Ancient History lessons and continuing the tradition of the 17th-century Latin School gave me a love of the 17th century which has come out in my poetry as an admiration for the Metaphysical poets and their use of wit.

Big School Two (with windows on left), 1850.

Most of our non-Latin pre-'O'-level lessons took place in the classrooms round New Hall: Room 1 (on ground level near the armoury), where English and History were taught; Room 2 (above Room 1), where Maths lessons were held; Room 3 (on ground level the other side of New Hall), where French and sometimes English were taught; and Room 4, where Geography was taught.

Lunches

We ate our lunches in the dining-hall near the Swallow Room (named after the Reverend Canon R.D. Swallow, Headmaster from 1876 to 1912). We sat on benches. Masters sat at the end of tables and ladled out food from a baking-tray placed in front of them, and plates with served helpings were passed down to the end. If a boy was deemed to have misbehaved he had to stand on the bench where he had been sitting so all could note his misbehaviour.

Cricket

Cricket had been played at Chigwell since 1875.[22] As captain of the Under-12 and Under-13½ cricket teams, both of which played on Top Field, I wrote out the names of our team for the notice-board, greeted the captain of the team visiting from another school, took part in the toss and shook hands with the opposing captain after the match had ended. I learned responsibility and hospitality skills that would stand me in good stead for running large staffs at different schools. I often played in matches on Top Field and once hit a boundary from the chapel end that bounced across the road and disappeared into the graveyard of the parish church.

Montgomery

Every morning we attended a service in the Chigwell chapel, now restored after bomb damage. It was adjacent to Top Field. It was on a garden seat by the chapel, facing a sunny Top Field in mufti, that Field Marshal Montgomery sat when I encountered him at the School on Sunday 18 October 1953, when I was fourteen. The previous week Godfrey Stott had set us a prose about Caesar which had to be turned into Latin, and we were told to write Caesar as Montegomerius. Among a dozen selected boys, I chatted to Montgomery, our Caesar, and walked to New Hall with him. Sitting near where I took the entrance exam, I heard him say memorably, making sawing movements with his right hand, "I went through the Germans at El Alamein like a knife going through butter."

New Hall and chapel from Top Field, 1979.

CCF

The early 1950s were still close to the end of the Second World War, and there was still National Service. Every Monday afternoon we changed into uniform and took part in the CCF (Combined Cadet Force). We wore an itchy khaki shirt, tie and battledress, and specially polished belt, boots and gaiters. We took part in parades and marched about. We learned how to take guns apart and reassemble them, and how to lie down and shoot at targets that flipped up for a few seconds and then fell back. We went on Field Days and corps camps, where we took part in small wars.

Call-overs

There was still a strong military dimension to school life. Morning and afternoon call-overs, when the register was centrally checked, were run on military lines. We were each given a number to call out, which we kept for the year. We filed past the master or praefect holding a clipboard and called out our number and the name of any boy immediately before us who was absent.

Speech Day

Speech Day was held on a Saturday in June. We wore suits and straw boaters and displayed a white rose in our lapels because as Archbishop of York Archbishop Harsnett was a Yorkist in the aftermath of the Wars of the Roses. On Speech Day there was always a morning service in Chigwell parish church, St Mary's.

St Mary's church

We thought of St Mary's church as a kind of adjunct to the School, a part of the School day-boys did not enter very often, like the boarding areas. It was originally built c.1160. Of this first church only the south wall (the wall facing the road) now survives, including a Norman doorway with a semicircular arch (that is ornamented with double chevrons, a panelled tympanum, a soffit and jamb), and also a window to its east. A north aisle and arcade were added in the 15th century and at the same time the chancel was lengthened and the bell turret added.[23] On Speech Days we sat in the south aisle, and at Advent or carol services I now sit towards the back of the north aisle opposite, and with a view of, the Norman doorway.

St Mary's church, Chigwell, c.2000.

The King's Head

The prize-giving part of Speech Day took place in the afternoon in New Hall in those days. (It now takes place in a marquee in the grounds of Chigwell Hall.) When it was over some of the senior boys repaired to the King's Head to express their attainment of adulthood.

We passed the 1547 King's Head every day. It was so familiar that it seemed to be part of the School. It was reputed to be The Maypole in Dickens' *Barnaby Rudge*. Imagining the year to be 1775, Dickens wrote vividly of the King's Head/Maypole: "An old building, with more gable ends than a lazy man would care to count on a sunny day; huge zig-zag chimneys out of which it seemed as though even smoke could not choose but come in more than naturally fantastic shapes imparted to it in its tortuous progress; and vast stables, gloomy, ruinous and empty. The place was said to have been built in the days of King Henry the Eighth; and there was a legend, not only that Queen Elizabeth had slept there one night while upon a hunting excursion, to wit, in a certain oak-panelled room with a deep bow window, but that next morning, while standing on a mounting-block before the door with one foot in the stirrup, the Virgin Monarch had then and there boxed and cuffed an unlucky page for some neglect of duty.... Its windows were old diamond-pane lattices, its floors were sunken and uneven, its ceilings blackened by the hand of time, and heavy with massive beams. Over the doorway was an ancient torch, quaintly and grotesquely carved.... In the chimneys of the disused rooms, swallows had built their nests for many a long year, and from earliest spring to latest autumn whole colonies of sparrows chirped and twittered in the eaves."

Dickens often came to Chigwell, and described his enthusiasm for it in an extract from a letter that forms the epigraph of this chapter. (The King's Head has been bought by Lord Sugar and leased out, and to some consternation its Tudor, Dickensian rooms were turned into an ultra-modern Turkish restaurant, Sheesh, which opened in January 2011.)

Sport

The older boys still played football in the autumn term and cricket in the summer term on Wednesday and Saturday afternoons. We now used the pitches on the forty-eight (now seventy) acres of grounds. Here we played in the Under-15 and Under-16 teams – I was captain of both these cricket teams – and in set matches. The Under-16 football coach in those days was John Dutchman, the Pegasus and England amateur international. At half-time at Ardingly he told us to shoot on sight of goal and in the second half, seeing their goalie off his line, I scored from the half-way line with the help of some swirling wind.

We played at the top of the long slope at first and as we grew older we progressed downwards towards the far end of the sloping grounds.

Those selected to play in the 1st XI eventually played on the 1st-XI pitch, the pitch nearest the Roding. I played both cricket and football for the 1st XI and changed in the isolated pavilion near that pitch.

Many of our games were on other schools' grounds. I played one of my better cricket innings in damp weather at Bancroft's Speech Day. The pitch was their grass quadrangle surrounded by a collegiate redbrick chapel and crenellated buildings. (Bancroft's was founded in 1737 and moved to Woodford Green in 1889.)

In the spring term we did cross-country running. The senior annual Bean race began in the vicinity of the 1st-XI pitch. We ran up to Vicarage Lane and headed off alongside ploughed fields, the route being indicated by senior boys in khaki CCF uniform with walkie-talkies. After a few miles of running alongside fields on uneven, frozen mud, avoiding hoof-holes filled with ice, we re-emerged near the top of Vicarage Lane, crossed the road into the field opposite the village shops and raced for the finishing line. Here stood a master with a clipboard to record our positions.

Walks

When the ground was too frozen for cross-country running we were sent on long walks, very often along Vicarage Lane to Chigwell Row, along Manor Road, back along Gravel Lane and past Rolls Park, the house of the Harvey family from c.1666 to 1841, which was eventually demolished in 1953.[24] These country walks passed fields, barns and isolated Georgian houses.

Cycling

During my senior-school career I cycled to Chigwell and back each day. From Station Road, Loughton I headed down Roding Road and turned into Avondale Drive. From there a path led across the "Recreation Ground", the mown grasslands and wet meadows, to the Roding. In this vast expanse of flood meadows and marshes could be found southern marsh orchids and yellow watercress, butterflies and dragonflies. Here in spring and summer were sedge warblers, skylarks, reed buntings and whitethroats, and there were always finches among the thistles and teasels. In the winter there were grey herons, little grebes, snipe and green and common sandpipers.

I pushed my bike across the humped bridge over the Roding and then rode up the narrow path between railings and netting behind the playing fields of Buckhurst Hill Boys School (now Guru Gobind Singh Khalsa College) and the RAF Station (which provided barrage balloon protection during the Second World War). The original moated manor house of Chigwell Hall, which was deserted by 1650, had stood there, and its moat had been filled in by the contractor building the RAF Station in 1937-8.[25] This path came out on the bend of Roding Lane. It was a long haul up through the overhanging trees (requiring us to pedal while standing up) past the hedged fronts of large houses to the School and the bike shed near the senior-school's marble pitch, a muddy area behind the Tuck Shop, adjacent to the road.

On the way back I worked up quite a speed down Roding Lane, and on late summer afternoons the sun shone through mottled leaves, flickering and flecking on my eyes as I free-wheeled and hurtled forwards, sometimes triggering a migraine, for which my mother gave me codeine.

Swallow Room

I spent two years in the Sixth Form taking 'A' levels. I was now based in the Swallow-Room library, where there was a long table under the dome and a bronze head of Hypnos (the goddess of sleep) with slits where the eyes should have been. (Today the library is in Big School, where drinks gatherings are held on events days.) There I was taught Latin by Donald Thompson, the last Headmaster to be thought of as the Latin Master.

Swallow Room Library, 1956, with Nicholas Hagger second from right.

Reception Room

Study time was often in the Reception Room in the Georgian house adjoining the first Latin Master's house. It then included the staff room and had been the second Latin Master's (and Headmaster's) house from 1772 to 1948. Here we sat at tables and worked responsibly in silence. Here I read Bowra's *Tradition and Design in the Iliad* very slowly, making extensive notes, not realising that one day I would need the Homeric background for my own epics, *Overlord* and *Armageddon*.

Calling

I took the entrance exam to Worcester College, Oxford in December 1956, shortly after the Suez operation, and was one of four out of a hundred who were awarded places. (In those days five per cent of 18-21-year-olds went to university in the UK.) I returned to Chigwell for the spring term of 1957, knowing it would be my last as my father wanted me to go into articles with a firm of solicitors for a gap year and prepare for the subject I was supposed to be reading at university.

Sitting on a garden bench alone in Lower Field in warm sunshine (very near the hedge that borders what is now Lord Sugar's garden) in March 1957, dipping into *The Faber Book of Modern Verse*, I read 'The Wreck of the *Deutschland*' and thrilled to the language. I took my eye off the two pages beneath me, basked in the warm sun and knew that I was going to be a poet. I had found my calling, that would involve an escape from Latin into English, just a few days before I left school.

In December 1957 I went to the Partisan coffee-bar where the Angry Young Men were known to congregate – I was with my fellow Chigwellians John Ezard (who would become Arts correspondent for the *Guardian*) and Ken Campbell (who would become an actor, director and playwright) – and I was already on a path that would take me away from Latin into English Literature.

Changes

In later years Chigwell turned into a wealthy area – especially in parts of Manor Road, Hainault Road and Chigwell High Road – and became part of the Golden Triangle of Loughton, Chigwell and Buckhurst Hill, the area of the old Chigwell Urban District Council that has featured in television series. During this transformation I visited Chigwell School many times, as a parent of two boys attending parents' evenings in New Hall and on Speech Days; as an Old Chigwellian attending Shrove-Tuesday reunions in Big School and the dining-hall; and as Principal of three feeder schools attending an annual reception followed by dinner in the dining-hall. My family's association with Chigwell School has now exceeded six decades and has been almost uninterrupted as my two younger brothers attended the School, my mother played in the orchestra, my two sons attended and I now have a grandson there. I have regular contact as a Principal of feeder schools, and when the Headmaster Tony Little left to become Head Master of Eton and held a farewell gathering for the Chigwell staff, I was the only non-staff invitee. Now my eldest son is a Principal of feeder schools.

In the past the Latin School was in ascendancy over the English School. In practically all educational institutions today the position has been reversed. The School has reflected this modern shift in emphasis but has managed to preserve a core of continuity, and Harsnett's traditional values have endured. There have been many changes and improvements over the years – many new buildings (including a Drama Centre) have been erected, the School now admits girls, Latin is not so dominant and Spartan severity has been replaced by friendliness and a more comfortable environment – yet the Chigwell School I visit today is still recognisably the School I attended in the 1940s and 1950s.

Woodford

"Along the Woodford road there comes a noise
Of wheels, and Mr Rounding's neat post-chaise
Struggles along, drawn by a pair of bays,
With Reverend Mr Crow and six small boys,
Who ever and anon declare their joys
With trumping horns and juvenile huzzas,

At going home to spend their Christmas days,
And changing learning's pains for pleasure's toys."
Thomas Hood, 'Christmas Holidays'

I occasionally went to Woodford (Old English for 'ford in or by the wood') during my school days. When my parents drove to our annual holiday we passed the shop doorway nearly opposite the Castle where stood a lady dressed (like Queen Mary) in a long mauve satin dress with a round matching hat. She was known as 'The Duchess of Woodford'. She had reputedly refused to believe that her son had been killed in the war, and every morning went to meet him at Woodford station. When he did not appear, she came to this doorway to wait for him.

Occasionally I was invited to tea by a classmate in one of the roads behind Woodford Green and beyond All Saints' church, such as Monkhams Avenue (where Clement Atlee lived in the 1920s and 1930s). All Saints' was near The Horse & Well, a 17th-century coaching inn in Woodford Wells whose name refers to mineral-water wells located nearby.

The White House: Col. Sir Stuart Mallinson

My main contact with Woodford Green was through the White House, which had been bought in 1926 by Col. Sir Stuart Mallinson, a colonel with the Royal Engineers who fought in Flanders and at Ypres. He bought more land and created an estate of twenty-six acres. He continued his father's business, which imported timber for manufacturing and distribution, and devoted his life to public service: creating sports facilities, clubs and local groups, helping Scouts and providing welfare for troops. The White House was visited by King George VI, who inspected the Home Guard on 23 July 1940, and by Prince Philip, who attended a garden party in aide of the National Playing Fields in June 1949.[26]

Sir Stuart was a friend of Churchill, MP for Wanstead and Woodford, who was a frequent guest at the White House and used it as his base during his visits, appreciating "a good table, vintage wine, fine cigars

(Havana brand), a First World War hero of commanding presence and a charming Lady".[27] On 27 February 1950, the day of the UK's General Election, the White-House chapel was taken over by secretaries linked to Conservative Party headquarters who analysed the election results. Field Marshal Montgomery was also a regular visitor and planted two trees in the Arboretum in 1953. (Churchill planted one.)

The White House, Woodford.

Every April Col. Sir Stuart Mallinson invited a professional cricketer to coach in the nets in the White-House garden and wrote to local schools requesting each to nominate a local schoolboy who would benefit from free coaching by a professional. I was somehow chosen by Chigwell School, and in April 1953 I spent a week in the White-House nets being coached by the Surrey opening batsman Laurie Fishlock. I can see the back corner of the White House, a lawn and two tree-clad nets side by side. My parents later received a typed letter with a comment Fishlock had made that was written in Mallinson's own hand: "Shows promise with bat and ball." A year later I made 38 not out for Chigwell at St Dunstan's, whose umpire was none other than Fishlock. He recognised me and we chatted between overs.

I was invited back to the White House the next two Aprils, and was coached by Ken Preston, the Essex fast bowler, and Barry Knight, the Essex all-rounder. In due course, Mallinson invited Graham Gooch and John Lever to coach cricket and Christine Truman to coach tennis. We shall see that I eventually got to know his son Terence Mallinson.

In the 1960s Sir Stuart became concerned over the upkeep of the White House and transferred the estate to the London Borough of Waltham Forest, which celebrated his generosity by renaming it Mallinson Park.[28] In 2000 the Borough leased the White House to the

Haven House Foundation, which created a centre of excellence to help the families of children with life-limiting or life-threatening conditions.[29] It has cared for and supported 350 families.

Churchill statue

Sir Stuart was behind the sculpting of a bronze statue of Churchill that was unveiled on Woodford Green on 31 October 1959. On that day Montgomery arrived with the uniformed Sir John Ruggles-Brise, Lord Lieutenant of Essex from 1958 to 1978. (I visited him at Spains Hall on 31 October 2001.)

Montgomery spoke before 5,000 people. With Churchill sitting on the small covered dais, he said: "It may seem to us today almost an impertinence to act as though we should ever need a reminder of Sir Winston's appearance or his achievements. This famous man to whom this statue is designed is still most happily with us, enjoying in dignity and quiet the evening of his splendid life. But that, alas, will not always be so. Future generations will not only need but will desire to know what he looks like, and it is most fitting that you in Woodford have decided to supply the answer. He did so much for the world but you helped him to take his place in the House of Commons when he was without a seat and without a party. He has received your unfailing loyalty for more than a quarter of a century. Woodford was his political Alamein."[30] He unveiled the statue and saluted first the statue and then Churchill, who sat beaming on the dais.

The unveiling of Churchill's statue on Woodford Green, 1959, with Montgomery saluting and Churchill beaming.

Churchill then went to the microphone and said: "I am deeply obliged to my old friend and comrade for the very kind things he has said. When I consider the war years of his own brilliant achievements and his own long career of devoted service to this country I reflect that of him it may well be said: 'I have built a monument more lasting than bronze.' I am most grateful to the people of Wanstead-Woodford for the signal honour you now do me. You have sustained and supported me throughout the 35 years I have had the privilege of representing you in Parliament."[31] Churchill continued to represent his constituency until October 1964, just months before his 90th birthday.

Col. Sir Stuart Mallinson represented the trustees of the statue committee at the unveiling. He had been instrumental in organising the sculpture and he was the first to arrive, accompanied by the sculptor, David McFall.[32] McFall had done an original life-size bronze cast of Churchill's head, which Sir Stuart purchased. As the cast had been produced in France rather than the UK the Tate Gallery was not entitled to buy it, and possession of the head is now shared between Terence Mallinson and his brother Justin, each holding it for a year in rotation.[33]

Wanstead

I hardly ever went to Wanstead in my boyhood. I have now and again passed the grasslands of Wanstead Flats and have reflected that the woodland of Wanstead Park was once part of Wanstead House, in its time one of the finest Palladian country houses and known as the English Versailles, sadly demolished in 1824. Because Wanstead House is no more I have left it in my imagination and have not regarded Wanstead Park as one of my special places.

Forest School, Snaresbrook invited my wife and me to attend the annual Shakespeare play every December for several years. Each year the evening began with a dinner-jacket reception at which champagne flowed, and there was an excellent opportunity to chat with colleagues from other schools.

I had a good rapport with Andrew Boggis, the Warden of Forest at that time, and recall gingerly walking in the corridor of Holly House in my hospital gown after a minor operation in December 2005, spotting his name on the door of the room next-but-one to mine, and putting my head round the door to say casually and cheerily, "Good evening, Mr Boggis." He was sitting in bed in his gown working on papers, and, surprised to see me, told me he was writing a speech. I said I hoped I had not interrupted his train of thought.

In January 2006 the national newspapers had headlines quoting him as urging: "Mr Blair, kindly get your tanks off our quadrangles." He had made the speech he was working on to the Headmasters' and Headmistresses' Conference, of which he was the new Chairman, and was defending independent education against government interference.

Claybury

Bizarrely, Claybury Asylum has featured in my affection. This psychiatric hospital at Woodford Bridge was opened in 1893, and at its peak had 4,000 patients. It had a chilling reputation. Every so often my father and mother would talk of someone who had been taken away in the night suffering from mental illness and put in Claybury. "Don't do too much cerebral work," my father used to say, "or you'll end up in Claybury."

In 1997 a public enquiry was held and Claybury was shut down. It was converted into luxury flats and renamed Repton Park. The main building where the inmates assembled is now an Esporta gym. I have been a member since 2001. I go once a week to walk, cycle, treadle, pull light weights and do sit-ups on a large ball, and I often reflect that my father was right. In a sense, I have ended up in Claybury.

Buckhurst Hill

> "There's Bucket's Hill, a place of furze and clouds,
> Which evening in a golden blaze enshrouds."
>
> John Clare, 'A Walk in the Forest'

We saw on p.44 that "Buckhurst" derived from the Anglo-Saxon '*boc hyrst*', 'beech wood'. The manor of Buckhurst was probably part of the manor of Barringtons (or Little Chigwell) until 1135. Then William de Montfichet granted "his wood of Bocherste" (*La Bocherste*) to the Cistercian Abbey of Stratford Langthorne (now in Stratford, East London). The abbey retained Buckhurst until the Dissolution. It was then leased by a number of private individuals until it passed into the possession of Chigwell Hall in 1799.[34]

History of Buckhurst Hill

Buckhurst Hill was within the ancient parish of Chigwell along with Chigwell Row until the 19th century. Much of it lay within Epping Forest. From the Roding the ground rose to 267 feet at Buckhurst Hill and then fell to 150 feet at Ching Brook, the western boundary of the ancient parish. The Loughton-Woodford road ran through it, and there were a few scattered houses.[35]

In the early 1800s much of Buckhurst Hill was farmland with the Bald Faced Stag (first recorded in 1725, but probably much older), King's Place (14th century, see pp.67-8), Monkhams Farm and a few cottages being the only inhabited buildings.[36]

Buckhurst Hill was formed as a separate ecclesiastical district from the parish of Chigwell in 1838, and became a separate parish in 1867. The church of St John the Baptist, Buckhurst Hill, was built to be a chapel of ease to St Mary's Chigwell, and was consecrated in 1837, the year the new ecclesiastical district was created, and after 1867 it was enlarged to cater for an increased congregation of local parishioners.

St John's church, Buckhurst Hill, 1868.

Railway

In 1856 the Eastern Counties Railway had extended its line from

Woodford to Loughton, and had built a station at Buckhurst Hill, round which small cottages and "villas" gathered. Queen's Road and Princes Road were built in 1856-7. Encroachments on Lords Bushes provided land for private houses such as Holly House (now a private hospital) and for the construction of Knighton Lane. But there was no proper road between Chigwell and Buckhurst Hill until 1890.[37]

Buckhurst Hill became a separate urban district in 1895, and was eventually merged with Loughton and Chigwell to form the Urban District of Chigwell in 1933.[38]

Extent today

Today Buckhurst Hill is part of the so-called Golden Triangle that includes Loughton and Chigwell. It includes (from south to north along the High Road and Epping New Road, which link it with Loughton and Epping) the Bald Faced Stag, St John's church, the Roebuck (a public house originally built c.1770 and rebuilt in 1871, now replaced by flats) and arguably the Warren (the headquarters of the Conservators of Epping Forest, which incorporates Little Standing and parts of the 16th-century Reindeer); and (from west to east) Princes Road, Queen's Road, and Palmerston Road which links it to Chigwell. It also includes Lords Bushes, a piece of Forest containing the Pulpit Oak and a large pond that is skirted by Princes Road and Knighton Lane; and (at the time of writing) a trendy pub nearby, the Three Colts.

Cricket grounds

Between the High Road and Epping New Road, at the top of the road known as Buckhurst Hill, is Buckhurst Hill cricket ground, the "top ground" which in the pre-television days of the 1950s attracted spectators who often sat four deep all round the ground on a Saturday afternoon. Sometimes they included my brother and me. The pavilion was a hut on the Forest side of the ground that was shuttered during the week.

I played cricket for Buckhurst Hill 1st XI on this "top ground" after I left Chigwell School. Alan Lavers, a former Essex all-rounder and now the captain of Buckhurst Hill, had invited me to play for his XI against Loughton at the Loughton cricket field during Loughton's cricket week in August 1955, and I had played against him for Chigwell School in 1956, when I hit him for two fours in an over. I was picked for Buckhurst Hill 1st XI's first match of the 1957 season. It was against Westcliff away, and, batting with Alan Lavers, I scored 40 out of a total of 121-7, an innings that secured my place for the rest of the season.

I can remember a dozen matches and innings I played on the "top ground". Every four I (or other batsmen) hit was greeted with applause. Five of our players were picked for the county. As no. 3, I often batted with our opener Bob Greensmith (brother of the Essex cricketer Bill Greensmith), who, when he died, at his request had his ashes scattered on the "top-ground pitch" on which he had played so many innings that had given him pleasure.

Buckhurst Hill top ground.

I also played on the "bottom ground" in Roding Lane, the continuation of Palmerston Road, some Sundays. Fewer watched there, but I can remember a lot of people sitting in deck-chairs all round the pavilion. My last game that season was during cricket week in August, and it took place on the "bottom ground". Tony Durley, one of our Essex players, and I had a long partnership of over 100 – he scored 85 and I made 31 – which nearly saved the game for Buckhurst Hill.

It was my last match for the club. I went up to Oxford in October

1958 and, though I played cricket for my college, I was involved in new activities and never returned to play for Buckhurst Hill. But in 1989 I employed Alan Lavers' daughter at Coopersale Hall, and Alan Lavers attended my 50th birthday there. I attended his memorial service, which was held at Chigwell. (Doug Insole, the former Essex cricket captain and England player, also attended. He startled me by telling me that in 1958 I was on his "watch list" to be picked to play for the county. At the time I had no idea.)

The Roebuck

My family sometimes held family gatherings at the Roebuck. I recall dining in the private Oak Room on the first floor on the eve of my younger brother's wedding in 1973, looking out at Scotch pines and sunset while cows horned round the cars below, and also making a speech in the same room at my aunt's 90th birthday party in June 1993, standing with my back to the window. My aunt, Margaret Broadley, had been Assistant Matron at the London Hospital. I also made visits to Holly House and had minor operations there, and often walked down Queen's Road to use the shops or see an osteopath with whom I was friendly.

In due course my wife and I vacated our house next to Oaklands, now called Oak House, and moved to the western part of Buckhurst Hill where, from my study window, I had a good view of Epping Forest.

7

Waltham Abbey, High Beach and Upshire

Waltham Abbey

"Through the prayer of his mother,
The body was carried on a bier;
At Waltham it is placed in the tomb,
For he was founder of the house."

13th-century Old French poet of *The Lives of Edward the Confessor* on Harold II[1]

The town of Waltham Abbey stands between the River Lea (the boundary between Essex and Hertfordshire) and Epping Forest. The Lea rises in marshes and flows through meadows to a plateau of London clay topped with sand and gravel. Cobbin's Brook, a tributary of the Lea, runs across it, and local legend claims that Boudicca poisoned herself with hemlock gathered on the banks of the Waltham end of the Brook. In the Middle Ages the Lea was drained and split into seven streams at Waltham, an operation that may have begun with Alfred's marooning of Danish ships (see p.46). The waterway closest to the Abbey's western side was used to power the grinding mill and came to be called Cornmill Stream.[2]

Waltham Abbey aerial map.

Cornmill Stream

The Abbey, Waltham Holy Cross, once the owner of Loughton, stands near the end of Cornmill Stream. There was a corn-miller in the town of Waltham Abbey until 1898.[3] The stream flows under a small, ancient humped-back bridge built for the Abbey and commonly called 'Harold's Bridge'. It is certainly 600 years old and may have provided the only passage across the stream for Harold, and for Tovi before him.[4] Over the years half the bridge fell into the stream. It was repaired by Churchwarden Bentley in c.1902.[5]

"Harold's bridge" (left) and three-arched gatehouse bridge (right) over Cornmill stream.

Cornmill Stream flows 300 yards down to pass under the post-Dissolution three-arched bridge beside the c.1370 gatehouse, and on to a weir, where it plunges underground. It was probably dug out by the Saxons to power a long-demolished Saxon mill to grind corn. It also probably flushed the sewers of the monastic buildings and provided transport for food

Weir beside Waltham Abbey, before (left) and after (right) the water plunges.

and grain by boat. Gazing down at the falling water on 30 June 1966 I conceived the idea of 'An Inner Home', the first poem I wrote that connected my poetry to history. I drafted the first sixteen lines that evening. (See pp.322-3.)

In the early 7th century Waltham (Old English *weald* or *wald*, 'forest', and *ham*, 'homestead' or 'enclosure', see p.44) was a small village in the centre of a royal hunting-park belonging to the kings of the East Saxons, and it continued to be royal property until the reign of Cnut.

Five Churches at Waltham

Until the archaeological work at Waltham Abbey of 1984-91, most people in the town of Waltham Abbey believed that the present church was Harold's church, and the majority of the people of the town of Waltham Abbey probably still believe this today. However, the present church was built in a style that differed from that in Harold's time, although some of the masonry is of about the right date. The archaeological work, which Peter Huggins led, established that the c.800 foundations were reused by Harold and were reused again by the Normans, and revealed that over the years there were five churches.[6]

Church 1

The first church at Waltham probably dates to the 7th century, a date based on radiocarbon dating (590-690) of a burial near the south door inside the present church which would have been outside the south-west corner of the first church.[7] A date of c.610 has been proposed, when the Christian King of the East Saxons was Sabert (or Sebert, 604-616).

Traces of Sabert's church have been found under the choir area of the present church: traces of a small timber building orientated to the present building – the evidence being packed flints in a trench that would have supported the sill beams of a ground-standing timber building[8] – and a jewellery bookclasp showing sea-eagles grasping a fish. The fish represents Christ as the Greek *ichthys* stands for *Iesos*

Christos Theou Yios Soter ('Jesus Christ, Son of God, Saviour'), and the eagle is a symbol for St John the Evangelist. The clasp was designed in Kent and has been dated to the 7th-century bishopric of Mellitus.[9] Sabert was the nephew of Ethelbert of Kent, and a Christian, and as we have just seen the fish was a Christian symbol.[10]

Church 2

A second church, a stone building, was built of Barnack stone from Northamptonshire round the timber-framed church during the 8th century when the Kingdom of the East Saxons passed to Offa of Mercia, c.790.[11] Offa's church was half the length of the present church, and was a *porticus*-type church with chambers on each side of the nave to contain tombs or altars.[12] It was intended to be a minster, a central church serving nearby villages. Priests went out to the villages for baptisms and burials and to preach, and the people came to the minster for Festivals.[13]

The second church was held, along with the manor of Waltham, from King Cnut by his standard-bearer, Tovi (Tofig) the Proud. We have seen (on p.47) how a life-sized black marble stone crucifix bearing a carved figure of Christ was found at Montacute, Somerset, of which Tovi was lord, was brought on an ox-drawn cart to Waltham after c.1016 and set up in the church to become an object of pilgrimage. Tovi is said to have rebuilt the church between 1016 and 1035[14] but Offa's church was already in existence and it is likely that Tovi did not refound or rebuild the church. At some stage the Holy Cross of black marble seems to have been housed underground and approached by pilgrims down a flight of steps.[15]

Church 3

We have seen (on p.47) that when Tovi died and his son fell into debt, his estate at Waltham, including the church of Waltham Holy Cross, passed back to the King, and that Edward the Confessor gave it to Harold Godwinsson, Earl of East Anglia and Essex, who, according to a Waltham chronicle, suffered a serious illness that seems to have been a form of paralysis. Harold asked that prayers for his healing should be said before the Holy Cross. When he recovered he built a third church on a grander scale from c.1053. The building work may have been begun when he was Earl of East Anglia, which included Essex, or after 1053 when he became Earl of Wessex and the most powerful man in the kingdom.[16]

This third church was dedicated in 1060. Harold's builders probably reused the foundations and stones of Offa's church. Harold's church had a nave the same length as the present one and aisles on each side. It was placed under a Dean and a college of 12 married priests. (In the pre-Norman English Church the clergy were allowed to marry.) Building work would probably have ended in 1066 when William I confiscated some of Harold's lands.[17]

Several parts of the present church can be attributed to Harold and belong to the third church: a wall with stones set in herring-bone fashion outside the east wall of the Lady Chapel and crypt, which originally formed the inside of the west wall of the south part of Harold's transept; a rain-water gully under the herring-bone wall; and base-course stones with pink mortar at shoulder height on the right at the bottom of the steps that lead down into the crypt.[18] Parts of the foundations of the ambulatory of the collegiate church (Harold's church which had a college of married priests) were discovered during an excavation in 1958.[19] (There had been an excavation of the cloisters in 1955 and there were further excavations outside the present church in 1958-62.)

There may be a description of the building of Harold's church in the anonymous *Vita Haroldi*, c.1216: "Foundations of a large church are rapidly laid; the walls rise; lofty columns at equal distances unite the walls with interlacing arcades or vaults; a roof of leaden plates keeps out the wind and the inclemencies of the weather."[20] However, this may be a description of the building of the church that became church 5 after 1177.

There is another story about a cross at Waltham. It involves the True Cross on which Christ was crucified. This was allegedly found under Golgotha by Helena, mother of Constantine the Great when she visited

Jerusalem. Remains of part of it were sent to Rome. These were found in 1492 walled up in Rome's Santa Croce in Gerusalemme, which occupied the site of the hall in the palace Helena occupied from 317 to 322. Popes gave fragments of wood from the True Cross to important pilgrims, including, when he visited Rome in 1056, to Harold, and Harold is said to have given his piece to Waltham Holy Cross.[21]

Church 4

Before, or at, the beginning of the 12th century Harold's church was pulled down and replaced by a fourth church that was built on Harold's foundations. The Barnack stone was reused, and new Reigate stone from Surrey, Kentish rag and Norman Caen stone were added. These new stones were probably brought by barge up the River Lea.

The fourth church had been begun c.1090 at the east end and was finished by c.1150 at the west end. About 1120 three chapels were added around the ambulatory. This church was cruciform with a tower and had two towers at the west end which were taken down about 1300. The west end was then rebuilt behind the 16th-century tower, and the Romanesque nave's western bays were mutilated to give pointed arches.

The fourth church had a long eastern chapel to which the Holy Cross may have been moved.[22] The Holy Cross attracted many pilgrims, who enriched the abbey. The abbey was now a valuable asset, and Henry I gave the manor of Waltham to his wife Maud of Scotland, and later to his next wife Adelicia of Louvain.

It has been suggested that the eastern chapel housed Harold's tomb, but this is unlikely as Harold had died in an invasion blessed by the Pope. There would therefore have been no Catholic cult of pilgrims seeking out Harold's tomb, and no special chapel to draw attention to Harold's remains.[23]

Church 5

A fifth church was built after Henry II was ordered to found three monasteries as part of his penance for the murder of Thomas Becket. Becket was murdered on 29 December 1170, and so the building of the fifth church began some time after c.1171 and probably in 1177 when, as part of his penance for his part in the murder of Thomas Becket, Archbishop of Canterbury, Henry II refounded Harold's church as a priory with a prior and 16 Augustinian canons regular (i.e. canons belonging to a monastic order). The building work continued until c.1242. In 1184 Henry II raised the church to an abbey, with an abbot, a prior and now 24 canons regular. The abbey grew to be the richest monastery in Essex.

The east end of the fourth church and added chapels were taken down and the chancel was extended as the central nave of the fifth church.[24] To the nave of the fourth church were thus added a choir and presbytery, new transepts – a second pair – and a tower. The first Lady Chapel may have been the ground floor of the tower east of the present building, the altar of which was consecrated in 1186.[25] The altar of Harold's church was removed to the east end of the fifth church, and a new altar was placed where the present one stands. The fifth church was now longer than Winchester Cathedral, and new monastic ranges and cloisters were added.

Waltham Holy Cross had therefore had its status upgraded from church (churches 1 and 2) to college (church 3), priory (in 1177) and finally abbey (in 1184). When we speak of the church of Waltham Abbey, strictly speaking we are referring to the church after 1184.

Waltham Abbey was subject to the King and Pope, but was excluded from the jurisdiction of the bishops. In the late 13th and early 14th centuries a lower chapel for funerals and an upper chapel for memorial services were built.

After the Abbey was dissolved in 1540, the Holy Cross vanished without trace and the flight of worn steps down to the Holy Cross was sealed off under the present church. Its present whereabouts is now unknown.[26] The Abbey buildings were leased to Sir Anthony Denny, an ambitious courtier who pulled them down to reuse the stones, and the present church and tower were left. In the reign of Edward VI the tower was struck by lightning and the present tower was built at the west end.

All this was gleaned from the archaeological excavations. An excavation to unearth the foundations and extent of the demolished Augustinian church (church 5, the one that had first 16 and then 24 Augustinian canons) took place in 1938 but had to be abandoned with the outbreak of war. The 1984 excavation was across the chancel of the collegiate church (church 3) to establish what remained and to determine the relationship between the collegiate and Augustinian foundations (the foundations of church 3 and church 5). The 1986 excavation focused on the collegiate aisle and ambulatory to establish the geometry of the east end. The 1987 excavation continued this work and focused on the number of apse bays and a fourth buttress. The aim was to see if there were any remains of the east end of an original collegiate church (church 3, Harold's church) that predated the apse and ambulatory.[27] The 1989, 1990 and 1991 excavations opened trenches in the grassland east of the present church to obtain information about the east ends of churches 2 and 3.[28]

A Walk round Waltham Abbey

I have wandered round Waltham Abbey, reflecting on its five churches.

Nave: zodiac

I have gazed up from the nave at the pier arches on either side which support the smaller arches of the *triforium* and the lesser arches of the clerestory. The simple Norman architecture of the church contrasts with the 1859-60 Burne-Jones rose and lancet windows.

I have glanced up at the signs of the zodiac on the ceiling. Designed by the architect William Burges and painted in 1860, the ceiling is based on the 13th-century ceiling of Peterborough Cathedral: the earth is the centre of the universe, and the twelve constellations of the zodiac revolve round it, the sun rising in each in turn. The ceiling is also a pictorial calendar showing the twelve months of the Year and their labours.

North aisle

I have wandered past the entrance to the tower, which has fourteen bells that Tennyson heard before he wrote 'Ring out, wild bells' in *In Memoriam*:

> "Ring out, wild bells, to the wild sky,
> The flying cloud, the frosty light;
> The year is dying in the night;
> Ring out, wild bells, and let him die."

I have gone through the 14th-century wooden screen and sauntered down the north aisle past the tomb of Captain Robert Smith, a merchant seaman who died in 1697. It shows a ship avoiding a rock, and weapons used at sea. I have looked at the Jacobean oak pulpit and sounding-board. I have turned right and stood in front of the altar rail and looked at the sanctuary that perhaps contains Harold's grave. (See pp.183-4.) I have been only half-aware of the ornamented reredos that tells the Christmas story behind the altar as I have mused on the 11th century.

Denny monument

I have turned right and stood before the Denny monument, which dates from 1600. Sir Edward Denny and his wife Lady Margaret, a lady-in-waiting to Elizabeth I (and to Queen Anne of Denmark and Queen Henrietta Maria), lie wearing armour and a fine dress. They are on their sides, one above the other, their heads supported by their left hands. Beneath them their seven boys and three girls (including twins with linked arms) kneel in prayer, praying for their parents' souls. Boys with swords are over 21, girls with ruffs are married. Sir Edward, the younger son of Sir Anthony Denny who leased the site of the medieval Abbey from the Crown after the Dissolution in 1540, sailed with Sir Humphrey Gilbert to claim Newfoundland for England in 1583.

Denny monument, Waltham Abbey, c.1600.

Both were buried elsewhere: Sir Edward in the family mausoleum beyond the east wall of the south aisle, where he was laid when he died in 1599 (1600 by modern reckoning as the New Year began on 25 March until 1752); and his wife in Bishop's Stortford.

Doom painting

I have ascended the steps to the Lady Chapel, which was built in the 14th century as a funeral guild chapel. For sixpence a year a guild member could have an annual memorial service in the chapel after his death. I have glanced at the 1930s stained-glass windows about Mary's life and have gazed at the 14th-century wall-painting above the altar.

It is a Doom painting, showing the Last Judgement.[29] Christ sits on a rainbow in the middle surrounded by seven angels blowing curved, Roman-style trumpets, and the souls of the dead are being weighed in scales against their accumulated sins below him. Red devils or demons drag the sinful to the mouth of Hell, which is like the mouth of the sea-monster leviathan, where Satan awaits them. On the monster's head are written sins: *Invidide* (envy) and *Lwste* (lust), two of the seven deadly sins.

On the right, the living await judgement, wearing clothes that represent all classes of society. St Peter welcomes the good to Heaven on the left. They are led by an abbot, possibly the Abbot of Waltham, and a bishop, possibly John of Waltham who became Bishop of Salisbury and died at the end of the 14th century. At the bottom of the picture the dead rise from their graves in accordance with *Revelation*, 20, 12-13.

14th-century doom painting, Waltham Abbey.

There was an earlier painting underneath this Doom painting for a small figure of Christ at the top survives from an earlier picture. This Doom painting is a secco: it was painted on dry plaster with pigments mixed in water, and the plaster was dampened when painting was taking place. A fresco, on the other hand, is painted on wet plaster and needs a warm, quick-drying climate (as in Italy, but not in England) to prevent the colour from spreading into the wall behind.[30]

Sitting before this Doom painting in natural light, contemplators seek to be illumined by spiritual Light. I have described Heaven and Hell in my two poetic epics, *Overlord* and *Armageddon*, and I cannot help wondering if I have been as much influenced by this Doom painting as by Dante.

Doom paintings spread after 1000, when the end of the world did not come as expected. The Church thought that in accordance with *Matthew* 25, 1-13 and 31-33 (which asserts that Christ will come in glory to judge the living and the dead) everyone must be ready to be called to Judgement at any time. From the 11th to the 16th centuries paintings of the Last Judgement appeared over the chancel arch of a church, for in a medieval church the congregation stood in the nave, which represented the world, and looked at the chancel, sanctuary and high altar, which were screened off and represented Heaven. To take communion, the congregation went through a door in the screen under the Judgement and reached the altar rail, symbolising the soul's hope of reaching Heaven. In a medieval church the walls were covered with paintings which priests used as a picture book to teach the illiterate.[31]

Guilds

In Waltham Abbey there was originally no chancel, and the Doom painting is in the small guild chapel built on the side of the nave in the 14th century. The funeral guild had been founded in the 1340s, and in return for a subscription of sixpence a year a guild priest conducted a member's funeral in the undercroft below (now the crypt and visitors' centre) and, as we have just seen, an annual memorial service in the guild chapel above on the anniversary of a member's death. Indicating the Doom painting, the guild priest would have contrasted the fate of those going to Hell and the likelihood of the member's going to Heaven.[32]

Parliament abolished funeral guilds in 1547, and the chapel became a vestry and church school until in 1875 (a free state school having opened in the town under the 18th century Education Act) it became a Lady Chapel. In the undercroft is a mutilated 14th-century carving of a headless Mary sitting on a chair of state. Christ's fingers can just be seen on the chain of Mary's cloak, but otherwise there is no trace of the Christ child. This is the Waltham Madonna that explains the renaming of the guild chapel as the Lady Chapel.

South aisle

I have wandered back down to the south aisle and looked up at small worn steps across the bottom of a small window, the remains of a staircase in a turret in the corner of the west front. I have gazed at the organ (given in 1819 by Thomas Leverton, who founded a local school). There Thomas Tallis, father of English church music, was organist during the Dissolution of 1540. I have seen grooves in a pillar that once held books on chains for the congregation and pilgrims to read: Cranmer's 1539 *Bible*, Erasmus's Greek *New Testament*, Bishop Jewel's book on the teachings of the Church of England and Foxe's *Book of Martyrs*, which was written in Waltham Abbey.

I have recalled the funeral of our MP, Sir John Biggs-Davison at Waltham Abbey in October 1988. I had known him for more than thirty years. He had given me a ticket to the crucial Suez debate in 1956. The Abbey was packed. The local dignitaries sat in the front. There were chairs down the side aisles and I sat on a bench with my back against the south-aisle wall. It was an ecumenical service for the whole community.

I have gone on to the west end and looked at the 12th-century font (which was reshaped in the 19th century) and the ancient doorway that was the outer doorway before the tower was built. It has a medieval Green Man on the northern capital.

Tower

I have left the Abbey and looked up at the tower. When the destruction of the Abbey was authorised, in 1544 the townspeople claimed the Abbey as their parish church. When the tower at the east end collapsed in 1552 the people carried many of the stones to the west end and built this tower to prop up the building: a black-and-white chessboard effect up to the top of the first window, then smooth stone up to the three narrow windows, the clock and the two top windows beneath the crenellations.

Gardens

The remains of the medieval Abbey are in the Abbey gardens. It was nearly four times as long as the present church. The east end of the Norman church – the apse and ambulatory – were demolished to create space for new monastic buildings. I have traced the cloister, chapter house, parlour, store-cellar, refectory where the canons ate and dorter where they slept. I have sauntered through the gardens to the 15th-century Welsh Harp, sat outside over a cup of tea and reflected on the stone marking the site of Harold's grave, which is among the open-air monastic ruins surrounded by grass. I have walked back to my car through the rose garden and herb garden and have pondered the evidence for Harold's burial at Waltham and for his body's being near the memorial slab.

Harold buried at Waltham

There has been a long tradition, as we are about to see, that Harold was buried at Waltham. There have been no excavations exclusively devoted to finding his tomb. The traditional view is that there was only one tomb, which was in Harold's church, church 3. The transept and apse of this church were demolished, and if the tomb was near the altar it is somewhere in the churchyard outside the present church, in the vicinity of the stone marker. If it was on one side of church 3 it may be under the floor of the

Coin with portrait of Harold II.

present church, possibly in the sanctuary.

If the tomb was indeed near the altar of church 3 it would have been close to the marker stone in the churchyard. This was placed c.1960 as an indication of where the incumbent at that time thought the tomb might be. It was a guess based on the knowledge of that time rather than an accurate location based on archaeological evidence.

When it became established in the 1980s that there were five churches, another view grew up that there was a new tomb in church 4, and another new tomb in church 5 at least 40 yards or more further away from the church. There is no evidence to support this view, which was championed by Dinah Dean, and it is now thought to be unlikely. See drawing below for the possible positions of these hypothetical tombs, for which there is no archaeological evidence.

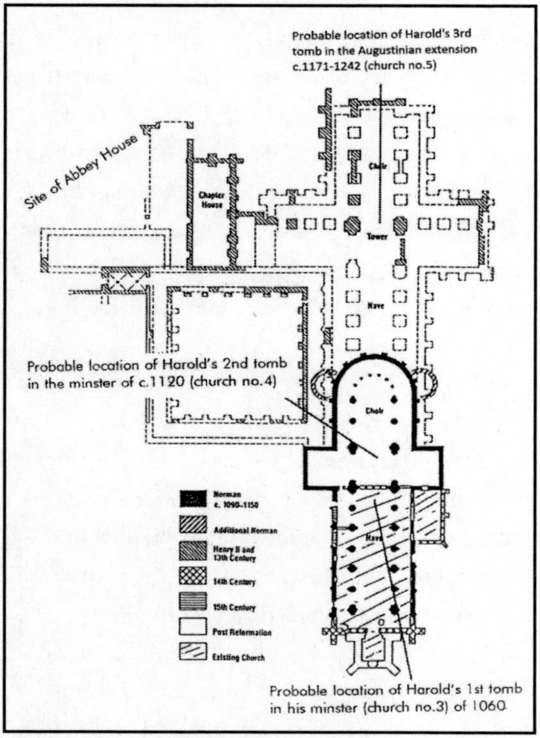

Possible positions of Harold's hypothetical tombs.

The Waltham Chronicle

There is no mention of Harold's burial in *The Anglo-Saxon Chronicle*. There is some evidence that after his death during the Battle of Hastings, Harold's body was taken back to the church he built, Waltham Holy Cross, and was buried beneath the high altar, in a grave that now lies outside the east end of the present church. The main evidence is in *The Waltham Chronicle*, *De Inventione Sanctae Crucis Nostrae* ("*The Discovery of our Holy Cross*"), a Latin text c.1177, a translation of which has been published in the Oxford Medieval Texts series.

It was written by a secular canon who entered Harold's college at Waltham during the reign of Henry I at the age of five,[33] given by his family to the Church to become a priest. As a child he was friendly with Turkill, an elderly canon, who told the author that Harold visited Waltham on his way from Stamford Bridge to Hastings, and had been followed to Hastings by two of the canons, Osgod (or Osegod) Cnop (or Cnoppe) and Aethelric (or Ailric), the child master.

After the battle these two canons went to William, Duke of Normandy, and begged to be allowed to take Harold's body back to Waltham. William consented. The two canons were unable to find Harold's body as the bodies around his standard were too dismembered to recognise. They went to Eadgyth Swanneshals, Edith with the swan's neck, and returned with her. She identified Harold's body from marks on it that she recognised. The two canons carried the body on a bier back to Waltham and buried it.

The author of *The Waltham Chronicle* claims, "They brought the body to Waltham and buried it with great honour, where, without any doubt, he has lain at rest until the present day, whatever stories men may invent." Harold would have been buried in church 3, either in the nave or in the continuous transept, which would put his grave at the east end of the present church or in the grassland to the east.[34]

The author then describes how he was present when, during the building of Henry I's church, church 4, Harold's body was disinterred, removed and then reburied: "I can now in my old age remember when

I was present when his body was translated for the third time, occasioned either by the building work in the church or because the brethren out of devotion were showing reverence for the body. It is generally well-known, and we have heard old men testify, that men saw with their own eyes, and touched with their hands, the marks of wounds visible on the very bones."[35]

Harold's body was "translated" (i.e. moved) three times within the author's memory. His tomb was in his own minster (the third church) of 1060, as we have just seen. There is no evidence that Harold's tomb was moved to a new location when the fourth church was built between c.1120 and c.1150, or into the Augustinian extension that began in 1177 (the founding of the priory or monastery), continued after 1184 (the raising of the priory to an abbey) and was finished with the dedication of the abbey in 1242 (the fifth church). There was no demand for Harold to have a bigger or better tomb in church 4 or church 5. There was no cult of Harold, just the cult of the Holy Cross, and the canons of Waltham Abbey would not have wanted to offend their Norman masters by drawing attention to Harold's tomb in order to attract pilgrims. They would have wanted the tomb to be as inconspicuous and unobtrusive as possible.

The author of *The Waltham Chronicle* is looking back as an old man on the c.1120 rebuilding of the church, and the third "translation" of Harold from his tomb. He joined the college at the age of five, had spent 53 years in the college and was writing in 1177, which means that he was not looking further back than to c.1124, when he was five.[36] He says he was present when Harold's body "was translated for the third time", but he also says that the "translations" (moves) were occasioned by the state of building work or out of reverence to the body. In other words Harold's body could have been temporarily removed and returned to the same tomb three times in the course of building work for church 4.[37] Suggestions that two of these three translations were from church 3 to church 4 and from church 4 to church 5 (work on which had not been begun in 1177 when the author was writing) can be dismissed. However, we shall see that there are later written traditions suggesting that his tomb was some distance from the present church.[38] (See pp.183-4 for the location of Harold's tomb and suggested locations for two later tombs.) Be that as it may, the writer of *The Waltham Chronicle* is clearly saying that he was an eyewitness of the wounds on Harold's body, and that Harold was definitely buried at Waltham Abbey.

Another child of Waltham, Laurence of Durham, wrote a poem in Latin recalling Harold's tomb, which is in an Appendix of *The Waltham Chronicle.* The English translation is: "Blessed father of your country, Harold marked out by your merits, you, our shield, fist and sword: now a mound covers you….In this tomb brave Harold rests."[39] Laurence left Waltham to become a monk, and later prior, of the abbey at Durham, but he clearly says in his poem that Harold was buried in a Waltham tomb.

Other chronicles

William of Malmesbury wrote in Latin *Gesta pontificum Anglorum, The Deeds of the Kings of the English*, c.1130, and had not been born when the Battle of Hastings was fought. He states that Harold's body was given to his mother, Girtha (or Gytha or Gutha), to be buried in the minster which Harold had built and endowed at Waltham.[40]

Henry II (1154-89) commissioned Master Wace to compile the history of the Norman dukes. In his *Chronicle of the Norman Conquest*, believed to have been prepared for Battle Abbey[41] c.1200, he states on folio 271 that Harold's body was carried to Waltham and buried. His work was completed by an anonymous continuator who wrote in the reign of Henry III (1216-72): "He that wishes to know this at Waltham, behind the high altar, can find this self same altar [i.e. the altar of the Holy Cross] and King Harold lying in the choir [i.e. of church 4]." The continuator is saying that Harold's body lay in the choir of church 4. This would put Harold's body to the west of the present stone marker outside the church.[42]

Coffin in gardens

A further claim that Harold was buried at Waltham came to light in the

16th century. After the Dissolution in 1540, the parishioners had been allowed to keep the church. A screen separated the nave from the monastic buildings, and the rubble of the demolished choir and presbytery was removed and the ground was laid out as a bowling-green. The tomb was alleged to have been in the presbytery of the Augustinian extension of the church in the late 12th and early 13th century, and according to a story told by Edward Walford in 1883[43] Harold's stone coffin was discovered by a gardener working for Sir Edward Denny, son of the Sir Edward Denny whose tomb I described on p.179 – he was one of the kneeling boys – and grandson of the Sir Anthony Denny to whom the rectory and manor had passed. The remains were exposed to the air and mouldered into dust.[44] The gardener's employer, Sir Edward, the Earl of Norwich, died in 1637 and was succeeded by his grandson, James Hay, the 2nd Earl of Carlisle.

There were claims that Harold's tomb was variously in church 3, church 4 or church 5. The incumbent of Waltham Abbey, Dr Thomas Fuller, claimed in 1665 in his *The History of Waltham in Essex founded by King Harold* [45] that Harold was buried "near the Earl of Carlisle's leaden fountain in his garden, then probably the end of the choir [i.e. of church 3], or rather some eastern chapel beyond it [i.e. of church 4]; his tomb of plain but rich grey marble, with what seemeth a *cross-florée* (but much descanted on with art) upon the same, supported with pillarets, one pedestal whereof I have in my house".[46] He adds, "As for his reported epitaph, I purposely omit it, not so much because barbarous (scarce any better in that age), but because not attested, to my apprehension, with sufficient authority."[47]

This has been taken as referring to Harold's third and final hypothetical tomb in the presbytery of church 5, the Augustinian canons' extension of the church in the late 12th/early 13th century (between 1177 and 1242).[48] There is such a stone in the floor of the north-chancel aisle of the present church. It is coffin-shaped, wider at the head than at the foot and six feet nine inches long, but there is doubt as to whether it is early enough to be Harold's stone, even if it were late 12th/early 13th century.

The pedestal that Fuller says "I had in my house" in 1665 was later in John Farmer's house in 1735. He says that this fragment "I have now in my house. It is a curious face or bust of grey marble, which by tradition always was, and is to this day, esteemed to be part of King Harold's tomb". John Farmer was the author of *The History of the Ancient Town and once Famous Abbey of Waltham in the County of Essex.* He also says: "It is without dispute that he [Harold] was buried in the garden, under a leaden fountain, where now there is a bowling-green, which formerly belonged to the Earl of Carlisle."[49] Farmer gives the epitaph that Fuller said was too bad to quote, which can be translated as

> "A fierce foe thee slew, thou a king, he a king in view,
> Both peers, both peerless, both feared and both fearless;
> That sad day was mixed by Firmin and Calixt;
> The one helped thee to vanquish, the other made thee to languish."[50]

The Battle of Stamford Bridge took place on 25 September, the feast day of St Firmin, and the Battle of Hastings took place on 14 October, the feast day of St Calixtus.

Another claim locates Harold's tomb on the site of Abbey House. This contradictory story about Harold's body was told of Sir Charles Jones, who owned Abbey House, the manor house of Waltham Abbey built by Sir Edward Denny, 1st Earl of Norwich and Sir Anthony Denny's grandson, from the stones of the pulled-down abbey buildings. A well-known 18th-century Irish jig, set as a song, was evidently based on Sir Charles, and included the words "For pray what would you more/Than mirth with good claret and Bumper Squire Jones?" *The Parlour Portfolio or Post Chaise Companion* contains the following anecdote, written perhaps 20 years before its publication date in 1820, about Sir Charles:[51] "Between thirty and forty years ago, the manor house of Waltham Abbey was inhabited by the famous Bumper Squire Jones. In digging to enlarge his cellar [presumably his claret cellar], the body of King Harold was discovered, as evidently appeared from

Haroldus Rex inscribed on the lid of the coffin. Jones thought he could not do greater honour to the corpse than by placing it at the head of the cellar where it had been interred, and whenever any of his friends were led by curiosity to see it, he made them offer libations to the memory of the deceased until they could not see it."[52] The house burned down soon after Sir Charles's death, and was demolished in 1770. Presumably the coffin was destroyed.

Stone marker

The memorial tablet or stone marker marking the alleged site of Harold's grave was placed in the churchyard in the 1960s. The assumption then was that a refounder of a minster would be buried to the east of the high altar, like canonised saints such as Edward the Confessor in Westminster Abbey and St Cuthbert in Durham Cathedral.

However, a founder, or refounder, was always buried several yards to the *west* of the high altar on a church's east-west axis, which puts the location of Harold's tomb before the apse (the semicircular recess at the eastern end of a church) and in the presbytery of church 3, away from the general public who were only allowed into the canons' church in groups to pray at the Holy Cross. Harold's tomb in the minster of

Marker stone for Harold's tomb foreground (left), with present Abbey east end behind it (right).

c.1120, the fourth church, would therefore have been in the demolished transept, at the beginning of the demolished apse. It was therefore much closer to the existing east wall than the memorial tablet. (See pp.183-4 for the probable location of Harold's tomb.)

Harold buried elsewhere

There is some evidence, from three authors writing in Latin and one in French, that Harold was buried elsewhere than at Waltham.

William of Poitiers, Archdeacon of Lisieux and William the Conqueror's chaplain, was not present at the Battle of Hastings but wrote in *Gesta Guillelmi II Ducis Normannorum et Regis Anglorum* (*Deeds of William II, Duke of the Normans and King of the English*, 1071-7) that William "gave him [Harold] to William Malet for burial, and not his mother, who offered an equal weight of gold for the body."[53] Harold had been friendly with William of Malet during his enforced stay in Normandy. Malet was uncle to Harold's queen Ealdgyth (or Alditha), and he was related to William of Normandy by his (i.e. Malet's) marriage to Hesilia Crespin.[54]

Benoît de Sainte-Maure wrote in the late 12th century, and seems to base his account on William of Poitiers' in *Chronique des Ducs de Normandie* (*Chronicles of the Dukes of Normandy*), adding: "But this William [Malet] was so often robbed of it [the body] that he gave it to be carried away where they might sell it as they pleased."[55]

The unknown author of *De Bello Hastingensi Carmen* (*The Song of the Battle of Hastings*) wrote in c.1071 that William refused the entreaties of William of Malet and of Harold's mother and commanded that Harold's body should be burned on the "top of a lofty rock". He says that the body was buried on the Sussex seashore under a cairn ("*aggere sub labidum*"),[56] perhaps at Bosham in Sussex, which is eight miles from Hastings. It was the Godwinsson family home, where his mother would have wanted him buried.

Vita Haroldi (*The Life of Harold*), written by an unknown author and commissioned by the Norman Abbot of Waltham Abbey, which had been refounded as a priory by Henry II in 1177 to replace Harold's college of secular canons, claimed that Harold survived the Battle of Hastings and became a hermit, first in Dover and then in Chester. Bishop Stubbs wrote that this work was an "untrustworthy legend" designed to prove that Harold was not buried at Waltham. The Norman author did not want a Harold cult to gather round Waltham and was at pains to make people believe that Harold was not buried at Waltham.

Consensus for Harold's burial at Waltham

However, a mass of further evidence indicates that Harold *was* buried at Waltham. Robert of Gloucester, a monk living at the time of the 1265 Battle of Evesham, records in his chronicle that Harold's mother brought his body to Waltham for burial.[57] Bede's *Ecclesiastical History of England* reports that William of Malmesbury says of William the Conqueror: "*Corpus Haroldi, matri petenti sine pretio misit, licet illa per legatos multum optulisset. Acceptum itaque apud Waltham sepelivit.*"[58] ("He sent the body of Harold to his petitioning mother without [requesting] payment, even though she would have offered a fortune [literally, much] through ambassadors. And so she buried [the body] she received at Waltham.")

Evidence[59] that Waltham was Harold's burial place can be found in William of Malmesbury, Hygden, Johannes de Oxenedes' *Chronica*, and the 13th-century poet who wrote lines in the epigraph of this chapter: "Through the prayer of his mother,/The body was carried on a bier;/At Waltham it is place in the tomb/For he was founder of the house." Also in the work of Orderic (or Ordericus) Vitalis, who added to William of Jumièges' *Gesta Normannorum Ducum* (*Deeds of the Norman Dukes*), and to William of Poitiers' *Gesta Guillelmi II Ducis Normannorum et Regis Anglorum* (*Deeds of William II, Duke of the Normans and King of the English*). Also in Peter of Ickham, *The Annales de Wintonia*, in Roger Wendover in *The Flowers of History* and in Strutt, Matthew of Westminster, William Pictavensis, Knighton, Bompton, Stow, Camden, Rapin, Thoyras, Rastell, Tyrell, Keighley, Turner, Lingard, Hume and others. All say the same, that Harold was buried at Waltham.

Both history and tradition suggest that Harold was buried in

Waltham Abbey, some distance from the east end of the present church – not as far as the 120 feet where the present memorial or stone marker stands according to one view, and west of the memorial according to another view. Stubbs says that the evidence is strong.[60] Harold was a nationalist who fought for Saxon England against invading Norwegians and Normans, and his defeat brought to an end the Saxon period.

I have spoken with Peter Huggins, who conducted the 1984-91 archaeological excavations, in an attempt to pinpoint a possible site for the tomb, which is likely to have been an inconspicuous slab to avoid offending the Normans rather than an elaborate tomb of the proportions of Edward the Confessor's in Westminster Abbey. There has never been an excavation for Harold's tomb. It is surely time for a case to be made to English Heritage, who own the site, for a survey with sub-ground radar and for a new excavation in the two most likely places where there may be remnants of Harold's slab.

I have sauntered to the stone marker of Harold's grave and contemplated the outline of the foundations of the demolished monastic buildings and I have reflected on the continuity of this Forest place. Waltham Holy Cross was a royal possession from the 7th century until Cnut, and again after Edward the Confessor and Harold. There were royal stables here in 1294 and enough stables to attract Henry VIII to spend five days staying at the Abbey in 1532 and to retain the stables until 1541, as we saw on p.66. It was the last Abbey in the country to be dissolved because it was Henry VIII's favourite place. I feel a sense of continuity spread from this place to the nearby town, Market Square and Sun Street, and feel I am rooted in history since the 7th century by gazing at these ruined stones.

High Beach

> "I love to see the Beech Hill mounting high,
> The brook without a bridge and nearly dry."
>
> John Clare, 'A Walk in the Forest'

High Beach church

I got to know the church of the Holy Innocents, High Beach properly in the 1960s, and especially when I returned from Libya in 1970. I sometimes drove up to the King's Oak and walked among the pillow mounds and looked at the view over the Lea into Hertfordshire. I sometimes walked down to the Turpin's Cave public house that was surrounded by grass and trees near a hollow where Turpin was reputed to have hidden. It was kept by a woodlander with fingers missing from one hand. Sometimes I drove up Earl's Path, over the Robin-Hood roundabout to High Beach church, "the church in the Forest", and parked my car by the low black rail. Sometimes I walked through the lych-gate past a yew and up the path and into the deserted church. I was always the only soul there.

The parish of High Beach was created in 1836 from part of Waltham Holy Cross. The first church of St Paul was built on Blencow's Green at the bottom of a hill on damp ground off Church Road, High Beach (see pp.200-3). In 1862 it was in bad repair and was abandoned. It was eventually demolished in 1885. The second church, the church of the Holy Innocents (named after two children of the Baring family who had died in infancy) was opened in 1873 and consecrated in 1883. It is a stone building in the Early-English style with an apsidal chancel, nave, transepts and a tower. It stands in a graveyard surrounded by silver birch and other Forest trees.

It is a woodland church with woodlanders lying in the graveyard, the Forest all round. I have passed the organ and font by the door and have noted the black and red Victorian tiles, which are identical to those in the scullery at Journey's End. I have advanced under the hammerbeam roof to look at the altar and embroideries of traditional parish cattle-brand marks (each a letter of the alphabet surmounted by a crown). I have taken in the pulpit and the lectern, which is in the form of an eagle. Sitting in a pew I have seen leaves caress the diamond windows in the wind, reinforcing the idea that the church is surrounded by Nature. I have looked back at the font. Here, while living in London, my wife and I had our two sons christened.

I have wandered out of the porch and turned left and gone down to the stile: on the other side of the low black rail three stone steps descend to the Forest. From that stile I have looked back and up at the spire towering above, which I reflected in 'A Crocus in the Churchyard'. Standing here, I received the images that became 'Two Variations on One Theme'. (See pp.333-7.)

High Beach church (left), and "three-stone-stepped stile" (see p.337).

Tennyson

Near the church is Arabin House, a privately-owned house now split into two, to one half of which I was invited to dinner during the 1990s. Tennyson is said to have visited its garden when he lived at High Beach. From 1837 to 1840 he lived at Beech Hill House, a short drive down Wellington Hill to Pynest Green Lane. The house was enlarged in 1850 and pulled down in recent times, but the stables have survived (now modernised and redeveloped). There he wrote part of *In Memoriam*.

Tennyson's silent decade

In 1832 Tennyson had been ridiculed by Coleridge: "The misfortune is that Mr Tennyson has begun to write verses without very well understanding what metre is." Coleridge said that Tennyson could "scarcely scan his verses". In 1833 his university friend Arthur Hallam had died in Vienna. Tennyson suffered a "silent and morose decade" from 1832 to 1842, when he published nothing. In 1835, though in the Lake District, he refused to go to Rydal Mount to see Wordsworth. In 1836 he met Emily and became engaged the following year. But no wedding would follow for another thirteen years.

Tennyson leaves Lincolnshire

Tennyson and his mother were forced to move out of the Rectory in Somersby in Lincolnshire, where they had been living. After the death of Tennyson's father in 1831 Mrs. Tennyson had rented the Rectory, which was too large for the new incumbent to live in. Then the patron of the church announced that the new incumbent would be replaced by his own son, who would live in the Rectory, and the Tennysons were told that they would have to leave.

Wanting to be near London while living in the country, Tennyson found High Beech House, High Beach between March and May 1837. The owner of the house was Sergeant Arabin, whose wife was related to Lincolnshire friends of the Tennysons.[61]

Tennyson at Beech Hill House

Tennyson came to Beech Hill House, High Beach, with his mother. Beech Hill House was a large house in a walled park with greenhouses and an ornamental lake, set on a height that commanded a view of Waltham Abbey. When it was enlarged in 1850 its name was changed to Beech Hill Park, but the house Tennyson lived in was much simpler. He had a study over the dining-room with a bay window and red curtains. He skated on a pond in the park. His mother had an income and they were able to afford three female servants and a liveried man indoors, and gardeners.

Nevertheless, he was restless and unhappy. In 1839 he wrote to Emily, "I have been at this place all the year, with nothing but that muddy pond in prospect, and those two little sharp-barking dogs. Perhaps I am coming to the Lincolnshire coast, but that I scarcely know. The journey is so expensive, and I am so poor."[62] There was a thunder-storm and his mother cried out, "Oh, I will leave this house; the storms are very bad here."[63] Tennyson wrote in a letter to Mrs Rawnsley, 28 January 1838, "Mrs. Arabin [of Arabin House] seems to me the only person about who speaks and acts as an honest and true nature dictates; all else is artificial, frozen, cold, and lifeless."[64]

Tennyson (left) and the site of Beech Hill House (right).

In spite of his misgivings he wrote part of *In Memoriam*, 'The Talking Oak' and 'Locksley Hall' there, and worked on the poems of his 1842 volume.

Tennyson and Dr Allen's insane asylum

Tennyson met walkers from Dr Matthew Allen's private insane asylum as he walked in the Forest. Since 1825 Matthew Allen, an enlightened pioneer in the treatment of mental illness, had had three houses in High Beach: Fairmead (or Fair Mead) House for men (which closed in 1859 and was subsequently demolished and replaced by the rebuilt Suntrap

Centre in Church Road), Springfield for women, and Leopard's Hill Lodge (now known as Lippitt's Hill Lodge) for the more severe cases. A John Clare Society paper gives details of Allen's three houses.[65] (See map on p.203.)

Within a year of Tennyson's arrival in High Beach, his brother Septimus Tennyson became a voluntary patient at Fairmead House for several stays. Tennyson stayed occasionally as a guest of Dr Allen, presumably at Fairmead House rather than Lippitt's Hill Lodge to support his brother rather than to be treated for his depression.

Lippitt's Hill Lodge.

James Spedding wrote in a letter about the fortnight Tennyson spent as a guest of Dr Allen, presumably at Fairmead House: "Alfred Tennyson has reappeared....He has been on a visit to a madhouse for the last fortnight (not as a patient), and has been delighted with the mad people, whom he reports the most agreeable and the most reasonable persons he has met with. The keeper is Dr Allen, with whom he has been greatly taken." [66]

Tennyson and Dr Matthew Allen both knew Carlyle and had other literary friends in common, and became friendly. Tennyson learned about madhouses from Allen, knowledge he put into 'Maud'.[67] Carlyle wrote an account of an appearance by Tennyson and Allen in London at the Sterling Club, founded as the Anonymous Club, in 1838: "Some weeks ago, one night, the poet Tennyson and Matthew Allen were discovered here sitting smoking in the garden."[68]

Tennyson's disastrous investment in Dr Allen's company

Tennyson came to regret his association with Dr Allen, who had formed a company to produce patented wood-carvings by machinery. The company was called The Patent Decorative Carving and Sculpture Company, and the device was christened a "Pyroglyph", but was later called "The Patent Method of Carving in Solid Wood".[69] He persuaded Tennyson to invest all the money from the sale of land left to him by his grandfather at Grasby in Lincolnshire, together with a £500 legacy from an aunt of Hallam's.

Tennyson handed over £3,000 to Allen in mid-1840. The security on Tennyson's investment was an insurance policy on Allen's life, a bond and the mortgage deeds of Fairmead House. Three of Tennyson's sisters added £4,000 between them.[70] At this point, despite his investment, in 1840 Tennyson was depressed and he and his mother were persuaded by a London doctor to move from High Beach to Tunbridge Wells.

The company failed, all the money was lost and Dr Allen and almost the entire Tennyson family were declared bankrupt in 1843. Tennyson could not afford to get married now. He had to postpone all thought of marrying Emily and had nothing from which to support himself.[71] In fact, Allen died in 1845 and Tennyson recouped some of his losses from the insurance policy on Allen's life.

It is said[72] that he returned to High Beach in December 1861 to stay with his friend Judge Arabin at Beech House (later renamed Arabin House) and that he wrote his 53-line poetic Dedication of a new edition of *Idylls of the King* to Prince Albert there. (Prince Albert had just died and the Dedication poem was a tribute written around Christmas and sent on 7 January 1862.)[73] It must be pointed out that there is no mention of Tennyson's writing this poem in High Beach in the main biographies or scholarly works.

John Clare

At Fairmead House or Leopard's Hill Lodge Tennyson may have met the poet John Clare, who was admitted into Allen's asylum with deteriorating mental health in July 1837. It is not clear to which house Clare was initially admitted but in the last year of his institutionalisation under Dr Allen he was living at Leopard's Hill Lodge (now Lippitt's Hill Lodge).[74]

Clare in Dr Allen's insane asylum

Clare.

Reliable inmates like Clare were allowed to roam at will in the Forest. It is possible that Tennyson met Clare in the Forest – they had literary friends in common, including Thomas Campbell – and that he was introduced to Dr Allen by Clare. However, as we have seen, Tennyson's brother Septimus was an inmate at Fairmead House, and Tennyson was almost a neighbour of Allen's, Beech Hill House being just beyond the woods behind Fairmead Cottage.

Clare's basic problem was penury. He had dug fields during the day and had copied out verses he had composed by candlelight in the evenings. He had been briefly taken up by the poetry world. It dropped him, and he now had seven children to support and insufficient income.

Clare's mind went, and his publisher, John Taylor, brought him to Dr Allen, who when opening his asylum in 1825 had pledged "to assist the disturbed and diseased mind to regain its tranquillity".

Clare's poems about Epping Forest

Clare was encouraged to walk in the Forest and write poems, free from having to provide for his large family, and he ceased to complain of his poverty. He wrote to his wife, "The place here is beautiful,...The country is the finest I have ever seen."[75] This mood is reflected in his poetry. Clare's punctuation was often non-existent, and the following excerpt has to be presented as it was written as any punctuation at the end of line 5 can change the queen from being Nature to being Mary:

"How beautifull this hill of fern swells on
So beautifull the chappel peeps between
The hornbeams – with its simple bell – alone
I wander here hid in a palace green
Mary is abscent – but the forest queen
Nature is with me – morning noon & gloaming
I write my poems in these paths unseen
& when among these brakes & beeches roaming
I sigh for truth & home & love & woman."[76]

This is from 'Child Harold', a poem whose title was clearly influenced by Byron's *Childe Harold's Pilgrimage*. The "hill of fern", "chapel" and hornbeams were up the road from where he was living. Mary Joyce was his first love, who had died unmarried in 1838, aged 41. Clare refused to believe that she had died and somehow imagined that he was still in a relationship with her and that she had been his first wife. He loved Epping Forest:

"I love the Forest and its airy bounds,
Where friendly Campbell takes his daily rounds:
I love the breakneck hills, that headlong go,
And leave me high, and half the world below;

I love to see the Beech Hill mounting high,
The brook without a bridge and nearly dry,
There's Bucket's Hill, a place of furze and clouds,
Which evening in a golden blaze enshrouds."

The poem from which these lines are taken, 'A Walk in the Forest' was almost certainly written at the early-18th-century public house, The Owl (which was demolished and rebuilt around 1977). Campbell was the son of the poet Thomas Campbell. The "brook without a bridge" crosses the garden of Fairmead Cottage, runs through what may have been Clare's lily pond and under the road, joins the brook that rises in Hill Wood and trickles across Fairmead Bottom and on to Connaught Water (when the water-table is high enough). "Bucket's Hill" is Buckhurst Hill. It would be interesting if "Beech Hill" referred to Tennyson's Beech Hill House – Tennyson put his address under his letter to Mrs. Rawnsley of 28 January 1838 as "Beech Hill" – but it is more likely to be High Beach, the area in the vicinity of the pillow mounds.

Locations of Clare's Epping-Forest poems

The locations of Clare's Forest poems were all within a quarter-of-an-hour's walk of each other. If Lippitt's Hill and Church Road form an L, The Owl was at the top of the down stroke, and Lippitt's Hill Lodge is at the bottom of the down stroke opposite Springfield. Fairmead House (now replaced by the Suntrap Centre) was 400 yards along Church Road on the horizontal stroke. Fairmead Cottage is 100 yards further along (a few yards from the site of a lily pond where Clare may have written 'Water Lilies' in 1841). The "brook without a bridge" rises at the back of Fairmead Cottage and flows into this pond to go under the road to join the brook that rises in Hill Wood near the site of Clare's small redbrick "chapel": the site of the old High Beach church on Old Church Plain, built in 1838 and demolished in 1872. Fifty yards further along the ground rises to what Clare thought of Fern Hill ("this hill of fern"), a ferny area (in his day) that is now covered with trees on the edge of Hill Wood, in Old Church Plain. In Clare's day it was covered with ferns, and Clare had to jump the "brook without a bridge" to reach the side of Fern Hill near Dairy Cottage, the scene of his poem 'By a cottage near a wood'.[77] (Confusingly, there is another Fern Hill that consists of 31 acres acquired in 1997 off Lippitt's Hill beyond The Owl, to the left before Blinds Lane.) He wrote in 'Sighing for Retirement', "I found the poems in the fields/And only wrote them down."[78] The whole of Clare's poetic output while at High Beach can be located along Lippitt's Hill and Church Road.

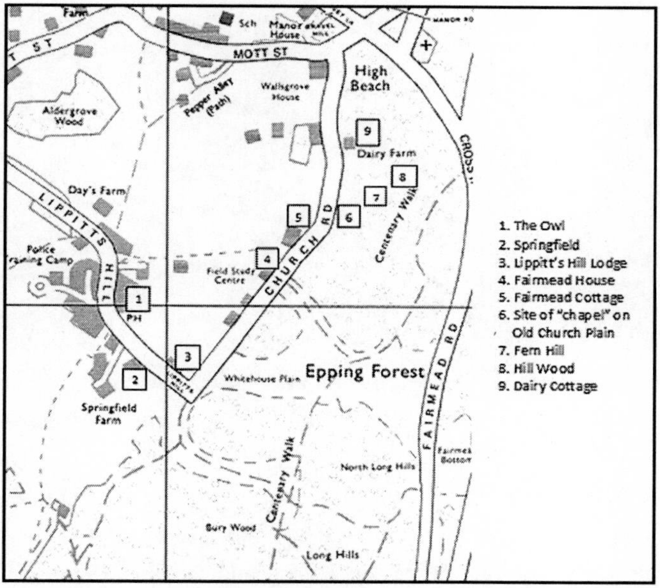

Map of Lippitt's Hill and Church Road, High Beach, with locations of Clare's Forest poems.

Fairmead Cottage and the Insane

I visited Fairmead Cottage in 2011 and talked with its owner, Austin Darby, to whose mother I had chatted before she died in 1967. Fairmead Cottage was the cottage behind Fairmead "to be used occasionally for noisy patients".[79] He showed me "the brook without a bridge" that passes through what used to be a lily pond beyond his lawn and took me over the road to show me the site of the "chapel" and the humps of graves now under holly bushes and leaves. He showed me the extension at the back of his property that his family believe was built by Allen with money from Tennyson's 1840 investment – "built by Allen and Lord Tennyson", as he put it. (He told me he was cutting the grass round the stables at Beech Hill Park, Tennyson's estate, the day English Heritage demolished the enlarged house Tennyson had occupied.) In 2011 his father-in-law owned Lippitt's Hill Lodge, and he said that Clare lived at Lippitt's Hill Lodge but was often at Fairmead Cottage.

Fairmead Cottage (left) and Austin Darby (right) holding bar that enclosed inmates, with the extension Allen built with Tennyson's money behind his head.

His own father had told him that there were double hedges (mentioned by others) between three of the properties in Allen's asylum – Lippitt's Hill Lodge, Fairmead House and Fairmead Cottage – and that the inmates were allowed to walk between these two prickly (presumably hawthorn) hedges and would thus be kept apart from the local people of High Beach. When inmates died they were not buried in the small church then on the other side of Church Road, but in the grounds of Fairmead Cottage. He told me that he had on occasion inadvertently dug up bones, that there were plenty of dead inmates in his garden and that all his family had heard their voices very often and had learned to live with them. He was convinced that the energies of the inmates still haunted the cottage. He had often heard a whistling of 'Greensleeves', which was reputed to have been composed by Henry VIII. He wondered why he had a ghost going back that far. He said that Fairmead Cottage was built without foundations, that it was constructed so that the earth was directly beneath its floors, a feature of pre-Tudor houses. To some, the cottage's possibly pre-Tudor origins might account for such dislocated energy.

The noisy inmates of Fairmead Cottage were locked in their rooms. Their doors opened outwards, and a bar on the outside of each inmate's door was dropped down into a groove on the outside of the door-frame so that inmates could not leave their rooms. He showed me such a bar. In his father's time the internal walls were still painted brown to hide the discoloration of paint caused by oil-lamps, and he said that the whole place was as dark and depressing as the inmates' moods. He gave me a stark picture of inmates' lives: they were barred in at night, forced to walk between double hedges by day, a rule that did not apply to Clare, and buried in unconsecrated ground when they died. To the Victorians, no insane soul was fit to enter Heaven, and therefore had to be buried in unconsecrated ground.

Clare at St John's, Buckhurst Hill

Clare wrote about a visit to the church of St John's, Buckhurst Hill in his notebook in 1841: "Easter Sunday, 1841. Went in the morning to Buckhurst Hill Church and stood in the churchyard, when a very interesting boy came out while the organ was playing, dressed in a slop frock like a plough boy and seemingly about nine years of age. He was just like my son Bill when he was about the same age and as stout made. He had a serious, interesting face and looked as weary with the working days as a hard-working man. I was sorry I did not give him the last half-penny I had and ask him a few questions as to his age and name and parents, but perhaps I may see him again." (Bill, one of his seven children, had been born in 1828 and would then have been over 12.)

Clare escapes the asylum

Dr Allen was sure that a small annuity or pension would restore Clare to health. There was an appeal for £500 for him, but it fell well short. Clare became gloomy and in his mind went back to his first love, Mary Joyce. On 18 July 1841 he met "some gypsies, one of whom offered to assist in my escape from the madhouse by hiding me in his camp".[80]

Two days later Clare left the asylum and walked from High Beach to Northborough in Northamptonshire, a distance of eighty miles in three days, without a penny in his pocket. During this time he was so hungry that he ate grass. He arrived home convinced that Mary was his wife and still alive, and felt "homeless".

In August he wrote to Dr Allen, expressing a wish to be a hermit, and received a reply: "Whenever you like a little change you are welcome to come here and get Bed and Board for nothing, and be at liberty to come and go as you choose, provided you do nothing to make you unpleasant as a Visitor. You might lead the life of a Hermit as much as you choose, and I would contrive to get you some place for the purpose."[81] Four years later Allen was dead.

Clare in a Northamptonshire asylum

In December Clare was put in Northamptonshire County Asylum for having spent "years addicted to poetical prosings". Nearly twenty years later he wrote to James Hipkins on 8 March 1860: "Dear Sir, I am in a Mad house. I quite forget your Name or who you are. You must excuse me for I have nothing to commu[n]icate or tell of and why I am shut up. I dont know. I have nothing to say so I conclude Yours respectfully, John Clare."[82]

Edward Thomas

The poet Edward Thomas lived at High Beech Cottage, High Beach, down the road from the King's Oak, from October 1915 to 1917. His unit, the Essex Artists Rifles Corps, were in huts and under canvas during training on the site of the nearby cycle track (now the Field Centre), where Barnes Wallis, the inventor of the bouncing bomb that breached the dams of the Ruhr Valley during the Second World War, was in charge of the latrines (which overflowed on to the Epping New Road).

High Beech Cottage was one of the two keepers' cottages on the edge of Paul's Nursery, which was still operational until c.1920. Forest keeper Butt lived there, and the cottages appear on a map of c.1945 as

"Keeper's Cottage". The "Keeper's Cottage" had been designed by the architect Edmund Egan, who designed his keepers' cottages in pairs. Helen Thomas occupied the rear keeper's cottage. Thomas rented it so that his wife could be near his unit, and she described the cottage as inhospitable. Thomas would often have walked from the cycle track to High Beech Cottage. The two cottages were demolished in 1960 and replaced by a more modern building.[83]

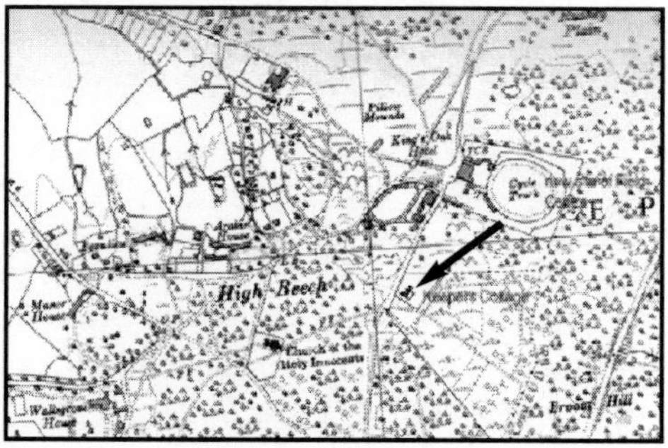

Forest keeper's cottage which Edward Thomas rented shown arrowed on map of High Beach c.1945 (top) and (bottom, at rear) in painting before it was demolished in 1960 (courtesy of Tricia Moxey).

The Owl, Edmund Blunden and Harry Roberts

Further along Church Road from Lippitt's Hill Lodge is The Owl, a public house which I visited before I left for Japan. In Japan I had lunch with the First-World-War poet Edmund Blunden, who said he would like to visit The Owl, which he associated with Clare, and Edward Thomas, his fellow First-World-War poet.

The Owl before demolition (see p.202).

I arranged to take Blunden to The Owl for lunch, and we fixed a day in August 1966 when we knew we would both be back in England. Unfortunately Blunden had to cancel at the last minute as he was unwell. I have a letter and a card from him about the arrangement. It is fortunate that he did cancel as that day (18 August) the double police murderer Harry Roberts, who had been living wild in Epping Forest while on the run, burst into The Owl and at knife point robbed everyone of their wallets, watches and jewellery. This ordeal would have had a detrimental effect on Blunden's fragile health.

Upshire

> "The general opinion, so unmistakingly evinced,
> that the Forest shall remain a forest and not be civilised
> into a park, is but the expression of a true instinct."
>
> Edward North Buxton, *Epping Forest*, p.21

Upshire is between Waltham Abbey and Epping. It includes the hamlets of Upshire, Copped Hall Green and Wood Green.

Warlies

The 18th-century Warlies Park House was named after Richard de Warley, who is recorded as owning land in Upshire in 1338. In the

17th century the house belonged to Samuel Foxe, son of the John Foxe who wrote *Foxe's Book of Martyrs*. In 1720 the estate was held by the Morgan family. Richard Morgan sculpted the landscape after the manner of "Capability" Brown and Humphry Repton and in accordance with the principles in Pope's epistle to Richard Boyle, Earl of Burlington: "In all, let Nature never be forgot..../Consult the genius of the place in all:/That tells the waters or to rise or fall." In 1848 the estate comprised 477 acres.

Warlies, Upshire.

In 1858 Warlies became the home of the Buxton family (the brewers of Truman, Hanbury and Buxton), who were involved in education and social reform. Sir Thomas Fowell Buxton succeeded Wilberforce as leader of the anti-slavery movement and fought for the Forest in the 1870s. His brother Edward North Buxton wrote *Epping Forest* and opposed the Maitlands' enclosures (see p.88).

Church of St Thomas

The church of St Thomas, Upshire was opened in 1902. It stands on higher ground than Waltham Abbey, on Horseshoe Hill, which is mentioned in 1414 as linking Copped Hall near Epping to the monastery at Waltham Abbey.[84] It was built on the initiative of Sir Thomas Fowell Buxton, who had built a local village school that he personally owned. After 1877 he had acted as Chairman of the Warlies School Board, and the first Christian services in the village had taken place at the Board school.

He, his wife Lady Victoria Buxton, an invalid, and his son Harold Buxton (later Bishop of Gibraltar) had evangelistic views and wanted a village church. Sir Thomas designated a sloping field on which it should stand and paid for architects to design the new church, which was modelled on the 15th-century Essex churches at Shenfield and

Theydon Garnon. His wife, Lady Victoria Buxton, laid the foundation stone in 1901. Sir Thomas told the villagers that the church and grounds would remain the property of himself and his successors but agreed that there should be a church council.[85]

This council ran the privately-owned church at a deficit, which was made up by a donation from his son Thomas Fowell Victor Buxton, known after Sir Thomas's death in 1915 as Sir Victor Buxton. Shocked by his death and faced with death-duties, in 1915 the Buxtons sold Warlies to Dr Barnado's Homes, who turned it into a school.

Lady Victoria died in 1917. Sir Victor was killed in a road accident in 1919 and succeeded by his son Sir Fowell, who transferred the ownership of the church to trustees and said he would be an ordinary member of the congregation. In 1923, still grappling with death-duties following his grandfather's and father's deaths, Sir Fowell announced that his family would no longer pay the chaplain's stipend or provide him with accommodation. Soon afterwards Sir Fowell moved to Woodredon. Warlies was now a Dr Barnado's home for girls, sixty of whom attended church services.[86]

Church of St Thomas, Upshire.

The church of St Thomas, Upshire was served from Waltham Holy Cross until 1956, when it was joined to High Beach parish, with the Rev. Joseph Crompton as the first vicar of the parish of High Beach and Upshire. High Beach was a remote and scattered rural village, whereas Upshire served new housing estates outside Waltham Abbey. Joseph Crompton tried to blend together the two dissimilar wings of this parish until his retirement in 1980. St Thomas' Upshire then reverted to being a daughter church of Waltham Holy Cross, while Holy Innocents, High Beach became the daughter church of St Mary's, Loughton.

In recent times, my wife and I have sometimes stopped at St

Thomas', Upshire for Sunday afternoon tea and home-made cake. We have sat in warm sunshine at tables in the churchyard, and I have reflected that we have occasionally celebrated family birthdays in the restaurant at the nearby Good Intent, and that Winston Churchill often visited Hubert and Lady Llewellyn Smith at their nearby home. He painted the row of 18th-century white weatherboarded cottages (which then had blue front doors) that sit on the brow of the hill towards Epping.

8

Epping and the Theydons

Epping

"And quiet Epping pleases well."
John Clare, 'Sighing for Retirement'

Epping is a market town surrounded by farmland, close to Epping Forest. In my youth I often wandered through the weekly market on a Monday. Cattle in pens made parking difficult. The cattle market dates back to 1253 – the day changed from Monday to Friday from 1575 to just after the First World War – but was discontinued in 1961.

Epping cattle market.

The Town of Eppinga

"Eppinga" began as scattered farms and a chapel on the edge of the Forest. The settlement was recorded in the 1086 *Domesday Book* and was in what is now Epping Upland.

Three manors were listed under Epping in the *Domesday Book.* The canons of Waltham Holy Cross held lands in the centre and south of the ancient parish of Epping before *Domesday Book*, and these lands formed the nucleus of the manor of Epping or Eppingbury, later known as Eppingbury and Priestbury. The two other manors were held by Count Alan (who owned part of Harlow hundred) and Ranulf, brother of Ilger, who held a manor in Nazeing and Epping that passed to the canons of Waltham Abbey in 1189. The canons of Waltham Abbey owned the manor of Epping from 1235.[1]

All Saints church, Epping Upland goes back to 1177, when Henry II gave it to the Augustinian canons of Waltham Holy Cross along with other property. The church has 13th-century features.

In the church there is a brass memorial to Thomas Palmer, Professor of Common Law at Cambridge, who lived at a moated farmhouse, Gills, less than a mile from the church and died in 1621. The arresting inscription in Latin on his memorial can be translated: "You who behold (this tomb) are dust destined to die. I am dust that is dead. Your fate is much worse than mine. The tainted world has you in its grasp, I am held by the starry heavens. Your life is death for you; my death is life for me. Learn how to die while you (yet) live, that you may be able to find life when you die. Thus will life not be burdensome, nor death sorrowful."[2]

The church was altered and restored (Pevsner says "badly over-restored") in the 18th and 19th centuries.

Epping Street

As the Forest was cleared, in the mid-12th century the settlement spread southwards to Epping Heath, later known as Epping Street. Henry VIII's grant of the right to hold a weekly market to Epping Heath in 1253 established a trading town.

Four roads converged at Epping Street in 1594: the roads from Harlow, Waltham Abbey (via Upshire), Stratford (via Chigwell, Abridge and Theydon Garnon) and Passingford Bridge.[3] There were no main roads through Loughton in 1594.

In the 17th, 18th and early 19th centuries there was development along the High Street and Hemnall Street. Epping was a stop for stage-coaches travelling from London to Norwich, Cambridge and Bury St Edmunds, and there were 26 coaching inns in the High Street, today's public houses The George and Dragon and The Black Lion being two of them. The coaches were superseded by a branch railway line from London in 1865.

St John's church, Epping was built in 1889, the year the 14th-century chapel of St John the Baptist, which belonged to Waltham Abbey until just before the Dissolution, was demolished. The new St John's was built in the style of a 14th-century church and became the parish church. A north aisle was added in 1908 and a tower was added in 1909 (paid for by Ernest James Wythes of Copped Hall). In 1912 the parish split into the parish of St John, Epping and the parish of All Saints, Epping Upland.

Copped Hall

I first visited Copped Hall in May 1984. It was a deserted ruin. I found the foundations of Heneage's Tudor hall overgrown with nettles and wrote 'Copped Hall' about a hall that had "copped it from time". (See pp.341-3.) I went again after it had been rescued in December 2001. I attended an exhibition of Eric Dawson's wartime artistic "cartoons" in the racquets court and then slipped away and toured the site. I wrote 'Copped Hall Revisited'. (See pp.343-5.)

Waltham Abbey holds Copped Hall, 1350-1537

We have seen that three manors were listed under Epping in the 1086 *Domesday Book*. Some of the estates listed in the *Domesday Book* as being in Waltham Holy Cross extended into Epping. The capital manor of Epping, known after the 12th century as Eppingbury and Priestbury, was in the possession of Waltham Abbey until the 16th century.

From 1150 to 1337 Copped Hall was held by the Fitzaucher family[4] in fee of (i.e. as a feudal benefice, or land held under the feudal system, from) Waltham Holy Cross (after 1184, Waltham Abbey) to be foresters in Waltham Forest. Their duty was to beat deer in the king's path when he hunted. The 12th-century medieval manor house of Copped Hall was 250 yards north-west of the present site in the parish of Waltham Holy Cross.[5]

Henry II (1154-89) granted two acres for the Hall and its surrounding garden. He owned Waltham lands in the vicinity of Copped Hall.

The name 'La Coppedehalle', or Copped Hall, was in use by 1258.[6] According to one view,[7] Copped Hall meant 'peaked hall', a reference to the two turrets or pinnacles on the medieval building which were coped with lead. Fuller associates its name with "two ancient and essential turrets".[8] According to another view[9] it meant 'the hall on the hill or the peak', *cop* or *copp* being Old English for the top or summit of a hill. According to yet another view '*cop*' referred to eminence or height, for Copped Hall stands 300 feet above sea level. Yet another view claims that it was named after 'Cobbing brook', the old name for Cobbin's brook, suggesting that it was really called 'Cobbin's Hall'.[10]

Copped Hall had grown to 60 acres by 1303 with 100 additional acres of arable land and 20 acres of meadow land.

During the Middle Ages Waltham Abbey enlarged its estates in Epping, Waltham and Nazeing. The manor of Epping belonged to Waltham Abbey in c.1235,[11] and in 1350 Waltham Abbey acquired Copped Hall.[12] In 1374 the abbot of Waltham Abbey extended the park by 120 acres towards Epping. The king stayed at Waltham and hunted and also sought spiritual refreshment, as did Richard II in 1381 at the end of the Peasants' Revolt. Now Copped Hall became a retreat or rest-house or place of retirement for the abbots of Waltham.[13]

Royal ownership, 1537-1564

In 1533 Thomas Cromwell recommended that Waltham Abbey should exchange Copped Hall park and the manor of Epping for Crown lands elsewhere.[14] With the Dissolution looming Abbot Fuller tried to save Waltham Abbey from the Dissolution by presenting Copped Hall to

Henry VIII.[15] Copped Hall was exchanged in 1536-7,[16] when it was stated that Henry VIII liked to stay there.[17] However, Epping manor remained with the Abbey until the Dissolution of 1540.

Henry VIII had been a frequent visitor to Waltham Abbey, and probably stayed at the monks' retreat at Copped Hall. We saw on p.72 that on 19 May 1536 he may have heard the cannon signalling the beheading of Anne Boleyn while sauntering in the yew walk there. Giving Waltham Abbey to Henry VIII of course did not save it, and the monastic buildings were pulled down soon after 1540.

Both Copped Hall, which had been owned by the Crown after 1536-7, and Epping manor were given to Mary by Edward VI, and she lived in her "poor howse at Copped Hall" while illegally saying Mass. In 1558 Mary annexed Epping and Copped Hall manors to the Duchy of Lancaster,[18] which already held Theydon Garnon. Copped Hall passed to Elizabeth I.

Sir Thomas Heneage holds Copped Hall

In 1564 Elizabeth I gave Copped Hall to Sir Thomas Heneage and his wife.[19] Between 1564 and 1568 Heneage enlarged the existing brick building that was probably L-shaped, to create a quadrangle (see p.73). The older part of the house was probably the entrance range and great hall, and a side wing with a chapel, and there was now a square

Sir Thomas Heneage (left) and site of Heneage's house (right).

courtyard enclosed on three sides by three-storeyed ranges, and on the fourth side by a single-storey loggia which led to the garden. In 1604 the Earl of Northumberland noted that the long gallery was 174 feet long, 24 feet wide and 23 feet high.[20] There were 103 rooms and hallways and 53 hearths.[21] (There were 67 rooms according to an inventory that was mentioned when I visited in 2001.)

Elizabeth I visited Sir Thomas Heneage and his wife at Copped Hall in 1568, and gave them Epping manor to hold of the Duchy of Lancaster in 1572.

Heneage's wife Anne died in 1593, and Sir Thomas remarried Mary, the Countess of Southampton, the mother of the 3rd Earl of Southampton, in 1594. (See pp.73-4.) He died in 1595.

Their heir was Elizabeth, Heneage's daughter by his first marriage. She married Sir Moyle Finch, who died in 1614. Elizabeth had been heard to say that she would give Copped Hall to anyone who could persuade James I to make her a Countess, the same rank as her stepmother. The ambitious Lionel Cranfield saw his opportunity. When he became Lord Treasurer, he secured Copped Hall by persuading James I to elevate Elizabeth to Countess in return for her surrender of Copped Hall to the Duke of Richmond, the King's relative. Cranfield then agreed to settle the Duke's £10,000 debts in return for Copped Hall. To raise the £10,000 he had to sell his own house, Pishiobury in Sawbridgeworth.

Cranfield settled the Duke's debts and in return received Copped Hall from the Duke of Richmond. Into the bargain he was himself made Earl of Middlesex in 1622. Elizabeth agreed to surrender Copped Hall without payment in 1623.[22] However, James went back on his word and made her Vicountess Maidstone instead of a Countess.

In 1628 Charles I made her Countess of Winchelsea, belatedly keeping his father's promise. Elizabeth still owned the manor of Epping, and built a new manor house, Winchelsea House, at the southern approach to Epping. She died in 1633. (In the early 18th century Winchelsea House's name changed to Epping Place. It became a coaching inn. In 1872 it was converted into two dwellings. The one nearer Epping was called Epping Place – a rebuilt house containing the basement of Elizabeth, Countess of Winchelsea's house – and the other was called Winchelsea House.)

The Epping manor was sold to William Grey, Lord Grey of Warke, in 1636. In due course the Grey family sold the Epping manor to Edward Conyers of Walthamstow, MP for East Grinstead, in 1734.[23]

Earls of Middlesex

Copped Hall had remained in the family of the Earls of Middlesex. Lionel Cranfield's public career came to an end when he was found to be guilty of corruption, stripped of all his offices and imprisoned in the Tower. In embittered retirement in Copped Hall he amassed a vast library, which he shared with Thomas Fuller, whose 1665 *History of Waltham Abbey* owed much to the books in the Copped-Hall library. He also entertained Charles II on several occasions after 1660.[24]

Copped Hall descended to Charles Sackville, Earl of Dorset and Middlesex, the Restoration poet, who often entertained Charles II and James II at Copped Hall and offered a night's refuge to Princess Anne as she fled on the arrival in London of William of Orange. Macaulay wrote, "On the following morning she set out to Epping Forest. In that wild tract Dorset [i.e. Sackville] possessed a venerable mansion, which has long since been destroyed. In his hospitable dwelling, the favourite resort of wits and poets, the fugitives made a short stay."[25] Sackville became a friend of William III and became Lord Chamberlain of the

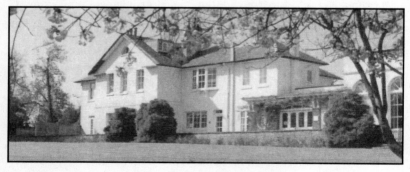

Coopersale Hall School.

Household. He gave Dryden a pension when Dryden ceased to be Poet Laureate.

In 1700 Sackville's extravagance led to his selling Copped Hall for £20,000 to Thomas Webster, later a baronet and MP for Colchester. In 1739 Webster sold it to Edward Conyers, lord of the Epping manor since 1734.

The Conyers

From now on Copped Hall passed down with the manor of Epping. It passed to Edward Conyers' son, John Conyers I, who demolished Heneage's Copped Hall and rebuilt a new Copped Hall from c.1748 to 1758 (no doubt applying the principles in Pope's epistle to Richard Boyle, Earl of Burlington to the grounds). He probably lived at Epping Place during the rebuilding. Copped Hall then passed to *his* son John Conyers II, who arranged for James Wyatt to redecorate the main rooms in 1775-7. He was host to Lord Palmerston on several occasions. In 1840 Copped Hall passed to his son Henry John, a keen huntsman. His estate now extended to 2,800 acres.

Henry John Conyers, as lord of the manor of Epping, was an ally of the enclosing Maitlands and among the first to enclose parts of Epping Forest. He approached his tenants and offered to lop firewood in the Forest on their behalf, and once this practice had continued for a few years the tenants discovered they had forfeited their right to lop as their own exercise of their right had lapsed.[26] The estate passed to his daughter Julia, who, on the death of her husband, Hon. Anthony John Ashley, in 1869 sold the estate – now over 4,113 acres – to George Wythes, the son of a Worcestershire farmer.

Ernest Wythes

George Wythes' son, George Edward Wythes lived at Copped Hall, and when George Edward died of a diffusive carbuncle in 1875,[27] George Wythes left his estate to his two grandsons. The elder grandson, George E. Wythes II had been dropped as an infant by a maid and crippled, and this misfortune reputedly led to his early death in 1887.[28] The younger grandson, Ernest James Wythes then inherited the entire estate.

Ernest J. Wythes enlarged Copped Hall in 1895. The centre of the west (garden) front now had four Ionic pilasters and an entablature, and the tympanum of the pediment was filled with sculpted figures, a sundial and a motto. The figures of Light and Shadow (*Lumen* and *Umbra*), motifs round the sundial which adorn the cover of my *A New Philosophy of Literature* (which presents the fundamental theme of world literature), date from this 1895 enlargement.

In the 1901 census Ernest Wythes was listed as living in Copped Hall with his wife, three small daughters, father-in-law, uncle-in-law and twenty-seven servants (twenty of whom were unmarried women).[29] The building work was finished in 1905. He laid out an elaborate Italian garden which was photographed for *Country Life* magazine.[30] The house was in its heyday from 1906 to 1917.

Copped Hall, (left) and Italian gardens, c.1909 (right).

Fire

Fire broke out at Copped Hall on Sunday 6 May 1917. It has often been said that the fire began when a hairclip was used as fuse-wire while the family were dressing for 8am Holy Communion at St John's church. It has also been said that the fire began as a result of an electrical fault, or a maid leaving a candle alight, or an abandoned cigarette-end.

At first the fire was ignored. Eventually the Epping fire brigade were called. The chief fire officer had to get out of bed and dress, harness the horses in the stables in Station Road, Epping, light the boiler and round up the only three men available to work the pumps and hoses, which were only capable of delivering one jet of water. All the doors and windows of Copped Hall had been opened to receive the water, and wind made the fire worse. In due course the Loughton fire brigade arrived.

Workers on the estate salvaged contents and put out some flames. Gardeners manned the hoses. Melted glass ran down the windows as if the house was crying. The rare books in the library were thrown into baskets, which were carried out. Ernest Wythes concentrated on clearing valuables from his wall safe. The fire burned until late on Monday evening.[31] By now Copped Hall had been gutted.

Copped Hall was never rebuilt. After the fire the Wythes family moved into Wood House, which had been built in 1898.[32] Churchill stayed there for two months in 1924, when he was fighting a by-election to be Epping's MP. The singer-songwriter Rod Stewart now owns Wood House and lives there.

Ernest Wythes served as a magistrate for fifty years. He was known as a man of few words. William Addison said of him: "He did much and said little. He must have been the quietest man ever to influence for so long for good the fortunes of Epping with so few words."[33] He died in 1949, leaving three daughters.

Rescue of Copped Hall

Vandals smashed up two Victorian wings of the gutted Copped Hall, and in the 1950s the Italian statuary, temples and ornamental stonework in the formal gardens were sold. The gates were sent to Washington. Lead statues went to an abbey in Anglesey and stone obelisks, balustrades and steps ended up in Bullwood Hall in Hockley, Essex (a women's prison until 2006 and now a men's prison).

The restoration of Copped Hall became urgent. Three developers put forward schemes that would have added unsuitable buildings had planning permission been granted. After I bought Coopersale Hall in 1988 I was asked by the then Chairman of the Council, Ann Miller, if I would consider taking on the restoration of Copped Hall and turn part of it into a school. To thwart plans to create a golf course and to protect Epping Forest, the Conservators of Epping Forest bought 785 acres of land surrounding the Copped-Hall estate.

In 1992 the Copped Hall Trust, a charitable trust whose leading light was the architect Alan Cox of Loughton, bought the ruin. Alan Cox found funding sources, and the first trustees – Alan Cox himself, Denys Favre, Lady Pat Gibberd, and Ann Bartlett – were committed to restoring Copped Hall to its 1758 glory at the end of John Conyers I's rebuilding, with the help of volunteers. The trustees sold parts of the stable block and outhouses to pay for interest on the two loans they had raised, and to mount events.

Stonework was returned to the gardens, and the West Essex Archaeological Group searched for the remains of the medieval and Elizabethan foundations.[34] The medieval hall was found to have been incorporated into Heneage's Tudor building. Roman pottery and medieval tiles were found. The trustees intend that Copped Hall should eventually be used for community purposes.

I returned to Copped Hall in May 2010 for an event to show recent restoration work. We drank wine in the saloon, which originally had a dance floor for balls and hosted social gatherings, and has a balcony overlooking the gardens under the pediment. I chatted to Alan Cox. He told me about the sundial on the pediment, and I wandered down steps into the grounds and looked back up and saw the Light and Shadow figures (*Lumen* and *Umbra*).

That evening I was not able to meet Denys Favre, then chairman of the trustees, later life president of the Copped Hall Trust, as he had gone to Oberammergau, though 95. However, I stood alongside him at John Silberrad's funeral in St John's church, Loughton on 26 September 2005. I had been a trustee of the Shakespearean Authorship Trust with Silberrad, an ex-barrister and son of Oswald Silberrad (a scientist who discovered that TNT could be used as a detonator), in whose house, Dryad's Hall, Woodbury Hill, Loughton, he had continued to live until his death. I had known him for more than fifty years.

At his funeral I found myself sharing the order of service with Denys Favre. A ladybird alighted on our order of service and then flew onto the floor of the aisle just as the pallbearers were loading the coffin onto their shoulders. "Get the ladybird out of the way," I whispered to Favre, who was between me and the aisle. He stepped out into the aisle, crouched (impressively nimbly for his years) and, with his back to the altar, made scooping movements with our order of service. The pallbearers were advancing on him with the coffin on their shoulders. Had they seen him? Would he be trampled underfoot? Would the pallbearers stumble, tilt the coffin and propel Silberrad into the aisle? "Quick," I urged. With one final scoop he swept the ladybird out of the aisle and towards my feet, stood up and returned to the safety of our pew as the coffin came by. That incident revealed a lot about the caring and determination of that first Copped Hall trustee.

Coopersale Hall School

I founded Coopersale Hall School, Epping (in the parish of Theydon Garnon) because the waiting-list for Oaklands School approached 150 and it dawned on my wife and me that it held a school-in-waiting. My mind was made up when a doctor approached me on the Oaklands steps soon after Easter 1988 and said, "I have two children on your waiting-list, I'm just the sort of parent you want, and all the local independent schools are full. Couldn't you start a new school somewhere nearby, teaching the same as you teach at Oaklands, and fill it from families like mine?"

Search for site

That summer I looked around for a suitable site. There were not many places available. I went to the 17th-century Coopersale House, for 200 years the home of the Archer family which produced a Governor of the Bank of England, Sir John Houblon. It had recently been the home of Rupert Murdoch, whose daughter Elizabeth had been in the Oaklands Kindergarten before we arrived. (The police had warned him of a plot to kidnap her, and Miss Lord had allowed a policeman to stand guard outside the Garden Room to make sure she would not be snatched during school hours.) The house had a shallow lake behind it, which would be a hazard for small children. I could not see where assemblies would be held, and I was not sure that I would be able to secure a change from residential to commercial use. I rejected Coopersale House.

In early May, on the Oaklands main field where a couple of dozen parents were rounding up children at the end of the School day, I was approached by Alan Fordham, an Oaklands parent and property developer, who said he had heard I was looking for a site on which to start a new school and would I consider his property, Coopersale Hall? I knew of the property but had been told it was not on the market. I visited him on 18 May and was immediately struck by the Hall's suitability.

Churchill

It was a Georgian building of the late 18th and early 19th centuries with (according to the Department of Environment's list of buildings of "architectural and/or historical interest") a "possible earlier core". Fordham told me it had been rebuilt in c.1776. It had an attached orangery that could be converted into an assembly hall capable of seating 250.

It had eight acres of lawns and gardens going back to the time of Charles Lyle, an England tennis player who in 1932 was created Baronet Lyle of Westbourne (and in 1945 Baron Lyle). Lyle, later president of the family firm of sugar refiners Tate & Lyle, had bought the house in 1912 and had opened the mature gardens to the public during the First World War. Some of the trees and shrubs had been supplied by Kew Gardens. Having been MP for Stratford from 1918 to 1922, Charles Lyle was MP for Epping from 1923 to 1924, when he made way for Churchill.

According to Fordham Coopersale Hall was the first house in Epping that Churchill came to in 1924. The transfer of the MP-ship from Lyle to Churchill via a by-election was agreed in Coopersale Hall's panelled dining-room (now the library), which has since acquired a wooden barley-twist fireplace, and Churchill then stayed for two months with Ernest Wythes in Wood House to fight the by-election.

Churchill in Epping, at by-election in 1924.

In 1940 Coopersale Hall was requisitioned from the Hudson family, who had succeeded Lord Lyle there, by the Canning Town Women's Settlement to provide a home for male civil defence wardens, which opened on 21 June 1942. The West Ham ARP (Air-Raid Protection) wardens could spend a fortnight resting and recovering their mental and physical health after their traumatic experience of nightly air raids.[35] Churchill sometimes left Downing Street, visited Blake Hall where the Battle of Britain was planned and North Weald where the pilots were based, and then spent a night at Coopersale Hall with the civil defence wardens, sleeping (according to an eyewitness who visited me) in the

Coopersale Hall before it became a school, front (left) and side (right).

upstairs bedroom with a pillared fireplace and a view of Epping from its window (now a classroom). In those pre-motorway days Coopersale Hall had 150 acres and stretched to the distant hills.

Decision to found a new school

Fordham told me all this while I sat with him in the dining-room. He reckoned I would be given planning change of use as the house overlooked the M11/M25 intersection and traffic noise when the wind blew towards the school had undermined its residential status. He said the property was not on the market but that he intended to move to Bishop's Stortford and would sell privately to me if I wanted it.

Holm-oak, Coopersale Hall.

I agreed to go ahead subject to my receiving planning permission. There was about to be a recession in the economy and opinion was divided as to whether I was brave or foolhardy, but I followed my instinct. I briefed the councillors and discovered there was a will to create a new independent school in Epping. On 3 November the Chairman of the Council, Ann Miller, rang me to say I had been granted planning permission. I told the Oaklands staff next day, after a fire-drill. There was applause.

Soon afterwards my wife and I were invited to dinner by Chigwell parents, and Dr Southern, Head Master of Bancroft's School, was present with his wife. As the six of us dined, Dr Southern said, "May I take this opportunity to tell you that we're opening a new Junior School, Bancroft's Prep, in September 1990." I said, "May I take this opportunity to tell you that we're opening a new Junior School in Epping, Coopersale Hall, in September 1989." There was a stunned silence.

History

I now researched the history of Coopersale Hall. I learned that it stands on land held by Ulmar before the Norman Conquest. Ulmar had been replaced in what is now Theydon Garnon by Eudo *dapifer* (Eudo the Steward), who is mentioned in the 1086 *Domesday Book*. When Eudo died in 1120 his honour (i.e. lordships, lands) escheated (i.e. reverted) to the Crown.[36]

Soon after his accession in 1154 Henry II gave part of Theydon Garnon – including, it is believed, the land of Coopersale Hall – to his chamberlain, Warin FitzGerold, who died in 1159. Warin FitzGerold was succeeded by his brother, whose descendant, Warin de Lisle, held Theydon Garnon in 1310. In 1368 the honour of Lisle reverted to the Crown and was merged in the Duchy of Lancaster.[37] From 1368 Coopersale Hall was part of the Duchy of Lancaster.

In 1558 the manors of Epping and Copped Hall were annexed by the Duchy of Lancaster, which also ran Theydon Garnon. The land round Copped Hall, including the land of Coopersale Hall, was all run by the Duchy of Lancaster. Coopersale Hall can therefore be said to have been part of the Copped Hall estate (the lands surrounding Copped Hall that passed to Elizabeth I in 1558). We have seen on p.215 that over 250 years earlier in 1303 the Copped Hall estate consisted of a park of 60 acres, 100 acres of arable land and 20 acres of meadow land.

In 1562 Elizabeth set up a commission to plant trees in "our park" at Copped Hall. The Commission were told to "repair yourselves as well to our Manor House of Copped Hall, being parcel of [i.e. part of] our Duchy of Lancaster in our County of Essex, as also to our park". Elizabeth I thought of Copped Hall as "a manor house" and it is likely that the park included Coopersale Hall, an earlier house whose pre-Elizabethan or Elizabethan dry cellars have survived beneath the c.1776 building. (These cellars were used as an air-raid shelter during the Second World War.)

Local tradition has it that the evergreen holm-oak at Coopersale Hall dates from c.1562, and that Queen Elizabeth I herself planted this tree, which has been called the "second most famous tree in Essex", after riding from Copped Hall. If scenes of *A Midsummer Night's Dream* were performed on different parts of the Copped Hall estate to celebrate Heneage's marriage in 1594 (see pp.73-4), it is possible that a scene was performed in the vicinity of Coopersale Hall's evergreen holm-oak.

The "earlier house" of Coopersale Hall may have been constructed in c.1540 as a home for the Chevely family. It was certainly in the ownership of the Chevelys in 1620 as an inventory (terrier) of the Theydon Garnon parsonage was signed as accurate by W. Chevely of Coopersale Hall in that year (according to an article on the early rectors of Theydon Garnon by Mrs. A.D. Bell which appeared in the *Essex Review* in 1926).

The present country house was built when in the ownership of Mrs. Chevely. *The Victoria History of the County of Essex* states that the hall, "which dates mainly from the 19th century, may incorporate parts of an earlier building".[38] Sales details that were produced by John D. Wood of Berkeley Square, London in 1988 for Fordham's sale while he negotiated with me speak of "an 18th-century country house and state: "The house dates from 1778 and is predominantly Georgian in style..., although the origins are Elizabethan and there is a tree in the Garden which is believed to have been planted by Elizabeth I." The 1778 date seems slightly late as Coopersale Hall is shown, and mentioned as the seat of Mrs. Ann Chevely, in the 1777 Chapman and André map, which was surveyed in 1774, see pp.x-xi. Fordham told me that the house had been dated, by an expert he called in, to c.1776, which fits better with the Chapman and André map. A picture from that time shows the gardener rolling the lawn near the evergreen holm-oak, which is half its size today.

Orchard Cottage, which was originally linked to Coopersale Hall at first-floor level by a bridge and is shown thus on the 1777 Chapman and André map, is thought to be c.1680 or older, and the 1988 sales details produced by a different agent stated that it was 300 years old and "set within Elizabethan grounds".

Several members of the Chevely family lived at Coopersale Hall. Jamineau Chevely proposed the building of an Essex ship (to which all the people of Essex would contribute wood, an idea which was rejected by The Board of Admiralty). He also proposed a reduction in the

National Debt, but is principally known for successfully resisting a fine of £500 on the people of Essex for not having two separate rooms for male and female invalids in its county jail, as required by a 1774 statute.

Coopersale Hall, seat of Mrs. Chevely, c.1776.

In 1790 Coopersale Hall was burgled. The burglars took old Roman coins, Venetian and other foreign medals, swords, plate, pewter dishes and silver spoons. The two thieves were caught, sentenced to death and eventually transported to Van Diemen's Land in 1793. The wife of one of them, Frances (or Fanny) Saville, was Jamineau Chevely's dairymaid. Bizarrely Chevely left £60, mourning clothes and a ring to her in a will he had made in 1791. In 1796 Fanny gave birth to a son who was baptised at All Saints' church, Theydon Garnon. The infant was named Jamineau Chevely after his father, who had had a child by the wife of one of the burglars. Jamineau Chevely senior died at the age of 65 on Christmas Eve 1796, soon after his son was born.[39]

In 1956 a bell-cote on the roof contained a bell dated 1816, and the entrance front was of this period. In 1815 Coopersale Hall was the home of John Worth, a prosperous East India merchant, who presumably installed both the front and the bell-cote.[40]

In the 1890s the artist Lucien Pissarro (who lived in Epping at 10 Hemnall Street from 1893 to 1897) painted several pictures of Coopersale Hall, which was then owned by Mr Edward Flux, a solicitor who gave his name to the private drive, Flux's Lane. Flux had been a senior partner in the London firm of E. Flux, Leadbitter & Neighbour of 144 Leadenhall Street. He had bought Coopersale Hall in 1891, and the 1901 census listed his servants: a groom, a kitchen-maid, a housemaid and a parlour-maid, all under the cook, Clara Ward. Flux sold the Hall to Lyle in 1912.

Founding

I was now committed to converting Coopersale Hall to a school that would take girls and boys to the age of eleven. I had decided that the first two classes would open in April 1989. I had to buy Coopersale Hall itself, Orchard Cottage next door and the 450-metre-long private drive, Flux's Lane (a single-width road with passing bays between an avenue of plane trees), from three different vendors, and put them together to reunify some of the Coopersale Hall estate to its former glory. Contracts for the purchase of Coopersale Hall and Orchard Cottage were exchanged towards the end of July 1988. The purchase of Coopersale Hall was completed on 17 November 1988, and the purchase of Orchard Cottage around the same time, soon after I received planning permission for a change from residential use. I now gave long interviews to the *West Essex Gazette* (now the *East London and West Essex Guardian*) and the *Epping and Harlow Star*. Contracts were exchanged

Nicholas Hagger at Coopersale Hall, November 1988.

on Flux's Lane on 9 December.

Oaklands had registered pupils for the new school. We were creating the structures of a new school from scratch without any existing staff. I chose a head, Frances Best, the Deputy Head of Woodford Green Preparatory School. I was determined to retain the country-house atmosphere. Responding to the newspaper articles, sixty teachers sent me CVs and applications, and we interviewed them all. I was impressed by the quality and enthusiasm of those who had come forward, and we selected twenty. I had run into Ann Miller, the Chairman of the Council, at an event at St Mary's, Loughton. She said, "I want to come and teach at your new School." At interview she agreed to take the top form.

I designed a new uniform in conjunction with the Head. I designed the School badge, which showed the evergreen holm-oak on the lawn that had reputedly been planted by Elizabeth I and was shown on the print of Mrs Chevely's c.1776 Coopersale Hall with a circular seat round the trunk. I installed new fire doors and improved the heating and furnishings of the building.

I set about widening the private road. I hired a JCB and a 10-ton lorry, and without any practical experience of road-making we doubled the width of the road. This involved creating an embankment down to the wooded stream at the bottom of the road. Quite simply, we changed the contours of Nature. I installed a septic tank the size of a small submarine with the help of the local fire brigade. This was a holding operation until I could install main drainage. The walled garden at the back of the School had head-high undergrowth, and this was cleared.

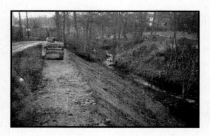

Creating an embankment to widen Flux's Lane.

We chose a new school secretary, a classmate at Woodford County High School of the Oaklands secretary (whose hair she had set on fire with a Bunsen burner in a science lesson). The Easter holidays were warm, and the front door was wide open as work inside the building progressed. A horse strayed up the road and wandered into the secretary's room, as if wanting to be registered.

We opened Coopersale Hall in April 1989 to 35 very young children. It was a golden summer and our charges spent mornings sitting at tables out on the terrace or on the lawn under the vast holm-oak. The Head was not starting full-time until September, and every morning I left Oaklands, drove through Epping Forest past Ambresbury Banks and visited the two class teachers and school secretary, and co-ordinated the building work. Elsewhere, particularly upstairs, conversion work proceeded apace.

Steve Norris

In May our new MP, Steve Norris, who had won the by-election caused by Sir John Biggs-Davison's death, came to look at the School for his son. He asked about Orchard Cottage, which was standing empty next to the school. I said it would contain classrooms in due course.

He said, "I'd like to live there."

I said, "Why don't you? We're not ready to use it yet. You can live there until we're ready."

Soon afterwards he arrived to open the Oaklands fête and immediately asked what rent I would charge. A thousand people were waiting for the fête to be declared open, and I suggested a rent seconds before introducing him.

He moved in as my tenant in September, and when people asked him where he was living he would say, "At Coopersale Hall. Haven't you heard about the new School that's just been created there?" Our new MP was a walking advertisement for the new School.

Organisation

During that summer I transformed the orangery, a large garage-like building that bizarrely had a polished dance floor, into the assembly hall and stage that is now part of the School. I designed the panelling. It was made and fitted by a carpenter I had taken on as a school keeper, a quiet, bespectacled fellow called John. There was a wooden Jacobean frieze round a small room at the end of the old building – grimacing figures and a Green Man – and we found more Jacobean carvings in the loft. I found a coat of arms among these that showed a knight's armorial helmet, and fixed it over the fireplace of the assembly hall, where it can still be seen.

Creating the panelling in the assembly hall, Coopersale Hall (left) and the coat of arms on the assembly hall's fireplace (right).

In July I organised the installation of new water and gas pipes up the 450-metre-long private drive. I bought the pipes and hired a JCB. Our in-house team of two dug a trench and lowered blue 125mm MDPE water-pipes in six-metre sections which they fused together with electrofusion equipment, and coiled yellow MDPE gas-pipes.

In the autumn term of 1989 we opened to 150 pupils with our new Head and staff overseeing a new intake. Each day I left Oaklands and sat with the Head and sorted out problems. I helped with anything of an insurance, legal or financial nature. I did the banking and returned to Oaklands for the afternoon.

Coopersale Hall School.

I set up a Parents' Association at the new School. There were no rules, and I found myself making the rules. I decreed that the chairman would be elected by a committee that would be composed of volunteers. The volunteers came forward. I designated three candidates, and the election duly happened. I was a benevolent dictator who set up new structures and then pulled away to allow them to run democratically. I had engaged Compass Services to run the lunches at both Schools, and so my wife and I had shed the weekly shopping we had done for the Oaklands lunches for seven years.

Steve Norris at Coopersale Hall School.

Tom Hammond

For a year I had tried to complete the purchase of the private drive from Tom Hammond, about whom the local residents had many stories.

He lived in a bungalow near the bottom of the drive. He elongated the transaction in an attempt to squeeze more money out of me. I would go and see him and negotiate. One evening I went to his bungalow and, finding the front door open, walked in. He was sitting with two men just inside the door, and the floor was covered with bundles of £20 notes. Keeping my eyes trained on his, I said, "Oh, I can see you're busy, I'll look in tomorrow."

For years Hammond had mysteriously stored goods in two corrugated-iron "barns" at the top of the road. At the bottom end of the drive a barrier, operated by Hammond's men, would go up and let lorries

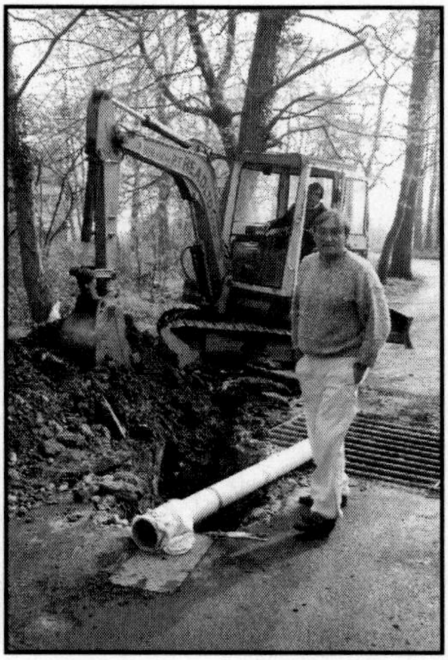

Work on private drive and Tom Hammond.

through late at night. I once looked in on one of them to meet Hammond, and found it stacked with chandeliers and lighting accessories. There was a shotgun propped in the corner.

The daily convoy of parents' cars driving up to the School at peak times soon flushed Hammond out. Now the "barns" stood empty. Having written in poems about Heracleitus's *panta rhei* ("everything is in a flux") I thought the name of the road had a metaphysical significance. I was there to impose order on the chaotic flux of Flux's Lane.

In January 1990 our tenants the Norrises were burgled. They lost a substantial amount of jewellery. Steve Norris rang me and asked if I could do anything to recover it. I visited Hammond in his bungalow and asked him to put word out in the East End that the jewellery should be returned as it was against our local interests to alienate our MP.

With an elaborate shrug, both hands fully extended, Hammond protested, "You've come to the wrong man, you might as well ask that tree." Soon afterwards, I received a postcard from the Seychelles festooned with stamps of fish and animals that left a tiny space for a message. Hammond's girlfriend wrote that she and Tom were enjoying a fortnight's break.

Extension

At Christmas we had put on a nativity play, which was attended by the new Chairman of the Council and Mayor of the Town Council. I had told them I was putting in a planning application to build a six-classroom extension, including a kitchen, and I had taken them to an exhibition of the plans in the staff room. In March I received planning

Back half of extension, Coopersale Hall.

permission to build six classrooms.

In the Easter holidays concrete was pumped into the footings, and building began. Our in-house team worked on the extension for two years to spread the cost. We built four classrooms and a new kitchen and toilets, and left the last two classrooms until 1996-7.

Throughout 1990-2 the recession deepened and I seemed to be the only person building in Epping. The Building Regulations inspector visited me every week to see the progress of the work. He told me, "I say in the office, thank goodness for Mr Hagger. If it weren't for him I'd have nowhere to visit."

We built slowly but steadily, and at the end of the recession we had a new block of classrooms and a brand-new kitchen.

Official opening by Lord Tebbit

The official opening of Coopersale Hall was performed by Norman (later Lord) Tebbit, who had been Secretary of State for both Employment and Trade and Industry, and Chairman of the Conservative Party in Thatcher's government. He had been blown up by the 1986 Brighton bomb, and security had to be tight.

Before the event a chief inspector of police visited me and walked the terrain. He said there would be a policeman at the bottom of the private drive and a helicopter hovering at the back. He said, "You've got a certain person near here. I knew him years ago at Wickford when he was with a gang of robbers. He was the safe man. Our security will take care of him."

Tebbit came on 9 July 1990. He got out of his car, a gentle man, and I showed him round the School together with the Chairman of the Council and his wife, the mayor of Epping, our resident MP Steve Norris (who had arranged for Tebbit to come) and his wife, my wife and the Head. (The Chairman of the Council told me that a neighbour of ours had been recognised as the masked leader of a gang of four who had taken £100,000 from a jewellers in Ilford. The raid had destroyed the shopowner's life as he was not insured and the loss caused his marriage to break up.)

We went out onto the terrace where guests were seated on either side of our table and the children and parents were on the lawn. A helicopter hovered at a discreet distance. I spoke for ten minutes about the evolution of the School and Tebbit's local connections. I dwelt on the link between Coopersale Hall and four 20th-century MPs: Lord Lyle, Churchill, Norris and now Tebbit. Tebbit spoke and then drew back two curtains to unveil a brass plaque. We went into the assembly hall for iced cake. Tebbit was applauded when it was time for him to leave.

Nicholas Hagger introducing Lord Tebbit at the formal opening of Coopersale Hall (left) and listening to Lord Tebbit speaking (right).

In the study I told him (perhaps prophetically) that schools like Coopersale Hall were the way forward. On 9 July, that very morning, Tebbit had been quoted in the *Epping and Harlow Star* as being against maintained schools (i.e. schools supported by public funds) opting out of local government control and becoming grant-maintained schools (i.e. schools funded directly from central government). Soon afterwards he was in favour of schools opting out of local government control, a view that must have been strengthened by the example of Coopersale Hall, which anticipated the growth of academies and free schools.

David Seaman

I first met David Seaman, the Arsenal and England goalkeeper, when he won the fathers' race at Sports Day. He was tall and spoke with a Rotherham accent, and he smiled a lot as he chatted. He opened the next fête for me, wearing a sweatshirt and shorts and sporting a moustache. I introduced him and after he had spoken a lengthy queue of small boys formed to obtain his autograph. Enrolments increased as Coopersale Hall was now associated with successful footballers.

Hammond, who had at last completed the sale of the private drive to me, looked in and asked me to introduce him as a farmer. I took him to PC Sims, who was standing by his police car, introduced him as a farmer and left them together.

Nicholas Hagger introducing David Seaman at a Coopersale Hall fête.

By the summer of 1991 the extension had made substantial progress. I widened the driveway and forecourt that led to the front door. On a Saturday morning I took delivery of six lorry-loads of crushed concrete, signed the dockets and directed the spreading of it by our in-house team.

Soon afterwards, in the autumn of 1991, Seaman came and played football with the Coopersale Hall School boys. We played on the field at the bottom of Flux's Lane, the touch-line lined by parents. I put on a track suit and we formed two sides: Seaman, me and ten boys; and the football coach and his assistant and another ten boys.

Thanks to the two energetic coaches, at half-time the other side were winning 5-2. I said to Seaman, "You may be an international, but we're being trounced by nine- and ten-year-olds. I'm going to have to put the ball in the air to keep our honour up. We'll go over the top. Get ready for some headers." I crossed four balls and Seaman headed four goals. The other side equalised in the last minute, and the match ended 6-6. The story was carried on the front page of next week's *West Essex Gazette*, and applications for the School rose dramatically.

Growth

From these beginnings Coopersale Hall grew steadily until it had in excess of 250 pupils. I met the staff the day before the beginning of each term, just as I did at Oaklands. Year by year the standards went up, and every three or four years there was an inspection. Local dignitaries came to our Prize Days, which were held in the assembly hall in the early days – they are now held in a marquee in the grounds – and among them for a few years was Eric Dawson, the artist who had exhibited his wartime "cartoons" at Copped Hall. One year Tony Little, Headmaster of Chigwell and later Head Master of Eton, gave out the prizes.

We fell into a pattern. Each year in the autumn term there was a fireworks night at the School. In the summer term there was a fête and Sports Day. There were always showbiz and sports stars among the parents: Bradley Walsh, Ronnie O'Sullivan, David Sullivan and several Tottenham and West Ham footballers.

In 1995 I bought the sloping field next to the school gates from Hammond, which meant more nightmare negotiations. I turned it into a football field. We levelled a pitch by digging into the slope and creating a grassy bank at the top. Soon afterwards, in 1996, I believe, we converted the garage block into two classrooms, and in c.2000 we added an upper floor to the squash court, turned the lower part of the squash court into a studio and installed two first-floor classrooms that linked by a corridor to Orchard Cottage, which, following the departure of the Norrises, had now been converted into four classrooms.

Travellers

In the summer holidays of 2004 we were invaded by gypsies who camped below our football field, on a strip that had until recently been owned by Hammond. They came on a Friday evening in the summer holidays. Residents alerted me to their arrival, and we all turned out to block the road and turn back the lorries carrying concrete. I was rung again and told that two of them were seen climbing into the school grounds.

On the Saturday morning I bought a sturdy chain and tied it to two trees at the bottom of the private road. I told the police that my road was a no-go area, and that we were controlling access. On the Sunday the entire Council together with the new MP, Eleanor Laing, paid a visit to inspect. Residents kept a vigil in shifts.

Eventually I decided to go in and confront the travellers. As I pushed open the high gate, a little girl ran to her father and handed him a knife with a long blade, which he took and held. "We own this field," he said, holding the knife by his side with the blade up.

"I'm afraid you made a bad decision," I said. "You see, unfortunately you haven't got access onto the road. If you want to come and go, you'll need a helicopter."

"But I haven't missed Mass for thirty years," one of the travellers piped up.

"Well, you will this Sunday," I said. "You'll be trespassing if you go to Mass."

I left relieved as the high gate shut behind me.

The residents then conferred in the road. One was sure that Hammond had sold them the field. One of the residents knew a fellow who was big in the East End and had a fearsome gang of Bosnians. There were negotiations. The big fellow swaggered into the travellers and said with great authority, "These people are *friends* of mine."

"Oh, I'm sorry," one of the travellers said, "I didn't know."

An arrangement was made for them to sell the field to a resident and they were gone by Wednesday afternoon. The resident duly bought the field, and Coopersale Hall returned to normality before the autumn term.

Before the arrival of the gypsies Hammond had been knee-capped with a sledge-hammer at the front door of his bungalow. He sold his bungalow and moved to a flat, where I visited him. A young East-European girl let me in and I commiserated with him about his knees. He asked me, "Why would anyone want to do that to me?"

He sat in his dressing-gown and told me he had throat cancer. He was clearly unwell, a shadow of his former self. Soon afterwards I heard that he had died in 2004 at the age of 70.

There was a high-profile funeral at St John's church Epping involving horse-drawn carriages. Mourners from the East End were dressed in black and white. He was buried in the new part of the Epping Cemetery, Bury Lane.

There were now no incidents involving Flux's Lane and life at Coopersale Hall was uneventful.

Matthew Hagger

We grew the School through three longish Headships: we changed Heads in 1997, 2006 and 2011. (The second Head had left in 2002 and returned in 2003.)

My son Matthew gradually replaced me from 2001 onwards, as he did at Oaklands, and I became more of a figurehead, appearing at Prize Days, at post-inspection celebratory dinners held in an Epping restaurant and at key events. I kept in touch with the School and joined the staff for some of their end-of-term lunches. It was increasingly my son Matthew who developed the School from the foundations I laid between 1988 and 2001.

In November 2007 the tennis-court was Astroturfed and opened as a football area. Ray Clemence, the former Spurs and England goalkeeper and later goalkeeping coach to the England football team, arrived to perform the opening ceremony. Our son Matthew presided over the occasion.

My wife and I were actually off Antarctica at the time, on the *Minerva*, which had been renamed *Explorer II*. That day we were woken by an announcement: "Good morning, ladies and gentlemen. Sadly, I have to tell you that our sister ship *Explorer I* has sunk in the Antarctic Sound. Our thoughts go out to the passengers and crew." Another announcement soon confirmed that the passengers and crew were safe, although their luggage was at the bottom of the sea along with their ship.

Meanwhile, back in England BBC television reported that "the *Explorer*" had sunk and mistakenly showed a picture of our ship, *Explorer II*. Matthew was rung on his mobile with news of this while he was sitting in the Head's office with Ray Clemence shortly before the opening ceremony. With the admirable self-control of a true professional who understands that the show has to go on he glanced at the message, that his parents seemed to have sunk in the Antarctic Sound, asked one of the office staff to find out as much information as possible and, resolving to pick up the pieces after the event, walked down to the Astroturf pitches with Clemence and made his speech.

20th anniversary

In 2009 we held a gathering to mark the twentieth anniversary of the founding of Coopersale Hall School. All past pupils were invited to a lunch in a marquee in the grounds, and two retired Heads and many past teachers attended along with the present staff. I addressed the guests about the founding of the School.

Quality

In 2011 there was another inspection and we had the best result we had ever achieved: many "outstandings" and "excellents". I attended Prize Day, which was held in a marquee, and was impressed at the homely, family relationship the pupils had with the staff. I studied the leavers' class in some detail. We had turned out fine pupils who were in demand at the leading local independent secondary schools.

New block

Once again we had applied for planning permission to build a five-classroom extension. We were given permission to build five classrooms and once again built through a recession. We built one classroom in 2010 as infill in the 1996-7 classrooms, and a block of the other four, including a lift, in 2011. We completed the building and widened the playground in the summer of 2011.

Coopersale Hall School's new block, with Matthew Hagger.

Rod Stewart, now a Coopersale Hall parent, began a three-month run of shows in Las Vegas in 2011. His family went with him. He was keen that his young son, who had been a pupil at the School, should not fall behind in his British education during his three months in the US, and Matthew arranged for him to have a video-link to lessons at the School 5,000 miles away: to download classwork, discuss it with the teacher and have it marked. This pioneering arrangement was widely reported in the national press and indicated how far the School had come since those early days when we were converting a country house into a new school.

Matthew Hagger outside Coopersale Hall School's new block.

On 30 November 2011 our new block of four classrooms was formally opened by Rod Stewart and Penny Lancaster, whose son, back from Las Vegas, resumed his place in the classroom to which he had been video-linked.

Coopersale Hall School was now the largest independent school of its kind to be founded in West Essex since the Second World War.

The Theydons

"The burial place of the Chevely family."

Inscription on a tomb in All Saints', Theydon Garnon churchyard, referring to the Chevelys of Coopersale Hall.

Theydon Garnon

From 1989, for a few years, Coopersale Hall's carol service was held at All Saints' church, Theydon Garnon, which is tucked away near the M25 between Theydon Bois and Abridge.

Theydon (*thaec dean*, 'thatch-reed valley' – see p.44) was split into three parishes: Theydon Bois, Theydon Garnon and Theydon Mount. The parish of Theydon Garnon stretches from Epping to Abridge and includes Coopersale Hall and Coopersale House. We have seen (on pp.55 and 226-7) that Ulmar held this land in pre-Norman times.

Robert de Gernon (a nickname meaning 'of the moustache') came from Normandy with William the Conqueror in 1066 and received gifts of land in Essex, but not Theydon Garnon. The Gernon family received Theydon Garnon in the reign of Henry III (1216-72), when Sir William Gernon married Beatrix, daughter of Henry de Taydon.

In the past Theydon Garnon was near important roads: the Roman road from Abridge, and the medieval road from London to Epping via Abridge. The bridge at Abridge had been the most important crossing of the River Roding for hundreds of years and had been a magnet for the historic core of the village, which clustered round it (such as the medieval buildings that now form the Roding restaurant).

Hugh Gernoun of Theydon Garnon (Gernoun) was granted a charter by Edward I in 1305 to hold a market every Thursday and a fair lasting three days every year. A copy of the charter hangs inside All Saints' church, as does a royal coat of arms showing a lion (England/Wales) and unicorn (Scotland). Royal arms were placed in churches between 1547 and 1553, just after the death of Henry VIII, to remind parishioners that, following the Reformation, the monarch was now the earthly Head of the Church of England. These arms were painted by a

Chigwell artist in 1762, and recognised George III as Head of the Church of England.

Theydon Bois

Theydon Bois, which grew up round the Green, had a different provenance. The name (pronounced 'boys') derives from Simon de Bois, who came from Normandy with William the Conqueror. His descendants held the manor in the 12th and 13th centuries. Due to the nearness of the Forest the view is still expressed that the name came from the French 'wood'.

One of Simon's descendants, also called Simon de Bois (or Boyes) of Theydon Garnon, so impressed Henry V (1413-22) with his skill in an archery contest at Havering-atte-Bower that he was commanded by the king to change his name to Archer.[41] Henry's command began the Archer branch of the de Bois family that in 1770 married into the Houblon family who lived at Coopersale House.

James Houblon had built the north aisle in All Saints' church in 1644, and his son Sir John Houblon was the first Governor of the Bank of England. In 1696 Sir John lent William III £200,000 to fight the war against Louis XIV.[42]

All Saints' church, Theydon Garnon

All Saints' church, Theydon Garnon was dated to the 13th century by Cecil Hewett, an authority on the dating of timber buildings from carpenters' joints. The original roof was of scissor-based couples,

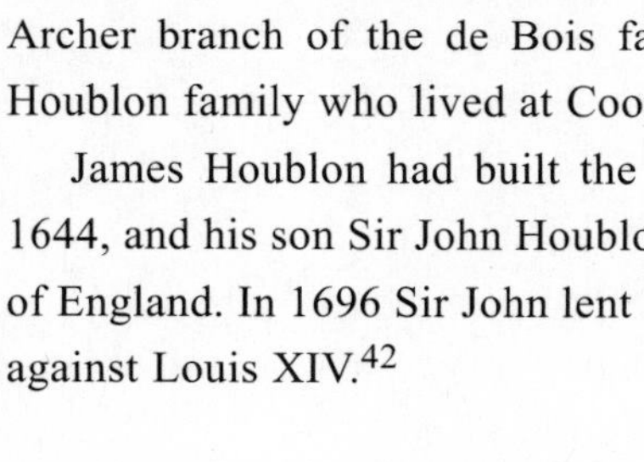

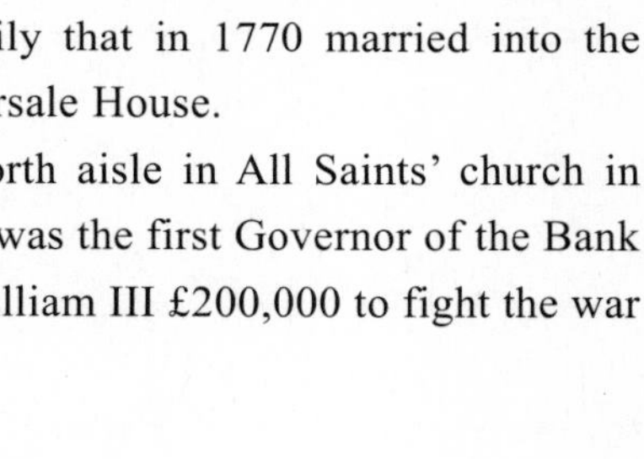

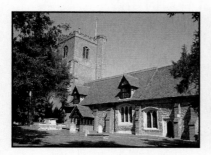

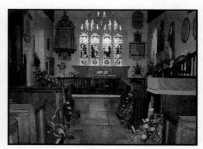

Theydon Garnon church outside (left), and inside (right).

notch-lapped, c.1200-50. The brick west tower is dated by an inscription on the south side, 1520.[43]

Sundial

On the outside, on the buttress over the south porch, are two sets of scratches. The lower set is a c.1520 sundial on a brick panel. It is under a dripstone to protect it from rain. Although clocks had been in use for 200 years, they were expensive and in the 16th century sundials were still used to tell time.

Mass marker

The upper set of scratches on stone – on the left side only and with a hole which held a metal rod – are the remains of a mass marker dating to c.1300. Mass markers used the shadow thrown by the sun to tell the specific times of day when mass was being celebrated. The sanctus bell was rung when the sun's shadow reached a particular scratch.[44]

Carol services

When I arrived for the carol services, I was always firmly escorted by a churchwarden or the rector to a seat in the 13th-century chancel. I sat on my own in a choir seat up near the altar, near the 15th-century stained glass of the three wise men visiting the infant Jesus. I faced the pulpit, with the deafening organ behind me. The pupils of the School and their parents sat on either side of the nave aisle and on the north side of the north aisle.

If I looked to my right and then sat forward I could the see the hatchments, an abbreviation of 'achievements'. Hatchments were paintings showing the achievements of local people of importance as coats of arms. They were carried in their funeral processions and hung outside their houses for several months, and were then placed in the church.

All Saints' church, Theydon Garnon, had always been Coopersale Hall's parish church, and in past times the owners of Coopersale Hall walked to the church for the Sunday-morning service. The M25 is now between the two, and has made such a walk impossible. But the churchyard bears witness to the attendance of the owners of Coopersale Hall. Between the south porch and the church gate is a large vault with a stone slab on top, on which is written "The burial place of the Chevely family".

Eventually the annual carol service was moved to Coopersale Hall's assembly hall, where it was easier to accommodate all children and parents and give everyone a good view of the nativity play. The rector (later, clergyman) now came to Coopersale Hall. By then the special link between Coopersale Hall and Theydon Garnon church had been revived.

Garnish Hall

The manor house of the parish of Theydon Garnon was the present Garnish Hall. It was built on the site of the Gernon family residence

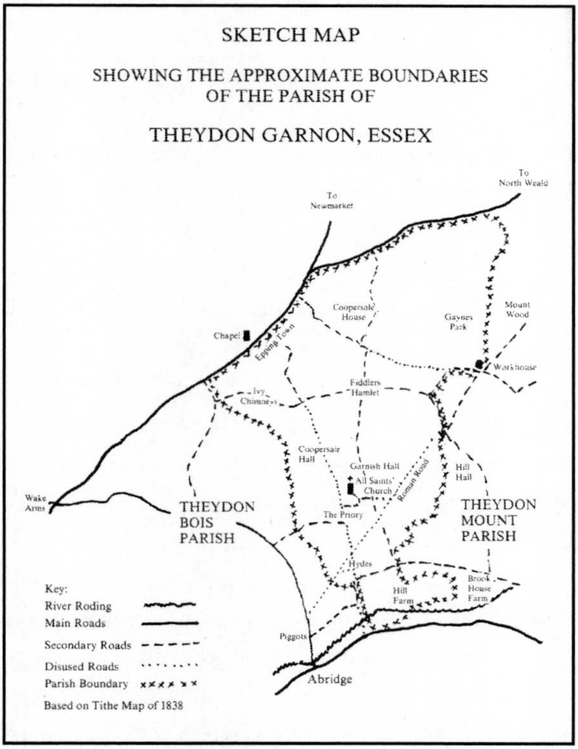

Map of Theydon Garnon parish.

(called Gernons Hall) in 1572. Over time, the name Gernon became Garnon and also Garnish. Elizabeth I visited the newly-built Hall during her royal progress in 1572, ten years after planting the Copped Hall park and possibly the evergreen holm-oak at Coopersale Hall. She probably visited All Saints' church and may also have been escorted to the seat of honour up near the altar in the 13th-century chancel where I sat.

Garnish Hall is now owned by Di Collins, the Leader of Epping Forest District Council from 2006 to 2011, who came to many of the Coopersale Hall prize days (at one of which, at least, Eleanor Laing MP made a speech and gave out the prizes). I visited her at Garnish Hall in February 1992 (and spoke at some length to Tebbit, who was a fellow guest). It was a timbered house that had been rebuilt c.1750, and there was a leaping log fire in the inglenook of the beamed main room. I returned in May 2006 for an event and met David Cameron, later Prime Minister, in a marquee on her lawn.

Theydon Mount

The parish of Theydon Mount adjoins the parish of Theydon Garnon, and Hill Hall is as near to Garnish Hall as Coopersale Hall.

Hill Hall

I first visited Hill Hall in 1996 when it was a burnt-out ruin. (It had been a women's prison that for a few weeks, when Holloway had to be vacated, incarcerated Christine Keeler, and was destroyed by fire in 1969.) I approached the Georgian façade and pediment, and wandered round the derelict rooms.

I looked at the wall-paintings: in the West Room, scenes from Hezekiah's life, and in the East Room, scenes of Cupid and Psyche in the style of tapestry hangings with fruit-and-foliage borders based on designs by Raphael. The Cupid-and-Psyche scenes follow Italian engravings by Augustino Veneziano: the departure of Psyche's sisters on the east wall, and Cupid and Psyche on the south wall. The theme of Cupid and Psyche is in Shakespeare's last two sonnets, a detail that has not escaped Oxfordians who believe that Edward de Vere – who was tutored at Hill Hall (see below) – was Shakespeare.

I went again in 2001 when Hill Hall was being converted into apartments. English Heritage had restored the wall-paintings, the Great Hall and the courtyard.

Hill Hall, c.1910.

Sir Thomas Smith

Hill Hall was rebuilt during the 1550s by Sir Thomas Smith, who completed the main part of the project in 1557 as we saw on p.74. Smith was Vice-Chancellor of Cambridge University and had gone into politics and served Protector Somerset. He had studied in Padua in 1540-2, and led an architectural group that was inspired by the Renaissance style, and in particular by France rather than Italy.

A Protestant, he was provost (i.e. Chairman of the Governing Body) of Eton from 1547 to 1554. He had fallen from favour with the fall of Somerset and the accession of Mary in 1553, and was forced to retire from his public positions to Hill Hall, where he pressed on with the restoration work. The reign of Mary was a dangerous time, and he was relieved to survive Mary's burnings of Protestants. He took as his crest a salamander in flames. The salamander was a mythical creature that was immune from fire, and the lizard-like salamander of the genus *Salamandra* was thought to be actually able to endure flames.

He had just ceased to be provost of Eton in 1554 when the young Edward de Vere was placed in his household, having been sent away by his father to what was perceived to be the relative safety of Smith's household during Mary's burnings. Smith had a vast library. Fifteen years later, in 1569, it was known to consist of 350 books, 300 of which were in Latin and Greek. He taught the young de Vere literature, art, poetry, grammar, history, legal jargon and the language of court and society: a Renaissance education. He spent time, presumably with de Vere, walking and hunting. De Vere left Hill Hall to become Lord Burghley's ward on the death of his father in 1562. Oxfordians, who regard Shakespeare as Edward de Vere, the Earl of Oxford, locate Shakespeare's early education at Hill Hall under Sir Thomas Smith.

In 1562 Sir Thomas Smith became Ambassador to France and in 1572 Secretary of State to Elizabeth I. In the mid-1570s he fell ill with what seems to have been a form of throat cancer, and the wall-paintings are thought to date from this time. King Hezekiah fell ill and pleaded with God to save him, and as a result his life was extended. Smith died in 1577, still in the process of improving Hill Hall.

Hill Hall in the 20th century

Hill Hall was given its 18th-century façade and pediment in 1713. It remained in the Smith family until the 20th century, but the wall-paintings were panelled over and were not exposed again until 1934. In 1938 three fragments of the Cupid-and-Psyche cycle were removed to the Victoria and Albert museum.

Mrs. Charles Hunter became tenant of Hill Hall and she commissioned Reginald Plomfield to remodel it in 1909-12. A society hostess, she invited such cultural figures as Rodin, the Sitwells and Henry James to Hill Hall. Hill Hall was sold to her in 1923, but she had to sell the Hall in 1925.

There were two more owners before it became an institution. During the war it was a maternity home, a billet for RAF officers, and an agricultural camp. It housed soldiers, and prisoners-of-war, and eventually became a women's open prison in 1952.

Church of St Michael, Theydon Mount

Near Hill Hall is the church of St Michael, Theydon Mount. The first church was at least 13th-century – the register of Rectors goes back to 1238 – and was destroyed by lightning in 1611. The present church was rebuilt in 1614 by Sir Thomas Smith's nephew.

Smith's tomb

I visited the altar tomb of Sir Thomas Smith in the chancel, on the south side of the sanctuary. His seven children kneel at a prayer-desk in front of the tomb. Smith lies stiffly reclining, with his head propped up on an elbow and hand, wearing a garter mantle. Round the arch under which he lies is written: "What ye Earth or Sea or Skies conteyne, what Creatures in them be, My Mynde did seeke to knowe, my Soule the Heavens continually." He was an early Metaphysical in distinguishing the mind's quest (the Earth) and the soul's quest (the Heavens). The salamander living in flames, symbolising his relief at surviving Mary's burnings, is on his tomb.

Sir Thomas Smith.

I looked at his reclining face and later compared it to the face in a large picture of him at Spains Hall, Finchingfield, the home of Sir John Ruggles-Brice, which I saw when I visited him in 2001. (See p.164.) The stained glass on the church's east window shows St Michael's war in Heaven against Lucifer, later called Satan, a theme in my two poetic epics.

Thanks to the Forest, Epping and the Theydons have retained some semblance of a rural setting, as (to a lesser degree) has Chingford, which was for centuries within the border of west Essex but is now on the edge of east London.

9

Chingford Plain

"I go too seldom to Chingford, where my books lie idle: and when I go have many things to look after."

T.E. Lawrence, letter to A.E. Chambers,
10 March 1923

The history of Chingford

Chingford (the Anglo-Saxon *cegingaford*,[1] 'the dwellers by the stumpy ford', Norman Cing(h)efort – King's Ford, see pp.44 and 366 – and medieval *Chingelford*, 'shingly ford', c.1242, see p.44) was originally a Saxon hamlet beside the River Lea. By the time of the Norman Conquest the parish of Chingford – bounded by the Lea on the west; by the Ching, scarcely more than a brook, on the east; by Walthamstow on the south; and by Chingford Plain on the north – comprised two manors: Chingford St Paul's (which was held by the Dean and Chapter of St Paul's Cathedral for 500 years) in the north-west; and Chingford Earls (originally named after the Earl of Essex, Henry Bouchier, who briefly owned it from some time after 1461 until 1483) in the south-east.[2]

Both manors passed to Henry VIII in 1544. In 1551 the fourteen-year-old Edward VI granted them both to Lord Darcy of St Osyth Priory. In 1552 Lord Darcy gave Chingford back to the king, who gave it to Mary. In 1554 Mary gave Chingford manor to Susan Tongue, one of the widowed ladies of her bedchamber.

Chingford Earls was later owned by the Boothby family from 1608 to 1774 and then by the Heathcote family until 1940. In 1839, the 1608 manor house was demolished and replaced by Friday Hill House, the manor house of the Heathcote family. After the Second World War the estate was bought by the London County Council and turned into a housing estate. The house remains and is used for Adult and Community Education by the London Borough of Waltham Forest.

Railway

Queen Victoria leaving Chingford station, 1882.

The rural isolation of Chingford ended with the advent of the railway in 1873, and a town grew up along Station Road. In 1882 Queen Victoria arrived at Chingford station to declare the Forest open to the people, as we saw on p.93. In the following years East-Enders came to the Forest at weekends and on Bank Holidays. Chingford ceased to be two manors surrounded by scattered farms and became the towns of North and South Chingford, which merged into one town that included Chingford Mount.

T.E. Lawrence in Chingford

Behind the town was Pole Hill, where T.E. Lawrence lived briefly. At Jesus College, Oxford he had become friendly with Vyvyan Richards, a fellow undergraduate who went to teach at Bancroft's School, Woodford Green in 1909. They used to camp under canvas on Pole Hill, and in 1912 Richards proposed that they should build a permanent hut there. A hut was built.

The day Lawrence left the army in 1919 he bought five acres of Pole Hill, and increased his holding to sixteen acres in the following years. In 1921 a grass fire destroyed the hut Richards had built – Lawrence wrote from Cairo to Eric Kennington on 1 October 1921, "My house in Epping has been burnt down" – and a replacement was built in the same year with help from Bancroft's boys.

Lawrence planned to retire from public life, set up a private press in the hut and print *Seven Pillars of Wisdom*. However, later that year Lawrence enlisted in the RAF under the name of Shaw, and in 1922 Richards left Bancroft's to live in South Wales. In 1923 Lawrence left the RAF and the following year went to live in Clouds Hill, a cottage at Moreton, Dorset. The hut on Pole Hill was used by Scouts and slowly fell into disrepair.

In 1929, stipulating that Pole Hill should become part of the Forest,

Lawrence sold all his land on Pole Hill to Chingford Council for £4,450 and the hut for £350 (the amounts he had paid for them). In due course Chingford Council transferred Pole Hill to the Conservators in return for other pieces of Forest land. The hut was dismantled and re-erected at the Warren in c.1936.[3]

T.E. Lawrence's hut.

Connaught Water

I got to know Chingford Plain in my boyhood. We sometimes went to Connaught Water in the late 1940s. In those days there were rowing-boats on the lake. Each had a number, and when a turn was up a man called through a megaphone, "Come in number three." (Or whatever the number was.) We used to feed the ducks. Here could be found mallards, teal, greylag geese, mute swans, moorhens, coots and other waterfowl.

Soon after we took over at Oaklands, my wife and I went with Mabel Reid to listen to the nightingales. From the road we headed to the right of the lake and stopped in a glade. We listened to the trilling of the nightingales for a good hour at dusk.

My wife and I went again to view the bats. Daubenton's bats skimmed low over the lake at dusk, seeking midgets and mayflies, and a small group of us learned about their habits and calls from an expert who had met us there.

Connaught Water.

Tennis

I used to cycle to the Connaught Tennis Club with my brother. Every April there was a tournament and some of the Wimbledon stars would take part. My favourite was Tony Mottram, Britain's no.1. One morning my brother and I watched him practise serving, looking through the mesh of the netting, and he beckoned us into the court and had us acting as ballboys. He had a row of tennis-balls and he served one after another, which we retrieved and returned to him, excited to be making ourselves useful to our nation's star player.

Fair and festival

Every Easter there was a fair, organised by the City of London, on Chingford Plain behind the Royal Forest hotel. There had been a fair there since1882, and Somerset Maugham set part of his 1897 story, *Liza of Lambeth*, at the Chingford fair. In the early days there were boat-swings, donkey rides and coconut shies. On Whit Monday, 1920 100,000 arrived at Chingford station to go to the fair.

I went in 1968, walked across the grass to the fair and wandered round the stalls. There were several roundabouts. In April 2011 the City of London announced that it would not be holding the 2011 fair because only three showmen applied to operate funfair equipment.

In the early 21st century the City of London's Epping Forest

Chingford fair.

Festival was held on Chingford Plain every September. For a number of years there was a railed-off central ring with bales of straw for spectators to sit on. There was an outer ring of stalls. In the central ring there were displays.

The highlight was a jousting tournament. In 2006 it was announced that we were in 1348, the year the Black Death spread northwards. Knights in armour on horses were introduced over the public-address system, including the Earl of Chingford and the Black Knight. There were two other knights. Ladies in the crowd were encouraged to offer favours (ribbons of support) to each of the knights. Then pairs of knights charged at each other on horseback and tilted with lances, each trying to knock the other off his horse to clatter in armour on the grass. Each victor chivalrously sought out and bowed to the lady who had favoured him.

In February 2011 the City of London announced that the Epping Forest Festival would not be held until further notice as the City of London's Epping Forest and Commons Committee (which manages Epping Forest) had embarked on a cost-cutting programme.

Queen Elizabeth's hunting lodge

On the brow of the hill overlooking Chingford Plain next to the Royal Forest hotel (which was once four storeys high but was damaged by a fire in 1912 and not rebuilt to its original height) is the grandstand built by Henry VIII known as Queen Elizabeth's hunting lodge. As we saw on p.66, Waltham Abbey had been dissolved in 1540 and was no longer available as a hunting base. The Royal stable there was still in use in 1541 but is not mentioned after that date.

1543 building

As we saw on p.66 Henry decided to create a Royal deer park in Chingford and between 1540 and 1543 300 acres were cleared of trees. He built Great Standing, this hunting lodge, between 1543 and 1544. It was mentioned in 1543 in a warrant to Sir Richard Rich for £30 to be paid to George Maxey for the "ffynyshinge as wall of(f) on great stondeinge", work probably overseen by the King's Master Carpenter.[4]

It was really three platforms, one above the other, with open sides to view the hunt and sloping floors to drain rainwater away. In 1544, as we have just seen, Henry acquired the manors of Chingford Earls and Chingford St Paul's to expand the deer park. There is no record of Henry VIII's hunting there after 1544. However it is known that he stayed at Copped Hall, and he may have visited the hunting lodge before he died in 1547.

1589 survey

We have seen that Great Standing eventually passed to Elizabeth I. There is a report of a survey of the condition of the building that was commissioned by Elizabeth in 1589. Robert Wroth, John Hill, Francis Stonard, Francis Stacye and William Rowe, all lords of Forest manors and Forest officers, were asked to co-operate with the Queen's Surveyor in compiling this survey.

Queen Elizabeth's hunting lodge.

They found the building to be in poor condition. The walls needed replastering, the roof needed retiling and the outbuildings needed new floors and windows.[5] The need for these repairs suggests that the hunting lodge had fallen into disuse after Henry's death in 1547 and the termination of the deer park (or "disparking") in 1553. It could be that following the report the grandstand was turned into a shooting-gallery to allow Elizabeth to hunt without getting on horseback. Beaters may have driven deer towards Great Standing so that the royal party could fire at them without having to gallop.[6]

Royal ownership

James I continued the hunting traditions of the Forest and hunted from Theobalds in nearby Cheshunt. It is assumed that he continued to use the hunting lodge until his death at Theobalds in 1625. It was probably not used much during the next 40 years. In c.1666 the Crown sold adjoining land to Sir Thomas Boothby which passed by marriage into the Heathcote family and descended with the manor, but the hunting lodge remained the property of the Crown.[7]

It was referred to in 1788 in a Return to the Land Commission by the Master Keeper of the Chingford Walk as "a Lodge House standing in Chingford Manor which is repaired by the Crown". The title of Master Keeper of the Chingford Walk belonged to the lord of the manor, who had an interest in the hunting lodge by virtue of his office as Master Keeper of the Chingford Walk. However, the work of the office was carried out by an Under Keeper who lived in the hunting lodge – having adapted the upper floor to serve as bedrooms – and was paid by the Crown.

The Crown still owned the hunting lodge in 1867, as was made clear in an agreement between the Reverend Robert Boothby Heathcote and the Corporation of London regarding waste land in the manor of Chingford Earls. Eventually Queen Victoria agreed that the hunting lodge should be vested in the Corporation of London.[8]

Bailiffs

The ground floor was always in three compartments, as can be seen from the braces between the interior uprights. A brick chimney-stack seems to have been built c.1666 when Sir Thomas Boothby acquired the land near the hunting lodge. Manor courts were held there in the 18th century. The building was first referred to as Queen Elizabeth's hunting lodge in the Chapman and André map of 1777. In 1817 it was retiled.

In 1833 a pamphlet, *The Mirror of Literature, Amusement and Instruction*, stated that it had been the home of Mr Heathcote's bailiff and his wife for 20 years and of his father for 50 years before that. The writer of the pamphlet visited the hunting lodge and reported that there was a log fire in the kitchen where sides of bacon were hung, and that there were tapestries on the first floor.[9]

In the 19th century, the Chingford part of the Forest began to be enclosed as happened in the Loughton part. The lord of the manor of Chingford Earls, the Reverend Robert Boothby, enclosed 50-60 acres and the lord of the manor of Chingford St Paul's, Richard Hodgson, enclosed 170 acres west of the hunting lodge, on which Station Road would later be built.

The arrival of the railway in 1873 brought crowds of East-Enders at Easter and Whitsun, and a tea garden opened at the hunting lodge, run by the bailiff's wife, Harriet Watkins. When the Corporation of London took over the hunting lodge in 1878, the Watkins family had occupied it for 120 years as bailiffs and Under Keepers paid by the Crown. The hunting lodge was restored between 1880 and 1882 to prepare for Queen Victoria's visit to Chingford station on the royal train (see p.93).

Tea garden

When her husband died Mrs. Watkins stayed on between 1882 and 1885, and moved the tea garden into the barn next to the hunting lodge so that visitors viewing the hunting lodge would not be obstructed by queues for tea. She left the hunting lodge in 1890, and from 1 January 1891 was replaced in the barn by John Butler, who had operated a tea tent near Connaught Water. The barn came to be called Butler's Retreat. When John Butler's marriage broke up his wife Hannah carried on the tea business.[10] The Butler's Retreat tea garden was reopened in 2012.[11]

Museum
On the initiative of Edward North Buxton, the hunting lodge was turned into a Museum of Natural History and Antiquities by the Essex Field Club. At first the Museum opened on the staircase and top floor as the Butt family had replaced the Watkins family on the ground and first floors.[12] The Epping Forest Museum then replaced it, and opened in the whole of the hunting lodge in 1928.

Sir William Addison
In 1987 I attended an Annual General Meeting of the Epping Forest Centenary Trust on the first floor of Queen Elizabeth's hunting lodge. It was chaired by Terence Mallinson, Col. Sir Stuart Mallinson's son, to whom I chatted about his father's cricket nets. Also present was Sir William Addison, sitting grandly in a wheelchair between sticks in the entrance hall of the hunting lodge, at the foot of the stairs up which Queen Elizabeth I is reputed to have ridden a white palfrey to celebrate the Armada victory.

He was 82 and I stood in front of him and reminded him that he sold me *Observer's* books in his Loughton bookshop when I was a boy. I said I was now running Oaklands and had some of his books. He told me he had written 17 books – his final tally was 19 – and talked about his ailments, and then said, "Come and visit me at home." I said I would, but did not take his home address. I was so busy in the late 1980s, running Oaklands School, writing my study of 25 civilizations, *The Fire and the Stones*, and founding Coopersale Hall School that I never got round to going, and in 1992 I was sad to hear that he had died.

Sir William Addison welcoming 'Queen Victoria', 1978.

Terence Mallinson

On 18 May 2005 I attended the Annual General Meeting of the Epping Forest Centenary Trust again. It was again held on the first floor of Queen Elizabeth's hunting lodge. I chatted to Richard Morris and then to Terence Mallinson (then 75), Chairman of the Trust, who, grasping that I now had three schools, asked if I would be a trustee. But I was just extricating myself from running Otley Hall, a historic house in Suffolk, and I was in the process of moving to Buckhurst Hill and had writing deadlines, and nothing came of his invitation. However, I took to attending the Trust's annual general meetings, which were now held at the Warren.

Normanhurst School

In 1965 Chingford joined Walthamstow and Leyton as part of the London Borough of Waltham Forest, ending a thousand-year association with Essex. Although its postal address now became London E4 it remained at heart an Essex county town on the edge of Epping Forest and that was how I thought of it in September 1996 when I was asked to buy Normanhurst School in Station Road, Chingford.

Rescue of School

On Monday 9 September I addressed a meeting of the Oaklands staff on the day before the autumn term started, and then went to Coopersale Hall to talk with the Head there. I inspected the tennis-court (since turned into an Astroturfed football area) and received a message that the Head of Normanhurst, Jeremy Leyland, wanted to see me urgently. I returned to my house next to Oaklands (now Oak House) and rang him.

He visited me at 2.30. We talked in the conservatory. He told me he had taken over the running of the school from his father, Eric Leyland, a children's author I had read as a boy who had also edited the *Children's Newspaper*. He said his father now had Parkinson's disease. He asked if I would "invest" in the School as the bank had declined to lend and he would be unable to pay the staff's salaries at the end of

September and was going into receivership.

He had called a meeting of the parents on Thursday 12 September to announce that the School would be placed in the hands of a receiver, and wanted to be able to announce that I would take over the ownership of Normanhurst from the receiver and would be retaining him on a salary. It soon became clear that we would have to buy four large Victorian houses that were already converted to school use, three of which were registered in Denmark.

Two views of the front of Normanhurst.

I took some figures away and quickly concluded that the School was fundamentally viable and had run into cash-flow difficulties due to certain management decisions. The Head had understandably been devastated by the recent death of his 25-year-old daughter, and things had been allowed to slide. I was very conscious that an entire staff, many of whom had families and mortgages, would be made redundant before the end of the week unless someone acted to save the School, and that my wife and I were the only rescuers who were in a position to act by Thursday. If we did not announce our take-over in three days' time, parents would withdraw their children and there might soon be no school, or revenue, to take over.

Having agreed to buy the School, I virtually lived in the accountants' boardroom for three days while advisers came and went and we made numerous calls to the bank, Denmark and other institutions whose representatives' voices were heard by all on speaker-phone. We now discovered that the staff had not been paid at the end of August, and that we would have to take on this additional expense.

We solved the problems as we went along, and by Thursday 12 September our Bursar, my former bank manager, Ken Jones, was able to meet the Normanhurst parents and announce that Normanhurst would now be a member of the Oak-Tree Group of Schools. There was applause when he finished and he was besieged by staff and parents seeking reassurance. We had rescued the staff and would be paying their salaries for the end of August. We had acted quickly and decisively and announced our rescue to the parents before any withdrawals.

History of Normanhurst School

I had toured Normanhurst (motto "*Filius viri pater est*", "The Child is father of the Man" from Wordsworth's "My heart leaps up"). It was a high-street school filling four turreted buildings that had a central porch. It was within walking distance of Chingford station, and a longish walk to Queen Elizabeth's hunting lodge. It had been founded in 1923 by Miss Rudge and Miss Rawson, in the Ridgeway, four years after T.E. Lawrence first bought land on nearby Pole Hill and rebuilt his friend Vyvyan Richards' hut-like retreat there. (See p.253.) Normanhurst had moved to its present site in 1929, and a photograph taken that year shows girls in pinafore dresses sitting at high desks, dipping their pens into ink-wells at one end of the School hall.

Normanhurst pupils, 1929.

During the Blitz a room off the old library was a bomb shelter and held 100 people in a space 20 feet by 12 feet. A number of bombs fell nearby, and Normanhurst was evacuated to Marazion, Cornwall; to a hotel near Praa Sands. Since the war Normanhurst had prospered under various Heads, including Jeremy's writer father. It took boys and girls from 2½ to 16 from Walthamstow, Leyton, Enfield, Bethnal Green and the City of London, and from Waltham Abbey, Epping and further afield in Essex.

Oak-Tree Group of Schools

In no time the Oak-Tree Group of Schools stabilised Normanhurst, which took on a new lease of life. We had a good relationship with Jeremy Leyland. With our Bursar I set out the parameters within which the School would function. I visited the School every morning and got to know the staff by chatting to them, and I reinforced the image of the School and proposed some steps that would raise standards. I formed an Improvement Committee which was a latent senior management team.

Nasser Hussain

Our first Founders Day (Prize Day) was held in Chingford Assembly Hall on 16 November. The Essex and England cricketer Nasser Hussain (later the England captain) had been asked to distribute prizes, and I had been asked to make the main speech. Wearing a suit, I greeted Nasser, who arrived in an old pale-blue sweater with a hole in one elbow, an open-necked shirt and baggy trousers. His wife was with him. I knew the older boys were hoping to secure his autograph, so to encourage them, sitting on the platform alongside him before a packed audience of 600, waiting to speak, I asked him to sign my programme, which he did to excited nudges from the older boys below.

Nicholas Hagger with Nasser Hussain at Normanhurst Founders' Day, 1996.

In my speech I emphasised that I was a local boy and that Normanhurst was on a new course. I talked of the benefits of the School's membership of a group of schools and dwelt on how parents and staff were in a partnership to lead the children forward. I found time to mention that I had played cricket for Buckhurst Hill 1st XI, and that five of our side had played for the county. Looking at the older boys, I said that I was hoping to come to Nasser's attention.

During the concert that followed Nasser and I sat together and we had a conversation about cricket. I asked if it was tense waiting to bat in a Test Match. He said, "It is. You're playing for England and there's a big crowd. You've got to keep your limbs relaxed. Physios don't help. Each individual has to handle his nerves in his own way." I asked what he would do when he stopped playing cricket, and he said, "I'm looking to be a commentator or a writer." I thought of John Arlott and Brian Johnston, and was sceptical. He said, "I might like to work in a school. I'll stay in touch." He added, "If you're in Chelmsford, ask for me at the pavilion door and we'll have a chat."

Nearly three years later, when he had become England captain, a letter arrived asking if I would buy tickets for a table at Lord's to support his Benefit Year, and I responded by taking a party of family members and school advisers on 12 October 1999. Nasser was now wearing a dinner jacket, and I chatted to him in the bar. We ate in the Long Room. One of my party won a cricket bat in a raffle, and gave it to me. It was signed by the Indian team.

After the meal I took my two sons up to the large visitors' dressing-room and then to the even larger home dressing-room which was used by the England team when they played at Lord's. There were getting on for a dozen men standing around in dinner jackets, savouring the atmosphere and sunk in memories. I took my stance at an imaginary wicket, tapping my bat against my right foot, and called for one of my sons to bowl, which Tony pretended to do. I executed a perfect, flashing cover-drive – and nearly took Nasser's head off. He had come forward, out of my eye line, to look at his name on the board of centurions, and he ducked just in time. "Just coming to the attention of the England captain," I said, and everyone laughed, including Nasser.

Over the years since then I have watched him as a commentator on television and I have been impressed by his fluency and by the clarity with which he expresses his views. He has the common touch for a new time which wanted a different kind of commentator from the well-born commentators of the past.

Growth

Normanhurst was a family school that gave individual attention within small class sizes, and during the first two years of our tenure the numbers rose steadily. Every school holidays we had a building programme to improve the classrooms. My daily visits to talk with the Head became less frequent in early 1997 as I was now overseeing the purchase of Otley Hall in Suffolk, a historic house that was open to the public for visits on open days, coach tours and conferences. It had to be renovated, and making one-night visits to Suffolk besides running Oaklands and Coopersale Hall left me relatively little time to spend on Normanhurst. Otley Hall was where the Jamestown settlement is thought to have been planned in 1606/7 and in October 1998 I visited Virginia and gave a lecture about the Jamestown settlement.

Lord Tebbit

In November 1998 Lord Tebbit, a former MP for Chingford, was invited to speak at Founders Day, which was again held at Chingford Assembly Hall. At 3pm, when the event was supposed to begin, there were 600 sitting in the hall and there was no sign of Tebbit. The Head was waiting with me at the door to greet him, and asked what he should do.

I said, "You go and start, and I'll bring him in."

The Head said, "What happens if he doesn't turn up at all?"

I said, "I'll take over from you."

"What will you talk about?"

"As it's Founders Day, I'll start with the founding of Normanhurst School, and I'll come up to the present very slowly and make it up as I go along. Have you got a better idea?"

At 3.15 Tebbit arrived in a large Range Rover. He got out and said, "Sorry I'm late, forgot about the Lord Mayor's Show." There had been a diversion.

I said, "It's, what, eight years since you opened Coopersale Hall and you don't look a day older." He laughed.

I led him down the left-hand aisle through the packed hall, and the Head interrupted his speech to greet him. As Tebbit sat down next to me on the platform I could sense his discomfort from the injury he sustained in the IRA's Brighton bomb. I watched as he jotted notes for his speech on his programme. Five minutes later he was speaking at the microphone about his school days and what they taught him, not looking at his notes and displaying his front-bench spokesman's skill in making a smooth impromptu speech from half a dozen hastily-scribbled headings.

In the interval before the second half we sat together and discussed England in relation to Europe and the attempt to split England into eight regions. He told me, "Blair's acting out someone's agenda." We discussed who might be behind this agenda. At the end I escorted him to his Range Rover and shut his door, and he sat with his hand on the ignition ready to start. I said out of the November dark by his open driver's window, "England's in a parlous state." Forty-five minutes later we were still talking about England in the dark, and whether there should be an ELF ("English Liberation Front") to save places like Epping Forest from insensitive foreign rule.

Iain Duncan Smith, Tebbit's successor as MP at Chingford and Woodford Green, found us in the dark. He wanted to thank Tebbit for visiting his patch and to say goodbye. He stood and listened the other side of the Range Rover, and occasionally chipped in with a comment. I said, "There's a plan to impose a world government on us and we know who's doing it." Tebbit said, "'Rockefellers'." As a result of that conversation, which contained many more observations than I have space for here, I decided to write *The Syndicate*.

Iain Duncan Smith

In the summer of 2001 the Head left to make a new life in Nottingham and was replaced internally. Iain Duncan Smith, now Leader of the Opposition, was our guest speaker for Founders Day in November. I led him to the platform and introduced him, and then the new Head.

Duncan Smith spoke directly and simply to the children. To illustrate the concept of leadership he told a story about a car heading to the West Country which became lost. The leadership of one of the

Nicholas Hagger and Iain Duncan Smith singing the School song at Normanhurst Founders' Day, 2001.

passengers put the car in the right direction. He explained that it was his job to lead his party in the right direction. At the end the School song was sung. Duncan Smith and I shared a programme. I said to him, "We've got to sing from the same hymn-sheet." He said, "That's what I'm telling my party to do."

Opening of new building by Duncan Smith

The roll at the School had risen to 253, nearly 100 more than when we took over. The growth can be seen in successive School photographs. These were taken on Chingford Plain. On a particular day every other year staging and benches were erected on the Plain in front of a wood, and the pupils walked in lines with their teachers. The Bursar and I drove down and walked from the car park across the brow of a low hill, from which we could see all the School's pupils in position, waiting for us. (During the taking of the first photograph after our rescue the original Head called out, "I'm going to be handing out a detention to anyone who speaks," and the Bursar and I exchanged glances that wondered if this applied to us.)

To cope with this growth, in 2002-3 we built a new two-storey L-shaped building of five classrooms, two libraries, two changing-rooms and toilets on the two sides of the playground farthest from Station Road. It was a very large and modern addition to the School, and Iain Duncan Smith opened it on 17 October 2003. Duncan Smith and I made speeches outside the building before local dignitaries and parents, and there was coffee afterwards in the hall. Duncan Smith had been in difficulties with his party – I remember telling him that it had just been announced that in a poll 67 out of 80 constituency chairmen supported him – and less than two weeks later, on 29 October, he was ousted as Leader.

I had heard evidence of an extra-party campaign against him. Shortly afterwards I was invited to a dinner at the House of Commons and was seated directly opposite him. I told him that he was forced out because those setting the political agenda Tebbit had referred to wanted all three party leaders to support Europe. "You were too critical of Europe for their liking," I told him, "although they must have appreciated your support for the invasion of Iraq." He listened and nodded but said nothing. In my experience, extra-party pressure is a subject that all politicians know about but are reluctant to talk about.

Church of St Peter and St Paul: carol services

The Normanhurst carol services were held at St Peter and St Paul, Chingford Green, which had been built in 1844. The original parish church, All Saints on Chingford Mount, had fallen into ruin, and its 12th-century font and 18th-century pulpit were moved to the 1844 church.

At the carol services of 2002 and 2003 the organ was played by a pupil, Simon Jacobs. I had paid him just as I had paid the organists at the other two schools' carol services. In July 2011 Simon Jacobs was the guest speaker at the Normanhurst Speech Day. (Founders Day had been renamed and moved from November to July.) He was now a professional musician attached to a church near New York, and he spoke as a role model to our pupils, demonstrating that they too could work their way to a position of responsibility. He told me that I was the first to pay him for playing music, and that I had given him the confidence to embark on his path.

A Thriving School

The new Head had retired and we had had three more Heads. Under the third of these, and under the day-to-day running of our son Matthew, the roll increased rapidly.

Normanhurst was now a thriving school on the edge of Chingford Plain and Epping Forest, with a catchment area that was increasingly from the more professional families in Chingford. It has adapted to the computerised 21st century, yet retains the family atmosphere of its origins after the First World War. It has led a charmed life. True to form, in the 2011 riots looters smashed windows to within a few yards of Normanhurst but did not touch the School.

By now North Chingford had become a well-to-do area within easy reach of Loughton, Woodford and Buckhurst Hill. It was an ideal place for a third school. Our triangle of schools connected Chingford, Loughton and Epping, and the lines of the triangle passed through Epping Forest, whose trees shaped the children's growth and education as they had once shaped mine.

*

Epping Forest and creativity

Epping Forest had reared me, and I had come to love its Forest places and had acknowledged them in my poems. (See Appendix.) Essex County Council had had a hand in my going to Chigwell under the Direct Grant system, and I had won a County Major Scholarship to pay for my education at Oxford. I had given something back to the county by taking over one school, founding another and rescuing a third one which had been within Essex until recently – by moving thousands of young souls forward while providing employment for more than 230 local families. The then Lord Lieutenant, Lord Braybrooke, had told me when he visited Coopersale Hall on the day of 9/11, 11 September 2001, that I had saved the Essex taxpayer the cost of educating the children in our care, and that the county was in our debt. But I did not see it like that. I was in the county's debt.

Such considerations paled beside the daily nourishment the Forest had given me as I wrote more than thirty-five books within its borders. My creativity was somehow linked to the Forest, and following my return to live within its ancient pastures my work had borne fruit. I was in a profound, lifelong, two-way relationship with the Forest, of giving and receiving. It had a presence that had shaped me and inspired me, and had provided my livelihood as I gave something back.

Epilogue: A Unified view of Epping Forest's History and Places

I have now completed my study of the interaction between the historical traditions of Epping Forest and the places they shaped. On p.5 I used the image of an oak tree. Epping Forest is rooted in the Ice Age, its trunk has grown in four segments over 2,000 years, and its leafy branches are the settlements of its Forest places.

Excavations of the evidential past

I have referred to several excavations in different places, attempts to make our interpretation of the past evidential. Much more can be done on the archaeological side. Full use should be made of new technology, including sub-ground radar, and there should be a new round of excavations at the hill-forts of Loughton Camp and Ambresbury Banks; and at High Beach round the pillow mounds. I have obtained LiDAR images of these, which show how the terrain in these places would look if the surface grass were stripped away. (See pp.284-7.) There should also be a new excavation at Waltham Abbey, to locate Harold's tomb. Many of the other places I have described and reflected on in this work would benefit from excavation. By sifting the evidence from a Universalist, whole perspective it should be possible to target areas where discoveries can be expected.

These days it *is* possible to work out where skeletons are buried. When I owned Otley Hall in Suffolk I asked Bill Kelso, the discoverer of Jamestown and excavator of more than 350,000 artefacts there, to dig for the skeleton of Jamestown's founder, Batholomew Gosnold (of the Gosnold family who lived in Otley Hall for 250 years), within the Jamestown Fort. He said that the Fort consisted of a triangle 140 metres x 140 metres x 140 metres, one corner of which was now in the River James, and that it would take him decades to dig the impacted ground in so large an area. I said that Gosnold would be buried in the centre of the triangle as all the ordnance of the Fort had been shot off for his funeral in 1607, including cannons in each of the three corners, and that out of politeness to the dead man they would have buried him where he could hear each salvo equally. Furthermore, the centre would be farthest from all the walls if the Fort was attacked by marauding native Americans.

Kelso followed my advice and eventually rang me from the US to say that he was sure he had found Gosnold: a perfectly-preserved skeleton of the right size wrapped in the English flag, dressed as a captain. We still await DNA evidence from Gosnold's sister's body to confirm the identification, but the skeleton has been exhibited in the Smithsonian Institute as provisionally being Gosnold's. Its discovery is proof that archaeological problems can be solved in the mind before any earth is scratched, long before excavations begin.

Present volunteers: Friends of Epping Forest and the Green Belt

The Forest is administered from the Warren, but much of the work of guarding the Green Belt can be found to have emanated from volunteers who are members of the Friends of Epping Forest.

Sir William Addison encouraged the formation of the Friends and became their first President. The Friends were formally established in 1969 to protect users of the Forest and the Green Belt from encroaching roads: most notably, the D-Ring road, later called the M16, and eventually the M25, which was to intersect with the A11 at Bell Common. The Friends successfully defended the Forest at public inquiries throughout the 1970s and achieved the 450-yard-long tunnel under Bell Common and the M11 and M16/M25 interchange that replaced it and has kept London-bound motorway traffic away from the Forest.

In later years the Friends blocked new encroachments on the Forest, working as a link between the Forest's administrators and the public, and organised the celebration of the centenary of Queen Victoria's 1882 visit to Chingford and High Beach.[1] After Addison's death the Presidency passed to Lord Murray, who several times used his influence in the Lords to defend the Forest. When he died in May 2004 he was succeeded by his widow, Lady Murray.

In 2011 the Friends focused on cattle. The City of London Corporation proposed to treble the number of cattle grazing in the Forest from 50 to 150 and to install four new cattle grids (two in High Beach, one in Ranger's Road, Chingford and one near Epping). The idea proved controversial. Horse riders claimed that the grids would be dangerous for horses, and the Friends expressed concern at the amount of tree clearance that would be needed to create new grazing pastures. The City of London, working with Essex County Council and the Boroughs of Redbridge and Waltham Forest, held a public inquiry chaired by an inspector of the Department of Transport, at which all parties gave evidence.

Every November from 2005 I attended a supper held by the Friends at the Hawkey Hall, Woodford. At the Friends' suppers I have chatted to Lady Murray; the current Superintendent of the Warren; Ken Hoy; Harry Bitten; Tricia Moxey; Richard Morris and Michael Chapman, Deputy Lord Lieutenant of Essex.

Conservators, Centenary Trust and the Duke of Gloucester

The administrative side of Epping Forest is thriving. On 25 June 2008 I was invited to a gathering of some 50 prominent local figures at the Warren (headquarters of the Conservators of the Corporation of London and once the site of Little Standing). We had come to celebrate the 30th anniversary of the Epping Forest Centenary Trust, which interprets the Forest for young people from Inner London and nearby communities.

In the presence of HRH The Duke of Gloucester, a successor to the Duke of Connaught as Ranger, and an equerry, and under the chairmanship of Terence Mallinson (Col. Sir Stuart Mallinson's son) we met to discuss how to reach more children and their families and involve them in Epping Forest. All the key people overseeing

The Duke of Gloucester meets 50 local figures at the Warren, 2008.

the management and administration of the Forest were there: the Lord Lieutenant of Essex, Lord Petre; the High Sheriff of Essex; the present and past Superintendents of the Warren; the Chairman of the Epping Forest and Commons Committee of the City of London; the Chairman of the Epping Forest District Council; the Mayor of the Borough of Waltham Forest; the director of The Suntrap Environmental Centre; verderers; county and district councillors, including Chris Pond; a City of London alderman; and Epping Forest Centenary Trust directors including Richard Morris.

It was a sunny evening. Drinks were served on the terrace of the Warren at 6, and we received the Duke and chatted. We then moved to the Conservators' boardroom for a presentation and later ate at crowded tables in the Warren's dining-room and discussed topics.

After the Duke left we all chatted in groups on the lawn outside. On the way out I took a look at Lawrence of Arabia's hut, which had been removed from Pole Hill in c.1936 and kept at the Warren as an outbuilding. (See pp.253-4.)

A unified view of Epping Forest, past and present

I returned to my base in western Buckhurst Hill a short distance from the Warren. Here I now sit in my study window looking out over my balcony at a panoramic view of Epping Forest that sweeps from Queen Elizabeth's hunting lodge to the spire of High Beach church (which is partly hidden by trees but clearly visible in winter). Immediately before

A view of Epping Forest across the old Fairmead deer park.

me is Henry VIII's Fairmead deer park. Fallow deer still invade the garden, an echo of the Tudor time. There are three oaks on the lawn, and a couple of fields beyond. Between them is a stream. LiDAR pictures (see pp.284-7) show clusters of circles in the ground with diameters of around five metres, suggesting that there was once a settlement near the stream of Iron-Age Celtic – or Roman, or Saxon – roundhouses. (As Chingford was a Saxon hamlet – see pp.44 and 366 – any settlement here might be Saxon.)

In this view of Epping Forest from my window, the Forest stretches, uninterrupted by road, from Chingford, skirting Loughton, to High Beach and Epping (encompassing the triangle of the three Oak-Tree schools). I sometimes gaze at this unified view of Epping Forest and, back in Henry VIII's time, dream of the King's procession from Poteles, the hunting lodge off King's Avenue, Palmerston Road, Buckhurst Hill, perhaps along these very pastures. I see them cross the Ching and process to Great Standing. Were these open fields once a green ride where beaters flushed out deer for the King's party to shoot at from horseback while they advanced towards their picnic lunch in Great Standing?

Forest wildlife

As I gaze, rabbits bound across the first field. They were perhaps introduced by the Romans and certainly by the Normans to feed their soldiers. Squirrels chase around tree-trunks. Foxes prowl round the garden, and there are traces of hedgehogs. A vividly-coloured grass snake of great length sometimes shelters in the bin shed. Hornets nest in the base of the nearest oak. Green woodpeckers flit over the lawn, and great and lesser spotted woodpeckers come to the bird-feeders every day. Three goldfinches swing on a feeder filled with niger seed. A heron alights near a pond filled with carp, beneath four levels of streams. Newts swim near the pondweed, and white lilies bask in the warm September sun. Four fieldfares flap off from a pine, new arrivals for the coming winter. Here come redwings, nuthatches, hawks, long-tailed tits, jackdaws, rooks, mistle-thrushes, and jays along with the more common blue and great tits, chaffinches, greenfinches, blackbirds and magpies. Robins, dunnocks and pigeons peck on the nearby ground. Two pairs of wild green parakeets have just flown into the oak tree nearest my window. Swallows and house martins skim the nearest field. Peacocks and small tortoiseshell butterflies settle on the herbs in the knot garden, and bees nuzzle in the lavender. Green and purple grasshoppers swing on blades of grass, clack and leap. At dusk bats flit.

This part of Buckhurst Hill is a paradise. The Forest is alive. It teems with wildlife. An abundance of Nature can be found.

The shaping Forest

Sitting in my window, I look across Henry VIII's Fairmead deer park at the sweep of the Forest which curves round like one entity, like a bushy hillside. My panoramic view encompasses thousands of individual trees through which I can glimpse permanent buildings: a hunting lodge, a spire. It includes a terrain crying out to be excavated, walks maintained by Forest administrators and trodden by volunteers, and an array of wildlife. I do not need LiDAR images to sense the four periods of history whose perspectives lie like hidden seams deep beneath the grass and autumn leaves, and the continuity of the historical tradition that shades present places, like an ancient oak in a modern garden. The curve of the Forest seems to enfold and protect each glimpsed lodge and spire to which its timbers once gave shape.

The Forest has not just shaped the places. It has shaped us woodlanders who dwell here as well. It has shaped me. I sometimes feel like "a much-gnarled oak",[2] and my books sometimes seem like the sprouting above ground of oak saplings imbued with sap. This book is stamped with the leaves and acorns of Epping Forest's long historical tradition.

From my window, a view of Epping Forest is at first sight a distant, static sweep of trees. Yet within it is a seething actitivy of animals, birds and insects which flit to and fro, driven by their own hidden purposes within Nature's dynamic system. To me, they glorify the present amid the resonant pastures of the past.

Timeline

List of dates of key events referred to in *A View of Epping Forest*

c.10,000BC	Mesolithic hunters.
c.4500BC	Neolithic farmers.
c.2300-1700BC	Bronze Age Beaker people.
c.700BC	Ambresbury Banks, Loughton Camp.
c.75BC	Catuvellauni harry Trinovantes.
55BC	Julius Caesar's first invasion of Britain.
54BC	Julius Caesar's second invasion of Britain.
	Caesar defeats Catuvellauni – at Ambresbury Banks?
AD43	Claudius's invasion of Britain.
	Aulus Plautius takes Camulodunum. Ambresbury Banks and Loughton Camp abandoned.
AD61	Boudicca's revolt against Romans.
	Suetonius Paulinus defeats Boudicca – at Ambresbury Banks?
AD211-17	Caracalla emperor.
c.460	Essex ceded to Saxons.
527-825	Kingdom of Essex.
c.610	Church built at Waltham (church 1).
c.790	Church at Waltham rebuilt (church 2).
878-92	Essex under Danelaw.
1016-1042	Essex again under Danelaw.
c.1030	Tovi houses Holy Cross at Waltham.
1052	Edward the Confessor promises throne to William, Duke of Normandy.
Before c.1060	Harold holds Loughton.
c.1060	Harold gives Loughton, Woodford and 15 other manors to Waltham Holy Cross by endowment.
	Waltham Holy Cross consecrated.
c.1060-66	Harold rebuilds Waltham Holy Cross (church 3).

c.1060-1540	Waltham Holy Cross (after 1184 Waltham Abbey) holds Loughton and Woodford.
c.1064	Harold swears an oath to William.
Jan 1066	Harold crowned as Harold II.
Sep-Oct 1066	Norwegian and Norman invasions of Britain, Harold killed.
1066-1075	William I owns canons of Waltham's lands in parish of Waltham.
1075	William I gives lands in the parish of Waltham to Odo of Bayeux, and the remainder of lands in the parish of Waltham to the Bishop of Durham.
1087	*Domesday Book*.
1088-91	William II owns lands in the parish of Waltham.
c.1090-1150	Church at Waltham Holy Cross rebuilt (church 4).
1091-1177	The Bishop of Durham holds lands in the parish of Waltham.
c.1124	Author of *The Waltham Chronicle* sees Harold's body temporarily removed from his tomb at Waltham Holy Cross.
1177	Waltham Holy Cross refounded as Augustinian priory.
c.1177-1242	Waltham Holy Cross rebuilt (church 5).
1177-89	Henry II owns lands in the parish of Waltham, gives two acres to Copped Hall and gives Coopersale Hall to his chamberlain.
1184	Waltham Holy Cross elevated to an abbey, becomes Waltham Abbey.
1189-1540	Land around Waltham Abbey held by abbot and canons, who bought the manor of Waltham from Richard I in 1189.
c.1200-1250	Theydon Garnon church built.
1348-9	Black Death.
1350-1536/7	Waltham Abbey holds Copped Hall.
1368	Manor of Theydon Garnon passes to Duchy of Lancaster.
c.1370	Waltham Abbey gatehouse built.

1381	Peasants' Revolt, attack on Waltham Abbey.
22 Jun 1381	Richard II meets rebels at Waltham Abbey.
1522	Manor of Loughton leased to John Stoner for 80 years.
1536/7	Crown owns Copped Hall.
1540	Waltham Abbey dissolved.
1540-3	Henry VIII erects 300-acre deer park at Fairmead.
1542-3	Henry VIII builds Great Standing, later known as Queen Elizabeth's hunting lodge.
Before c.1551-3	Mary Tudor, future queen, lives at Copped Hall.
1553-8	Mary Tudor owns Loughton.
1554-62	Edward de Vere, later 17th Earl of Oxford, tutored by Sir Thomas Smith at Hill Hall.
1557	Hill Hall's rebuilding completed.
1558	Duchy of Lancaster holds Epping, Copped Hall and Theydon Garnon.
1558-1613	Duchy of Lancaster holds Loughton.
1562	Elizabeth I sets up Commission to plant trees in Copped Hall park. Possible planting of Coopersale Hall's evergreen holm-oak.
1564	Elizabeth I gives Copped Hall to Sir Thomas Heneage.
1577	Wanstead House held by Robert Dudley, Earl of Leicester.
1589	Survey of Queen Elizabeth's hunting lodge.
May 1594	Heneage's marriage to the 3rd Earl of Southampton's mother at Copped Hall – for which Shakespeare writes *A Midsummer Night's Dream*?
c.1600	Denny tomb, Waltham Abbey.
1603-4	Edward de Vere, 17th Earl of Oxford, becomes Lord Warden of the Forest of Waltham.
1605	James I visits Loughton Hall.
1608	Lady Mary Wroth of Loughton Hall with William Herbert, 3rd Earl of Pembroke, by whom she has two children.
1610	Ben Jonson dedicates *The Alchemist* to Lady Mary

	Wroth.
1613	Sir Robert Wroth buys Loughton manor from Duchy of Lancaster.
1620-9	Founding of Chigwell School by Archbishop Harsnett.
1737	Dick Turpin hides in Epping Forest.
c.1748-58	John Conyers I rebuilds Copped Hall.
c.1776	Coopersale Hall rebuilt as the seat of Mrs. Ann Chevely.
1812	The Duke of Wellington's nephew marries the chatelaine of Wanstead House, becomes Lord Warden and permits enclosures of Epping Forest.
1825-61	William Whitaker Maitland, lord of the manor of Loughton, encloses 1,377 acres of Epping Forest.
1837-40	Tennyson lives in Beech Hill House, High Beach.
1837-41	John Clare at High Beach.
1840	Tennyson invests in Dr Allen's company.
1843	Dr Allen bankrupt, Tennyson family ruined.
1856	Eastern Counties Railway comes to Buckhurst Hill and Loughton.
1858	The Buxtons own Warlies, Upshire.
1861	William Whitaker Maitland dies and is succeeded by his son Rev. John Whitaker Maitland.
Jan 1862	Two fields sold by John Whitaker Maitland to Edward Vickers.
1864-5	John Whitaker Maitland, lord of the manor of Loughton, encloses 1,100 acres of waste land within Epping Forest.
1865	Railway reaches Epping.
	Thomas Willingale taken to court by John Whitaker Maitland.
1866	Three of Willingale's relatives imprisoned.
1867	Buckhurst Hill becomes a separate parish.
	Matthew Arnold visits British School, Loughton.
1870	Thomas Willingale dies.
1871	Corporation of London wins test case on enclosures in Lords.

1873	Church of the Holy Innocents, High Beach opened.
1875-8	Corporation of London buys 19 Epping-Forest manors.
1878	Epping Forest Act gives Corporation of London the right to administer Epping Forest as Conservators at The Warren and to own Queen Elizabeth's hunting lodge.
1881	Lopping peters out.
6 May 1882	Queen Victoria visits Chingford and High Beach.
1883	Connaught Water created by draining swamp.
1883-4	Lopping Hall built.
1889	Bancroft's School moves to Woodford Green.
1901-2	Church of St Thomas, Upshire built.
Before c.1914-29	Howards live at Fir Bank (later Oaklands).
1915-17	Edward Thomas lives at High Beech Cottage, High Beach before dying in France.
6 May 1917	Fire at Copped Hall.
1919-29	T.E. Lawrence owns 13 acres of Pole Hill, Chingford.
1921	T.E. Lawrence's replacement hut built (later placed in Warren).
1923	Normanhurst School founded.
1924	Churchill wins by-election at Epping.
1926	Col. Sir Stuart Mallinson buys The White House, Woodford Green.
1929	Normanhurst School moves to Station Road, Chingford.
1937-44	Old Oaklands is based by Trap's Hill.
1943	Nicholas Hagger comes to Loughton.
Sep 1944	New Oaklands opens at Albion Hill.
Apr 1945	Churchill speaks at Loughton war memorial.
May 1945	Nicholas Hagger first meets William Addison.
Sep 1947	Nicholas Hagger starts at Chigwell School.
Oct 1951	Churchill visits Loughton.
Oct 1953	Montgomery visits Chigwell School.
Oct 1959	Churchill statue unveiled on Woodford Green.
1969	Friends of Epping Forest established.
May 1982	Centenary of Queen Victoria's visit in 1882.

Sep 1982	Nicholas and Ann Hagger own Oaklands School.
1988-9	Nicholas Hagger founds Coopersale Hall School.
Apr 1989	Coopersale Hall School opens.
1989-94	Steve Norris MP lives at Coopersale Hall School.
Jul 1990	Lord Tebbit formally opens Coopersale Hall School.
1992	Rescue of Copped Hall.
	Sir William Addison dies.
1996	Nicholas and Ann Hagger own Normanhurst School.
Nov 1998	Lord Tebbit distributes Normanhurst prizes.
Jul 1999	Tony Little, later Head Master of Eton, distributes Oaklands prizes.
Jul 2001	Matthew Hagger becomes Managing Principal of Oak-Tree Group of Schools.
Nov 2001	Iain Duncan Smith MP distributes Normanhurst prizes.
Oct 2003	Iain Duncan Smith MP opens new block at Normanhurst School.
2004	Lord Murray dies.
Jun 2008	HRH The Duke of Gloucester, Forest Ranger, visits The Warren.
May 2009	20th anniversary of Coopersale Hall School.
Jul 2012	75th anniversary of Oaklands School.

APPENDIX

1

LiDAR maps of Epping Forest places

LiDAR images show land without grass or trees. These images show ancient settlements as they would be if all grass, vegetation and foliage were removed

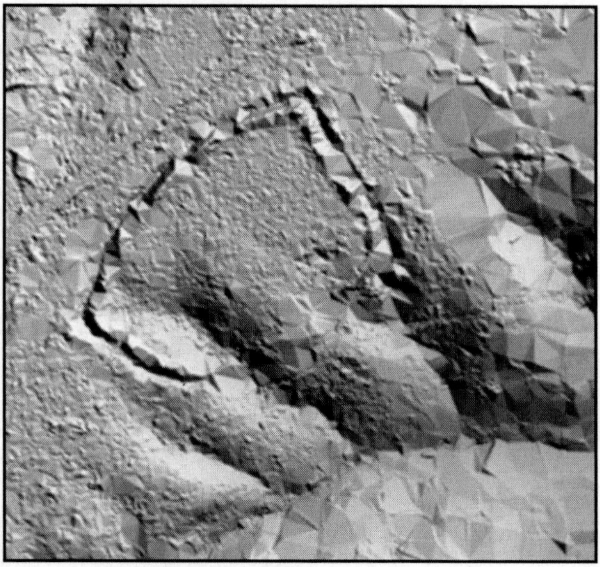

1. Ambresbury Banks, LiDAR image.

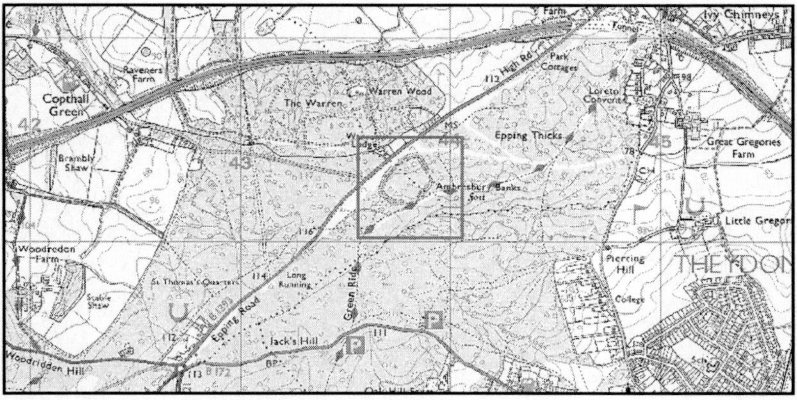

2. Map showing Ambresbury Banks.

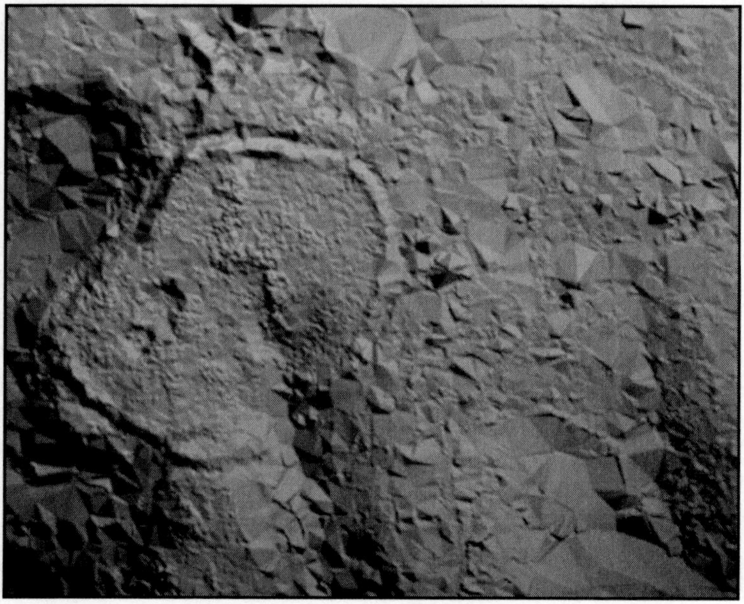

3. Loughton Camp, LiDAR image.

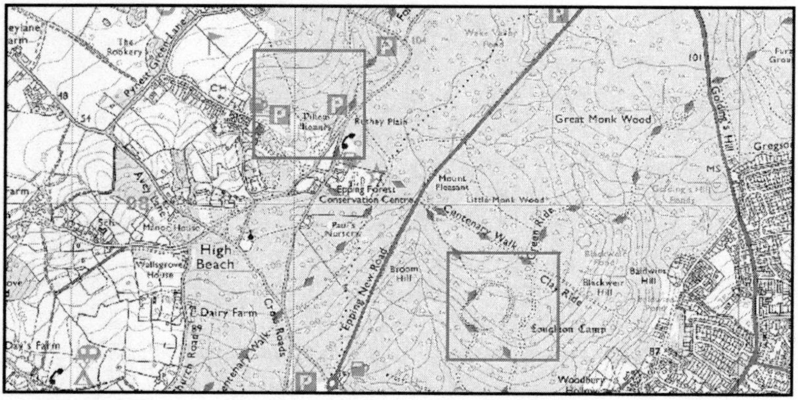

4. Map showing Loughton Camp (right) and High Beach pillow mounds (left).

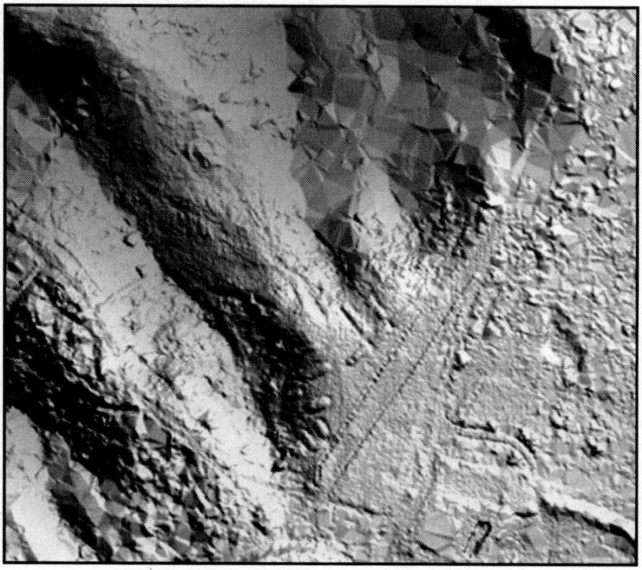

5. High Beach pillow mounds, LiDAR image (see 4, map).

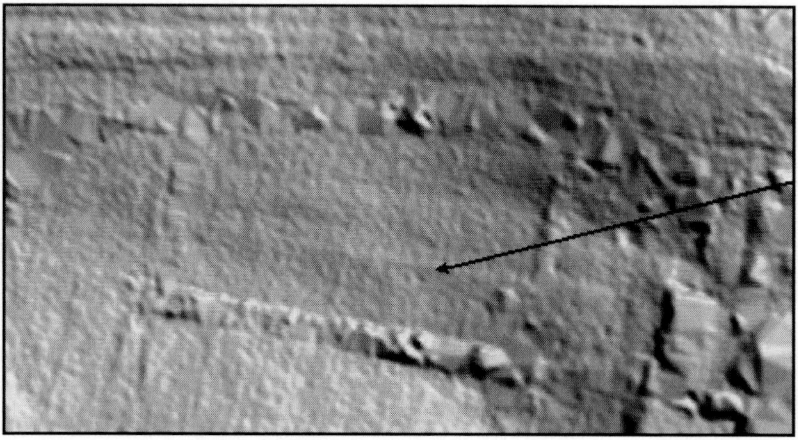

6. Part of Fairmead deer park, Buckhurst Hill, LiDAR image, showing faint circles the size of roundhouses (example arrowed).

2

Epping Forest Places and Nicholas Hagger's Poems

The following poems and extracts taken from Nicholas Hagger's *Collected Poems*, *Classical Odes* and his two poetic epics *Overlord* and *Armageddon* refer to the Forest places of Part Two. Their detail supplements his view of Epping Forest. (Poems taken from the first two of the above volumes have extensive notes referring to sources, and these can be found in those two volumes.)

Nicholas Hagger's *Collected Poems* contain nearly 1,500 poems and *Classical Odes* contain more than 300 classical odes, and many of his poetic works, in particular his shorter lyrics, draw on the Forest. This Appendix contains a selection of his Forest poems that echo themes in this book.

Loughton

A Green Country

Apples are green under a fluttering flag,
Green are my daughter's eyes, green is her breath.
Green are the children among brambles and ferns,
"Oi-olly-ocky," they yodle, "I see Liz,"
Stealing on tiptoe like scrumping thieves.
And let us run together now, across the road, down the hill
to the Forest,
To where the stream trickles from the long arched tunnel,
And, legs astride it, hands on the curved walls, walk
bow-legged
And stand under the grating overflow, as if in a Hellish
dungeon.
I took you there, and found a Victorian penny.
O this Blackweir pool, where I fished up green frogs
in flour-bag nets!
We scuffled up through leaves, leaving the water boatmen and
dragonflies,
And at a meeting of green paths plunged right, into beeches,
I held your hand and said, "Look, the banks,"
And we ran on back into blackbirds and sticklebacks and
newts,
And there, still under water-lilies, was the pond I had not
found for two decades,
The Lost Pond!

Apples, pears, wasps.
I came from the Essex flats, green fields round beech thickets.
When the daisies were humming with bees, I lay under
summer skies.
I see a clearing where I kicked a ball, where my father swung

his lame leg
And scored with a toe-punt. There I picnicked with two boys from the first form.
I ran through the Forest in the summers.
I caught caddice in the ponds, I had a glass aquarium that cracked at the top,
And green slime slopped down the sides. Near a fallen apple tree
I grew tall to the trembling of leaves. Upstairs, under green eaves,
I sniffed my death. I said to my brother
"I will live to be a hundred," clicking and reshutting the small black cupboard door
Until a voice from downstairs called "Go to sleep."

Brown is the earth of this Clay Country, and hard under frost,
Hard are the fields around Chigwell where we were sent on walks,
Stepping over iced hoof-marks in the frozen mud,
O those glistening stiles and brown dark thorns!
Crisp are the leaves of the heart in winter
When the bonfires smoulder no more. Bright is the air,
Remote the golden suns smashed across the icy pool of the sky.
Fingers are numb, cheeks pink, breath misty, clear.

I and my grandfather walked for tobacco in fog,
He fell and blood streamed from his white hair.
He had a stub of a finger he lost in a Canadian saw-mill.
Later my father took me for a walk. As we left the gate
The siren wailed. We wheeled to a white white flash,
The whole street shook, the windows clattering out.
Five bombs had fallen. Two houses up the road were

annihilated
And the cricket field had a hole in it. The war –
I lay in a Morrison shelter and read books, swapped
foreign notes,
While in the blue air puffs of smoke ended pilots.
When I moved home, I carried my battleship.

Red bricks and lilacs droop over the wooden shed.
On our rockeries, young hearts have wept and bled.
Ivy, and a garden hose.
A home is a rattling front door,
A broken flowerpot under a scarlet rose.

Green are the clumps of Warren Hill, green and
scummy pond,
Green are the Oaklands fields, green round buttercups,
Green are those fields where children squat in camps,
Green is the ride down Nursery Road, purple the thistles,
Green are the Stubbles and the open heath,
Green is Robin Hood Lane, green past Strawberry Hill,
Green and brown are the two gravel pit ponds,
Green is High Beach, green around Turpin's Cave where
beechburrs cling to hair,

Green round Lippitt's Hill and the Owl, green the fields
beyond,
Green back through Boadicea's camp, where you climbed
the brown mud walls,
Brown are the leaves round the hollow tree we climbed,
Green along Staples Hill, where we shuffled through leaves
to the brown stream,
Green past the Wheatsheaf, green up to Baldwin's Hill
Where we ran down to Monk Wood, and you were remote
from me;

Green holly, green beech leaves, green oaks, and only the trunks and banks are brown.
Green to the Wake Arms, green to the Epping Bell,
Green down Ivy Chimneys, green up Flux's Lane
Between the poplars and the farmers' fields
Green are the trees round distant Coopersale Hall,
Green are the fields of Abridge and Chigwell,
Green is Roding Valley before hilly Debden,
Green fields, wide open, back into cratered Loughton,
A green country with hosannah-ing pollards, arms raised in jubilation.
And green is that gate, green the lime trees that hide the green porch door,
Green is that house of echoes. O how you despised my cradle!
You found the buildings false, the people mean and ugly,
But couldn't you feel the kiss in the swishing wind?

From *The Flight, August 1970*
Collected Poems

Pear-Ripening House

A gable behind lime trees, a green gate
Which says "Journey's End". In the porch we wait
By the grained door, then go by pebbledash
Garage and shed which have seen small boys bash
Centuries before lunch against Australia,
Past roses (at square leg), a dahlia,
And a splurge of storm-beaten daisies, for
The old pear tree tumbles by the back door.

Now in this room peep – under four black beams,
Sloping ceilings – for the mirror where gleams
The yearning of a reaching out to moons,

Where flit the ghosts of a thousand afternoons.
This, and the black Victorian clock that cowers
Between two prancing horses, measured the hours
Of falling generations, crops of pears,
The sunsets and winters up and down the stairs.

Here floats a battleship on a lino sea;
The day war ended, this was ARP.
Here slides the ghost of a brooding schoolboy,
A fire-warmed clerk reading in lonely joy.
Here flits a brief affair, a wedding eve,
Here steals a separation. The shadows grieve.
Families, funerals....A Parthenon,
This house is permanent, we are the gone.

Now thirty years are less than the straggly twines
That were honeysuckle. And still the sun shines!
Dressing for church is the green of last spring's
Lilac; young ambitions and hankerings
Are now the floatings of a dandelion clock.
What meaning had they? Is Time just the block
And blackened stump of a hewn sweet chestnut?
Cascading ivy that drowned a summerhut?

Young wants and hankerings have a meaning
To the hard-skinned ego's slow mellowing.
The journey through maturing hours and years
Ends in wrinkling pith and pitying tears.
Cores fill with heavy juices from one flow
Whose sap softens to soul the hard ego.
All life ripens to drowse back to the One:
Fruit and old men fall earthward from the sun.

Ripe pears return pips to the ground, and sow

A next life's genes, patterned on this one. Know
That soul inherits genes from its last spring now
To gush a vision of buds upon a bough.
Leafy lives fill with the sap of all that's green
And are God's mind, whose code is in each gene,
And grow centuries of purpose into fruit
And show: soul ripens so new seeds can shoot.

We journey through a house and garden, shore
Up, improve, order and pass on the law
Of growth and fruit. The long way gives ample
If we soften to the universal
Sun. We journey, pick pears and paint old wood,
Teach sons. Seed is the end of parenthood:
The hard, small pear on the tree on the lawn,
And a ripe pip sprouting in a distant dawn.
4 August 1974; revised 23 March, mid-April, 26 May 1980
Collected Poems

In Loughton, Within Western Civilization

I leave the brick house where I live and work,
Shut the front door, go out through the porch, see
Malcolm up a ladder, scraping old leaves
Out of the gutter. Grinning, he shows me
His right hand, red blood trickling to the wrist.
He works for me. Concerned, I pull a face,
Offer Savlon, a plaster. He says, "When
I've finished." Loyal fellow. I grimace.

Two thousand years back he'd have been a slave.
Now he's my concern, I look after him.
I crouch into my BMW,
Drive down the leafy High Road – gardens, trim

Gabled houses on either side – and reach
The second parade of shops, turn and stop
On the yellow line, risking a fine, dart
Into the chemist's and queue: stand, loll, hop.

I ask if my wife's tablets are ready.
The prescription is still with the doctor.
I see rows of jars for those who have been
Brought drugs by the pharmacy's messenger.
Mine are missing. They will look for them when
Someone visits the surgery in an hour.
I pass all kinds of bathroom soaps and gels,
Shampoos, salts and foams to wash, bath or shower.

I leave by a door that has a throstle,
Cross to the newsagent, hand in my script –
My newspaper order, the days set out,
Some "full", some "part", with discount tokens clipped –
To the Pakistani and then walk through
The former fountain with a drinking-cup
On chain, drive on and queue at traffic-lights
And look at the Loughton where I grew up.

Trees overhung kerbs where there are now shops
In those days. I look at the Post Office,
The bank where I, a boy, was given a mound
Of foreign coins, some holed, some square – what bliss!
Gone is the café where I'd meet a friend
To talk poetry. I turn and park before
The spot I found Grandpa lying in fog
In the road I lived in during the war.

The war. I remember the flying bombs,
I hear the crash that knocked the windows out

Of the house in front of which I'm now parked
In my black car. In the High Road I scout,
See where my war-time school stood, since pulled down,
The war memorial where I saw Churchill.
And in the vanished White Shop Gladys weighs
Potatoes on brass scales in mittens – still.

I saunter past the site of the razed church
Where Sundays dragged like the clock on its wall.
I wander to the Holly Bush where I
Talked literature, and look at Lopping Hall,
The Loughton I returned to from Oxford.
I walk back to the bank, now changed, and smile
At Lyn the cashier, who tells me about
Tommy's wife dying of Alzheimer's. Vile!

I take my money from the till and walk
Back to my car in the footprints I made
As a youth from Oxford and first married.
The corners have memories that don't fade.
It is not as quaint as some villages,
But I will never escape its echoes.
I must pull up my new roots in Suffolk
And return to this place that my soul knows.

How could I have left these familiar streets?
In my car I return to my house, eat
Lunch from a tray and watch a minister
Squirm through a statement like a fog and cheat,
Using words to mislead and to deny.
I see my counsel on the screen, and think
Democracy's just a button away.
I connect with the System in one blink.

I ring my accountant for new accounts.
A fax bears a message from Suffolk life.
An e-mail's in the post I've just brought in,
Which I open. And then I see my wife
Hold my grandson she's picked up from nursery.
He kicks his legs as if swimming in sea.
I get down on hands and knees and play bo.
He kicks in recognition, beams at me.

This is how we live in the new century:
A simple, everyday life in memories,
In the marketplace with those I employ
Among all those who buy my services,
Those I patronise, whose labours I buy –
A town where familiar faces in shops,
Where the past invades the present and days
Drift by with little things, and aging stops.

Loughton, once one of seventeen Lordships
With which Harold endowed Waltham Abbey,
Later the *Domesday Book*'s Lochentuna
And Waltham's Lukitone* manor briefly,
Gifted to the Duchy of Lancaster
In the fourth and fifth years of Mary's reign –
Like grass growing through pavement flagstone cracks,
Ancientness breaks through my mind from time's drain.

Loughton, such an undistinguished place, on
The tube from London yet with leafy roads.
If this were Rome or Ephesus, I'd see
The houses as rich in mod-cons, with loads
Of gadgets, and marvel at the standard –
The frozen food, phone and instant TV,
Electric light, wonders old Europe lacked.

It's a life of comfortable luxury.

I delight in merging place and idea,
In showing how a concept rose from streets
That are now marble blocks, or brick houses,
In the thinginess of poetry: hewn feats.
I sculpt an ancient town but laterally
Chisel the work of a philosopher
Who once lived there and was inspired by it,
Could not have carved his work without its spur.

What's the idea behind this modern place?
Community, souls leaving houses, blessed,
Going to work on the tube or by car,
Teaching children, walking in the forest
In leisurely weekends, drinking, eating –
Chinese, Indian, French – at restful pace;
An everyday life that is for all time:
Eternal verities rooted in place.

I have made the familiar strange and see
The universal – streets of Pompeii –
Behind particular Loughton, and felt
The rootedness of growing in memory.
This place was my cradle, will be my grave.
I found better towns – in country, by sea;
None rivalled the familiar atmosphere
Of Loughton, which I've loved devotedly.

O Loughton, your chemists, banks and restaurants,
Your newsagents and shops that rest on clay,
Are a little life, like the cricket-ground
I played on one packed-crowd Bank Holiday.
On the rim of your three-sided crater,

Among your forest ponds I heard a call
From a far destiny and responded,
Wrote verses while bustling round Lopping Hall.
February 26, 2002; revised March 20-22, 2002;
April 16, 2005
Classical Odes

* Loughton was Lukintune to the Anglo-Saxons, Lochintuna (or Lochentuna) to the Normans in the *Domesday Book* and Lukitone to Waltham Abbey. (See pp.55 and 383.)

Two Glimpses of Churchill

And over fifty years on I recall
The bare-headed Churchill, wearing a coat,
Holding a microphone, braving drizzle
(Like Themistocles after Salamis),
Standing at the war memorial by
The Loughton cricket field before a crowd
In an open-air election address,
Congratulating his constituents
On surviving rockets and flying bombs
And saying that if he was called away
During the election (a reference to
Potsdam), Mrs Churchill, who stood upright
Beside him, would take his place. And I saw
A banner, "Hitlers come, Hitlers go, but
There will always be a Churchill." I heard
The cheers, was there at an event that has
Receded into history like a town
Seen after take-off from the air. I did
Not know how fickle a people can be.
Overlord, Book 12, lines 997-1015

O Churchill, you who were my MP in
The war, whose constituency Hitler
Attacked with V-1s and V-2s, so I
Lay awake at night listening for the whine
Of doodlebugs, the silence and the crash
That obliterated houses like mine –
Hitler whose bombers blew out our windows;
You who I heard speak at the Loughton war
Memorial on your way to Potsdam
When you stood on the first step with your wife,
And who, entering the High School, in nineteen
Fifty-one stopped and signed my autograph
Album and beamed at me under your hat.
Armageddon, Book 5, lines 1-13

Among Loughton's Sacred Houses

I

I park in Brooklyn Avenue, a long
Way back from the High Road, linger, loiter
Outside the house I came to when just three,
Semi-detached with a concrete area.
I recall sitting on the stairs inside,
Could go up on my bottom, heaved and strove.
I see myself sitting in my high-chair,
My mother in the kitchen, by the stove.

I hear a deep voice on the radio
Read the war news, then see myself in bed
Listening in terror after lights-out for
Doodlebugs, and once heard in mounting dread
A knocking underneath, a broken spring.
I thought there was someone below my feet
And was too paralysed by fear to look,

And cowered in the safety of my sheet.

And I came to this gate with my father,
Where I'm standing, fifty-nine years ago.
The sky lit up with a white flash, windows
Behind broke, bits of glass fell, lay below.
I see my father turning in the dark,
Saying "Come on, back in" in a low shout,
Limping-running back towards the front door
While I chant with glee, "The windows are out."

A string of bombs had hit the cricket field.
We lived in the V-bomb corridor then.
My father told me stories at bedtime
Of "Peter and his dog", when the siren
Went off at the police station – air raid!
And I was led by hand to the shelter
Somewhere downstairs in there, lay on a rug,
Was read to as we waited for thunder.

From here I walked to school, first Essex House,
And then to old Oaklands across the road;
And walked back with Robin Fowler's mother.
My shoelace came undone there, as she strode
By her bike she stooped and tied it. That night
I tried, fumbled lace and mucked up my bow.
In old Oaklands garden I lay inside
The Morrison shelter in the sun's glow.

Grandpa, white-haired, one finger missing, came
And sat gnarled by the fire, and one tea-time
Went to the shops in fog, did not come back.
I was sent out and found him, nose in grime,
Towards the High Road, lying on the ground.

He had stumbled and cut his head. I "woke"
Him up and led him back through the thick fog,
Bleeding, now wonder: did he have a stroke?

I see my father's study, he sits by
A desk, green curtains drawn, light on. I stand
While he tells me the twins have died. Will I
Help tell my younger brother, hold his hand?
Filled with importance and responsible,
Wondering if I should grieve, they'd not known me
As they'd never left hospital, I nod,
Am haunted by that room which I still see.

II

I drive to the school my grandson went to
And stand outside the green home we bought, see
Myself hold a grey battleship. Up there
Wires hung from the skirting-boards, ARP
Telephones had stood on the bare floorboards.
A hot May afternoon, and I hear words
From my birthday party in the garden.
Robin Fowler gave me a book on birds.

I said, "I've got this book." "No, you haven't,"
My mother said menacingly, laying
Jammed bread on a clean, white tablecloth I
Sat at with other small children, watching.
A blob of damson jam dropped on the cloth.
I see my mother in a summer dress
Pinch salt and rub it on the purple stain.
I could lean in and rub the salt, touch, press.

I see the bedroom where I used to read,
Up there on the right, where I dreaded creaks,

The streetlight reassuring on the wall;
And then I moved to the back room that speaks
Of my brother. We shared a black cupboard –
Rickety, a door catch that clicked
And whispered round it from our twin beds till
One of our parents called up, "Go to sleep."

I recall being ill and the gas fire
By which I would read all Dostoevsky.
Dr Walker came, I ate arrowroot,
A poached egg on mashed potato. I see
My mother cook on the old kitchen stove,
Red and black tiles on the floor: Welsh rarebit,
And on Sundays a sizzling sausage pie;
High tea at six, the nursery dimly lit.

As I had younger brothers and sisters
Nurses came to stay, my former bedroom
Had a bath, nurse's chair and baby clothes.
I saw a baby being bathed in gloom,
In a half-oval white bath that slotted
In a metal holder on folding legs,
Filled from a blue enamel jug's water
Boiled on the coke boiler near piled clothes-pegs.

I think of summers in the back garden,
The grey enamel tub we put pears in.
My father up a ladder hands pears down
For me to pull off twigs and leaves, wipe skin;
And also apples from the apple-tree
To take to the cellar, arrange in rows:
First pears, not touching, topped with newspaper,
Then Cox's orange pippins above those.

I recall how we dressed for church in suits –
The clock ticked too slowly on the church wall;
How we walked to my grandmother's and sat
In her large pink armchairs, while in the hall
Her clock struck each hour's quarter sonorously,
And told our news, my aunt nearby, her skills
No longer at the London Hospital
Where I saw Queen Mary by daffodils.

III

I stand in Station Road, mind in nursery.
I sit left of the fireguard and coal fire.
My mother holds her hands towards the coals,
I feel warmth on my cheeks as I aspire.
Coals glow red-hot, orange, I see faces
As low flames dance and sparks fizzle on soot.
To her it was normal but it haunts me:
The simple homely warmth of hand and foot.

I recall the room on the half-landing
Where my father lay during his last hours,
Grasped my hand, how when we raised beer tankards
Together, he choked out his failing powers.
I stood by him when he lay still and dead
And saw the Council Offices through glass,
The workplace he walked to, and early stars
Beyond the pear-tree's branches, twilit grass.

I see the Brook Road gate, my grandmother
Walking beside me with her stick "to say
Goodbye for the last time", at eighty-nine.
She died soon after, when I was away.
Memories whirl through my head as I stand
By the knobbly lime-trees I used to prune

With a long-arm. I was snapped on that path
With my brother, in sandals, one hot June.

I see my father and my mother peer
Round the side wall, though they are both long dead.
My father limps and smiles, smoking his pipe,
Holding a pail, and smooths his balding head.
My mother clutches the Moses-basket,
A baby lies inside, playing with hands.
They smile at me from a far place, and I
Smile back. They're gone. Only the house still stands.

The tears are in my eyes as I loiter
On the once tree-lined kerb of Station Road
And look in from outside on vanished youth,
Look across sixty years. How much I've owed
Them, I would ring the bell, go in and stand
In the same places, but all would have changed.
It's better to keep fresh in mind from then
Those faces so familiar, now estranged.

I went away, I left them, fled at first
To Oxford, then Iraq, Japan. Surely
I'd left them earlier, changing from law
(Their world) to poetry, self-discovery,
Culture, my world of walks in the Forest,
Deep ruminations by glades, leafy brooks
On literature, and a mountain of texts
On my bed, to be read, Europe's best books.

The gate to this house proclaimed "Journey's End".
It called me to a journey with a goal,
To search and research through history's ages
And find in myself, and awake, my soul.

I travelled deep into cultures and mind,
Soul-climbed through regions, religions, up stone,
Philosophers of east and west, poets
Who've anything to say and who have known,

And now I'm at my journey's end I stand
Where my climb for lost knowledge was begun
And think how the very name on the gate
Urged me to start a journey to the One.
This place was a call – poetry a method,
A trellis rose-like souls can climb and grow –
And a pledge that one day all journeys end
As mine has now I stand in sun, and know.

With memories like these which still haunt me, how
Could I retire anywhere but this place?
This Loughton where some houses are sacred
Holds dear and troubled memories I retrace.
And so I've come back to such memories,
Will never leave Loughton except for weeks
Here and there in Cornwall, Italy, Greece.
I embrace Loughton and have her for keeps.

Memories of one's childhood are limpid-clear,
They have the power of images and seem
To come not from this world but from beyond
Everyday's phenomenal screen – from dream:
Faces so vivid I could lean and touch,
Hands held over the nursery fire, still kind;
And coals that will never grow cold again.
The Loughton I embrace is in my mind.
February 20, 2003; revised August 24-25, 2003
Classical Odes

In Addison's Essex

I read in Addison's *Essex Heyday*
How Lady Mary Wroth held Loughton Hall
For forty years, leased it from King James' Queen,
How bravely Sir George Lisle went to the wall,
How Edward de Vere became Lord Warden
Of Waltham Forest in the very year
Harsnett, Chigwell's vicar, published his book
From which Shakespeare named spirits in *King Lear*.

I leaf through illustrations, black and white,
Of Essex village greens and country sleep,
High streets, beached boats, stage coaches, hens pecking,
All seventeenth-century, walkers and sheep,
A spire, old halls and tombs, how life was in
Essex in its heyday when hay was forked
On carts to feed horses and parsons strode
With benign tolerance for all that talked.

It's a paean in praise of all that's old.
The epigraph quotes Webster on old wine,
Apples, wood, linen, soldiers, old lovers
Who "are soundest": a county like a shrine
From top to bottom of the social scale,
Seen from post-war Labour Britain to say
Through family records how Puritans
Slowly replaced the medieval way.

Beneath the social conflicts – Civil War –
Everyday life went on in halls, manors
And farms among lords, their employed, servants,
Cottagers, workmen, weavers, sheep-farmers.
We glimpse English economic history:

Vagrants, inns and ale-houses, how Merrie
England's feudal grandees were confronted
By puritans who scorned their pedigree.

He saw the hidden movements of an age,
A verderer haunted by the Forest.
I think of how he stood in his bookshop
After the war, in a dark suit, with zest,
Hook-nosed, balding, hair round his ears, tall, grave,
A JP, and stooped to give me advice
As I, in short trousers, held out a book
Token – the first writer I knew, and nice.

I have gone some way down Addison's way,
Am steeped in Essex and Forest buddings.
From him I sense the pressure of the past
Under paving-stones, on crests of buildings
And in the earthen walls of Loughton Camp
And Ambresbury Banks, two Iron Age Forest forts
And houses once owned by Essex worthies
Of whom he wrote and is now one; and courts.

I last saw him at Chingford's Great Standyng –
Henry the Eighth's, Queen Elizabeth's grand
Hunting lodge – at a Forest reception.
He was in a wheelchair, smiled, shook my hand
As I told him I ran Oaklands. He sat
Grandly with sticks and talked of his ailments
And invited me to his home. He died
Before I went and heard his strong accents.

Now he has joined the rich-textured pattern,
The criss-crossed design of the past he'd found,
Knighted for serving Essex and history,

A man on eminent, distinctive ground
Who'll be known for hundreds of years to come
In his locality, but not outside,
A local man who unearthed his county
And through his books served as a Forest guide.
September 2, 2001; revised September 3, 7-8, 2001
Classical Odes

Orpheus-Prometheus in the Blackweir Region of Hell

We looked in this Blackweir pond at stickleback
And minnows with green and silver bellies,
At water beetle, skimming dragonflies –
Looked down through the bars, and then picked blackberries.

As a boy I climbed into the round tunnel,
Crouched underground, under this high-barred grate
Where the pond overflows in a cascade down,
Heard voices echoing up to this dungeon gate.

Now squatting beneath the bars within my mind,
Watching gnats dance from an awful torture cell,
I look up at blue sky from a dark tunnel.
Will there ever be an opening in the Gates of Hell?
18 November 1972
Collected Poems

Clouded-Ground Pond

On Strawberry Hill, a break in forest trees.
We park on mud and cross the road in breeze:
A brown pond, yellow lilies. It is cool.
We could stay all day here at the Horseman's Pool,
But it is near the road. We take the track

Past logs and stones in clay, turn into brack-
en, hawthorn, beech. And now, beyond holly,
A pond amid gorse and birch, and a fallen tree.

It has seen the agonies of the seasons:
How fathers died in autumn; the reasons
Young men married, were exiled, lived alone,
And their returns. This pond has also known
The stealings-up through sawing grasshoppers,
And secret comings far from eavesdroppers.
It has sensed small girls crouch in these gnarled roots,
And dreamt of the netting of speckled newts.

A touch of sadness taints the autumn tint.
Like a daughter leaving till spring, a hint
Of absence skips round the deep gravel pit.
Across its quiet eternal stillness flit
The changing shadows of dragonfly time,
Newt and lily months. Sticklebacks stir slime.
This gravel is honey, this cloud is cherry
And the heather and gorse smell of strawberry.

Now time disturbs the eternal with raindrops,
Voices. Ducks clack, dogs splash, a robin hops,
Frogs watch and plop in mud, a rustle rolls
Through the silver birch near where, in spring, tadpoles
Cluster like thorns round submerged sticks. At noon
The shimmering mirror, teeming with June,
Can blaze into nothing, while two hearts bound
As a face drowns in clouds to gasp on: ground.

Four worlds make contact in beauty, and when
The ground reflects a leafy, clouded sky, then
All four dance in the mirror of a pond.

Through layered leaves, the groundless soul beyond
Reflects clouds of spirit, and, in high moments,
The sun's divine air, blinding experience
Of the first source when all say yes and see
The One that shines within layered complexity.

Sadness and joy are one to this still Tao
Whose horn of plenty, like a watery bough,
Gushes buds, leaves, petals, and pours faces
From warm clouds into each self and all places.
Six months are one ripple that smoothes away
All sad twigs till the dancing, wintry day
Restores a universe like a green shower:
The Tao-self renews the earth, stroking the hour.

As old genes teem new lives, Tao's hidden sun,
Which joined the heights and depths and fused into one
The clouded ground, is now this lily, it
Gushes from clouds, is blown with pure sunlit
Wind, and rooted in mud, yet still, pours All.
The lily on-in water is a call
For Essex men to leave their cars and say "Yes"
To grounded roots in cloud-bordered stillness.
4 August 1974; revised 23 March 1980
Collected Poems

Oaklands: Oak Tree

I look out of my study window at
Green trees in chestnut flower, with candles that
Snuggle round a corner of green field, in the sun
On which blackbirds hop and two squirrels run,
Iron railings, where magpies and jays flit,
Where a woodpecker and a bullfinch sit.

Closer, two goldcrests swing near nuts, like thieves
And buttercups tint yellow between green leaves.

A Paradise, this field, where all aglow
I lay a childhood through a life ago,
Near the shady oak puffed at an acorn pipe,
And watched bees hum in clover when all was ripe.
A log, a pond, a horse, and everywhere,
Nature dances in the flower-filled air,
And among butterflies it is easy to see
A human gathers pollen like a bee.

A Paradise of sunlight and skipping feet
As swallows skim and swoop in the summer heat,
As a robin pecks in grass near children's speech,
The green only broken by the copper beech.
Here birds and flowers and insects perch and run,
And humans grow like berries in the ripening sun.
And tiny heads grow large like bud from stalk,
Like the spring bluebells fluttering round the Nature Walk.

It teaches that man is part of Nature's care,
That a boy can become a man without moving from here,
As a bud becomes the fruit of this apple tree,
Or this downy chick the nesting blue tit's glee,
As a grub hatches from pond slime into dragonfly;
This field is full of transformation's cry,
Of bees and birds and boys and girls and showers,
Observe your true nature among these flowers.

See the great oak like a druid tree – divine,
Filling with acorns that will make a soma wine,
And give the sight of the gods to all bound by sense,
faces across the fence.

Your true essential nature must include
This Tree of Life that pours spirit as food
Into the world, like acorns into leaves, and feeds
A horn of plenty that pours out souls like seeds.
August 1985 (?); revised 14 September 1993
Collected Poems

At Oaklands

I

I stand at the old gate that bees nest in,
Look at the school I came to in war time,
A redbrick Victorian pile deep and wide,
A massive castle, four-storeyed, sublime:
Gables, protrusions to which I added
After I bought it twenty years ago,
Two extensions and half-room at the front,
A place children run to, faces aglow,

As I did once. I walk round to the back,
Survey the tennis-court, grassed in those days,
And the lawn where the jungle gym once stood
That I'd climb and "King of the Castle", gaze.
I think of the school photo, me in it,
Fourth row back, perhaps six, against ivy
And trees where I've now built a house: small boys
With strong faces and girls with plaits, lively.

I probe the tennis-court where summer fêtes
Began with country dancing, where I spoke
To crowds, introduced Geoff Hurst, who told me
As we walked later underneath the oak
His World Cup final hat-trick was unique,
That was the last final England would reach.

I think of play-time, how I used to crouch
Near boys and girls, from haunches talk to each.

I take the path down past the Garden Room,
Three wood buildings, two of which I brought in,
One which I renewed, walk through iron railings
To the field where I lay as a boy, thin.
From under the oak tree of the school badge
The whole field shimmered yellow, hummed with bees
I picked, held a buttercup to a chin
Which shimmered yellow love of butter, cheese.

I think of how we played rounders here, how
I belted a whopper and ran round posts;
How we made camps at war-end, dragged branches,
Blocked exits, held friends prisoner, break-time hosts.
I sat at a table under this tree
And miked sports' days' running races, and warned.
Rachel Hunter ran barefoot with mothers
While Rod Stewart lay on his front and yawned.

I think of the fireworks nights I've controlled
Near the caravan, watched the rockets go
Whooshing up the night sky to oohs and aahs
And a fire as big as a bungalow
Shooting high flames, scattering smuts that float.
I think of a barbecue by this tree
For the School's fiftieth. Here five hundred queued
And Jack Straw, once a pupil, wrote to me.

He was told not to skate on the iced pond
At the bottom of the field, naughtily
Disobeyed, fell in and was led blubbing
To stand disgraced outside Miss Lord's study.

I opened fêtes before the caravan,
Stood with Norris and Vicki Michelle, when,
Stunning, she hung on my arm, said, "Leesten
Very carefully, ze fête ees open."

I go down to the second field and see
Where once a week, wearing a blue track suit,
I played football with the boys. The West Ham
Goalie McAlister passed ball to boot,
And later Dutchman, hero of my youth
Who won the Amateur Cup at Wembley.
I mowed both these fields, starting outside, rode
Round in decreasing circles, happily.

The far pond I had excavated, then
A dozen of us puddled mud with bare
Feet to seal the bottom. Now ducks nest on
The island I made, there's weed, in sun's glare
Newts and tadpoles, and dragonflies flit round.
Water-boatmen skate on the calm surface.
All round, hawthorns and trees shimmer. I love
Such spots, where the foxes live, the wind's kiss.

II

I walk back past huge logs like garden seats,
A squirrel skitters, two magpies, a jay;
Climb the stone steps I moved ten yards, shifting
Huge York-stone slabs with garden fork one day;
And go to the two white Wren doors I found
In Architectural Salvage, that had come
From St James', Piccadilly, and enter
The School past Miss Lord's old study, succumb:

There Ann, my wife, was Head for fourteen years.

I go upstairs past framed cigarette cards, flowers
I bought and hung, which remind me of when
I was in hospital aged seven, spent hours
In bed making sets of fifty from mixed
Fish, reptiles, trees, kings that slope up this wall.
I go up to Mabel's room, the nursery
When the Howards hung their coats in the hall.

Here was my desk, that day through that door strode
Alan Donald, new uniform and rules,
Proudly to the front, a smart example
Of how we should all stand at our new schools.
Poor Mabel, I hear her with her eye-shade,
Saying "Shh, an owl" on a Nature-walk.
I listened for nightingales with her, learned
To love Nature in Paradise and talk.

I go down to the assembly hall, which I
Painted one weekend with parents' help, rolled
The ceiling white, leaning out from high steps,
Amateurish, then brushed the mouldings gold.
Here I have held so many staff meetings,
Christmas lunches, and sat for hours and bent
Through Parents' Association shopping-lists,
What sausages to buy for their event.

I sat here in a circle on the floor
When a naughty boy struck a match daftly.
I recall an assembly, I sat there
When Miss Lord spoke of the League of Pity
From the stage, since replaced by my brother's
Mother-in-law when she chaired the PA
Before our time. I acted on "those" boards
When for our parents we put on a play.

I return to the study, where Miss Lord
Stuffed wads of notes – fees – through a cushion patch
(Once in the kitchen oven, and cried out
"Don't light it" as the old cook struck her match),
An improvised safe from a bygone age.
I wander out and stand under the blue
Acacia cedar that scatters needles,
Look down on the brick house I built, first drew.

I linger by the window-sill where Rod
Stewart sat, waiting to collect Renée
And a dozen mothers would form a line,
None speaking to him, he in shorts, *risqué*.
A childhood's memories stir, how I jumped off
A speeding bus at the foot of the hill
When it passed my stop, football boots dragging,
And was led grazed and bleeding past this sill.

III

I look at the grounds, now in spring blossom,
The flowers out under a blue summery sky
And children filing up in green sweaters
Marshalled by a coy schoolmistress who's shy.
And I know this place is a place where souls
Like mine come and take root, trust, grow a knack,
And love these surroundings and half-lost scenes
That can't be forgotten, that bring me back

As it brought back my lost friends – Peter Liell,
Jennifer Fish, Gordon Roberts – who say
They had a lifelong devotion to those
Who fussed over them, set them on their way.
This is a green place, the cradle where I
Found my soul's seed-bed, learned to grow and thrum,

A place where my heart longs to roam, with woods
That are mine when the holidays have come,

Where I can wander to my heart's delight,
Find each leaf or flower I drew as a child,
See all manner of creatures – spiders, toads,
Hedgehogs, voles, bullfinches, owls in the wild.
I think of how the Spurges were here when
The apple-tree trunks were all painted white
For Florence's wedding to Booth Harris
From across the road, in Victorian light.

I think of the Howards here in one war.
In the next war Belgian refugees came.
One day I arrived with the caravan
Our tractor drew across a rounders game.
Oaklands, you have a spirit that reflects
The spirit that each of us strives to free,
Of zest, shared play, excitement and wonder,
Rootedness mirrored in the great oak tree.

I have sat in my window and gazed at
A decorated raw-clay, handled jug
With blue borders, given to my mother by
Composer Percy Sharman as a hug;
Have looked at the reliefs: eight white children
In Regency clothes skip and dance and jog,
Three holding hands, while under a white tree
A boy plays a flute near a prancing dog.

I've looked out of my window at the school
Playground and seen some eighty children play,
Running, skipping, dancing, all acting out
Something they've seen as urgent as the day,

A scene glimpsed in their imagination
As do these boys on my jug-urn who stamp
As I did once when I was a lad here
And ran in the field, made a wartime camp.

As a schoolboy here I saw on waste ground
Opposite Albion Hill a JCB
Scoop earth and pile it near me. Something small
Glinted in sun, I bent and saw "SC",
Picked from mud and wiped a bronze coin, a worn
Bald head, and later took it to Seaby
Who said "It's Caracalla" – the brutal
Emperor who ruled in the third century.

Caracalla spread Rome's citizenship
To almost all who lived in the empire.
I've thought that through him Providence called me
To learn how all world governments conspire;
But now I think that bronze coin was a call
To make my fortune from this ancient hill,
A nudge to buy my old school, see and care
("SC") for tiny souls' acorn-like will.
February 16, 2003; revised February 18-21,
September 1, 3, 2003; February 18, 2004. Classical Odes

Chigwell

At The Old Chigwellians' Shrove-Tuesday Dinner

I look at the field and classrooms that lit
My school days and go to the Swallow Room
And stand with a glass of red wine beneath
The dome that lifts each whisper to a boom
And am greeted with great cheer and smiles by

Retired men, once my classmates, my co-slaves,
By Leng and Godfrey, Dutchman beams and heads
Through a packed throng as cheery Hoppit waves!

I take my reserved *Châteauneuf* red wine
And stand at a long table. The chaplain
Asks us to hold Tommy Farr "close to God"
As he is in hospital once again.
I sit with Hoppit, opposite Egan;
We retell memories across the table,
How we walked four miles down the Appian Way
And I nearly died in Paestum's temple.

"I changed his life, and he changed mine," I say
To Egan, and describe how Hoppit saw
A party of girls on St Peter's steps,
How he talked to one he'd marry, adore;
And how I swapped my tuck for his Greek coin
From Corinth, with a horse's head I brought
Into my Oxford viva, and won one
Of four places a hundred hopefuls sought.

Yarning and reminiscence fume with wine.
Egan retells how his class "mucked about"
In their Maths lesson, held a mock funeral
For Rose, who'd gone to hospital "with gout".
"They're dressed in khaki and they have a box
For a coffin, blow a bugle. Rose nears,
Opens the door. One says, 'It's Lazarus
Come back from the dead.'" We laugh, the wine

There is *bonhomie, camaraderie.*
I am with men who knew me as a boy.
I turn and ask a bearded man, Gaymer,

"Are you Bunny's brother?" He fills with joy.
"Yes," he says, "I was ten years younger." He
Died, I say. "Yes, forty-five years ago.
In a plane crash over Northumberland.
He was navigator – and my hero."

I say I recall Bunny coming back
In uniform, red-cheeked, fair hair curly,
And talking about his life: "I'm smoking
Like a fish and drinking like a chimney."
Then he realized and put what he'd said right.
"The plane refuelled in Cyprus," he says, stilled.
"EOKA put a bomb on board. Blew up,
A mid-air explosion. Five men were killed."

And now I'm sombre amidst the laughter,
The English thanes with flowing mead and wine,
I am like a First-World-War veteran
Recalling a colleague who'd hit a mine,
Or Hamlet who once knew Yorick, and now
I no more set the table on a roar.
He shakes my hand, pleased to meet one who knew
His brother forty-five years back or more.

The interlude is over, once again
Laughter crowds in, lost people as they were:
Hutchin, the gaunt white Reverend Wallace,
Norwood, who'll soon be a priest, and de Boer.
Rooted like roses in a rose garden,
We bask in warmth, genial friendship, good cheer
And reminisce in treasured surroundings
And recreate a past we all hold dear.
Conceived February 27, 2001; written February 28, 2001
Classical Odes

Waltham Abbey

An Inner Home

"The forest which surrounds them is their godhead."
(From a review by Mr. Geoffrey Gorer of *Wayward Servants,*
a book on the Mbuti pygmies in the Ituri rain forest, N.E. Congo.)

I have followed the Waltham stream:
Winding through sunny meadows,
Stilled by lilies and reeds
It seems a long way from
King Harold's rough-hewn bridge
And Edward's two arches,
Till under the Abbey's tower
On either side of stone
Under two modern humped bridges
With a sudden tugging of weed
The stillness overflows
To plunge in a cascade down
And froth into gentle channels
And trickle underground
And I turned away in a panic,
There was weed in my hair and toes.

That child, who, sick from fleeing a baying form,
Lay on the humming Stubbles near the Witches' Copse
Like a sacrificial victim near Stonehenge,
And, seeing a six-spot burnet, suddenly felt secure,
Walled round and alone in a forest enclosure;
That child seemed a long way from that adolescent
Who, sick at having seen the universe
In a string of bubbles blown through a child's wire-ring,
Stood in Loughton Camp among writhing pollards

Like nerve tracts rising to a memory rooted in
The skulls of Boadicea's unconscious dead,
And, under the dark grey cortex, distinctly heard
The silence beneath the distant hum of cars
And knew himself under the patter of falling leaves;
And that young man, who, retching at one last sigh,
Stood where he fished as a child with sewn flour-bags
And skidded to the island on an icy slide
And stared past his reflection in the gravel pit
As if seeking an image in an unconscious mind,
Until his darkness split, and in the autumn sun
The pond blazed in an unknowable revelation,
He said Yes, and, looking back through the blinding leaves,
He longed to be a statue between the two ponds
And gaze for ever on the thrusting of those trees;
Or that poet, who, sick with impending exile,
Having driven round Lippitt's Hill to Tennyson's estate,
Crunched broken glass in the littered Witches' Copse
Alone in the centre of a living mandala,
And knew, although before him was approaching stone,
Like a hermit enfolded in a godhead he projects
He would always be enfolded in this Forest,
In this unchangeable image of an inner home.

Like the tree-enfolded face a still stream reflects
Below humped bridges where waving weed is pressed
Before it plunges down and is lost in foam.
13–16 October 1966; revised in 1968 (?)
Collected Poems

With Harold at Waltham

I walk through the stone arch, and by the stream
Which brims over the weir, plunges into gloom,
And beside the Abbey to the old altar's dream,
Now in fresh air, and stare at Harold's tomb.
Here Harold was brought, identified by his belle,
Edith Swan Neck, after the arrow in his eye,
Here he lay by the nave he built, as the old order fell
To the Norman horde – French Danes with a Latin cry.

The last of the Saxons. Under Canute the Dane
A carpenter had a dream that all should dig
Forty cubits for a buried cross, it sounds insane
But a black flint crucifix was found – quite big –
And the Lord of Waltham, Tovi the Proud, inflamed,
Claimed it as treasure, loaded it on an ox-cart.
The oxen only moved when Waltham was proclaimed –
Then people were cured, blood gushed from a stone like a heart.

Miracle or superstition? Accident? Providence?
Tovi vowed he would serve the cross and fate,
And his lands passed to Athelstan, his son, and thence
To Edward the Confessor, who gave his estate
To Harold Godwinson, on condition there should arise
A monastery there – we stand on holy moss.
Harold was broad, tall, handsome, strong and wise,
And cured of paralysis by the holy cross.

The finest man in England was elected King
And beat the Norwegians at Stamford Bridge, but then
Prayed here before Hastings: the figure, bowing,
Looked down from the cross sadly, an ill-omen,
The Saxons rushed on William crying, "Holy cross."

The cross disappeared in the Dissolution, and yet
In this oldest Norman church, I still sense loss,
I can still sense Harold and the Norman threat.

The cross – a dream, superstition, miracle, shield?
What can we make of it now when so many doubt?
Carpenter guided to a hill, a cross that healed,
And the Doom painting in which Christ sits and looks out
While two angels blow trumpets and the dead rise
From graves and are weighed in scales near a demon choir –
Was this the old order's folly? Look with Bayeux eyes –
The Normans were superior in their Roman Fire.
7–9 September 1985
Collected Poems

At Harold's Waltham Abbey

I

I look up at the crenellated tower,
The clock and squares of black flint, and go through
The arched door and take in the three-tiered aisle
With six sand arches and ceiling in blue,
See the smashed heads on the reredos
Which a maniac, while running amok, cleaved
With two axes, see the seventeenth-century
Pulpit with three panels hacked out and heaved.

I take a guidebook, stuff coins in a box,
Sit in a pew and gaze at sand limestone,
The Norman dogtooth round each arch, the imps
That grimace near the arches, perhaps groan;
The seven-petalled stained glass, the polished flag
Floor. I peer at the ceiling and make out
Signs of the zodiac, labours of the month,

Four elements, past and future; no doubt.

I wander to the Denny tomb, where lie,
Heads on elbowed-up left hands, Sir Edward
Who fought for his Queen and sailed with Gilbert,
And his wife Joan, Queen's maid of honour, hard,
And their ten children underneath. I cross
Black grave slabs to the black marble Smith tomb,
And floor indent for brass: mitred Abbot,
Right hand raised, pastoral staff turned in, in gloom.

I go to the boy of sixteen who died
Of smallpox in 1684, see
His chipped nose and sliced medallion under
His chin, then return to the sanctuary
And count seven heads chopped off the reredos
And a lamb's head hewn off near an angel
Beneath three Burne-Jones stained glass windows, find
A taped window in the Lady Chapel.

I sit beneath the fifteenth-century "Doom"
Wall-painting of Christ sitting in judgment.
Seven angels blow the Last Trump, the dead rise
From their graves and are weighed in scales and sent
Left to Heaven or right to Hell's jaws or fire.
All souls can choose: to axe or know true glee.
I go to the crypt, browse through cards, pamphlets,
Books. A white-haired old lady watches me.

I say, "I've looked in to see the damage."
"It's terrible. I saw him led away.
I arrived at the end, police were here.
He started at the Riverside Café,
Lived on a river boat, had two axes,

Smashed every window while an old lady
Sat terrified, then came here. He stood on
The altar, hacking. Police fired gas. *Débris*....

"He knew what he would hack, he targeted
The boy and did two hundred thousand pound
Worth of damage. He's locked up now, appears
Next month. They've been on hands and knees and found
Every splinter from the pulpit's panels,
Pieced them together, superglue technique!
It will all be restored, but will take time.
I'm a volunteer, sit three days a week."

I leave the crypt and sit by the pillar
With marks where all the parish books were chained:
The Great Bible, Erasmus' Paraphrase,
Bishop Jewel's *Apology*, Foxe's strained
Book of Martyrs. Our society's violent.
I look for Barnack, Caen and Reigate stone,
Purbeck marble (fresh-water snail shells massed),
Kentish ragstone, Beauvilliers – they're all shown.

I sat nearby at the memorial
Service for Biggs-Davison, our MP.
It was packed, I sat next to Pam Giblett,
Who as my mother's "help" used to bath me.
I recall he gave me a ticket for
A Commons Suez debate: Eden's stark
Statement on a three-power plan (collusion).
Now there's a new Suez: war with Iraq.

This is an ancient seat of five churches.
The first, built by East Saxon King Sebert
Of wood,'s under the choir. Then Offa built

A stone church that's under this one, whose dirt
Bore the large black cross found in Montacute,
Brought by Tovi the Proud, Cnut's adviser.
Harold rebuilt it in a T-shaped plan
And was entombed before the high altar.

His church was replaced by this one, the fourth,
Which Henry the Second made a priory
Enlarged it as penance for Becket's death
And then an Augustinian abbey.
Here Cranmer talked with King Henry the Eighth's
Advisers, formed the Church of England's fight.
This was the last abbey to be dissolved.
Sir Edward Denny's father leased this site.

Harold, Earl of East Anglia and Essex,
Stood for England at Hastings, set the tone.
Tallis, organist here, was the father
Of English church music. Fuller, unknown
Vicar here, wrote *The Worthies of England*.
This Abbey's central to Essex's grace
And cultural life. I would like my remains
To leave for burial from this hallowed place.

I have four claims to East Anglian fame.
I ran schools and founded Coopersale Hall;
Gave Otley Hall a transatlantic thrust;
Journeyed through cultures and stars to the All,
Light-centred history and philosophy;
Wrote poems on the Western world's rupture
But stayed true to my Englishness. I lay
This puzzle ring upon the high altar.

II

I wander out, pass Harold with a sword
Up near the mass marker and find the raised
Slab that marks the altar's position in
The fifth church and the stone behind, time-grazed,
That marks where Harold's said to be buried.
But he was not canonized, so his tomb
Would have been westward, in the two-bay choir.
I saunter westward, think of Hastings' gloom,

How Harold was cured of paralysis
By the black stone cross here that was well-known,
Raised a minster on the edge of the huge
Waltham Forest, bringing bargeloads of stone
From Caen, prayed here before mounting his horse
And riding to Hastings; and how, after,
Edith Swan-Neck found him and brought him here,
Buried him (it's said) near the high altar.

I think, William of Poitiers and Benoit
Both said Duke William gave Harold's body
To William Malet; I think of *The Song
Of the Battle of Hastings*, which said he
Was buried on the seashore; of William
Of Malmesbury, who said that Harold's mother
Buried him here; of *The Life of Harold*'s
View he lived on, a hermit in Chester.

The seashore....Archaeologists would dig
An unmarked grave at Harold's Bosham church,
Under the Saxon chancel arch shown on
They Bayeux Tapestry, to do research,
Test headless legless bones for DNA,
Match Y chromosomes with male descendants,

Show Harold slain by sword, not an arrow,
Head cut off, cut up by four knights. False scents?

The Waltham Chronicle says he was found
By Edith Swan-Neck when the carnage ceased.
She brought him here. His first tomb was before
The present altar, then he was moved east
Within the two-bay choir, now grassed, and then
Just west of this raised slab under the tower
Of the fifth church which has since been pulled down.
The Abbey fell to ruin, like its power.
"They brought the body to Waltham, buried

"They brought the body to Waltham, buried
It with great honour, where, without a doubt,
He has lain at rest till the present day,"
The *Waltham Chronicle*'s author spells out.
It was moved three times within the author's
Memory (since 1124), a mix
Of place-change and repairs. I read, "Harold
King of England, *obiit* 1066."

O Harold, you were an English hero,
The last king of the Saxons, who opposed
The take-over from Europe in your time
By Norman William with his "Brussels-posed"
Laws. You prayed at this place before you rode
South to Hastings to defend Englishness
And, when shot in the eye you expired, your
Saxon life-style was swept out by "progress".

I walk through meadow to the arched gatehouse,
The Augustinian Abbey's frontage,
And follow the river where mallards swim

As in the fourteenth century to a bridge
And stand and see it brim quite still one side,
Then by an iron wheel "cascade down" and flow
Rapidly underground with the same rush
My first historical poem would show.

That was thirty-six years ago. Where did
My lifetime go since I stood here that day,
As much a poet as I'm now? A man
Fishes with rods. "Caught anything?" I say.
"A hundred and two roach," he smiles. I've caught
Poems like roach. I sigh. My life, estranged,
Plunges and froths. I've lived my life against
This majestic place which, though hacked,'s not changed.
February 7, 2003; revised February 7-9, December 16, 2003
Classical Odes

High Beach

A Crocus in the Churchyard

Hoofs clop clop clop between the silver birch
That hide the arrowed spire and this Forest church.
Come through the lych-gate, down steps by the yew:
Where the bracken tangles, wood-pigeons coo.
On this green carpet, pause: a nightingale
Sings through eternity by a black rail.
A crocus blooms where every heart believes
That unknown faces mean more than autumn leaves

The aisle is quiet, tiptoe to the chancel.
Altar, pulpit, stained glass, lectern eagle,
Hammerbeam roof, a tiled Victorian floor,
The font and cattle brands, organ by the door.

Here on the wall two marble tablets state
The Ten Commandments, and how to contemplate.
Red and black, a life like scullery tiles;
Where a robin hops, a wife is wreathed in smiles.

"No graven images", "no gods but me",
No murder or covetous adultery.
A time when no host wanted, it would seem,
And manna was not yet a juicy dream.
A city smile is like a warm pillow,
Here girls are like a shower of pussy willow.
A rooted life, like the evergreen yew:
No glass or redbrick spoils each woodland pew.

The church is faithful to its hillocked dead.
Whether poet, agent, or Department Head,
Their deeds, like bluebells on a mound of moss,
Attest a Britain like a marble cross.
They, like bent gardeners in their commonwealth,
Cut bellbind and preserved their belief's health,
Conserved the diamond lead window standards
From the stones of revolutionary vanguards.

Silver birch, bracken and folk who seldom sinned
Now feed the silence under this March wind.
Shh! rest in the eternal; hear a snail
Dragging beneath the warbling nightingale.
Here rustling moments are time's muffled thieves;
Faces under hillocks, unlike old leaves,
Are compost so a crocus can proclaim:
To glimpse a Golden Flower is man's true aim.

Under this hillock, a decaying heart
Feeds the roots of a crocus and takes part

In the lost blowings of time from a windless
Ecstasy's silence and brimming stillness,
And, filled with dews, can, like an art-work, hold
A mirror down to Nature and still gold
Sunshine so posthumous meaning can wave
From fields of silver light beyond the grave.

Under the spire that towers from the slate roof
With arrowhead and vane like rational proof,
Look up at a high tripod which can view
White clouds that scud across the darkening blue,
And startle God at His theodolite,
As, measuring the angles of clouds and night,
He takes a reading of time's speed and flow
And calculates the centuries still to go.

Death has its beauty. A hearse, a squirrel's tail,
And your coffin is lowered by this black rail,
Between laurel and holly. For companions,
Unknown Belshams, Cookes, and rhododendrons.
A crocus under buds, now blink and brim
At dew-dipping finches, a tinkling hymn,
Snug in grass, safe from brambles; and in fine rain,
Gaze at the still arrow on the windless weathervane.
24 March 1974; 17 February 1980
Collected Poems

Two Variations on One Theme
1. Time and Eternity

I held her hand at this Omega gate,
She wanted to paint the yew,
And now the moment has blown away
Like dandelion fluff on blue.

Now, on the High Beach forest church
The passing clouds and years
Are like pattering footsteps in the porch
Or the silence under bedsit tears.

In the city I am scattered like poplar fluff
Blown on the wind of echo,
But here I breathe, with the quiet of stone,
The white light these dead men know.

Oh bury me behind this grave,
At the low black rail,
That all who have suffered and been brave
May pass the yew and wail
For all whom golden hair enslaves,
Till the past is a squirrel's tail;
Then, like the boom in childhood caves,
Oh hear beneath the breeze
The mystery that flows through stars and seas,
Where the autumn bracken waves.

2. The Bride of Time

I

Time held a dandelion that day,
Blew the clock by this yew;
Now the moment has blown away
Like fluff across the blue.

To the porch of this forest church
The passing clouds are years;
Pattering feet feed silver birch
And silence under tears.

In the city men are scattered
Like poplar fluff, and waste;
Moss enfolds all who are shattered:
An embrace that is chaste.

All who are broken and are blown
On the wind of echo
Here breathe in the quiet of stone
The light these dead men know.

Eternity connives at pains
Which mould spirits that sinned,
But trembles when tears ooze from veins,
Consoles like whispering wind.

II

Listen beneath each gentle gust,
Hear the meaning of life;
The silence of the after-dust
Taunts like a flirting wife.

Seek her, she hides yet will be found,
Cooing from leafy den;
This nothingness empty of sound
Pregnantly woos all men.

Nothingness round an empty tree
Is full of rustling love.
A something woos men passionately
Like a cooing ring-dove.

A black-hole womb sucks in dead things
And then thrusts out new grass,
But waves of light and angels' wings

Swirl down where ebbed fins pass.

This black-hole void preserves all souls
Like fish in tides of love.
Expanded souls are like a sea
Sucked out from a foxglove.

Eternity lets all men know
She loves stillness not haste,
Yet preserves tides fish-spirits flow
Before their bodies waste.

III

Eternity blows in the breeze,
Yearning for years and graves.
Hear her soul pant through stars and seas
Where sighing bracken waves.

O carve two verses on a grave
Before this low black rail,
That all who suffer and are brave
May pass the yew and wail

For all whom golden Time enslaves
Till Time's a squirrel's tail;
That, like a pshsh in childhood caves,
Trembling a leafy veil,

The wind may whisper through these trees
With a soothing shsh of "still",
Drop to a hush, reveal and freeze
A hidden Void of will:

"Eternity blows like a bride,

Billowing springs and graves.
Her meaning foams through star and tide,
Teases where each leaf waves.

Seek her secret beneath the breeze,
Leap this three-stone-stepped stile:
Hear silence surge though years and seas,
Know her mystery, then smile!"
14 November1972; revised 21–22 June 1980
Collected Poems

Epping

At Ambresbury Banks, Epping

I park on Jack's Hill, take the forest walk
A quarter of a mile to Ambresbury Banks,
Turn in through trees and see the Iron-Age folk
Cooking pots near one of the earthwork flanks,
Weaving osiers on a wattle hurdle,
Making nettle twine, one feeding a fire,
Some dressed as peasants, Boudicca with spear,
One in a toga, all avoiding mire.

The circular earthworks are still daunting,
An Iron-Age walled encampment from around
500 BC. I'm near the food tent.
"Yes", a girl says, "Boudicca on this ground
Fought her last battle against Suetonius
When the Iceni rose, smarting, with staves:
Her husband's estate seized by the Romans,
She flogged, her daughters raped by Roman slaves."

While Governor Suetonius was in the west

She sacked Colchester, scorched the countryside,
As her hordes marched on London, defeated
A legion of veterans with smarting pride
And burned London to blood-reddened ashes.
In a few days seventy thousand souls
Were massacred or else tortured to death.
The Romans lived in fear of their patrols.

The Roman Governor turned south. She then
Sacked Verulamium, fell back to this place
According to tradition. The Romans,
With military skill, weaponry and pace,
Slaughtered Boudicca's boxed-in army. Some
Eighty thousand Britons bleached in the sun.
The militaristic British uprising
Against the Roman Empire was now done.

From here Boudicca fled across Copped Hall
With her two daughters, down to Cobbin's Brook
Which meanders near Epping Upland's hills
To the Lea at Waltham. There in a nook
Of great beauty, now with an obelisk,
In despair the Queen ate poisoned berries –
Hemloch? – and died; now stands in a chariot
With her daughters and two rearing horses.

I see the toga-ed Suetonius, Tony
The Curator, and shake his hand and peer,
Ask him if he is going to pursue
The laughing Boudicca with pointed spear.
Do you believe it happened here? I ask.
"In Northampton," he says, shaking his head.
"The geography in Essex is different.
There were hills round a plain and many dead."

He doubts this was a military fort.
"It was a residential settlement,
Univallar, with just one ditch all round,
Moat twelve feet wide, walls twelve feet high, ascent
Too elaborate for an animal-pen.
The main gate was on the west of this ring.
All this was open, there were no trees then,
There would have been sheep where we are standing."

His assistant David, in peasant's smock,
His face painted with Celtic curly lines,
Shakes my hand. He says he likes the legend
And does not want to "shake" the way it twines.
I meet a lady wearing sack vestment,
Face blue with woad and ochre scrivenings:
"I think the legend came from Warlies Hall,
The folly by Upshire village." Shakings!

She says that in the eighteenth century word
Of Boudicca went out from there to spread
The fame of the park: "It was invented,
That's my view." I am quite disappointed.
I walk with my daughter, stand on the camp's
High wall, look down at the valley within.
Did Suetonius' defile continue here,
Did he fight Boudicca near here and win?

And standing on the bank I now assert
Imagination over likelihood.
Epping has hills, this was on the way back
To Iceni East Anglia. This wood
Is the massacre site! I can hear cries,
See eighty thousand Britons lying dead,
Their bones whitening in the sun as the weeks

Tread by, in the once-open space ahead.

Historical likelihood and caution
Are the imagination's enemies.
How romantic to see the fiery Celt,
Yellow hair flowing, lead her legionaries
Against the occupying Romans, chew
Poison berries as raped daughters caress.
The truth is, no one knows where this happened.
These earthworks tantalize with their stillness.

The Iron Age is lost in the mists of time,
The Britons who lived here were simple folk,
Primitive beside the conquering Romans,
While Pheidias carved stone built huts of oak;
Sheep farmers who left no written record,
No writings on their lives in biting breeze.
And now my mind is rooted in these banks,
My consciousness grips legend like these trees.

History without imagination's dead,
A set of facts, no pattern or detail.
History informed by imagination
Comes alive, people wear hood and ring-mail,
Characters who flit through a forest glade
As if greeted a mere moment ago,
Ghosts in smocks, sacks, robes, togas. History mixed
With legend haunts like oak and mistletoe.

I am a traveller through the past centuries,
I journey in my mind back to a time,
Alight in a forest clearing like this,
See faces that scratched a living through grime;
And then resume my journey to legend,

See the Grail, living wars and raping slaves.
The beings imagination conjures
Are more alive than faces seen in graves.
July 21, 2001; revised July 22-26, 2001
Classical Odes

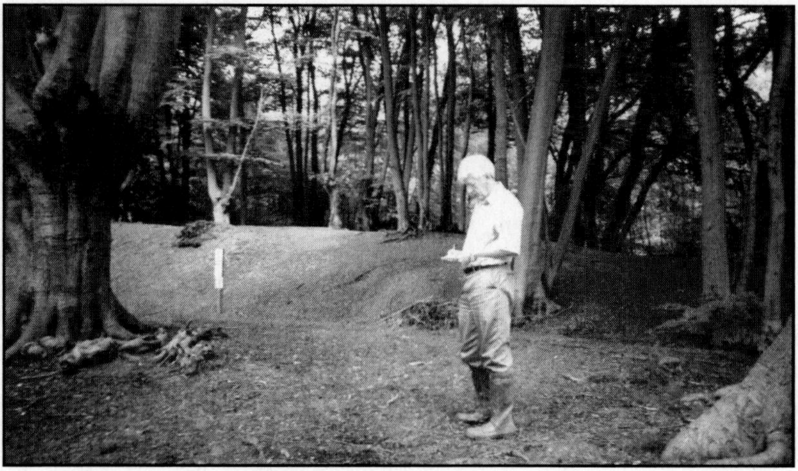

Nicholas Hagger writing 'At Ambresbury Banks, Epping' (see p.337) inside Ambresbury Banks, 21 July 2001.

Copped Hall

Turn off the Epping road well before dark.
A clearing leads to ornate gates, there park
And walk through pines past many a bluebell,
Over a hill till the great large-chimneyed shell
Of the third Copped Hall looms up, all overgrown.
Boarded up with corrugated iron and stone.
See the eighteenth-century pediments, as the light fades
Go to the tangled garden, and sunken balustrades.

The first Fitzauchers' hall passed to the Waltham abbots;
Then the King so Mary Tudor took Mass on this spot;

Then to Heneage (a present from his guest, the Queen),
Who rebuilt it and married the mother – hence the Dream scene –
Of Shakespeare's WH; to Suckling; Sackville;
Till Conyers built this shell that survived till
It was destroyed when a hair-clip used as fuse wire
As the household dressed for church, lit the final fire.

O Edwardian glory – four-columned pediment,
Italian gardens where walled terraces went,
Stairways, iron gates, fountains, figures of stone,
Parterres, summerhouses where caryatids moan,
Conservatory and ballroom, no clop of hoofs,
A grandeur of pavilions and domed roofs –
But now decay, a roofless shell again,
And desolation in moonlight, or this fine rain.

Alas for great hall, like this ancient seat
That stood against time and then crumbled to defeat,
Alas for past grandeurs like this stone shell
In which a style challenged the dark, then fell.
Salute the vision and energy of its prime
Which kept an estate going in a ruinous time.
As civilisation lost dignity, it saw
A way of life perish, now home for the jackdaw.

Now see the ruined foundations of Heneage's hall;
Elizabeth stood with Shakespeare by this wall,
And saw his Dream performed in the Long Gallery
At the wedding of his Theseus to Countess Mary.
How overgrown the yew walk now, climb through
To a ruined tower, headless marble statue.
Time, like a clump of nettles, winds about
Past glories and stings the hand that reaches out.

There are two forces – order and chaos.
Out of the forest: a fine house, gain from loss
Yew walks, stone steps, square gardens and statues,
And candles blaze against twilight's night blues
And a play is acted, all are in good cheer,
Then the ground moves and gigantic cracks appear,
The house is abandoned or razed, the people go –
Or else burnt down by fire, and the nettles grow.

But its scenes are retained for ever in these walls,
The voices that laughed linger as history falls,
Those images are present to our mind now,
We see a queen, a wedding, a frown, a bow,
And for all eternity each triumph matures
This Hall copped it from time, but its art endures.
Like Greek – or Roman stone, or art of Copt –
This ruin embodies events, as if time had stopped.
30 May 1984; revised 19 September 1993
Collected Poems

Copped Hall Revisited

We drive from the Upshire entrance along
A muddy lane, cross the M25
And approach the eighteenth-century ruin.
Tall chimneys, faded yellow stucco thrive
Despite empty windows, ivy wisping
Round bits of scaffolding near the roof's snort.
We park and walk through a wall gate and take
A muddy track down to the racquets court.

Inside a cheery throng, mid-morning wine
And *canapés*, and pictures on each wall.
I shake Eric Dawson's gnarled hand and look

At his water-colour cartoons, see all
Are of visitors to Copped Hall and one
Shows Henry the Eighth surveying them, thuds
An impish sense of humour, like his cars
Splashing an old lady sweeping out floods.

I wander past his memory of Cairo,
Bored men sitting in the mess in khaki;
Then see an exhibition on Copped Hall,
How it was acquired by Waltham Abbey
For the abbot's own use, and how Heneage
Rebuilt it beyond where the yew walk heads.
"An inventory's been found," a lady says.
"It had sixty-seven rooms, forty-eight beds."

I slip away from the local gathering
And squelch through mud in boots to the yew walk
And recall how Henry the Eighth paced round
On the nineteenth of May and would not talk
And when the cannon banged to signify
That Anne Boleyn had lost her head he rode
To Theobalds, Waltham Cross, a free man
To meet his new love Jane Seymour, the toad.

I turn left and see on a wooded mound
A sole pillar, all that's left from the hall
That Heneage built, see the Long Gallery –
Not nettled now, just woodland soil and sprawl –
Where *A Midsummer Night's Dream* was performed
In sunshine, not this dark December air,
When he wed the Countess of Southampton
And they climbed these steps that now lead nowhere.

This place is still redolent with history.

Henry the Eighth stayed on here with the monks
And built the Great Standyng on Chingford Plains,
His hunting lodge, from here from felled oak trunks
So he could watch hunts there. I walk back, glad
That the Copped Hall Trust now safeguards this clay.
A strimmer tells me, "We are twenty-four
Volunteers, we cut the grass each Sunday."

I founded a school on this hall's estate
Where a Queen rode on horseback and planted
A tree that's now our badge, worn on blazers.
I look to this pillar and scratch my head.
It's all that's left of a grand hall that ruled
The landscape, chimneyed cottages with slates,
In terms of which all local people lived
And touched their forelocks as they passed its gates.

This place is a magnet though nothing's left
Of Heneage's hall save a pillar, steps
And buried bricks. And though the splendid house
Is a ruin, open to winds, its reps,
Local volunteers, are tidying up
Have removed unpaid, committed, umpteen
Nettles so locals can walk and reflect
On when the place was host to king and queen.
December 2, 2001; revised October 10-12, 2002. Classical Odes

At Coopersale Hall: Founder's Day

I

At the double white gates I turn, look back,
Recall the narrow road with passing bays
Down to the cattle-grid. It's now two-way,
I had to widen the valley's side, raise

Half a road's width, use land machines, then tar.
I found six tarrers cowering in their cab,
They'd just been told they'd be shot if they worked
By a local gangster who sought to grab.

I walk the wide, gravelled forecourt, recall
The first time I came it was overgrown.
I counted in the lorries, signed dockets,
Saw crushed concrete spread, then pea-shingle sown,
Raked into a parking area. I go
To the front door. That first day of my rule,
The door open, a horse entered the hall
As if to register at my new School.

That first day....The carpentry done, a boy
And girl pictured holding hands by the gate.
I chatted to parents who crowded round,
Thanked them for trusting I would keep this date.
The Council'd made me widen a slip road,
Put great screens up with fire doors, spend, spend, spend.
It was a golden summer, girls in gold
Dresses I'd designed, sunshine without end.

I look at the holm-oak Elizabeth
The First planted, it's said, when she rode out
From Copped Hall on a summer's day like those.
I hear the playing children laugh and shout.
Some crowd to me with questions, beaming, still.
I think of all the fêtes held on this lawn,
One when I stood and spoke into a mike
While Seaman waited in shorts, smiling brawn.

The stream, the bridge, the grounds beyond, the trees,
Rare shrubs planted by Lyle, Epping's MP....

I walk through tots on the terrace and pass
The plaque on Tebbit's opening, again see
The lawned throng I spoke to, sit with Norris
While Tebbit speaks, in pain, despite his gaze,
From wounds that still weep from the Brighton bomb.
I am lost in memories as in a maze.

I see my black-and-white print of the lawn
Of the old hall in Mrs Chevely's time
And a gardener in a cocked hat pulling
A roller, and the holm-oak, small, sublime,
Has a ringed seat round a trunk that's narrow,
Unlike the massive girth it boasts these days.
Children run and leap, skip or talk in groups,
Happy in the sun among flowers that blaze.

I enter the hall, which I once panelled –
I designed the wood, said how it should go –
To cover the orangery's brick walls.
I renewed the floor, put this staging so,
Led prize-givers through rows of seats all packed:
Little, whose smile now rules Eton, benign.
Here I've hosted fourteen Christmas lunches
Amid teasing staff, laughter, flowing wine.

Many a time I've stood at end of term
Here, made a speech, given gifts to leaving staff.
The day before term's start I've sat, elbows
On table, talked on our aims, made all laugh.
I wander through to the small lobby-room
With medieval carved frieze, grimacing
Figures, oaten pipes, Green Man, where I gave
The Lord Lieutenant lunch and talked court things.

I amble to the panelled library,
Look fondly at the barley-twist fireplace
With a wooden hood and a Tudor man
On top, a hatted head with Wolsey's face.
This was the staff room, I've held meetings here
And drinks gatherings for staff and guests, blends
Before prize days, and chatted to them all.
I've spent happy hours drinking here with friends.

This was the room where Churchill was received
By Epping's MP, Lyle, when he talked through
Taking over the MPship from him.
This was the first house in Epping he knew,
And during the war he stayed at the Hall,
Then a rest-home for officers wounded.
An eyewitness told how he saw Churchill
Walk down a passage upstairs, stooping head.

I go upstairs to the room Churchill used,
With columns both sides of its white fireplace,
As his bedroom when he came out to stay
From Downing Street, and visited the face
Of the battle of Britain – planners at
Blake Hall, North Weald pilots, wounded troops here.
Across fields Epping hangs on the skyline,
The same view he saw, full of country cheer.

II

I take the path – by the brick extension
I built all through the long recession when
The Council's building inspector thanked me
For keeping him in work, no one built then –
Pissarro painted, to the walled garden
I found head-high, now playground, and fig-trees.

The old greenhouse that decayed was pulled down.
I look at my kitchen, my new rooms please.

I peer inside the squash court I floored in,
Made two-storey, connected by staircase
To the place next door. Here I held a tea
For the gaunt Ofsted team like an embrace
And introduced nervous staff, broke the ice.
There are classrooms over my head these days
Where squash balls were belted by owners' friends
And officers in convalescing stays.

I stroll past Orchard Cottage, now classrooms
Here Norris lived as my tenant. I reach
Back: he sat by his portrait and picture
Of him speaking just after the Queen's speech
In the Commons. We discussed Major's slide.
He was Minister for Transport, and proved
It with: "If you see any road works cones,
Ring my mobile and I'll have them removed."

One day he washed his car in shorts, and stopped
As I left school to talk Thatcher and brutes.
I go on to the pond that Tony dug
As I directed, now replete with newts,
Pond weed and ducks, and a small boat with oars
For sitting in, reflecting in the shade
Of trees that ring. I look at butterflies,
Birds that flit, thickets, sun shafts in the glade.

I go out past the garage, now classrooms,
To the field I bought, levelled with a slope,
Where there are football goals with nets for boys
And an athletics track, a place of hope.

Here I've been on the mike on hot sports days
And athletes crowded round to hear who'll reign
As champion, before proud parents. I love
The two lines of poplars that flank the lane.

Way down the lane, beyond the cattle-grid,
Is the communal field where I once played
Football with boys of ten, Seaman and I
On one side, on theirs two coaches I paid.
At half-time we were five-two down. I told
Seaman, "You may play for England, but you're –
We're – being trounced by boys. I'll cross. You head."
He headed four in, and we forced a draw.

I return to the ancient tree and stand.
Memories crowd in, a thousand faces peer,
All earnest, doing their best in their own way
Over a dozen years, on their way, cheer.
I founded a school like mitred Harsnett.
Its life spans my books, measures me and calls
That Classical Man climbs like gnarled ivy
Up the old stones of institutions' walls.

This land, Ulmar's before the Conquest, then
Given to Warin FitzGerold by Henry
The Second, then left to Warin de Lisle,
Formed part of royal Copped Hall till the Chevely
Family built their seat here and stayed two
And a half centuries till Jamineau's stir:
Burgled, he willed cash to the burglar's wife.
Their cellars hold Churchill's air-raid shelter.

After the Chevelys, a motley crew: two
Reverends – Newman, Howman – who let to Green,

Ingham, Ainslie, More, Worth, Howes, Cam, Berkeley,
Then Baily, Willett, Blott all owned this scene,
Then Edward Flux, whose name's in Flux's Lane,
Then Lyle, then Normans', Greens' and Fordhams' rule
Till I, citing two motorways' wheel-roar
When borne by wind, turned it into a school.

So many memories crowd in, voices
That ring in my ears, deafen with their words,
Recalled at the same time, all talk across
Each other, sing for attention like birds;
Faces that passed through as I watched them go.
A lifetime went but their voices have stayed
Clear in my head though their bodies have gone.
I hear joyful children's laughs, hear them fade.

I, the founder, am alone by my stones.
For the founder, Founder's Day's every day.
My day is one of many when I've come.
Little found a ready-made place and way;
I made an institution where souls grow,
Are shaped, and I've helped shape thousands of spruce,
Polite, bright local children who've passed through
This great Hall I turned over for their use.
February 10, 2003; revised February 13-16, 2003
Classical Odes

Five hours ahead that day I, your poet,
Greeted the Lord Lieutenant of Essex,
Lord Braybrooke, at the school I founded in
Epping Forest in cream, eighteenth-century
Coopersale Hall, and after a tour lunched
With him under Jacobean carvings
Of grimacing faces and a Green Man,

Discussed the founding of America
From my Otley Hall in 1607
And our surrender of America
At Yorktown by his famous ancestor
Lord Cornwallis, whose surrender sword he
Owned and kept in his house by Audley End.
I waved him off and went to the Head's room
Where Ken the Bursar said, "I've just been rung.
A plane's flown into New York's Twin Towers."
And later Robin told me, "Down your lane
I put the radio on and heard two planes
Had flown into the World Trade Center's towers."
News of the attack on America
Instantly pervaded the leafy lane
And building built in the year the US
Declared independence and came to birth,
Borne on air waves to our provincial life
From the capital of the Western world.
This poet wanly recalls the moment
Bin Laden flung down his gauntlet and crowed
With hubris swollen by his suitcase bombs;
When the world changed and a new Age began,
When provincial peace was now outmoded
By the aim to prevent Armageddon.
Armageddon, Book 1, pp.40-1, lines 1753-1783

Theydon

At Theydon Garnon Church

I note the tower and thirteenth-century nave,
Enter through the fifteenth-century porch, late,
And walk down the aisle to the frontmost pew
And sit with the Rector. Behind me wait,

Fidgeting, wriggling, a school. The sun streams
Through stained glass St George and roses. I loll
And gaze at the Royal Coat of Arms till
All stand to sing the first Christmas carol.

In past years I was sat in the choir stall
Before the organ, which boomed in my ear.
It is a release to be off the aisle.
I think of when it was a brisk walk here
From Coopersale Hall, when its great acreage
Stretched to where the horizon meets the sky
Before the motorway cut Hall from church.
I squint in blinding sun, blinded by eye.

A reading, a carol and shepherds walk;
Angels; three kings proffer gifts; a descant.
Robert de Gernon – "with the moustache" – came
With the Conqueror and a descendant
Got this village by marriage in the reign
Of Henry the Third. I gaze at the grey
Marble canopied tomb by the altar
Of one who witnessed the first Tudor day.

Hatchments hang either side of the south door,
Paintings with lozenge frames, arms, crest display
Heraldic 'achievements' of local men.
I think of what my lozenge should portray:
A rampart, sphinx, pen, bell, winged horse and waves,
Oak tree and three acorns (three-school insight,
One founded, two run, all owned), moated hall,
Poems like bound corn-sheaves, a rayed sun's Light.

Another carol, and the tableau forms.
Like Houblon (fifty-pound notes bear whose scrawl)

Who lived at Coopersale House, or Shake-speare
Who staged *Midsummer Night's Dream* at Copped Hall
In whose (then) grounds I founded my school, I
Have defined myself through risk and now claim
Some social standing, sit in the front pew
With the Rector who's blessed – almost some fame.

In the churchyard I find the weathered vault
Of several Coopersale Hall Chevelys.
In an old print from Anne Chevely's day
The gardener's shown rolling a lawn with his
Roller. Jamineau Chevely was burgled,
Two were transported to Van Dieman's Land.
He willed the wife of one (his dairymaid)
His furniture, cattle and dairy stand.

I stand outside, apart from milling boys.
Elizabeth came to this Tudor tower
And saw the sundial hang from those scratch marks
And, high up the buttress, the mass marker
Where the sun's shadow told the time of Mass.
I join a time when Rectors were devout,
Put on the cloak-like cope in Kyrkeby's brass
And foresee Tudor pride and Stuart doubt.
Conceived December 12, 1996; written January 2, 1997;
revised December 26-27, 2000
Classical Odes

At Hill Hall, Theydon Mount: Mind and Soul

I drive through woodland up to the Mount's church,
Dismount and walk up to the gates and look
Beyond the muddy track to the distant
Pediment and eighteen windows – and hook

My mind to a day nearly five years back
When it was a burnt-out ruin and I
Wandered round its derelict rooms, and saw
The wall-paintings on plaster cracked but dry.

Here lived Sir Thomas Smith, who rebuilt it
In Renaissance style (Somerset's esprit)
From a design by John of Padua,
Whom he met while travelling in Italy,
Having acquired it when he remarried
Philippa, widow of Sir John Hampden.
He never raised his tenants' rents, sued or
Evicted them, a perfect gentleman.

This man, described by Eden as "the flower"
Of Cambridge, served Somerset, and impressed;
A Protestant, was forced to retire when
Mary acceded. He survived – his crest
A salamander living among flames –
And busied himself rebuilding, though sore,
His home and tutoring Edward de Vere
Who had been placed in his household when four.

Was the Hall I saw the original
De Vere knew in his boyhood? It's denied.
That Hall had walls two thin, bricks set in loam
And not in mortar, like the House of Pride
That was "without morter laid". This new Hall
Was rebuilt in two phases, a tiny
Bit remains of what the boy saw. Older,
He returned here, saw Cupid and Psyche.

The boy was removed here in Mary's reign,
To the home of the provost of Eton,

After the persecution of Ridley
And Latimer, and Wyatt's rebellion,
And the beheading of Lady Jane Grey
Whom his father John de Vere supported.
It was wise to send the boy to a house
Where he'd be safe from Catholic bloodshed.

Carew said Smith was next to Plato in
Mastery of style, grace of language at court,
Spoke Latin, Greek, Hebrew, French, Italian,
Was the foremost scholar of Greek and taught
De Vere grammar, history, legal jargon,
Language of court and university
From his library of three hundred books –
Literature, art and his favourite: poetry.

Here de Vere was taught to love learning: sums,
Buildings, God, the stars. Smith assisted when
His father received the Duke of Finland,
Sent by his brother Eric of Sweden
Who'd proposed to the Queen; wrote to Burghley.
De Vere saw national diplomacy
And caught secrets at first hand until Smith
Retired to hawk, hunt, sort his library.

Writing on government and Parliament,
On the constitution after Mary,
He compared England with other countries.
A monarchist, he saw democracy
In which degree was preserved – Crown, nobles,
Yeomen at one for country's good, no foes.
Did Edward de Vere learn his thinking: "Take
But degree away…what discord follows!"?

I see the young de Vere roam round these lanes,
Love these hills between lessons, and join, shy,
In 1561 the Queen's progress
To Castle Hedingham, and catch her eye.
I stand in "Shakespeare Essex" where the mind
Behind the nom-de-plume soaked in Smith's praise
Of Paduan theatre and his wisdom,
And wrote him into wise men in his plays.

Here de Vere's tutor, before he became
Elizabeth's Ambassador to France,
Walked past the West and East Rooms' wall-paintings
That showed the early English Renaissance
King Hezekiah's life, scenes of Cupid
And Psyche in hung tapestry style, sets
Of fruit-and-foliage borders recalling
The Cupid in Shakespeare's last two sonnets.

I see de Vere leave to be Burghley's ward,
I see him return for Smith's funeral,
Now back from Padua. Now Hill Hall passed
To Smith's brother George, became a dreadful
Open prison where Christine Keeler served
A few weeks. Its main association
Was no longer Tudor constitution
But undermining government, treason.

I look into the church. In the chancel
I see Smith's figure, dignified and wise,
In Garter mantle and (perhaps placed by
De Vere) round the arch under which he lies
This: "What ye Earth or Sea or Skies conteyne,
What Creatures in them be, My Mynde did seeke
To knowe, my Soule the Heavens continually."

His mind sought earth's knowledge, his soul Heaven's leak.

And now on this Hill I reflect on how
I've combined mind and soul in all my work,
Turned mind on earthly civilizations,
The Age, human foibles; set soul to lurk
And watch for leaking Light. Mind and soul, I
Follow this many-sided man who weighed
Democracy and scholarship. We both
Hail a forewielder of our world-view's spade.
Conceived September 15, 1996; written March 11, 2001;
revised March 17-18, 2001; August 2, 2003. Classical Odes

Chingford

At Queen Elizabeth's Hunting Lodge

An L-shaped lodge, at first just wood and roof
With no side walls, just cloths and flags hanging
From rails on hunt days, top floor for viewing,
First floor for shooting, ground for cooking.
I push a side door to the beamed kitchen,
Notice pitsaw marks where a trunk's been split,
Amble past trenchers, spice, dried fruit and eggs,
And manchet rolls, bran extracted, unslit.

I see a wild boar's head, boiled in water,
Laid in a grate, basted with wine, now glint
Black and yellow sauces; and chicken breasts,
Gammon and joint; see mortises that hint
That a partition once kept the servants
From mingling with royals and silver-voiced,
Linger near a diminished-haunch tenon
In a gap between joist and binding joist.

I ascend the stairwell, seven sets of five
Shallow steps, each with a breath-pause landing.
This Great Standing was finished when Henry
Was portly, needed pauses for breathing;
One of four lodges on his royal estate.
It's thought he never came here, was too ill.
It's said Elizabeth the First rode up
These stairs on horseback, showing immense skill.

I wander round the large one-roomed first floor
Where archers shot from openings, and admire
The diamond-lead windows that now enclose.
I see the concrete nineteenth-century fire
Surround, in wood an apotropaic
Daisy wheel to ward off evil spirits,
See brasses of the two monarchs laid out
With crossbow, display boards, Tudor outfits.

I read, hunters quested the hart (the male
Red deer) at dawn with lymers (hounds with fine
Noses) and scooped up fumes or crotties (deer
Droppings) in hunting-horns, set them in line
At the hunt breakfast for the Lord to choose
From the largest which large stag was quested;
The largest buck (male fallow deer) was found
From widest tracks, heaviest antlers instead.

Then they coursed the hart, tired him out and brought
Him to bay (self-defence with his antlers).
The red deer gave more sport than fallow deer
As it knew tricks to escape through waters
So the hounds lost their scent. The hunters drove
The deer to near perookez (enclosures)
On Chingford Plain and released them in groups

To be shot at by the standing archers.

When the hart was spayed and dead the hunters
Skinned and quartered it, grolicked (cut open)
The deer of highest grease (juiciest, fattest),
Dipped bread in its guts, fed it to the ten
Dogs as their reward, then took off their clothes,
Shoes, hose and washed their thighs, legs and bodies,
And drank and went to sleep – not in this lodge,
There were no sleeping-quarters, just rushes.

I go on up the stairs to the top floor,
One long room where all could be known by dress:
The Lord, nobleman, clergyman, merchant.
The timbers came from Chelmsford, lines profess.
The fire surround says "1879".
This room was later a manorial court,
A forest-keeper's office, then his home,
A farmhouse, long after the sport and mort.

I read this was Mrs. Wilkins' tea-room
On Easter Monday 1897
When fifty-one thousand people came out
By train to walk in forest glade and den.
I look out at the "fair mead" that's "well green"
With "tall trees" and a running brook and see
Viewers go down the stairs for hunt breakfast
In a tent, sit or stand to eat with glee.

I see Elizabeth the First arrive
In fine dress, met by twelve ladies in white
Satin on ambling palfreys and twenty
Yeomen in green on horseback to have sight
Of hart. On entering the chase she's met by

Fifty archers in scarlet boots, yellow
Caps, with gilded bows. Each gives her, peacock-
Feather-winged, a silver-headed arrow.

I see her close the sport, cutting the throat
Of a buck while all round lean courtiers talk.
The venison's parcelled in the kitchen,
Ridden to the local gentry, who squawk
With delight at a royal gift. I see
A royal estate never completed,
This Fairmead lodge, Waltham Abbey lodge built,
Two more planned, left, and then the king is dead.

By then he had two hundred hunting parks.
I see an awesome spectacle planned here:
Two hundred deer killed in one afternoon,
The Tudors' amphitheatre with a cheer.
This Forest was close enough to London
For favoured guests to ride out, shoot and fell
One or two deer – the Queen a mere fifteen –
While musicians played from up the stairwell.

I smell the Tudor time, the frame freshly
Painted in white lime-wash and hung with bright
Tapestries, coloured drapes, flags and bunting;
Smells of cooked food wafting from the ash-white
Ground-floor fireplace as she arrives; the stench
Of the dead deer lying in lines as she
Slits down a buck to show it's of high grease
As huntsmen blow the mort on horns in glee.

When he became Keeper of the Forest
Of Waltham and of Havering, here came
Edward de Vere, to this Fairmead standing

Not far from Copped Hall Park, to check the game
And organisation of the parokes;
Here oversaw the running of the deer
In the new park in Waltham Forest so
There were enough deer on hunting days here.

I stand at the foot of the stairs where I
Greeted Addison in wheelchair with zest,
His sticks beside him as he tilted back.
This place is a symbol of the Forest,
A monument to a time when this mead
Was run for the monarch's benefit, deer
Herded into corrals and shot by bolts
As they bolted for the wild, weak with fear.
February 5, 2003; revised February 5-7, December 16, 2003
Classical Odes

At the Chingford Carol Service: Christian Religion

I stand at the back of the Chingford church:
Twelfth-century font and seventeenth-century chest.
The Head whose appointment I announced from
A Founders Day stage, surprising our guest
And five hundred, comes in and shakes my hand,
I go to the front pew and sit and wait
For the Deputy Mayor. The church has filled,
Parents, staff and pupils all sit sedate.

Prayers, carols, readings follow rapidly
And Joseph stifles giggles with Mary.
Now shepherds, angels and wise men parade
And, smirking, form a tableau, fidgety.
The choir sing '*Gaudete*', among them bald,
Lean Osprey, who can't have long left as he

Has leukaemia. This is his last full day.
Dead by Easter? Now he sings lustily.

The organist, a thirteen-year-old boy,
Plays with a billowing that is full-blown.
Encouraged by his volume, all sing loud.
The vicar asks who has a mobile phone
And says on his, when it works, he can reach
Everyone in the world by internet,
But it's not as good as meeting someone
Face-to-face and speaking to them direct.

The children are all round me, I am like
The head of a vast family that's strong,
I am among faces that smile at me,
Eyes that catch mine. It's my school, I belong.
All sit in pews and raise their souls to God
Who also has a mobile phone, can scroll
To all mankind on his prayers' internet,
Yet know all face-to-face, touch each one's soul.

The service is over. Children snigger
And stand with parents, who think them lovely,
While I walk to the young organist who
Crescendos Lefébure-Wély's Sortie.
Offord watches, already a pale ghost.
I speak to him, he is matter-of-fact
And praises the round talent of this boy
Who acts and plays and swots with suave impact.

The bald are dying and the fuzzy young
Are full of hope and express their talent,
Squeeze out patterns that cascade through a church
And stir a congregation to assent.

And I connect to the charged atmosphere –
All has been renewed since a wartime bomb
Damaged the chapel – as young encounter
Anew all that the dying retire from.

Were the Gospels historical reports
Or creations that were literary?
The star was the conjunction in the west
Of Jupiter-Saturn in 7 BC,
November; the census was announced by
Augustus that same birth year, and dragged on.
Herod's slaughter's been found in a mass grave,
A hundred dead infants at Ashkelon.

The Nativity story did happen.
The Church retells it and keeps it alive
Through plays. Children dress up and are brainwashed.
We foist religion's trappings on, connive
With, the young at legends, perpetuate
Our culture in young minds, shared heritage.
The historical event's now a myth –
A manger-birth in an angel-raised age.
December 12, 17-18, 2000. Classical Odes

Buckhurst Hill

At Connaught House

I

An L-shaped front with chimneys, I go through
The front door, left to the bare sitting-room
And gaze across Epping Forest at Queen
Elizabeth's hunting lodge that's in gloom.
I pass on, saunter round the swimming-pool,

Sunset on its Roman columns, and yield
To its steamy warmth and blue. Windows look
Out on the sloping lawn to the first field.

I wander through the empty house, the small
Kitchen, study, out to the garage wing
To be a library, soak in stables,
The vegetable garden and outbuilding,
Then go back in and climb the airy stairs,
Stroll in and out of bare bedrooms, to west
At each window snatch views of late-sun trees,
The side gate that leads out to the Forest.

Below, round a fountain of three Graces,
Are the twelve wedged beds of the rose garden.
Two circles, a cross, four side paths all make
A Union Jack seen from air, the union
Of England, Scotland, Wales which Europe would
Undo for twelve regions, as if twelve beds
Had primacy over paths and Graces
In the pattern, whose threefold fountain heads

Show: Britannia with Welsh and Scot nymphs; or
Three goddesses of fertile grounds, sisters –
Aglaia, Euphrosyne and Thalia:
Brightness, Joyfulness and Bloom, three daughters
Of Zeus and Hera, bestowers of charm
And classical beauty in poetry;
Or Existence, Being, Void who, arms joined
In sunlit O, show the One's unity.

I clasp a popping stone in my right hand
A hundred and seventy million years old;
A round pebble, split in two halves, each stamped

With identical ammonites, whorled gold.
The hard surface hides two matching spirals,
Soft molluscs coiled in shells as hard as chrome
That have endured through time, one raised, one grooved:
Two hearts that fit together in one home.

This will be our new house, I hold the plans,
Trace over the pool my new study suite
With filing-cabinets, trace six bedrooms,
See each nook filled with my knick-knacks, my seat;
Stairs up to the roof space. This will be where
I grow old in my triangle of schools,
Walk down to Connaught Water, one with trees;
A Forest person looking at toadstools.

The Ching valley is spread out in the dusk.
The sloping grass falls away to the brook
Which rises in Hill Wood near High Beach church
And drains woods on its way past crow and rook.
I see High Beach spire in a tree-top sea.
Down in a trough is Connaught Tennis Club
Where I cycled as a boy and retrieved
Practice serves by Mottram, a scampering cub.

Edward the Confessor gave that Chingford
Parish, within Waltham's half-hundred's doze,
To St Paul's, gift the Conqueror confirmed.
It was known as King's Ford as the meadows
Were called King's Meads and the Lea the King's Stream.
The Normans (who wrote Kent as Chent) spelt it
Cingheford. This view is of Anglo-Saxon
Lands held by the first English – exquisite!

There's no history here, just an Essex place.

I have put off my grandeur and expense
To live simply in a large house, write books,
Contract my hand to what I know, dream, sense.
I've finished with outside things and must make
My peace with my new works, get up to date,
Think, see, imagine all that's in my head
In prose and verse like Hardy at Max Gate.

I wander down the sloping garden grass
To the long lily pools, all linked, stepped down,
And in spite of early dusk feel the warmth
Of a new summer creeping in green-brown,
Flecked buds and scent of flowers speared by rabbits;
And I have chosen this to grow old by
Near my young family, son and grandson,
All school work shed, now an observing eye.

From here I could walk through the Chingford woods
Past Fairmead Bottom, Loughton Monks and go
To High Beach church where my boys were christened,
Wheel through Theydon down to Abridge, follow
The Roding that rose near Dunmow and runs
Through marshy green fields sunsets wash with joy,
Under Chigwell Lane, out to Roding Lane
And the bridge I crossed so much as a boy.

I think of the brown river as it brims
Under that bridge, and I think back to when
I walked with Mabel to the humped-back bridge
And was a boy cycling to school again
Across the flood meadows and pushed my bike
To the other bank's towpath and shade's cool,
Rode the track past the barrage-balloon site
And up the narrow hill to Chigwell School.

We walked two miles towards the Loughton bridge.
On the far side where Chigwell Hall once stood,
Willows; our side, thistles with bearded seed,
Purple loosestrife and nettles. Life was good:
A flock of whitethroats, pipits. And we found
Viper's bugloss, teasle, burdock. I squealed:
Purple mallow! A civilisation
Is like a mallow growing in a field....

The Roding from its Dunmow source to Thames
Is fed by tributaries from this Forest
And pastures, water-meadows and marshlands
Round ancient Saxon towns, Essex's best.
This Forest clay holds oaks, spruce and hornbeam.
I love the trees that cradle my paddock,
I love the brown-sedge reed-swamps, yellow flag,
Ditches with gypsy-wort, poisonous hemlock.

This swathe is my country: I can recite
A hundred names of woods of which I'm fond:
Woodman's Glade, Magpie Hill and Cuckoo Pits,
Kate's Cellar, Peartree Plain and the Lost Pond,
Each of which has old memories for me.
Strawberry Hill, the Stubbles....Here among rooks
I'll live like Chaucer's reeve on a far heath
And devote my last years to my last books.

II

From the pools on my land I look across
A valley our wooded landscapes thrive on.
We woodlanders live round bushed trees, old ponds
In this county where most names are Saxon –
Epping, Loughton, -ing "people of", -ton "town" –
In ancient royal forests in the wild

Among rabbits, hedgehogs, shrews and foxes
That I looked on in wonder as a child.

Here in the seventh century was the kingdom
Of the East Saxons of the seaxe, curved sword
Still on the Essex shield, whose Christian king
Saebert or Sigeberht found heavenly reward
Laid in a wood-lined burial chamber
To dissolve in acidulous Southend soil
Among things he took to the next world: wood
Drinking-cups, buckles, crosses of gold foil.

The Forest had a powerful lure for us.
We ran as soon as we had sight of trees
Banked, humped on the skyline, and then were drawn
By growing trunks, leaves fluttering in the breeze.
The Roding and these Forest streams and ponds
With sticklebacks and tiddlers that we caught,
And lilies, glint an ancient way of life
When cloth-capped children newted as a sport.

When this Forest ceased to be royal, was placed
Under the City of London's fat wing,
The Crown appointed a Ranger to watch
The bye-laws, rights of pasture and grazing:
The Duke of Connaught, Victoria's third son
Prince Arthur, who lives on in Ranger's Road,
Gave his name to the Water and this house,
Linked the Crown to these woods and this abode.

Exhausted like Propertius and Horace
I, with urbane and modest good humour,
Will retire from the bustle of the court
I have peeped into as an observer,

And will live in this sacred grove, less far
From London than Otley but far enough,
And hear news of those who pursue laurels,
Smile in blissful retirement, mind still tough.

When I was young we were agog: Angry
Young Men challenged the Establishment's mien
In plays and novels, questioned the icons
That were ruling us – Churchill and the Queen.
Osborne lambasted and then turned Tory.
Now I record with no little regret
The old order's long decay and passing,
Lament an England I cannot forget.

I look back at the timber-gabled house.
It is a palace of art: library
With all books in perfect order; records
In filing-cabinets, found easily;
A view between the Forest and the stars;
Apart from mankind where I can conclude
Within the triangle of my three schools;
A place where I can work in solitude.

I think of Joash Woodrow, great artist
Who withdrew from the world forty-five years
Ago and filled his family home in Leeds
With three thousand five hundred drawings, fears,
Paintings, hopes, sculptures, proof inspiration
Springs from solitude, not the public eye.
I too have known obscurity's great joy:
To write innovative works that don't lie.

What think my peers of my range, breadth and scale?
A few whose verses neither scan nor rhyme

Are indignant I took such care and feel
Affronted (threatened?) by my upstart crime:
Gigantic size, vast scope in verse and prose;
Disqualify my findings as steep hills,
Ignore my forests that demean saplings.
All should be small, doodles like daffodils.

So few know the great secret I exist.
I am ignored by all verse and prose hacks.
The press, radio, TV don't stoop to know.
All recoil from my truths like plague attacks
And quarantine them so they can't infect.
But I don't mind, like a forest that's oak
I put out leaves, shed them and then sprout more.
From this high place I see tiny men's smoke.

My purpose is my poems, my backbone.
I go about my business every day
And stanzas (like this one) float through my mind,
I set them down and understand and say
What my life means with freshness, clarity
And exactness, and measure my progress
By the growth of my work, which, now unknown,
May convey to future souls our "isness".

I've spent my life whittling at big ideas
And cramming them into eight-line stanzas
Like masted ships into midget bottles,
Trimming edges to make them fit so as
To please the eye. When books are no more read
And surface image has swept depth aside
My carved miniatures may seem messages
Like those tossed from where exiled Ovid died.

III

I amble by the pools in the garden.
Western philosophy is like a spring
From Parmenides and Heracleitus,
At first a splutter, then a trickling,
Now gushing Plato, Aquinas and Kant,
Locke, Hume and Leibniz filling pools, more near;
Now Positivists and Existentialists
And Universalism, the end one here.

Pools balance: Plato and Aristotle;
From them, Rationalists and Empiricists;
Lower down, Idealists and Realists;
Lower still, recent Intuitionists –
I love the Vitalists (Bergson, Whitehead)
And Existentialists like Heidegger,
Husserl – and Logical Analysis
That denied meaning (Wittgenstein, Ayer).

Pumps recycle the flow back to the start.
Now all's still, I see bathed in my end pool
The stars of the Western universe caught
In this puddle like flecked duckweed, the Rule
Reflected, disturbed by a webbed-toed newt,
And in its centre, distant, floats the moon
As twilight darkens into early night,
Reflecting unseen sunlight where I swoon.

I look into this mirror for a few
Of two hundred billion stars on the tree
Of our galaxy, heavenly Milky Way.
In my mind's puddle I can also see
A hundred billion galaxies that fill
The glittering universe that is missing

To man's telescopes, moon- and Mars- machines
That ply empty space and give it meaning.

O Western universe, the spring between
My sleeves flows like yours through these pools to sigh
As Horace's Bandusian water gushed
And can reflect your patterned starlit sky
And all the movements of philosophy
And can when running show the trickling run
Of Western direction, but above all
Reflect the night-sky of the darkening One.

The spring in my consciousness and these pools
Reflects the river that winds through my mind
Past the humped bridge I wheeled my bike over,
Near where a lorry knocked me from behind
Off my bike into the grass verge and past
My grandson's nursery where tots sing and bash;
Near where the Chelmer sometimes floods the road
At Great Easton and leaves a water-splash.

I see a dandelion, a yellow flower
As bright as morning sun, beyond Time's Word;
And a stem from the same root with round down,
Spores that will be blown by wind and scattered,
Seeds that will land, take root and grow new plants.
Being was once a round ball that was whole,
Then blown into planets. An artist's works
Are blown out like fluff near his golden soul.

Being was the gold Light's separate ball,
A wind blew and scattered each galaxy.
Ours has now become our stars and our earth
While the gold Light still shines eternally.

My works were once on a round ball of fluff,
A latent perfect clock beside my flower –
My gold soul – and will be dispersed, take root.
My flower's changeless, outside time's changing hour

The One pervades the twilit and night sky,
Leaks through the star holes, drips Light to the earth,
Rains on the Forest trees, frosts, dews the grass,
Constitutes all that's green, has form, had birth.
The universe is a well-ordered whole,
Cosmos that pours Being into our lives.
I love the sticky buds, chestnut candles
That light my way, show how Being connives.

I think of the Otley Hall knot garden:
Two infinity eights on their sides, twined.
I think, love and infinity are one,
A boundlessness beyond "before", "behind".
Add timelessness, a white seed hovering
Above the twisting knot of what's beneath,
And love's a tangled order whose sinews
Transcend a Tudor shape, soul's modern sheath.

The Western universe is meaningless
Unless it's seen with a poet's keen eye.
In my garden water's pumped down leats, pools
And's pumped back up to flow again. I sigh,
I watch the circular movement, aware
I pour in energy, more takes its place.
The flow within me's from Being to form
In an endless cycle that I embrace.

In Connaught House I will pour energy
Into new works, my spring endlessly new.

Like Hardy I'll do both poems and prose,
Take solitary walks to the past and chew
Down the Forest path to Connaught Water,
Reinvent myself, open to the One
That greens the Western universe's plains
And prinks the Forest flow from skull to sun.

I have a layered fourfold eye that peeps
Through body, mind, soul and spirit and sees
Past, present, future and eternity,
England, Europe, the globe, the One through trees,
History blend with politics, vision, Void
Or Great Zero, I co-exist with nought.
At Connaught House I co-naught and perceive
The trickling flux that erodes wood and court.

I stand by the bay-tree near my spring, look
In my pool still as mirroring mind, find
Dandelion and down, moon and fluffy stars
Which are all one when imaged in pure mind
Or before space-time when all was One seed
Enfolding Light, Void, Being, Existence;
Know a laurelled poet's still mind reflects
The Oneness of the universe through sense.
April 10-11, 2003, revised February 3-7, 9, 18, March 3, 8, 2004; April 10, 16, 2005
Classical Odes

Notes and References

(OS = Ordnance Survey)

Prologue: History Shaping Places

1. *The Fire and the Stones; The Light of Civilization; The Rise and Fall of Civiliations.*
2. *The Secret History of the West; The Syndicate.*
3. *The Secret Founding of America; The Secret American Dream.*
4. *The Last Tourist in Iran; The Libyan Revolution.*

PART ONE

The Roding Valley and the Stirrings of History

1. Celts and Romans

1. OS grid ref. TQ 456 963, *Transactions of the Essex Archaeological Society*: vol. 13, 1981; the finding of a hypocaust suggests a bathhouse rather than a villa.
2. M.W. Hanson, *Loughton's River, The Roding and its Ancient Meadows*, p.8.
3. For Durolitum, *see* http://www.pastscape.org.uk/hob.aspx?hob_id=408199&search=all&criteria=fort; *see also* Stephen Pewsey, *Chigwell and Loughton, A Pictorial History*, 'Early History'.
4. *The Victoria History of the County of Essex*, vol. III, p.197 and vol. V, p.151.
5. OS grid ref. TQ 4495 9732, *English Heritage County Scheduled Monument List*, March 1996.
6. OS grid ref. TQ 4725 9770, *English Heritage County Scheduled Monument List*, March 1996; and OS grid ref. TQ 47 97, Eleanor Scott, *Gazetteer of Roman Villas in Britain*, Leicester University archaeological monograph, 1983.
7. Archaeological Sites Index, http://www.digital-documents.co.uk/archi/sales.htm.

8. Edward North Buxton favoured "Beach" in his 1884 *Epping Forest*: "It is popularly supposed that these trees gave the name to the place; this is an error, the true meaning of the word being the *High Beach* or *Bank*." William Addison in *Epping Forest, Figures in a Landscape*, pp.76-8 supports this view. Philip Morant favoured "Beach". "Beech" was favoured by Dr Reaney in his *Place Names of Essex:* "There is little doubt that the name has reference to the famous beeches here." Addison points out that beeches at High Beach when the name first appeared were too dispersed and too common to mean anything. Reaney's view is preferred by *The Victoria History of the County of Essex*.
9. Pamela Greenwood, Dominic Perring and Peter Rowsome, *From Ice Age to Essex*, p.8.
10. For c.3350-2600BC, *see* Dr Michael Grant and Dr Petra Dark, 'Re-evaluating the concept of woodland continuity and change in Epping Forest: biological and sedimentary analyses', Kingston University, *see* http://science.kingston.ac.uk/ceesr/content/palaeo/Introduction.htm.; for c.2340BC, *see* C.A. Baker, P.A. Moxey and Patricia M. Oxford, 'Woodland Continuity and Change in Epping Forest', *Field Studies*, 1978, vol. 4, p.666; *see also* Georgina Green, *Epping Forest through the Ages*, p.6.
11. Baker, Moxey and Oxford, *op.cit.*, p.666. One of these studies took place 700 yards from Ambresbury Banks, in Lodge Road, Upshire.
12. *See* http://www.themodernantiquarian.com/site/2139/ambresbury_banks.html. Early Iron-Age pottery has been found at Ambresbury Banks going back to 800BC, *see* Baker, Moxey and Oxford, *op. cit.*, 647.
13. Baker, Moxey and Oxford, *op.cit.*, p.647.
14. J.A. Alexander, M. Aylwin Cotton, R. Robertson Mackay and S. Hazzledine Warren, 'Ambresbury Banks, an Iron Age Camp in Epping Forest, Essex: a report on excavations of 1933, 1956, 1958 and 1968', Essex Archaeology and History, vol. 10, 1978, pp.191-200.
15. *See* William Addison, *Portrait of Epping Forest*, pp.152-3 for the 1956 and 1958 excavations.
16. Alexander, Cotton, Mackay and Warren, *op. cit.*, pp.200, 202.

17. Tony O'Connor, Museum Officer of the Waltham Abbey Epping Forest District Museum, in conversation.
18. Tony O'Connor, in conversation.
19. This idea, expressed by Tony O'Connor, is touched on in Pamela Greenwood, Dominic Perring and Peter Rowsome, *From Ice Age to Essex*, p.14.
20. Stephen Pewsey, *Epping and Ongar, A Pictorial History*, p.xiv.
21. Alexander, Cotton, Mackay and Warren*, op. cit.*
22. Alexander, Cotton, Mackay and Warren*, op. cit.*, p.196.
23. Kenneth Neale, *Essex in History*, p.6.
24. Neale, *op. cit.*, p.8.
25. Caesar, *De Bello Gallico (The Conquest of Gaul)*, V,18. *See* Caesar, *De Bello Gallico (The Conquest of Gaul*, pp.137-8.
26. Caesar, *De Bello Gallico (The Conquest of Gaul)*, p.138.
27. Caesar, *De Bello Gallico (The Conquest of Gaul)*, V,21. *See* Caesar, *De Bello Gallico (The Conquest of Gaul)*, p.139.
28. Caesar, *De Bello Gallico (The Conquest of Gaul)*, V,21. *See* Caesar, *De Bello Gallico (The Conquest of Gaul)*, p.139.
29. Caesar, *De Bello Gallico (The Conquest of Gaul)*, V,9. *See* Caesar, *De Bello Gallico (The Conquest of Gaul)*, p.134.
30. R.T. Brooks and E.A. Fulcher, *An Archaeological Guide to Epping Forest*, pp.5, 10.
31. Ramon L. Jiménez, *Caesar against the Celts*, p.128.
32. Graham Webster, *The Roman Invasion of Britain*, p.46. *See also* http://books.google.com/books?id=1G4LXaH-WXkC&pg=PA46&lpg=PA46&dq=graham+webster+the+roman+invasion+of+britain+ambresbury+banks+caesar&source=bl&ots=ad9j9EdiKw&sig=F4fKuvvqlL48eJHmnMnclVArAfM&hl=en&ei=7pjfTc7IPISFhQf8t9TSCg&sa=X&oi=book_result&ct=result&resnum=1&ved=0CBUQ6AEwAA#v=onepage&q&f=false.
33. *Rambles in Essex* by "Pathfinder", London and North Eastern Railway, 1930s, revised edition 1946.
34. Lionel Munby, *The Hertfordshire Landscape*.
35. Barry Cunliffe, *Fishbourne Roman Palace*, pp.108-9; and John Manley,

AD43, The Roman Invasion of Britain, A Reassessment, pp.114-5.

36. Cassius Dio, book 60; translation from J.G.F. Hind, *The Invasion of Britain in AD43*, *Britannia, 20,* pp.1-21, quoted in John Manley, *AD43, The Roman Invasion of Britain*, p.55.
37. Alexander, Cotton, Mackay and Warren, *op. cit.*, p.202.
38. OS grid ref. TQ 426 912, *Britannia*, vol. 2, 1971.
39. OS grid ref. TQ 45 96, Eleanor Scott, *Gazetteer of Roman Villas in Britain*, Leicester University archaeological monograph, 1983.
40. OS grid ref. TQ 457 963, *Essex Society for Archaeology and History*, vol. 26, 1995, 238-58.
41. OS grid ref. TQ 462 973, *Essex Society for Archaeology and History*, vol. 18, 1987.
42. OS grid ref. TQ 456 963, *Transactions of the Essex Archaeological Society*, vol. 13, 1981.
43. OS grid ref. TQ 454 961, Hugh Toller, *Roman Lead Coffins and Ossuaria in Britain*, Oxford: British Archaeological Reports, 1977.
44. OS grid ref. TQ 457 964, *Essex Society for Archaeology and History*, vol. 19, 1988; *Britannia*, vol. XXII, 1991.
45. OS grid ref. TQ 4788 9885, *Essex Society for Archaeology and History*, vol. 20, 1989.
46. OS grid ref. TQ 4735 9786, Hugh Toller, *Roman Lead Coffins and Ossuaria in Britain*, Oxford: British Archaeological Reports, 1977.
47. OS grid ref. TQ 47 97, Eleanor Scott, *Gazetteer of Roman Villas in Britain*, Leicester University archaeological monograph, 1983; and OS grid ref. TQ 4725 9770, *English Heritage County Scheduled Monument List*, March 1996.
48. OS grid ref. TL 449 001, *Cambridge Antiquarian Society Proceedings*, 1965.
49. OS grid ref. TL 438 001, *Cambridge Antiquarian Society Proceedings*, 1965.
50. OS grid ref. TL 474 031, W.R. Powell, (ed), *The Victoria History of the Counties of England: A History of the County of Essex*, vol. 3, Roman Essex London: Oxford University Press for the Institute of Historical Research, 1963.

51. OS grid ref. TL 465 002, *Transactions of the Essex Archaeological Society*, vol. 14, 1982.
52. OS grid ref. TL 4625 0580, *Essex Society for Archaeology and History*, 2001.
53. OS grid ref. TL 460 037, Vivien G. Swan, *The Pottery Kilns of Roman Britain*, HMSO, London, 1984.
54. Archaeological Sites Index, http://www.digital-documents.co.uk/archi/sales.htm.
55. Tacitus, *The Annals of Imperial Rome*, trans. by Michael Grant, p.319.
56. Alfred Leutscher, *Epping Forest, Its History and Wildlife*, p.19.
57. *The Victoria History of the County of Essex*, vol. V, p.114.
58. 'At the Edge archive: Boudica – the case for Atherstone and Kings Cross', *see* http://www.indigogroup.co.uk/edge/boudica6.htm.
59. Philip Morant is referred to in Addison, *Portrait of Epping Forest*, p.151.
60. 'Seax Archaeology – Unlocking Essex's Past', *see* http://unlockingessex.essexcc.gov.uk/custom_pages/monument_detail.asp?kids=1&monument_id=301. *See also* http://www.themodernantiquarian.com/site/2139/ambresbury_banks.html.
61. Quoted in R.T. Brooks and E.A. Fulcher, *An Archaeological Guide to Epping Forest*, p.9.
62. William Winters is referred to in Addison, *Portrait of Epping Forest*, p.151.
63. OS grid ref. TL 436 004, W.R. Powell, ed., *The Victoria History of the Counties of England: A History of the County of Essex*: vol. 3, Roman Essex London: Oxford University Press for the Institute of Historical Research, 1963.
64. OS grid ref. TL 452 021, Vivien G. Swan, *The Pottery Kilns of Roman Britain*, HMSO, London, 1984.
65. OS grid ref. TL 451 011, *Cambridge Antiquarian Society Proceedings*, 1965.
66. OS grid ref. TL 47 03, *Historical Map & Guide: Roman Britain*, 4th Edition, Ordnance Survey, 1994.
67. OS grid ref. TL 444 008, *Cambridge Antiquarian Society Proceedings*, 1965; OS grid ref. TL 448 018, *Cambridge Antiquarian Society*

Proceedings, 1965; and OS grid ref. TL 448 027, *Cambridge Antiquarian Society Proceedings*, 1965.

68. OS grid ref. TL 451 034, *Cambridge Antiquarian Society Proceedings*, 1965.
69. OS grid ref. TL 452 022, *Cambridge Antiquarian Society Proceedings*, 1964.
70. OS grid ref. TL 429 016, *Cambridge Antiquarian Society Proceedings*, 1965.
71. OS grid ref. TL 434 016, *Cambridge Antiquarian Society Proceedings*, 1965; and OS grid ref. TL 431 009, *Cambridge Antiquarian Society Proceedings*, 1965.
72. Ambresbury Banks, *The Victoria History of the County of Essex*, vol. V, p.151.
73. High Beach, *The Victoria History of the County of Essex*, vol. III, p.197.
74. *Essex Naturalist*, vol. xxi, pp.214-26.
75. OS grid ref. TL 382 005, *Britannia*, 1975, *Transactions of the Essex Archaeological Society*, vol. 9, 1977, *Britannia,* vol. 7, 1976; and OS grid ref. TQ 383 999, *Transactions of the Essex Archaeological Society*, vol. 12, 1980.
76. OS grid ref. TL 3819 0055, *Essex Society for Archaeology and History*, vol. 23, 1992.
77. OS grid ref. TL 3817 0055, *Transactions of the Essex Archaeological Society*, vol. 14, 1982.
78. OS grid ref. TQ 383 990, *Essex Society for Archaeology and History*, vol. 23, 1992.
79. OS grid ref. TQ 419 975, A.H.A. Hogg, *British Hill-Forts: An Index*, Council for British Archaeology Reports, British Series, 62, Oxford 1979. The grid reference for the hill-fort at High Beach is distinct from Loughton Camp (OS grid ref. TQ 4188 9752) and Ambresbury Banks (OS grid ref. TL 438 003).
80. OS grid ref. TL 438 004, Colin Haselgrove, *Supplementary Gazetteer of Find-Spots of Celtic Coins in Britain*, Institute of Archaeology (Occasional paper/University of London, Institute of Archaeology, no.11a), 1978; and OS grid ref. TL 44 00, Colin Haselgrove,

Supplementary Gazetteer of Find-Spots of Celtic Coins in Britain, Institute of Archaeology (Occasional paper/University of London, Institute of Archaeology, no.11a), 1978.

81. OS grid ref. TL 46 02, *Frere*, 1961.
82. OS grid ref. TQ 44 94, *Frere*, 1961.
83. OS grid ref. TQ 37 93, *Frere*, 1961.
84. OS grid ref. TQ 462 973, *Essex Society for Archaeology and History*, vol. 20, 1989.
85. R.T. Brooks and E.A. Fulcher, *op. cit.*, pp.13-15. *See also* Addison, *Portrait of Epping Forest*, pp.152-3.
86. *See* http://www.themodernantiquarian.com/site/2139/ambresbury_banks.html.
87. OS grid ref. TQ 4495 9732, *English Heritage County Scheduled Monument List*, March 1996.
88. OS grid ref. TQ 44 97, Eleanor Scott, *Gazetteer of Roman Villas in Britain*, Leicester University archaeological monograph, 1983.
89. OS grid ref. TQ 416 871, Eleanor Scott, *Gazetteer of Roman Villas in Britain*, Leicester University archaeological monograph, 1983, *Essex Society for Archaeology and History*, vol. 16, 1983-4, and *Britannia*, vol. XIX, 1988.
90. OS grid ref. TQ 3755 9500, *Essex Society for Archaeology and History*, 1998, and *Essex Society for Archaeology and History*, vol. 26, 1995, 238-58.
91. OS grid ref. TQ 416 873, *Essex Society for Archaeology and History*, vol. 17, 1986, and *Essex Society for Archaeology and History*, vol. 20, 1989.
92. OS grid ref. TQ 41 88, *Historical Map & Guide: Roman Britain*, 4th ed, Ordnance Survey, 1994; and OS grid ref. TQ 419 875, H. Sheldon & L. Schaaf, 1978 A survey of Roman sites in Greater London, in *Collectanea Londiniensia*, Middlesex Archaeological Society Special Paper 2, ed J. Bird, H. Chapman, & J. Clark, pp.59-88, *see* http://ads.ahds.ac.uk/catalogue/adsdata/arch-726-1/dissemination/pdf/ewell/ewell_eus_report.pdf.

2. Anglo-Saxons and Normans

1. Della Hooke, *The Landscape of Anglo-Saxon England*, p.47.
2. Andrew Reynolds, *Later Anglo-Saxon England*, p,67; drawing on *The Origin of Anglo-Saxon Kingdoms*, ed. by S. Bassett.
3. Della Hooke, *The Landscape of Anglo-Saxon England*, p.47.
4. *The Victoria History of the County of Essex*, vol. V, p.151.
5. Leutscher, *op. cit.*, p.20.
6. P.J. Huggins, *The Church at Waltham, An Archaeological and Historical Review*, p.23.
7. Huggins, *op. cit.*, p.23. For Tovi's grant of lands to the church at Waltham, *see The Victoria History of the County of Essex,* vol. II, p.166 and vol. V, p.155.
8. *The Victoria History of the County of Essex,* vol. V, p.155.
9. *The Victoria History of the County of Essex,* vol. IV, p.118.
10. Thomas Kittson Cromwell, *Excursions in the County of Essex comprising a Brief, Historical and Topographical Delineation of Every Town and Valley*, p.30, states (in spellings that are sometimes incorrect) that Harold endowed Waltham with the manors of Northland in Waltham, later Northfield; Aelwartone (Alderton); Lambetithe (Lambeth, or Lambourne); Lukintune (Loughton's two manors regarded as a single manor); Nethleswell; Nessingham (Nazeing); Passefelde in High Ongar; Tippedene (Debden); Upminster; Walde (South Wealde); Wallifare in Boreham; Woodford; Brickendune Hicche in Herfordshire; Warmeley in Hertfordshire; Abricksey in Bedfordshire; Meluhoe in Bedfordshire; and West Waltham in Berkshire – a total of 17 manors.
11. Edwards, *op. cit.*, p.34.
12. *See* W.C. Waller, *Loughton in Essex*, p.2, and http://www.epping-forest.co.uk/placenames.htm. Loughton is first mentioned in Edward the Confessor's charter of 1062 which granted estates to Waltham Abbey. The chronological references to Loughton in historical documents are as follows: Lukinton or Lukintune (c.1062), Lochintuna or Lochetuna (c. 1086), Luketune, Luketon or Lukitone (13th century), Loketon or Lughton (14th century), Loghton (1384), Loughton or Lucton (16th century) and Luction (17th century).

13. W.C. Waller, *A Brief Account of the History of the Manor and Parish, from Domesday to 1900*, p.4.
14. *The Victoria History of the County of Essex*, vol. IV, p.262: http://www.british-history.ac.uk/report.aspx?c.
15. *The Victoria History of the County of Essex*, vol. V, p.155.
16. *The Domesday Book*, ed. by Thomas Hinde, pp.97-106.
17. *The Victoria History of the County of Essex*, vol. V, p.156.
18. *The Victoria History of the County of Essex*, vol. V, p.156.
19. *The Victoria History of the County of Essex*, vol. V, p.155.
20. *See* http://www.britannica.com/EBchecked/topic/425178/Odo-of-Bayeux.
21. *The Victoria History of the County of Essex*, vol. V, p.155.
22. *The Victoria History of the County of Essex*, vol. V, p.156.
23. *The Victoria History of the County of Essex*, vol. V, p.157; and p.118.
24. Leutscher, *op. cit.*, p.22.
25. Leutscher, *op. cit.*, pp.22-3.
26. Quoted in Leutscher, *op. cit.*, p.30.
27. Leutscher, *op. cit.*, p.28.
28. Bruce Hunt, *A Guide to Epping Forest*, http://www.maps.thehunthouse.com/Epping/Transcription_of_Guide_to_Epping_Forest.htm. Also White's *Directory of Essex*, 1848. *See* http://www.historyhouse.co.uk/placeE/essexe11a.html. *See also* http://www.friendsofeppingforest.org.uk/appx.htm .
29. William Addison, *Epping Forest, Figures in a Landscape,* p.1.
30. Nick Holder, report for the Corporation of London, quoted in *The East London and West Essex Guardian*, 15 September 2011, p.18.

3. Medievals and Tudors

1. Benedict Gummer, *The Scourging Angel*, devotes three pages to Essex; Philip Ziegler, *The Black Death*, has only three references to Essex; Lawrence Raymond Poos*, A Rural Society after the Black Death: Essex, 1350-1525*, focuses on the years after the Black Death.
2. Edwards, *op. cit.*, p.38.
3. Quoted in Edwards, *op. cit.*, p.38.
4. Quoted in Edwards, *op. cit.*, p.38.

5. Neale, *op. cit.*, p.82.
6. Alison Weir, *Henry VIII: King and Court*, p.284.
7. Alison Weir, *op. cit.*, p.295.
8. David Starkey, *Six Wives*, p.454.
9. *The Victoria History of the County of Essex*, vol. V, p.167.
10. William Addison, *Epping Forest, Figures in a Landscape*, pp.56-7.
11. William Addison, *Epping Forest, Figures in a Landscape*, pp.51-2, 57.
12. *The Victoria History of the County of Essex*, vol. IV, p.29. *See also* Elizabeth Ogborne, *The History of Essex*; and Thomas Kittson Cromwell, *op. cit.*
13. *The Victoria History of the County of Essex*, vol. IV, p.29.
14. P.J.S. Perceval, *London's Forest: Its History, Traditions and Romance.*
15. William Addison, *Epping Forest, Its Literary and Historical Associations*, p.8.
16. Ken Hoy, *Getting to Know Epping Forest*, 2002 edition, p.33, for 1341; and 2010 edition, p.83, for 1367. Both dates are mentioned in *The Friends of Epping Forest Newsletter*, Summer 2009, p.8.
17. *The Victoria History of the County of Essex*, vol. V, p.168.
18. *The Victoria History of the County of Essex*, vol. V, p.168.
19. Leutscher, *op. cit.*, p.64.
20. William Addison, *Queen Elizabeth's Hunting Lodge and Epping Forest Museum*, p.1.
21. Leutscher, *op. cit.*, p.64.
22. Edward North Buxton, *Epping Forest*, p.51.
23. *The Victoria History of the County of Essex*, vol. V, p.122.
24. Sylvia Keith, *Nine Centuries at Copped Hall*, p.9.
25. Keith, *op. cit.*, pp.9-10.
26. Stewart Trotter, *Love's Labour's Found.*
27. *The Victoria History of the County of Essex*, vol. IV, pp.118-9.
28. W.C. Waller, *An Extinct County Family, Wroth of Loughton Hall*, E.A.T. n.s. viii, p.154; quoted in *The Victoria History of the County of Essex*, vol. V, p.119.
29. William Addison, *Epping Forest, Figures in a Landscape*, pp.135-7.
30. *See* http://www.luminarium.org/editions/forest.htm.

31. *Oxford Guide to Literary Britain & Ireland: Loughton*, ed. by Daniel Hahn and Nicholas Robins. *See* http://www.answers.com/topic/loughton#ixzz1Wb2qarOm.
32. For a more detailed study of Lady Mary Wroth, *see* Sue Taylor, *Lady Mary Wroth*.
33. *See* http://www.luminarium.org/editions/forest.htm.
34. William Addison, *Epping Forest, Its Literary and Historical Associations*, p.52.
35. William Addison, *Queen Elizabeth's Hunting Lodge and Epping Forest Museum*, p.3.
36. Quoted in James A. Brimble, *London's Epping Forest*, p.52.

4. Enclosers and Loppers

1. *The Victoria History of the County of Essex,* vol. IV, p.114.
2. *See* http://seax.essexcc.gov.uk/result_details.asp?DocID=314828.
3. Robert Hunter, *The Epping Forest Act 1878*, p.13.
4. Pratt, *op. cit.*, p.12.
5. William Addison, *Epping Forest, Figures in a Landscape*, p.143. For Rev. John Whitaker Maitland, *see* http://www.archive.org/stream/transactionsess01socigoog/transactionsess01socigoog_djvu.txt.
6. Barbara Pratt, *The Loppers of Loughton*, p.4.
7. William Addison, *Epping Forest, Its Literary and Historical Associations*, p.220; and Pratt, *op. cit.*, p.12.
8. Richard Morris, *Who Actually Saved Epping Forest?*, p.10.
9. Brimble, *op. cit.*, p.157.
10. Ken Hoy, *Getting to Know Epping Forest,* 2010, pp.116, 130: the sand and gravel were dug from the Strawberry Hill Pond in the 1880s and the Blackweir (or Lost) Pond in 1895, which is why the Blackweir (or Lost) Pond is not marked on Buxton's map of 1885.
11. Pratt, *op. cit.*, pp.10-11.

PART TWO

Forest Places

5. Loughton

1. Census, 1801; quoted in *The Victoria History of the County of Essex*, vol. IV, p.110.
2. Chris Pond in *The Buildings of Loughton and Notable People of the Town*, 2010 ed, p.59 dates Oaklands to c.1885 and says its architect was probably Edmund Egan.
3. William Addison, *Essex Worthies*, p.170. Addison locates the school at Albion House, probably a reference to Albion Hall which occupied nos. 9-11 Albion Hill. Also Chris Pond, *The Buildings of Loughton and Notable People of the Town,* 2010 ed., p.59.
4. *The Valuation of Norwich*, ed. by W.E. Lunt, p.521; quoted in *The Victoria History of the County of Essex*, vol. IV, p.118
5. Chris Pond, *The Buildings of Loughton and Notable People of the Town*, 2001, p.52.
6. Kelly's Directory of Essex (1845, 1862); White's Directory of Essex (1848, 1863), E.R.O., E/ML51/1. Quoted in *The Victoria History of the County of Essex*, vol. IV, p.126.
7. Richard Morris, *From Clouds to Quinine, The Howard Family of Tottenham, Buckhurst Hill and Loughton*, Loughton and District Historical Society booklet, 2004, p.15.

6. Chigwell, Woodford and Buckhurst Hill

1. *The Victoria History of the County of Essex*, vol. IV, pp.24-5.
2. *The Victoria History of the County of Essex*, vol. IV, pp.24-5.
3. David Ballance, *The Buds of Virtue*, p.91.
4. *See* Encyclopaedia Britannica, online, http://www.britannica.com/EBchecked/topic/110931/Chigwell.
5. Robert Miller Christy and May Thresh, *History of the Mineral Waters and Medicinal Springs of the County of Essex*, p.43.
6. Nathaniel Salmon, *The History and Antiquities of Essex*, p.34. Salmon gives the *Domesday Book* spelling as *Cinghewella.*
7. *The Victoria History of the County of Essex*, vol. IV, pp.20-1.

8. *The Victoria History of the County of Essex*, vol. IV, p.21.
9. *See* http://www.britishlistedbuildings.co.uk/en-118584-chigwell-grammar-school-chigwell.
10. Godfrey Stott, *A History of Chigwell School*; http://www.chigwell-school.org/ourschool/history/index.html.
11. Stott, *op. cit.*, pp.174-5.
12. Stott, *op. cit.*, p.27.
13. Stott, *op. cit.*, pp.26-7; Ballance, *op. cit.*, p.18.
14. William Addison, *Epping Forest, Its Literary and Historical Associations*, p.58. Also Stott, *op. cit.*, pp.152-3.
15. Stott, *op. cit.*, pp.154, 159.
16. John Aubrey, quoted in Ballance, *op. cit.*, p.33.
17. Stott, *op. cit.*, p.97.
18. Stott, *op. cit.*, pp.95-6; Ballance, *op. cit.*, p.43.
19. Stott, *op. cit.*, p.96.
20. Stott, *op. cit.*, p.97.
21. William Addison, *Epping Forest, Its Literary and Historical Associations*, p.58; Stott, *op. cit.*, p.123.
22. Stott, *op. cit.*, p.102.
23. *The Victoria History of the County of Essex*, vol. IV, pp.33-4.
24. Richard Morris, *The Harveys of Rolls Park, Chigwell, Essex*, pp.4, 38.
25. *The Victoria History of the County of Essex*, vol. IV, p.26.
26. Thomas Crusz, *A Brief History of The White House & Mallinson Family*, pp.5, 8, 9.
27. David A. Thomas, *Churchill, The Member for Woodford.*
28. Crusz, *op. cit.*, p.6.
29. Crusz, *op. cit.*, p.10.
30. *Express and Independent*, 6 November 1959; quoted in Winston G. Ramsey with Reginald L. Fowkes, *Epping Forest Then and Now*, p.241.
31. *Express and Independent*, 6 November 1959; quoted in Ramsey with Fowkes, *op. cit.*, p.241.
32. *Express and Independent*, 6 November 1959; quoted in Ramsey with Fowkes, *op. cit.*, p.241.
33. Crusz, *op. cit.*, p.10.

34. *The Victoria History of the County of Essex*, vol. IV, p.28; M.W. Hanson, *Lords Bushes, The History and Ecology of an Epping Forest Woodland*, p.10.
35. Hanson, *Lords Bushes, The History and Ecology of an Epping Forest Woodland*, p.12.
36. *The Victoria History of the County of Essex*, vol. IV, p.18.
37. *The Victoria History of the County of Essex*, vol. IV, p.19.
38. *The Victoria History of the County of Essex*, vol. IV, p.18.

7. Waltham Abbey, High Beach and Upshire

1. *The Lives of Edward the Confessor*, poem in Old French with English translation, *see* http://www.archive.org/details/livesedwardconf00luargoog; quoted in William Winters, *The Burial of Harold at Waltham*, p.9.
2. Ramsey with Fowkes, *op. cit.*, p.475.
3. *The Victoria History of the County of Essex*, vol. V, p.164.
4. Revered J.H. Stamp, *The History of the Ancient Parish and Abbey Church of Waltham Holy Cross,* a lecture, 1904; quoted in Ramsey with Fowkes, *op. cit.*, p.477.
5. Ramsey with Fowkes, *op. cit.*, p.475.
6. *The Archaeological Journal*, 1992, vol. 149, pp.282-343, P.J. Huggins and K.N. Bascombe, 'Excavations at Waltham Abbey, Essex, 1985-1991: Three Pre-Conquest Churches and Norman Evidence'.
7. Huggins, *op. cit.*, p.12.
8. Huggins, *op. cit.*, p.12.
9. Huggins, *op. cit.*, p.17.
10. Dinah Dean, *The Five Churches of Waltham Abbey, Essex*, p.1.
11. Dean, *The Five Churches of Waltham Abbey, Essex*, p.1.
12. Huggins, *op. cit.*, pp.10, 12.
13. Dean, *The Five Churches of Waltham Abbey, Essex*, p.2.
14. *The Victoria History of the County of Essex*, vol. V, p.171.
15. Ramsey with Fowkes, *op. cit.*, p.477.
16. *The Archaeological Journal*, 1989, vol. 146, pp.478-9, within pp.476-537, P.J. Huggins, 'Excavations of the Collegiate and Augustinian

Churches, Waltham Abbey, Essex, 1984-1987'.

17. *The Archaeological Journal*, 1989, vol. 146, p.478, within pp.476-537, P.J. Huggins, 'Excavations of the Collegiate and Augustinian Churches, Waltham Abbey, Essex, 1984-1987'.
18. Huggins and Bascombe, *op. cit.*, p.296; Huggins, *op. cit.*, p.10.
19. *The Archaeological Journal*, 1989, vol. 146, p.478, within pp.476-537, P.J. Huggins, 'Excavations of the Collegiate and Augustinian Churches, Waltham Abbey, Essex, 1984-1987'.
20. *Vita Haroldi*, ed. by W. de G. Birch. Quoted in *The Archaeological Journal*, 1989, vol. 146, pp.478-9, within pp.476-537, P.J. Huggins, 'Excavations of the Collegiate and Augustian Churches, Waltham Abbey, Essex, 1984-1987'.
21. Dinah Dean, *The True Cross*, p.5.
22. Huggins, *op. cit.*, p.5.
23. Huggins and Bascombe, *op. cit.*, p.320, quoting Rosalind Ransford, *The Early Charters of Waltham Abbey, 1062-1230*, p.xxiv.
24. Huggins, *op. cit.*, p.5.
25. Dinah Dean, *The Gilds and Gild Chapels of Waltham Abbey*, p.4.
26. Ramsey with Fowkes, *op. cit.*, p.477.
27. *The Archaeological Journal*, 1989, vol. 146, p.478, within pp.476-537, P.J. Huggins, 'Excavations of the Collegiate and Augustinian Churches, Waltham Abbey, Essex, 1984-1987'.
28. *The Archaeological Journal*, 1992, vol. 149, p.284, P.J. Huggins and K.N. Bascombe, 'Excavations at Waltham Abbey, Essex, 1985-1991: Three Pre-Conquest Churches and Norman Evidence'
29. Colin Berry and Dinah Dean, *The Waltham Abbey Doom Painting*, pp.1-3.
30. Berry and Dean, *op. cit.*, pp.4-5.
31. Berry and Dean, *op. cit.*, pp.3-4.
32. Berry and Dean, *op. cit.*, p.4.
33. Dinah Dean, *Evidence of the Burial of King Harold II Godwinsson at Waltham Abbey*, p.2.
34. Huggins, *op. cit.*, p.25.
35. Quoted in Dean, *Evidence of the Burial of King Harold II Godwinsson at Waltham Abbey*, p.3.

36. Huggins, *op. cit.*, p.25.
37. Huggins, *op. cit.*, p.25.
38. Dean, *Evidence of the Burial of King Harold II Godwinsson at Waltham Abbey*, pp.4-5. Huggins, *op. cit.*, contradicts Dean in seeing only one tomb, and not three. I have followed Huggins.
39. Quoted in Dean, *Evidence of the Burial of King Harold II Godwinsson at Waltham Abbey*, p.4.
40. William Winters, *The Burial of Harold at Waltham*, p.3.
41. *Master Wace, His Chronicle of the Norman Conquest from the Roman De Rou*, c.1200.
42. Huggins, *op. cit.*, p.26.
43. Edward Walford, *Greater London: A Narrative of its History, its People, and its Places.*
44. Ramsey with Fowkes, *op. cit.*, p.477.
45. Thomas Fuller, *The History of Waltham-Abby (sic) in Essex founded by King Harold*, p.259.
46. Quoted in Winters, *op. cit.*, p.15.
47. Quoted in Dean, *Evidence of the Burial of King Harold II Godwinsson at Waltham Abbey*, p.6.
48. Quoted in Dean, *Evidence of the Burial of King Harold II Godwinsson at Waltham Abbey*, p.6.
49. Quoted in Winters, *op. cit.*, pp.15-17.
50. Quoted in Dean, *Evidence of the Burial of King Harold II Godwinsson at Waltham Abbey*, pp.6-7.
51. William Shackell, *The Parlour Portfolio or Post Chaise Companion*, vol. 2, 1820.
52. Quoted in Dean, *Evidence of the Burial of King Harold II Godwinsson at Waltham Abbey*, p.7.
53. Quoted in Dean, *Evidence of the Burial of King Harold II Godwinsson at Waltham Abbey*, p.1.
54. Quoted in Winters, *op. cit.*, p.7.
55. Quoted in Dean, *Evidence of the Burial of King Harold II Godwinsson at Waltham Abbey*, p.1.
56. Quoted in Winters, *op. cit.*, p.4.

57. Quoted in Winters, *op. cit.*, pp.5-6.
58. *See* http://www.ebooksread.com/authors-eng/british-archaeological-association-central-commit/the-archaeological-journal-volume-v-42-tir/page-50-the-archaeological-journal-volume-v-42-tir.shtml.
59. Quoted in Winters, *op. cit.*, pp.7-8, 13.
60. William Stubbs, *The Foundation of Waltham Abbey: The Tract de Inventione Sanctae Crucis Nostrae in Monte Acuto Et de Ductione Ejusdem Apud Waltham, 1861*, pp.30-31, note 90; quoted in *The Victoria History of the County of Essex*, vol. V, p.174.
61. Robert Bernard Martin, *Tennyson, The Unquiet Heart*, pp.135, 228, 233.
62. Quoted in Addison, *Epping Forest, Its Literary and Historical Associations*, p.176. Also http://highbeachchurch.org/WhosWhoatHolyInnocents.aspx.
63. Quoted in Edmund Gosse, *The Life of Tennyson*, *The North American Review*, vol. 165, no. 492, November 1897, pp.513-526. *See* http://www.jstor.org/action/doAdvancedSearch?q0=Perhaps+I+am+coming+to+the+Lincolnshire+coast%2C+that+I+scarcely+know.+The+journey+is+very+expensive%2C+and+I+am+so+poor&f0=all&c1=AND&q1=&f1=all&wc=on&Search=Search&sd=&ed=&la=&jo. Also Harold Nicolson, *Tennyson*, p.137. Also Addison, *Epping Forest, Its Literary and Historical Associations*, pp.176-7.
64. *Tennyson and His Friends*, ed. by Hallam, Lord Tennyson, p.27.
65. L.S.H. Young, *John Clare and High Beech*, John Clare Society newsletter no. 7, April 1984. *See* http://johnclareephemera.blogspot.com/p/john-clare-and-high-beech.html.
66. *Letters to Frederick Tennyson*, ed. by Hugh Joseph Schonfield, 6 November 1841, p.55; quoted in Christopher Ricks, *Tennyson*, p.164.
67. Martin, *op. cit.*, pp.236-7.
68. Quoted in Charles Richard Sanders, *Carlyle and Tennyson*, PMLA, vol. 76, no. 1, March 1961, pp.82-97. *See* http://www.jstor.org/action/doBasicSearch?Query=%28Some+weeks+ago%2C+one+night%2C+the+poet+Tennyson+AND+Matthew+Allen+were+discovered+here+sitting+smoking+in+the+garden.%29+AND+iid%3A%2810.2307%2Fi219653%29&gw=jtx&prq=%28Some+weeks+ago%2C+one

+night%2C+the+poet+Tennyson+AND+Matthew+Allen+were+discovered+here+sitting+smoking+in+the+garden.%29+AND+iid%3A%2810.2307%2Fi219653%29&Search=Search&hp=25&wc=on.

69. Ricks, *op. cit.*, p.164; Jonathan Bate, *John Clare, A Biography*, p.432.
70. Bate, *op. cit.*, p.432.
71. Addison, *Epping Forest, Its Literary and Historical Associations*, pp.177-8.
72. Quoted in Ramsey with Fowkes, *op. cit.*, p.380.
73. *Tennyson, A Selected Edition*, ed. by Christopher Ricks, p.675.
74. Bate, *op. cit.*, p.428. A number of books, including Ken Hoy, in *Getting to Know Epping Forest*, pp.99-100, claim that Clare lived at Fairmead House but do not give a source. This view may have begun with Henry Walker, *The Leisure Hour*, 1883.
75. Addison, *Epping Forest, Its Literary and Historical Associations*, p.161.
76. *The Later Poems of John Clare, 1837-1864. See* http://xtf.lib.virginia.edu/xtf/view?docId=chadwyck_ep/uvaGenText/tei/chep_3.2537.xml;chunk.id=d42;toc.depth=1;toc.id=d4;brand=default;query=how%20beautiful#1.
77. Young, *op. cit.* Ken Hoy, *op. cit.*, p.102, also locates Clare's "fern hill" in Old Church Plain.
78. *The Later Poems of John Clare, 1837-1864*, I, p.19.
79. Bate, *op. cit.*, p.425, quoting Allen's plans, Essex Records Office, Q/Alp3/2.
80. Frederik Martin, *The Life of John Clare*, Journal, Sunday 18 July 1841. *See* http://www.fullbooks.com/The-Life-of-John-Clare5.html.
81. Margaret C. Barnet, *Matthew Allen, M.D. (Abderdeen) 1783-1845*, p.24. *See* http://www.ncbi.nlm.nih.gov/pmc/articles/PMC1033439/pdf/medhist00156-0024.pdf. Also Addison, *Epping Forest, Its Literary and Historical Associations*, p.166.
82. John Wareham, *The Poetry of John Clare*, English Association Bookmarks, no. 39. *See* http://www.le.ac.uk/engassoc/publications/bookmarks/39.pdf.
83. I am indebted to Tricia Moxey for the information about Edward Thomas

and the keeper's cottage in this paragraph. Ken Hoy in *Getting to Know Epping Forest*, p.92, claims that Thomas was billeted at Fairmead House (now the Suntrap Centre), which was used for army accommodation during the 1914-18 war, just before he went to France in 1917, but he does not give dates or a source. Addison, *Epping Forest, Its Literary and Historical Associations*, p.227, states that Edward Thomas was stationed in "huts" erected close to the King's Oak, and that Helen Thomas rented "one of the two cottages [i.e. the keepers' cottages] close to what was then Paul's Nursery. It was the farther one from the road."

84. Richard Padfield, *A History of St Thomas' Church, Upshire*, p.1.
85. Padfield, *op. cit.*, pp.1-7.
86. Padfield, *op. cit.*, pp.11-16.

8. Epping and the Theydons

1. *The Victoria History of the County of Essex*, vol. V, pp.118, 127.
2. Jim Angel, *Guide to All Saints, Epping Upland*, p.15.
3. Norden's *Map of Essex*, 1594; quoted in *The Victoria History of the County of Essex*, vol. V, p.116.
4. Raymond Cassidy, *Copped Hall, A Short History*, p.4; Hoy, *op. cit.*, p.186; Keith, *op. cit.*, p.2.
5. *The Victoria History of the County of Essex*, vol. V, p.122; Cassidy, *op. cit.*, p.4.
6. Cassidy, *op. cit.*, p.3; Keith, *op. cit.*, p.iii.
7. *The Victoria History of the County of Essex*, vol. V, p.121; Cassidy, *op. cit.*, p.3.
8. Thomas Fuller, *The History of Waltham in Essex founded by King Harold*, 1655, p.262; quoted in *Victoria History of the County of Essex*, vol. V, p.123.
9. Cassidy, *op. cit.*, p.3.
10. Cassidy, *op. cit.*, pp.3-4. Keith, *op. cit.*, p.3.
11. *The Victoria History of the County of Essex*, vol. V, p.127.
12. *The Victoria History of the County of Essex*, vol. V, p.122.
13. Addison, *Portrait of Epping Forest*, p.13.
14. *The Victoria History of the County of Essex*, vol. V, p.118.

15. Addison, *Epping Forest, Figures in a Landscape*, p.26; Keith, *op. cit.*, p.9.
16. *The Victoria History of the County of Essex*, vol. V, p.122.
17. *The Victoria History of the County of Essex*, vol. V, p.123.
18. *The Victoria History of the County of Essex*, vol. V, pp.118, 122.
19. *The Victoria History of the County of Essex*, vol. V, pp.118-9.
20. *The Victoria History of the County of Essex*, vol. V, p.123.
21. Keith, *op. cit.*, p.17.
22. Keith, *op. cit.*, pp.19-20.
23. *The Victoria History of the County of Essex*, vol. V, p.119.
24. Thomas Gower, 30 June 1660, "The king dined yesterday at Copt Hall, today at Roehampton, returned both days in terrible rain and thunder, so as the fine weathers and day clothes are come back utterly spoiled, and the brave gallants looked like drowned rats or as if they had been rolled in puddles….The Earl of Middlesex feasted them magnificently at his house at Copt Hall, after they had spent the morning hunting with great content in Waltham Forest. P.S. The king went yesterday to Copt Hall to hunt the buck; the lords invite the king very oft, and the two Dukes, and he is very freely merry with them, and he will not have them provide above ten or twelve dishes for them at most." Quoted in Keith, *op. cit.*, pp.28-9.
25. James Cotter Morison, *Macaulay*, p.148. *See* http://ia600404.us.archive.org/30/items/macaulay00moriuoft/macaulay00moriuoft.pdf. Quoted in Keith, *op. cit.*, p.31.
26. Keith, *op. cit.*, pp.50-1.
27. Keith, *op. cit.*, p.54.
28. Keith, *op. cit.*, p.55.
29. Keith, *op. cit.*, p.56.
30. *Country Life* magazine, 29.10.1910. *See* http://www.countrylifeimages.co.uk/Image.aspx?id=4f16c2d6-57e0-4fec-9d60-6a535833eeb0&rd=2|%20prints_garden||1|20|70|150.
31. Keith, *op. cit.*, pp.70-1.
32. *The Victoria History of the County of Essex*, vol. V, p.124.
33. Quoted in Keith, *op. cit.*, p.60.

34. Keith, *op. cit.*, p.84.
35. *Times*, 'Rest Home for Air Raid Wardens', 22 January 1942.
36. For Ulmar, *see* K.S.B. Keats-Rohan and David E. Thornton, *Domesday Names: an Index of Latin Personal and Place Names in Domesday Book*, entry for Ulmar, 24 references. For Eudo *see The Victoria History of the County of Essex*, vol. IV, p.262: http://www.british-history.ac.uk/report.aspx?c.
37. *The Victoria History of the County of Essex*, vol. IV, p.262: http://www.british-history.ac.uk/report.aspx?c.
38. *The Victoria History of the County of Essex*, vol. IV, pp.258-62.
39. Palmer, *op. cit.*, pp.33-6.
40. *The Victoria History of the County of Essex*, vol. IV, pp.258-62.
41. William Palmer, *They Were Here*, pp.47-8.
42. Palmer, *op. cit.*, p.58.
43. Nikolaus Pevsner, *Essex*, p.384.
44. Palmer, *op. cit.*, pp.8-10.

9. Chingford Plain

1. *See* http://www.websters-online-dictionary.org/definitions/Chingford.
2. *See* http://www.british-history.ac.uk/report.aspx?compid=45469.
3. Quoted in Ramsey with Fowkes, *op. cit.*, p.351.
4. Addison, *Queen Elizabeth's Hunting Lodge and Epping Forest Museum*, p.14.
5. Addison, *Queen Elizabeth's Hunting Lodge and Epping Forest Museum*, p.3.
6. Addison, *Queen Elizabeth's Hunting Lodge and Epping Forest Museum*, p.3.
7. Addison, *Queen Elizabeth's Hunting Lodge and Epping Forest Museum*, p.3.
8. Addison, *Queen Elizabeth's Hunting Lodge and Epping Forest Museum*, p.4.
9. Addison, *Queen Elizabeth's Hunting Lodge and Epping Forest Museum*, pp.5-6.
10. Addison, *Queen Elizabeth's Hunting Lodge and Epping Forest Museum*,

pp.6-7.

11. *See* http://www.guardian-series.co.uk/your_local_areas/9188155.WANSTEAD__Cafe_owners_to_take_on_historic_tea_rooms/.
12. Addison, *Queen Elizabeth's Hunting Lodge and Epping Forest Museum*, pp.9-10.

Epilogue: A Unified view of Epping Forest's History and Places

1. Ken Hoy, *A History of the Friends of Epping Forest, 1969-2009*.
2. 'February Budding, Half Term', 11 November 1972, in Nicholas Hagger, *Collected Poems,* p.155.

Bibliography/Reading List

Addison, William, *Epping Forest, Figures in a Landscape*, Robert Hale, 1991.

Addison, William, *Epping Forest, Its Literary and Historical Associations*, J.M. Dent, 1945.

Addison, William, *Essex Worthies*, Phillimore, 1973.

Addison, William, *Portrait of Epping Forest*, Robert Hale, 1977.

Addison, William, *Queen Elizabeth's Hunting Lodge and Epping Forest Museum* booklet, Corporation of the City of London, 1978.

Alexander, J.A., M. Aylwin Cotton, R. Robertson Mackay, and S. Hazzledine Warren, 'Ambresbury Banks, an Iron Age Camp in Epping Forest, Essex: a report on excavations of 1933, 1956, 1958 and 1968', Essex Archaeology and History, vol. 10, 1978, pp.189-205.

Angel, Jim, *Guide to All Saints, Epping Upland*, All Saints Epping Upland Parochial Church Council, 1987.

Archaeological Journal, The, 1989, vol. 146, P.J. Huggins (with contributions by K.N. Bascombe and R.M. Huggins), 'Excavations of the Collegiate and Augustinian Churches, Waltham Abbey, Essex, 1984-1987'.

Archaeological Journal, *The,* 1992, vol. 149, pp.282-343, P.J. Huggins and K.N. Bascombe, 'Excavations at Waltham Abbey, Essex, 1985-1991: Three Pre-Conquest Churches and Norman Evidence'.

Baker, C.A., P.A. Moxey and Patricia M. Oxford, 'Woodland Continuity and Change in Epping Forest', *Field Studies* (1978), vol. 4, pp.645-69.

Ballance, David, *The Buds of Vi*rtue: *The Story of Chigwell School*, James and James, 2000.

Bate, Jonathan, *John Clare, A Biography*, Picador, 2005.

Bede, The Venerable, *The Venerable Bede's Ecclesiastical History of England: also the Anglo-Saxon Chronicle*, BiblioBazaar, 2009.

Berry, Colin and Dinah Dean, *The Waltham Abbey Doom Painting*, Waltham Abbey Parochial Church Council, 1995.

Brimble, James A., *London's Epping Forest*, Country Life, 1950.

Brooks, R.T., and Fulcher, E.A., *An Archaeological Guide to Epping Forest* booklet, Conservators of Epping Forest/Corporation of the City of London,

1979.

Buxton, Edward North, *Epping Forest*, Edward Stanford, 1884, 1923.

Caesar, *The Conquest of Gaul*, trans. by S.A. Handford, Penguin, 1951.

Cassidy, Raymond, *Copped Hall, A Short History*, Waltham Abbey Historical Society, 1983, 2005.

Cassius Dio, *Books 56-60*, vol. 7, Loeb Classical Library, 1989.

Christy, Robert Miller and May Thresh, *History of the Mineral Waters and Medicinal Springs of the County of Essex*, Essex Field Club, Simpkin, Marshall, 1910.

Cromwell, Thomas Kittson, *Excursions in the County of Essex comprising a Brief, Historical and Topographical Delineation of Every Town and Valley*, Longman, Hurst, Rees, Orme, and Brown, [et al.], 1818-1819.

Crusz, Thomas, *A Brief History of The White House & Mallinson Family*, Haven House Children's Hospice booklet, 2011.

Cunliffe, Barry, *Fishbourne Roman Palace*, Tempus, 1971, 1998.

De Sainte-Maure, Benoît, *Chronique des Ducs de Normandie*, *Chronicles of the Dukes of Normandy*.

De Inventione Sanctae Crucis Nostrae, The Discovery of our Holy Cross, or The Waltham Chronicle, An Account of the Discovery of Our Holy Cross at Montacute and Its Conveyance to Waltham, trans. and ed. by Leslie Watkiss and Marjorie Chibnall, Oxford Medieval Texts, Clarendon Press, 1994.

Dean, Dinah, *Evidence of the Burial of King Harold II Godwinsson at Waltham Abbey*, Waltham Abbey Parochial Church Council, 2001.

Dean, Dinah, *The Five Churches of Waltham Abbey, Essex*, Waltham Abbey Parochial Church Council, n/d.

Dean, Dinah, *The Gilds and Gild Chapels of Waltham Abbey*, Waltham Abbey Parochial Church Council, n/d.

Dean, Dinah, *The True Cross*, Waltham Abbey Parochial Church Council, n/d.

Domesday Book, The, ed. by Thomas Hinde, Guild Publishing, 1985.

Dunnett, Rosalind, *The Trinovantes (Peoples of Roman Britain)*, Sutton Publishing Ltd., 1975.

Edwards, A.C., *A History of Essex*, Phillimore, 1958, 1978.

Faber Book of Modern Verse, The, ed. by Michael Roberts, Faber and Faber, 1936.

Farmer, John, *The History of the Ancient Town and once Famous Abbey of Waltham in the County of Essex*, 1735, available from Amazon, print-on-demand, publisher unknown, 2010.

Fuller, Thomas, *The History of Waltham-Abby (sic) in Essex founded by King Harold*, Reproduction of original in the Bristol Public Library, reference Wing F2442, microfilm from Miami University library.

Grant, Dr Michael and Dr Petra Dark, 'Re-evaluating the concept of woodland continuity and change in Epping Forest: biological and sedimentary analyses', Kingston University.

Green, Georgina, *Epping Forest through the Ages*, 20/20 Publications, 1982.

Greenwood, Pamela, Dominic Perring and Peter Rowsome, *From Ice Age to Essex, A history of the people and landscape of East London*, Museum of London, 2006.

Gummer, Benedict, *The Scourging Angel, The Black Death in the British Isles*, Bodleyhead, 2009.

Hagger, Nicholas, *A New Philosophy of Literature*, O Books, 2012.

Hagger, Nicholas, *Classical Odes*, O Books, 2006.

Hagger, Nicholas, *Collected Poems*, O Books, 2006.

Hagger, Nicholas, *The Fire and the Stones,* Element, 1991.

Hagger, Nicholas, *The Last Tourist in Iran*, O Books, 2008.

Hagger, Nicholas, *The Libyan Revolution*, O Books, 2009.

Hagger, Nicholas, *The Light of Civilization*, O Books, 2006.

Hagger, Nicholas, *The Rise and Fall of Civilizations*, O Books, 2008.

Hagger, Nicholas, *The Secret American Dream*, Watkins, 2011.

Hagger, Nicholas, *The Secret Founding of America*, Watkins, 2007.

Hagger, Nicholas, *The Secret History of the West*, O Books, 2005.

Hagger, Nicholas, *The Syndicate*, O Books, 2003.

Hanson, M.W., *Lords Bushes, The History and Ecology of an Epping Forest Woodland*, Essex Naturalists number 7, Essex Field Club, 1983.

Hanson, M.W., *Loughton's River, The Roding and its Ancient Meadows*, Epping Naturalists' Trust and Epping Forest District Council, 1986.

Harsnett, Samuel, *A Declaration of Egregious Popish Impostures to With-Draw the Harts of Her Majesties Subjects from Their Allegeance, and from the Truth of Christian Religion professed in England, under the Pretence of casting out Deuils*, 1603, Lightning Source, 2010.

Hawkes, C.F.C., and M.R. Hull, *Camulodunum: First report on the excavations at Colchester, 1930-1939*, The Society of Antiquaries, 1947.

Hooke, Della, *The Landscape of Anglo-Saxon England*, Leicester University Press, 1998.

Hoy, Ken, *A History of the Friends of Epping Forest, 1969-2009*, Friends of Epping Forest, 2009.

Hoy, Ken, *Getting to Know Epping Forest*, Friends of Epping Forest, 2002, 2010.

Huggins, P.J., *The Church at Waltham, An Archaeological and Historical Review*, Waltham Abbey, 2000.

Hunter, Robert, *The Epping Forest Act 1878,* Davis and Son, 1878.

Jiménez, Ramon L., *Caesar against the Celts*, Spellmount, 1996.

Shackell, William, *The Parlour Portfolio, Or, Post-Chaise Companion; Being a Selection of the Most Amusing and Interesting Articles and Anecdotes That Have Appeared in Magazines, Newspapers, and other Daily and Periodical Journals, from the Year 1700 to the Present Time*, 2 vols., 1820, print-on-demand available from Amazon, publisher unknown.

Keats-Rohan, K.S.B., and David E. Thornton, *Domesday Names: an Index of Latin Personal and Place Names in Domesday Book*, Boydell Press, 1997.

Keith, Sylvia, *Nine Centuries at Copped Hall*, S. and J.A. Keith, 2007.

Later Poems of John Clare, The, 1837-1864, ed. by Eric Robinson and David Powell, Clarendon Press, Oxford, 1984.

Letters to Frederick Tennyson, ed. by Hugh Joseph Schonfield, Hogarth Press, 1930.

Leutscher, Alfred, *Epping Forest, Its History and Wildlife*, David and Charles, 1974.

Lives of Edward the Confessor, The, compiled by Henry Richards Luard, Longman, Brown, 1858.

Manley, John, *AD43, The Roman Invasion of Britain, a reassessment*, Tempus, 2002.

Manning, S.A., *Portrait of Essex*, Robert Hale, 1977.

Martin, Robert Bernard, *Tennyson, The Unquiet Heart*, Faber and Faber, 1983.

Mirror of Literature, Amusement and Instruction, The, 1833; many volumes published in the 1820s and 1830s, reprinted by FQ Books, 2010-11.

Morant, Philip, *The History and Antiquities of the County of Essex*, 2 vols., 1763 and 1768, EP Publishing [for] Essex County Library 1978.

Morison, James Cotter, *Macaulay*, Harper & Brothers Publishers, 1901.

Morris, Richard, *From Clouds to Quinine, The Howard Family of Tottenham, Buckhurst Hill and Loughton*, Loughton and District Historical Society booklet, 2004.

Morris, Richard, *The Harveys of Rolls Park, Chigwell, Essex*, Loughton and District Historical Society, 2005.

Morris, Richard, *Who Actually Saved Epping Forest?*, Loughton & District Historical Society, 2010.

Munby, Lionel M., *The Hertfordshire Landscape*, Hodder and Stoughton, 1977.

Neale, Kenneth, *Essex in History*, Phillimore, 1977.

Nicolson, Harold, *Tennyson, Aspects of his Life, Character and Poetry*, Doubleday, 1962.

Ogborne, Elizabeth, *The History of Essex*, Longman, Hurst, Reese, Orme & Browne, 1814.

Origin of Anglo-Saxon Kingdoms, The, ed. S. Bassett, Leicester, 1989.

Oxford Guide to Literary Britain & Ireland, 3rd edition, ed. by Daniel Hahn and Nicholas Robins, Oxford University Press, 2008.

Padfield, Richard, *A History of St Thomas' Church, Upshire*, St Thomas' Parochial Church Council, Upshire, 2002.

Palmer, William, *They Were Here: People and Events at All Saints' Church, Theydon Garnon, Essex, from the 12th century onwards*, Muriel Palmer, 1987.

Perceval, P.J.S., *London's Forest: Its History, Traditions and Romance*, J.M. Dent & Co, 1909.

Pevsner, Nikolaus, *Essex*, 2nd edition, Penguin Books, 1954, 1996.

Pewsey, Stephen, *Chigwell and Loughton, A Pictorial History*, Phillimore, 1995.

Pewsey, Stephen, *Epping and Ongar, A Pictorial History*, Phillimore, 1997.

Pond, Chris, *The Buildings of Loughton and Notable People of the Town*, Loughton & District Historical Society, 2003, 2010.

Poos, Lawrence Raymond, *A Rural Society after the Black Death: Essex, 1350-*

1525, Cambridge University Press, 1991.

Pratt, Barbara, *The Loppers of Loughton* booklet, Barbara Pratt Publications, 1981.

Rambles in Essex by "Pathfinder", London and North Eastern Railway, 1930s, revised edition, 1946.

Ramsey, Winston G. with Reginald L. Fowkes, *Epping Forest Then and Now*, Battle of Britain Prints International, 1986.

Ransford, Rosalind, *The Early Charters of Waltham Abbey, 1062-1230*, Woodbridge, Boydell Press, 1989.

Reynolds, Andrew, *Later Anglo-Saxon England*, Tempus, 2002.

Ricks, Christopher, *Tennyson*, University of California Press, Berkeley and Los Angeles, 1972, 1989.

Salmon, Nathaniel, *The History and Antiquities of Essex*, J. Cooke, 1740.

Starkey, David, *Six Wives: The Queens of Henry VIII*, Chatto & Windus, 2003.

Stott, Godfrey, *A History of Chigwell School*; W.S. Cowell Ltd., 1960.

Stubbs, William, *The Foundation of Waltham Abbey: The Tract de Inventione Sanctae Crucis Nostrae in Monte Acuto Et de Ductione Ejusdem Apud Waltham (1861)*, Kessinger Publishing, 2009.

Tacitus, *The Annals of Imperial Rome*, trans. by Michael Grant, Penguin, 1956.

Taylor, Sue, *Lady Mary Wroth*, booklet, Loughton and District Historical Society, 2005.

Tennyson and His Friends, ed. by Hallam, Lord Tennyson, Macmillan, 1911.

Tennyson, A Selected Edition, ed. by Christopher Ricks, University of California Press, 1989.

Thomas, David A., *Churchill: The Member for Woodford*, Routledge, 1994.

Trotter, Stewart, *Love's Labours Found*, Geerings of Ashford, 2002.

Valuation of Norwich, The, i.e. the ecclesiastical valuation carried out in 1252-54 by the Bishop of Norwich with the Bishop of Chichester and the Abbot of Westminster, ed. by W. E. Lunt.

Victoria History of the County of Essex, The, vol. IV, University of London, 1956.

Victoria History of the County of Essex, The, vol. V, University of London, 1966.

Vita Haroldi, ed. by W. de G. Birch, London, 1885.

Wace, Master, *His Chronicle of the Norman Conquest from the Roman De Rou*, c.1200, BiblioBazaar, 2010.

Walford, Edward, *Greater London: A Narrative of its History, Its People, and its Places*, Cassell & Co., 1883-4, 2009.

Waller, W.C., *Loughton, Essex: A Brief Account of the History of the Manor and Parish, from Domesday to 1900*, ed. by Richard Morris, published by Richard Morris, 2002.

Waller, W.C., *Loughton A Hundred Years Ago* (the text of *An Itinerary of Loughton 1905-1912*), ed. Richard Morris and Chris Pond, The Loughton and District Historical Society, 2006.

Waller, W.C., *Loughton in Essex*, only 12 copies printed, Alfred B. Davis, Epping, 1900.

Waller, W.C., *Notes on Loughton 1890-95*, ed. Chris Pond, The Loughton and District Historical Society, 2001.

Waller, W.C., *Notes on Loughton II: 1896-1914*, ed. Richard Morris, The Loughton and District Historical Society, 2002.

Waltham Chronicle, The, *see De Inventione Sanctae Crucis Nostrae*.

Webster, Graham, *The Roman Invasion of Britain*, Barnes and Noble, 1981.

Weir, Alison, *Henry VIII: King and Court*, Jonathan Cape Ltd., 2001.

William of Poitiers, *Gesta Guillelmi II Ducis Normannorum et Regis Anglorum, Deeds of William II, Duke of the Normans and King of the English, 1071-7*, published in *Emmae, Anglorum Reginae, Richardi I. Ducis Normannorum, Filiae, Encomium. Incerto Auctore, sed Coaetaneo. Item, Gesta Guillelmi II. Ducis Normannorum*, Lightning Source, 2010.

Winters, William, *The Burial of Harold at Waltham*, Waltham Abbey Historical Society, 2008.

Wright, Thomas, *The People's History of Essex,* 1861.

Young, L.H.S., *John Clare and High Beech*, John Clare Society newsletter no. 7, April 1984.

Ziegler, Philip, *The Black Death*, Penguin Books, 1969, 1998.

Index